Arguing for a General Framework for
MASS MEDIA
SCHOLARSHIP

Arguing for a General Framework for
MASS MEDIA
SCHOLARSHIP

W. JAMES POTTER
University of California, Santa Barbara

Los Angeles • London • New Delhi • Singapore • Washington DC

For information:

SAGE Publications, Inc.
2455 Teller Road
Thousand Oaks, California 91320
E-mail: order@sagepub.com

SAGE Publications India Pvt. Ltd.
B 1/I 1 Mohan Cooperative
   Industrial Area
Mathura Road, New Delhi 110 044
India

SAGE Publications Ltd.
1 Oliver's Yard
55 City Road
London EC1Y 1SP
United Kingdom

SAGE Publications Asia-Pacific Pte. Ltd.
33 Pekin Street #02-01
Far East Square
Singapore 048763

Printed in the United States of America

Library of Congress Cataloging-in-Publication Data

Potter, W. James
Arguing for a general framework for mass media scholarship / W. James Potter
       p. cm.
Includes bibliographical references and index.
ISBN 978-1-4129-6470-8 (cloth)
ISBN 978-1-4129-6471-5 (pbk.)
    1. Mass media—Research—History. 2. Mass media—Research—Methodology. I. Title.

P91.3.P682 2009
302.23072—dc22   2008028743

This book is printed on acid-free paper.

08   09   10   11   12   10   9   8   7   6   5   4   3   2   1

Acquisitions Editor:	Todd R. Armstrong
Editorial Assistant:	Aja Baker
Production Editor:	Astrid Virding
Copy Editor:	Gillian Dickens
Typesetter:	C&M Digitals (P) Ltd.
Proofreader:	Scott Oney
Indexer:	Kathy Paparchontis
Cover Designer:	Candice Harman
Marketing Manager:	Carmel Schrire

Brief Contents

PART V: EXPLAINING THE MEDIA EFFECTS FACET

PART VI: CONCLUSION

Detailed Contents

PART II: EXPLAINING THE MEDIA ORGANIZATIONS FACET

Socialization of Workers
    Structural Characteristics
    Professionalism
    Routines
    Media Logic
    Learning Values
    Learning Processes
    Shaping the News Formula
Conclusion

PART III: EXPLAINING THE MEDIA AUDIENCES FACET

PART IV: EXPLAINING THE MEDIA MESSAGES FACET

Preface

Developing a scholarly field is like solving a puzzle while at the same time designing it. Scholars start with a fuzzy, naive vision for what their phenomenon of interest is, that is, what they are trying to explain. To sharpen that vision, they work piece by piece to provide a good explanation for the components of the overall phenomenon. Using reason, insight, speculation, and observation, they must create the pieces that will reveal the full picture. Over time, they work on refining each piece, which leads them to break the components of the full phenomenon down into subcomponents and sub-subcomponents. This produces a greater and greater number of smaller and smaller pieces. This quest to create more pieces results in greater precision and refinement of the micro units, but it tends to draw the focus away from the big picture that tells us which pieces are more important and where the gaps are.

The generating argument in this book is that the scholarship about the mass media has grown so large and become so fragmented that it is very difficult for scholars to understand, much less appreciate, the incredible array of great ideas and findings that have been produced. This difficulty has less to do with the scatter of forums for this information—across a dozen scholarly associations with their own journals and conferences; dozens of book publishers; hundreds of citizen action groups with their own reports and Web sites; and reports to funding agencies. Instead, I argue that the difficulty in making sense of all this information can be traced to a lack of perspective. By *perspective,* I mean a common platform from which to observe all this scholarship. A well-known illustration of perspective is the Saul Steinberg sketch that appeared as a cover of the *New Yorker* magazine and on posters throughout the country. The artist takes the perspective of a New Yorker living on the Upper East Side of Manhattan. In the sketch, this neighborhood takes up about a third of the picture and has a lot of detail for landmarks in the Upper East Side. Another third of the sketch is the rest of Manhattan with its border of the Hudson River. The remaining third of the sketch depicts what lies west of the Hudson River, which is a squiggly line for the Mississippi River, a few bumps for the Rocky Mountains, and then the Pacific coastline. The sketch depicts the idea that Upper East Siders care most about their own neighborhood and know a fair amount about the rest of Manhattan, but, while they know there is something else to the United States, all that something else is relatively unimportant or at least unknown to them.

The more I read the mass media literature, the more I have come to see our field as a large number of distinct neighborhoods each with a few scholars who understand their home neighborhood very well. The scholars in a particular neighborhood get so engrossed in a few theories, research questions, and methods that the familiar grows so large that it blocks the view of other neighborhoods. Scholars lose sight of the overall phenomenon of the mass media.

This perception of our field started becoming clear to me several years ago. In the everyday conversations I was having with my media colleagues, I developed a sensitivity to what scholars felt they knew and what they did not talk about when it came to the mass media. In short, I was trying to understand the perspective from which they viewed our scholarly phenomenon of interest. For example, one colleague, who was trained in experimental psychology, saw the media in terms of particular content elements that could be treatments to generate differences in groups of participants; he knew very little about many other mass media areas such as content narratives or audience construction. Another colleague regarded the media as something that consumes people's time, so she conducted research only on motives for using the media; she knew very little about other mass media areas, such as physiological responses and structures of the mass media industries. Other colleagues who were critical mass media scholars saw the media primarily in terms of something that causes harm to society in one or two ways (such as negative images of certain groups of people); they knew little about many areas of mass media such as their positive effects or cognitive processing of information. Each scholar had become fixed in a perspective that foregrounded his or her special area of interest and blocked out a view of the larger phenomenon.

New scholarly fields are typically built from the ground up; we need to start with exciting, vital neighborhoods. The field of mass media scholarship has built many of these. But a field needs larger structures that are required for more general tasks that scholars within one neighborhood cannot accomplish by themselves. We need cities, states, and regions, but we have little comprehension of these in our field. For example, reviews of the literature are typically at the neighborhood level. This is because most of the research is at the neighborhood level, so it is relatively easy to summarize research on most topics. However, we need more reviews of the literature that synthesize the summaries from across neighborhoods. We need to leverage our findings to higher levels of generality by knitting together the best thinking from across many neighborhoods. This is needed to add conceptual strength to a field that has been built primarily on empirical strength. Until we can build greater conceptual strength, we will continue in a state of fragmentation where there is little sharing of definitions for key constructs, little sharing of measurement instruments, and little acknowledgment of—much less testing of and building onto—existing theories. Because of this fragmentation, scholars who attempt to read beyond their neighborhoods will continue to feel fatigue when trying to figure out what the meanings of key terms are, the validity of different methods, and the value of different theories. This is a significant barrier to building a scholarly field as defined by a community of scholars with common goals and a sharing of knowledge.

It is my goal in this book to energize mass media scholars to think well beyond their home neighborhood of expertise and to think more globally about the entire phenomenon of the mass media. In the first chapter, I make a case for why this is so vital. The remainder of the book, beginning with Chapter 2, lays out a picture of what such a general framework would look like. In that chapter, I use the metaphor of a bicycle wheel as a device to illustrate the nature of scholarly fields and to organize my critique of how the thinking and research about the mass media can be better organized and thereby made more useful.

The next four parts of the book each deal with one of the facets of mass media scholarship: media organizations, media audiences, media messages, and media effects. The part of the book on media organizations contains four chapters. Chapter 3 introduces a knowledge structure for thinking about mass media organizations. Chapter 4 focuses on business strategies, Chapter 5 on marketing strategies, and Chapter 6 on employment strategies.

Part III deals with the audience facet of the mass media phenomenon and is composed of five chapters. Chapter 7 presents the big picture perspective on audiences. Chapter 8 focuses on cognitive algorithms and how they are so important as an explanatory device for audience thinking and behavior. The next three chapters each deal with one of the three information tasks of filtering (Chapter 9), meaning matching (Chapter 10), and meaning construction (Chapter 11).

Part IV shifts attention to the content facet of the mass media phenomenon and is composed of four chapters. Chapter 12 introduces a general knowledge structure for thinking about media content. Chapter 13 presents information on patterns of content found in the mass media and looks at the general conventions underlying the production of that content. Chapter 14 examines message formulas and conventions across major genres. This section concludes with Chapter 15, which presents a critique of the scholarship about mass media messages.

Part V focuses on the effects facet and is composed of three chapters. Chapter 16 introduces the effects line of thinking. Chapter 17 takes up the issue of how to organize all the hundreds of documented media effects. Chapter 18 presents a critique of the methods used to generate the large literature of media effects.

Part VI consists of a single chapter. In Chapter 19, I review the major ideas of the general framework in order to leave the reader with the big picture.

How I Wrote This Book

The seeds for this book were planted in my mind while I was still in graduate school and reading the mass media scholarly literature for the first time. As every student does, I asked myself, "How does this all fit together? How much of this literature do I really need to read? What are the most important questions and studies?" My initial answers to these questions were very naive and partial, but those intuitively derived answers helped me get through (although not very well) many reading lists.

It took a long time to read even the shortest articles, and I was always worried (with good reason) that I was not getting enough out of those readings.

With more reading came more questions—but better questions. Also, my answers seemed more reasoned, more elaborate, and more useful to me. After finishing my graduate degree and becoming a faculty member, I gradually narrowed my reading to focus on particular topics so that I could design particular research studies. One area of interest was media violence, but after conducting a good deal of research on this topic, I felt I might be losing my perspective because my reading had become more and more focused on sub-sub-areas. So I began to broaden my reading and was amazed at how many good insights had been published on the topic of media violence. I tried to organize this scholarship in my 1999 book, *On Media Violence,* in which I synthesized from that literature an explanation of why media incorporate violence in their stories and how that violence affects individuals and society. After publishing that book, I wanted to broaden my perspective even more to look at a wider range of harmful effects of mass media exposures. I did a great deal of thinking and reading about media literacy and began working on *Theory of Media Literacy,* which ended up being published in 2004. As I was writing that book, I became bothered by how fragmented our literatures were and how many scholars typically ignored the research of other scholars working in other sub-areas of mass media scholarship. I myself was not immune from this problem. The more I read across sub-areas, the more I found important publications that I failed to cite in my own published work, although at the time I was writing those manuscripts, I had made every reasonable effort to find all studies published on my topic. The literatures of mass media are spread across so many disciplines, worldviews, journals, publishers of books, monographs, government reports, working papers of consumer groups, and so on that it is very difficult to arrive at a feeling that one has located all relevant materials on a given topic.

Then with the advent of electronic catalogs of very large numbers of journals, books, and other sources of information along with desktop computerized searches, it seemed that the access problem might be solved. But this is not the case. Electronic searches rely on the skillful use of keywords, and there is such diversity in definitions of key terms used by mass media scholars that the use of a single set of keywords almost always results in the identification of only a partial set of relevant publications. This led me to think about what it is that mass media scholars truly share—or should share. To try answering this question, I attempted to read all the mass media–related research published in journals (at least in the mainstream media journals) in order to form in my mind a picture of what the current topography of that literature looked like. I had done this in another form earlier in my research career when I conducted a content analysis of eight journals with two researchers who were then graduate students at Indiana University—Roger Cooper and Michel Dupagne. That project was a formal content analysis with specific variables and tests for reliability that ended in the publishing of several articles and setting off a debate about whether mass media research was scientific or prescientific (W. J. Potter, Cooper, & Dupagne, 1995; Sparks, 1995a, 1995b).

Then about a decade later, I wanted to take another broad look at the mass media literature, but this time I wanted a more qualitative feel for the big picture that emerges from the mass media literature rather than precise counts of various features. So over the course of an intense summer, I read through all the mass media articles published in mainstream communication journals over that past decade. I also read several dozen books published on mass media topics over that decade.

What first struck me as I read through all this work was that there were far more lines of research than I expected to see. Also, certain lines of research (on specific theories or generated by certain named scholars) were a lot smaller than I expected (particularly with cultivation and social cognitive theories), while other lines of research were more extensive than I expected (particularly with the third-person effect). There were new names of scholars that had already generated a fairly impressive line of research. However, most of the literature had the feel of scholars grappling with a very wide variety of theoretical and methodological issues.

The more I read, the more I came to feel that the mass media literature was still largely exploratory, even beyond 2000, when the research field was more than five decades old. By this I mean that scholars were still struggling with how to define key constructs such as cognitions, emotions, attitudes, beliefs, perceptions, behaviors, exposure, attention, audience, and even the term *mass media*. Also, a good deal of the research was not guided by a formal theory that could have helped the researchers with definitions of key terms, deduction of tests, and replication of results. Instead, a good deal of the research was question driven, where the authors reviewed a small portion of literature to try to position their study but not enough to build significantly on previous hypotheses, measures, and findings. These studies typically concluded with a call for more research in the area as well as a litany acknowledging the current study's limitations—many of which could have been avoided had the authors reviewed a larger swath of literature and found a closer study to replicate and thus learn from *that* study's litany of limitations. The value of this large literature lay in the creativeness in the speculations; however, there were very few "rallying points" where scholars built studies on the acceptance of the same definitions of key terms. On the surface, it *appeared* as if people were using the same definitions when they were using the same terms, but a careful reading of an article usually revealed that each author had his or her own specialized meaning. This was a criticism Steve Chaffee made in the late 1980s, which led him to publish *Communication Concepts 1: Explication* (1991) and to persuade scholars to explicate several dozen major terms commonly used in communication scholarship so as to build a shared basis of clarified meaning.

Although much of the literature was exploratory in nature, there were many examples of programmatic research clearly driven by theories. These theory-driven studies tended to arrange themselves according to different research traditions from the more established social sciences. Three of these literatures were fairly substantial—studies from psychological, sociological, and political traditions. Smaller literatures include economics (use of resources by the media industries and people interacting with those industries), education (evaluation of learning outcomes), and anthropology (ethnographies of cultures). There are also literatures developed by scholars from a humanistic worldview who use a different set of research tools, such as critical analysis, textual analysis, and argumentation from a clearly presented ideological position.

What impressed me the most was the growing size of the literature spread out across so many topics—all related to the mass media. However, at the same time I was concerned about how I could distill all these reading experiences down into a clear map of the literature. I was very concerned that after many months of reading, I did not have any clearer vision of a map than I had before. Over the next year, I thought about what I had read and tried to organize it for myself and for the students I would be encountering in upcoming media courses. I tried to induce patterns, and I tried different forms of comparing and contrasting studies to arrive at some meaningful groupings. Some organizational ideas gradually started forming and continued to form over the next year. Then in the fall of 2004, I went back to reread the same literature, but this time I was more evaluative, that is, I was looking for ideas that were most useful to help shape organizational schemes such that the resulting synthesis would be a good attempt at capturing the breadth of research as well as theorizing and at the same time be able to highlight patterns to illuminate the terrain of that scholarship. I was driven by the following questions: How can all this mass media scholarship be integrated into a meaningful framework that could feature most prominently the best thinking and research? Can a framework emphasize integration over fragmentation to showcase how ideas driving differing lines of research can be used to buttress one another? Can such a framework be constructed to reveal a map of scholarship in a way to direct researchers toward the most pressing topics? Can a framework help move us toward a strong community of shared definitions and shared context of thinking?

I attempted to synthesize such a framework to see if the questions posed above could be answered in the affirmative. During the next year, I began writing my ideas in book form. This manuscript represents a ninth major revision from that first effort. With each revision, I saw things differently. Throughout this process, I learned a great deal through feedback from students, reviewers, and presentations at various universities around the country. Also, I am amazed that as my context on the scholarly field changes, the reading of a particular article for the sixth time, for example, leads me to see things in a very different way than when I read that article for the fifth time.

In constructing this general framework, I employed a five-step procedure culminating in a synthesis. First, I analyzed all the scholarly literature I could find that was somehow relevant to the mass media. This came largely from scholarly journals and books. Of course, there is so much written that I am under no illusion that I have read the full inventory. But I am relatively confident that if an idea was important to more than a few isolated people, I was able to note it. By analysis, I mean that I searched each piece of writing for key ideas of definition, prediction, and explanation.

Second, I grouped those ideas to create a structure. The largest structure focuses attention on what I came to believe were the four major facets of the mass media: organizations, audience, messages, and effects. Within each of these four groups, I continued with subgroupings, and sub-subgroupings. Refer to the outlines at the beginning of each chapter to see those structures.

The challenge in grouping findings together lay in deciding which elements in a piece of writing to use in the groupings. If I was using a key term to structure the grouping (i.e., if a particular term appears in a study, it is included in a group), I had to be careful that the authors using the same term were attaching the same meaning to it. This forced me to clarify definitions for commonly used terms and also to construct other terms in order to help me organize all of these ideas into coherent groups.

Third, I evaluated the ideas. Evaluation essentially involves the comparison of something (in this case, an idea from the literature) to a standard. The standard I used was utility; that is, how useful was an idea in illuminating the nature of the mass media phenomenon. Using this evaluation procedure, I screened out a lot of ideas that did not seem to have much utility. I must acknowledge that I had a fairly high standard for utility because there is a limit to the size of the book I could publish. Many ideas that have utility are not acknowledged in this book because my focus here is on providing a general framework. Many of those "screened out" ideas have high utility at a more detailed level, where they serve to elaborate explanations.

Fourth, I used induction to look for patterns across ideas within each section, and then across sections. Within sections, I was interested in looking for trends and novel patterns across the findings of different studies. Across sections, I was interested in looking for consistency in an arc of explanation. A significant challenge lay in looking for patterns across studies. A good deal of the mass media literature presents equivocal results. While almost all of the published literature presents findings that have been found to be statistically significant, the matter of substantive significance is not so salient in many studies.

Fifth, I used synthesis to assemble the ideas from the literature (that were evaluated as useful) along with my own insights gained through grouping and induction into a coherent whole. When working on this synthesis, I had to be more than a clerk who cuts out the ideas from different literatures and pastes those various ideas together in a long list. The central challenge of synthesis was to use as many of the most important ideas from the literature as possible and to assemble them into a coherent whole. In constructing the synthesis, I uncovered many gaps in the literatures. Rather than fill these gaps with a statement such as "More research needs to be done in this area," I tried to bridge over these gaps with reasoned speculation. Therefore, some of the propositions I put forth in this theory have no empirical support. However, that is the nature of theorizing; I hope researchers will find those ideas worthy of testing. If so, this general framework will serve a heuristic function of generating additional research along particular lines of inquiry.

In creating the synthesis, I was particularly influenced by the ideas of cognitive psychologists (especially John Bargh and Robert Wyer) who have done a great deal of work concerning the human mind and how we process information. I have also relied heavily on the ideas of British sociologists (especially John Thompson and Anthony Giddens) and historians (especially Harold Innis and Marshall McLuhan) who take a longer and broader view of the media across history and cultures to examine profound macro effects on the context of our everyday lives. On the more humanistic and critical side of scholarship, I have not been impressed much with the ideas of the major scholars of the Frankfurt school (such as Horkheimer, Adorno, or Marcuse) because they are too focused on a negative criticism of the media industries. The media industries create culture in all sorts of ways, some positive, some neutral, and some negative. I prefer instead the more reasoned approaches of scholars such as Stuart Hall and David Morley. Also, as for semiotics, I have found the work of Saussure, Peirce, Foucault, Eco, and Derrida too abstract and technical for this synthesis, preferring instead the ideas of Volosinov and Propp. And last, but far from least, I have benefitted from the ideas of scores of media scholars who are too numerous to mention here but whose names and ideas are featured prominently in the following chapters.

What I have presented above might appear to be a linear process progressing from step one through step five to a final product. That was not the case. It was a process of trying to do early steps first, but the steps were performed in every order in mini-cycles of thinking and writing. Every few months, I usually completed a full cycle of drafting out a full set of chapters. At the end of such a long cycle, I had learned so much that the entire project looked very different to me, thus requiring a total revision starting with a major restructuring of approach, altering the sequence of chapters—dropping some, adding some, and combining some with others. This was the hermeneutic approach; in creating a draft of the entire project, I did the best I could in crafting each piece, but once all the pieces were assembled into a whole and I was able to see the "big picture" revealed as all the pieces were put in the puzzle, I wanted to rework the picture. In all, I created nine distinctly different drafts of the manuscript, revising it significantly each time, although the revisions on the later drafts were less major—but still substantial.

Conclusion

This general framework attempts to provide an integrated explanation of the mass media as an industry, the messages that are produced and marketed, the audiences for those messages, and the effects of those messages on individuals and larger social structures. This framework attempts to organize past and current thinking in a way that allows us to take stock of where we are and critique those ideas in a way that will help us gain a better understanding of who we are as a scholarly field and what we can do to strengthen our research community as well as our contributions to the general public.

I hope that the audience of researchers will find three characteristics of this book valuable. First, there is a prescriptive list of key terms and their definitions that form the foundation of this framework. These were derived through a careful analysis and synthesis of the literatures. This can focus researchers' attention on a common set of definitions. Sharing these definitions widely can serve to build the scholarly field faster. But even if some researchers disagree with certain definitions, their criticism will be clearer building off of those presented here rather than building off of primitive definitions where we inaccurately assume a shared meaning. Second, the patterns presented in this book will show researchers where their efforts will make the greatest impact, that is, important areas where there is yet little research. Third, this framework will present a complex of integrated ideas that can help form a stronger context for positioning their findings.

I ask that readers of this framework take a look at it in its entirety before making judgments about the value of any of its parts. There are elements in this theory that will appear strange or even anathema to different readers. This is because I have tried to craft a truly general framework, and this required not only the inclusion of a great many findings but also the inclusion of characteristics from different types of theories (covering laws, axiomatic, and systems), purposes (organization, prediction, and explanation), ontological positions (realism to actionalism), epistemological positions (logical positivist to constructivist), and scholarly traditions (experimental psychology, economics, sociology, political science, education, and critical/cultural approaches). At times, my approach is very mechanistic. This is because certain parts of the phenomenon appear to be that way. At other times, my approach is very open to the highly individualistic interpretations made by audience members. I regard humans as complex creatures who at times do process information like machines while at other times are able to take creative paths to completely original readings of messages and subsequent behaviors. Humans exhibit a wide range of potentials; after all, it is humans who have created the great variety of ontological, epistemological, and worldview positions! Therefore, it seems disrespectful of the human condition to wall off some of these options when creating a system of explanation about how people process media messages.

My ultimate goal for this book is to energize mass media scholars to take the next step in building our scholarly field. This next step emphasizes breadth of perspective in clarifying the big picture. It favors convergence over divergence. It privileges the sharing of definitions, conceptualizations, and operationalizations over the creation of new ones. This is not to say that I do not value divergent and creative thinking; that is essential to building a scholarly field, and this has been the strong point in the development of the mass media scholarly field up until now. But at this point in time, the marginal utility of developing another conceptualization is much smaller than assembling our best conceptualizations into a more powerful system of explanation.

Some scholars will find the insights presented here helpful and will want to use those definitions and ways of thinking in designing their research studies. For these scholars, this framework will provide a useful map to guide their selection of research topics that will have the greatest leverage on increasing our knowledge about the phenomenon. Other scholars will undoubtedly disagree with my vision; their oppositional stance will serve to challenge the assumptions, definitions, and propositions I present in this framework. The resulting argument and debate will also serve to increase our knowledge about the mass media. I welcome these debates—not only to argue my positions (as I will likely try to do) but also as an opportunity to broaden my perspective.

SAGE Publications gratefully acknowledges the following reviewers:

Sahara Byrne (Cornell University)
Roger Cooper (Ohio University)
Dennis K. Davis (Pennsylvania State University)
Dale Kunkel (University of Arizona)
Dana Mastro (University of Arizona)
Mary Beth Oliver (Pennsylvania State University)

PART I

Introduction

CHAPTER 1

Why Do We Need a General Framework?

Mass media scholars have accomplished a great deal over the past six decades. Our wide-ranging exploration of our phenomenon of interest has produced a very large literature of published work that is full of creative insights and empirical findings. However, the development of this literature has altered our challenge. The thesis underlying all the arguments in this book is that we cannot continue to do the same things and expect to continue making good progress in increasing our understanding of the mass media. We must evolve as a field by putting old challenges behind us and prepare to meet the newly emerging challenges. Now is a critical time for such an evolution as we are coming off the successes we achieved in the past by using what I will call a Generating-Findings perspective, where all topics, assumptions, explanations, and methods have been useful tools in generating an incredible variety of findings.

Now we are reaching a point of fragmentation where we need to take stock much more formally of what we have produced and assemble the vast array of individual findings into synthesized structures of knowledge to meet the needs of our three major constituencies. The first constituency is the mass media scholar. We need to organize findings so as to develop a higher profile scholarly field and guide the use of our limited resources in the most efficient manner possible to conduct future studies that will make the most difference in ratcheting up our knowledge of the mass media phenomenon. A second constituency is the student in higher education. Mass media courses are highly popular, but too often, the knowledge taught in these courses is a boring history of thinking long since discredited, a glitzy overview of so-called "new" media without contextualizing them in the larger phenomenon of mass media, or a myopic set of training experiences for entry-level jobs in the media industries. What is missing is a big-picture overview that is both complete and practical. And the third constituency is the general public, who has irrational fears of and expectations for the mass media. The general public—like students—needs a big-picture understanding of how the mass media organizations work, why they produce the content messages they do, and how exposure to those messages affects them and the people around them.

Beginning with this chapter, I show how a shift from the past Generating-Findings perspective to a Mapping-Phenomenon perspective is not only desirable but also essential if we as scholars are to serve all three constituencies better. This argument is elaborated in all subsequent chapters, where I show the advantages of such a shift and also provide some concrete guidelines and conceptual tools to help bring about such a shift.

In this chapter, I lay the foundation for the book by showing how the Generating-Findings perspective has been necessary to get us to this point. I then critique this perspective by showing that it has now reached a point of significantly diminishing returns and that it is time for an evolution into a new perspective that will better meet our current—and especially our future—challenges as an emerging scholarly field. Labeling it the *Mapping-Phenomenon perspective,* I will show how this perspective can be a useful tool in guiding this evolution in thinking and practice.

Generating-Findings Perspective on the Mass Media

The 20th century was a period of great technological development that spawned industries that have come to be known as the mass media. Parallel to the growth of the mass media has been an interest in examining those media as an economic, political, social, psychological, and cultural phenomenon. This research has been predominantly Generating-Findings in nature; that is, it is characterized by inductive processes and wide-ranging debates where the purpose has been to ask as many questions as possible and to try as many approaches, methods, and designs as possible to see what generates the most useful answers to which questions.

Growth of Mass Media Research

Up until near the end of the 19th century, a few technological channels were used to disseminate messages to a broad range of people. The mass media were newspapers, magazines, and books. Then in the span of a few decades, technological innovations pushed forward, with business entrepreneurship bringing about the newer mass media of film, recordings, and radio.

With the growing importance of each of these new media, the public expressed a growing concern about their impact on the culture. There was more scholarly activity in addressing questions such as the following: Could these channels be treated as a set of "mass" media? Can we identify patterns in their development that would help us understand their fundamental nature, their values, and their operating principles? How do these media construct and maintain their audiences? How do the media produce their content, and what is the nature of that content? What are the intended and unintended effects on audiences? Which media, types of messages, and message elements are especially influential in bringing about which effects? And are there certain types of audience members who are especially influenced by the media?

These questions became more pressing as television reached virtually complete household penetration shortly after midcentury, and scholars began conducting a great deal of research about the effects of such a powerful medium. Then, in the last few decades of the 20th century, newer technologies caught the attention of vast audiences as major content providers turned these newer channels of information distribution into mass media. These include cable TV, satellite TV, household computers, low-cost Internet connections, and digital gaming.

Throughout the 20th century, these questions attracted the attention of a wide range of scholars. Psychology scholars, who were primarily interested in how humans think and make sense of their world, began using mass media messages as stimuli in experiments. Political scientists, who were primarily concerned with how humans acquire and use power in social situations, began studying how people running for political office used the mass media to influence public opinion and voting behaviors. Scholars of literature, who were primarily concerned with how humans reconstruct their experiences and extend them in stories they tell one another, began studying how people use the mass media to restructure and disseminate those stories.

By the last decades of the 20th century, many scholars shifted their interest primarily to the mass media and relegated other concerns to a secondary role. Professional societies formed, journals were created to showcase media scholarship, and universities created programs to teach students about the mass media and train new generations of scholars to study it (Chaffee & Rogers, 1997; Lowery & DeFleur, 1988). Scholars had their thinking and practices shaped by a Generating-Findings perspective, which valued breadth over depth and divergence over convergence. All questions about the media were useful because scholars were trying to identify the perimeter and contours of this new field of study. Scholars could justify a new research study by simply stating, "No one has yet done a study on X." All methods were tried as scholars attempted to figure out which designs generated the most interesting insights about the mass media and which measures captured the most interesting concepts. Scholars looked for patterns in data distributions and patterns across studies to try to tap into the essence of the mass media. Thus, the inductive process underlay most scholarly activity.

Inductive Process

Most of the research in the Generating-Findings phase was inductive in nature. That is, individual research studies were typically motivated by questions rather than by a priori reasoned systems of explanation. Researchers collected data, and then looked for patterns in those data. When they found a pattern—such as a statistically significant treatment difference across means or a relatively strong degree of association among variables—they reported their findings as a suggestive answer to their research question. I say *suggestive answer* because the inductive method requires continual replication of studies to build greater evidence of a pattern until readers of the literature can have greater confidence that the pattern is robust enough that it is worthy of their attention rather than an anomaly of a particular measurement device, sample, or treatment.

Using this inductive approach, scholars could ignore no question because they could not be sure which question would tap into a rich mine of insight. The posing of any question was valuable because so little was known about the mass media. The results of just about any research study had good potential for contributing to knowledge.

Also, no approach, method, or assumption was considered out of bounds; all were tried for their usefulness in addressing all kinds of questions. All kinds of assumptions about the mass media, their content, their audiences, and their effects were tested to see which were the most useful. All kinds of constructs with all kinds of definitions were tried. All kinds of pairs of constructs were tested to see what was related to what. This brainstorming activity was necessary to "feel our way in the dark" and find out where the boundaries and contours of the phenomenon were.

To help in this Generating-Findings process of examining the new phenomenon of the mass media, scholars imported ideas and methods from other fields. This is understandable because other fields—particularly the more established social sciences and humanities—had theoretical and methodological traditions that they had been using as tools to examine the mass media within the context of their own scholarship. Media scholars found it very helpful to use these tools and continued to import these ideas heavily even into the late 20th century (Reeves & Borgman, 1983; Rice, Borgman, & Reeves, 1988).

Debates

The development of our research field has been characterized by debates on many scholarly topics, particularly debates about paradigms and about conceptualizations of effects, audiences, and content. This is understandable. When scholars import ideas from different fields, they must debate which of those imported ideas fit best within the context of mass media scholarship. Therefore, these debates have been a salient characteristic of our Generating-Findings phase.

Paradigms. The paradigm debate serves an important function of challenging us to think about the assumptions we make about the nature of our phenomenon of interest (ontology) and the limits on our ability to access the meaning of that phenomenon as humans and scholars (epistemology; see Kuhn, 1970a, 1970b). As for ontology, the paradigm debate is a disagreement over the nature of the human mind, that is, the degree to which we have free will. On the one side of the debate are scholars who regard the human mind as a machine that is an orderly system; this position is referred to as mechanistic determinism. On the other side of the debate are scholars who regard the human mind as an ever changing organ that allows people complete freedom to make a wide array of interpretations of any stimuli; this position is referred to as actionalism.

Mechanistic determinists regard the human mind as a wonderfully complicated machine that is hardwired to perform a great variety of tasks quickly. This "wiring," which makes the brain efficient at doing certain tasks, also constrains the brain from doing other tasks. Under this conception, the existing architecture of the brain can be reworked—through conditioning—to perform certain functions even better. Humans can be programmed to think better, which usually means more rationally, more logically, and more efficiently.

As a machine, the human brain employs standard parts; that is, the similarities across human brains are so striking as to be uniform. The differences across human brains are so minor and rare that they are regarded as characteristics of illness or nonnormal brains. This uniformity allows researchers to study one brain and conclude that the patterns found there represent the patterns that would be found in any other human brain. Thus, we have developed an educational system with standard treatments in the belief that the more individuals work with the standard treatments in exercising the mind, the better their thinking processes will be. There is also a negative side to this programming; when antisocial messages become widespread in a culture (drugs are fun, violence is a successful way to solve problems, consumerism leads to a happy life, and the like), the population is conditioned to hold antisocial beliefs, and this weakens society as people act on these beliefs.

The scholar who is most strongly identified with this ontological position of mechanistic determinism in the 20th century was B. F. Skinner. He argued that in order for the study of the human mind to be a science, scholars must accept the assumption that human behavior follows certain laws—that is, "we must expect to discover that what a man does is the result of specifiable conditions and that once these conditions have been discovered, we can anticipate and to some extent determine his actions" (Skinner, 1953, p. 6). Skinner recognized that this position would be offensive to many scholars. "It is opposed to a tradition of long standing which regards man as a free agent, whose behavior is the product, not of specifiable antecedent conditions, but of spontaneous inner changes" (p. 7). Skinner believed that humans have little real capacity for choice or self-motivated behavior. Everything that happens in the world is determined by prior physical causes acting according to invariable laws.

While strict behaviorism had an enormous influence on the field of psychology during the middle part of the 20th century, its influence has waned in favor of more cognitive approaches to explaining human thinking and behavior. However, most cognitive approaches still exhibit elements of mechanistic determinism. For example, in their chapter on theories of learning in the *Handbook of Cognition,* M. E. Young and Wasserman (2005) viewed human learning primarily in terms of making associations. They said that "associative learning is more than acquiring simple stimulus-response association. A sophisticated cognitive machine must be able to learn associations between configurations of stimuli, associations between sequences, the precise temporal relations among events, hierarchical relationships, and how much attention to pay to the variety of features, dimensions, and events extant in the environment" (p. 162). While their conception of human learning is not limited to simple stimulus-response (S-R) connections, the idea of association still dominates their view.

Bargh (1997) updated this mechanistic determinism position by saying, "Because of social psychology's natural focus on the situational determinants of thinking, feeling, and doing, it is inevitable that social psychological phenomena will be found to be automatic in nature" (p. 1). Thus, the examination of automatic processes governing human thinking and action extends the view that humans are machine-like. Bargh is not a strict behaviorist like Skinner because he disagrees with Skinner's position that cognition plays no role in the stimulus control of behavior; however, the inclusion of cognition does not weaken Bargh's view that stimuli can determine humans' responses in an automatic fashion. Barsalou (1992) concurred by saying, "Like behaviorists, most cognitive psychologists believe that the fundamental laws of the physical world determine human behavior completely. . . . The illusion of free will is simply one more phenomenon that cognitive psychologists must explain" (p. 9). Bargh went as far as to say that most of what people think, feel, and do is primed by cues in the environment so much so that he argued for changing the focus from social cognition to social ignition.

Over time, scholars holding to this mechanistic determinism view have elaborated their position to try to explain the vast array of challenges the human mind encounters in everyday life. Their explanations are more involved and more complicated, but at base, they still reveal a view of the human mind as a machine.

In contrast, actionists regard the human mind as a vastly complicated system with a wide-open architecture allowing individuals—and even requiring individuals—to solve a wondrously wide array of problems in a fully creative manner. Each person is a free agent in constantly creating his or her own interpretations of every-day reality. At any given decision point, people are free to take any option. Because there are so many decision points in the process of solving everyday problems, each person constructs a highly idiosyncratic sequence every day. With actionalism, expla-nations for human actions focus on human goals and intentions rather than external factors. For example, Giddens (1981) criticized the social science perspective—what he called the orthodox consensus of communication research—for treating indi-vidual behavior as "the outcome of structural causation or structural constraint—as though it derived directly from social forces" and that "we are driven by influences of which we are unaware" (p. 57). He argued that most of what we do is intentional, and "we are aware of our reasons for doing it. All human agents know a great deal about the conditions of their activity, that knowledge not being con-tingent upon what they do, but constitutive of it" (p. 57).

Scholars also differ on epistemological beliefs. Some scholars with a positivist view follow the ideas of Comte, who believed that observations about human behavior can be made (and need to be made) in as scientific and objective a man-ner as possible. In contrast, scholars with a constructivist view (following from the ideas of Kant) believe that humans cannot be both the object of study and the instrument of observation in an objective manner, and thus observations of the social world are highly subjective and idiosyncratic to the human observer. The constructivist position is illustrated in the writings of Hall and Newcomb, who believe that humans create meaning for themselves as they encounter experiences, such as media messages.

The debate over paradigms is reflected in debates about the use of particular research methods. The central question is as follows: Is it better to use social scien-tific or humanistic/critical methods to study the media? Livingstone (1993) has argued that "perhaps more than any other field of social science research, mass communication research has been dominated by key theoretical and methodologi-cal oppositions that underlie the fierce debates and splits within the field. These oppositions include critical versus administrative research, the study of texts (which itself is conducted in very different ways) versus the study of audiences, and the use of qualitative versus quantitative methods" (p. 5).

The paradigm debates have been featured prominently in three major publica-tions: the 1983 "Ferment in the Field" issue of the *Journal of Communication*, *Rethinking Communication* (Dervin, Grossberg, O'Keefe, & Wartella, 1989), and the 1993 "Ferment in the Field II." The 1983 "Ferment in the Field," which includes 35 essays by 41 authors from 10 countries, was the first major forum to bring the paradigm debate into mainstream consideration by communication scholars.

Rethinking Communication (Dervin et al., 1989) is a two-volume publication of 60 papers delivered at the 1985 annual meeting of the International Communication Association (ICA), where 80 scholars participated in sessions dealing with para-digms used by communication scholars. In the first volume of *Rethinking Communication,* the editors explained that their call for papers for the ICA confer-ence said, "Clearly, among us we have charted some radically different paths to scholarship. The diversity is so great, the positions sometimes so intense, the commitments so in opposition that it might be easy to conclude that the field is quickly moving toward a state of incompatibilities" (p. 9). The editors finished their call for papers on an optimistic note, saying that it was their hope that the papers would go "beyond polemics in the sense that they transcend superficial differences and polarities and allow us to gain a greater understanding of the fundamental ways in which we differ and the ways in which some of our differences may not so much differ as enrich" (p. 9). However, looking at the five major essays and the 24 commentaries in which scholars reacted to the ideas in the major essays, it appears that the former was achieved to a much higher degree than the latter. The five major essays each critiqued what they called the dominant paradigm of a social scientific, quantitative approach to studying communication. In the 25 commentaries published in that first volume, the authors either supported some of the ideas in the five major essays or argued against them. There were no attempts at synthesis. Instead, the set of 30 essays presented two themes: in the words of the editors, "first, the challenge to established lines of authority in social science generally and American communication studies in particular; and second, the development of an extraordinary pluralism of theoretical and methodological viewpoints" (p. 14).

The second volume of *Rethinking Communication* is subtitled *Paradigm Exemplars* and consists of 30 chapters written by communication scholars, each of whom typically focused inwardly on his or her own research interests and presented a brief summary of what he or she produced as findings on a small part of the overall communication phenomenon. Few scholars attempted to relate their work to a particular paradigm in any extended manner (Hay, McPhee, and Murdock), and a few acknowledged a paradigm while arguing that it was very difficult or impossible to relate their work to an established paradigm (Marvin, Schwichtenberg, and Sillars). These essays have been characterized by the editors as showing "the fractious nature of the debates among different perspectives in the field" and that as the field became more fragmented, "genuine dialogue among positions had become increasingly rare" (Dervin et al., 1989, p. 13).

These forums were very successful in demonstrating many issues in the paradigm debates. However, with no synthesis or summary chapters, they left readers in the midst of a controversy. Clearly, divergence of thinking was valued over convergence.

The debates are not limited to the deep issues of paradigms but also range over more concrete issues such as how the phenomenon of mass media is to be defined, what constitutes an effect, the nature of audiences, and content. These debates are important because they illuminate essential issues of defining a scholarly field. However, they are not useful if they remain scattered and fail to move toward a convergence of thinking.

Conceptualizations of the Mass Media. There continues to be a debate about how the mass media should be conceptualized. Many people define them by *size* of audience (J. Thompson, 1995; Webster & Phalen, 1997). Some point out that the mass media should be defined in terms of the *kind* of audience (Blumer, 1946; Lowery & DeFleur, 1988; McQuail, 2000), but others disagree (Cantril, 1940). And some scholars define the mass media primarily in terms of a channel of distribution of messages (Janowitz, 1968; Traudt, 2005; Turow, 1989). This lack of agreement among scholars sets up confusion about what our focal phenomenon is. There are also debates about the facets of the mass media phenomenon and their nature—especially the facets of effects, audiences, and content.

Media Effects. As for the effects facet, there are some scholars who conceptualize media influence as being powerful and others who conceptualize it as weak. For example, Fortunato (2005) pointed out that there are "two dichotomous perspectives of mass media effects. A more direct effects perspective contends that mass media messages are powerful in influencing the audience. The indirect, or limited effects, perspective where the uses and gratifications theoretical model is grounded, contends that mass media messages are not an overwhelming influence and are only one potential factor in influencing behavior as the message is interpreted by the individual audience member" (pp. 32–33).

Nature of Audience. There has also been a long-standing debate about whether the audience is active or passive (Biocca, 1988; Eastman, 1998; Himmelweit, Oppenheim, & Vince, 1958; Power, Kubey, & Kiousis, 2002; Schramm, Lyle, & Parker, 1961). To illustrate this point, Power et al. (2002) said there have been two schools of thought. One is the passive audience perspective, which includes the S-R approach, Payne studies, the Frankfurt school of critical theory, cultivation theory, and spiral of silence. The other is the active audience perspective, which includes uses and gratifications, poststructuralist influence, and the Birmingham school of cultural studies.

Meaning in Content. Another debate is concerned with the issue of whether meaning resides in the media text or in the mind of the audience members. Experimental psychologists place the locus of meaning in the texts they select for their treatments. In contrast, critical and cultural scholars argue that meaning resides in the audience (S. Hall, 1980; Radway, 1984). For example, S. Hall (1980) argued that television programs do not have a single meaning but instead are what he called "open texts," which are subject to different readings by different people. H. Newcomb (1984) reinforced this position by saying that messages do not speak for themselves and that we cannot predict a viewer's response by looking solely at the message or text. Instead, it must be understood that viewers constantly interact with the messages in a kind of dialogue. As H. Newcomb and Hirsch (1984) pointed out, there is usually a wide diversity of opinion about any given show, and even those people who share a common reaction to a particular program often have very different reasons for doing so. They explained that viewers bring "values and attitudes, a universe of personal experiences and concerns" to the texts, and by so doing, a viewer "examines, acknowledges, and makes texts of his or her own" (pp. 69–70). These multiple readings of television shows are made possible because viewers are individuals who bring different values and social histories to the task (Allen, 1987).

Related to the debate over where meaning resides is the debate about the nature of human language. This debate focuses on beliefs about whether language is denoted shared meaning or is made up of individual interpretations. The famed

French linguist and critical scholar Ferdinand de Saussure (1983) viewed language as a structured system of symbols that have shared meanings among a common linguistic community. He viewed linguistics as "a science which studies the role of signs as part of social life" (p. 15). Barthes (1968) followed up on this position in his examination of how the mass media promulgate what he called systems of signification, which are widespread sharings of meaning. In contrast, Volosinov (1986) reacted against what he called the "abstract objectivism of Saussure" and argued that in the everyday world, language is a living thing that changes shape and meaning given different contexts. In his work, Volosinov focused on how people struggle over establishing meaning in everyday language. Other critical scholars—most notably Morley (1992) and Radway (1987)—are aligned with this position. Both Morley and Radway argued that individual interpretation is important and that individual interpretations are influenced in large part by the context in which the messages are experienced.

Development of the Field. Media scholars have also debated conceptions about the traditions that have shaped the history of media effects research. Pietila (1994) said there are three: mass communication research (a social science approach to effects), the New Left (media's dependency on economic, political, and ideological forces, which leads to problems of social power and equality), and the cultural version (a symbolic process that produces meaning). Jensen and Rosengren (1990) saw five traditions: effects research, uses and gratifications research, literary criticism, cultural studies, and reception analysis.

Large, Fragmented Literature

Now in the early 21st century, the published research literature that examines some aspect of the mass media has grown to a very large size and covered a great many topics. This is a positive outcome of the Generating-Findings perspective. However, there is also the negative characteristic that the literature is fragmented. This criticism has become more prominent over the past two decades (C. R. Berger, 1991; Hardt, 1992; Jensen & Rosengren, 1990; McQuail, 1989; Pietila, 1994; Power et al., 2002). This literature continues to be plagued by little synthesis across studies, little programmatic research, many theories but with a small proportion of the literature that is theory-driven research, and little translation of ideas and methods from other fields where they were originally developed for other purposes.

Many Studies. There are about 6,200 articles published in scholarly journals on the topic of mass media *effects* (W. J. Potter & Riddle, 2006). Therefore, it is likely that the literature on all facets of the mass media (not just effects) comprises more than 10,000 studies. Furthermore, this should be regarded as a very conservative estimate when we consider that scholarship is published in other communication journals as well as journals from contiguous fields, such as psychology, sociology, political science, education, and marketing. There is also a considerable amount of media scholarship published in books and another large body of work that is presented at professional conferences and not published in books or journals.

Even this very conservative number of 10,000 scholarly pieces is a huge number, considering the amount of effort required to design, conduct, and publish a single study. This is powerful evidence that the phenomenon of the mass media has been of great interest to researchers. But there are also other problems besides its large size that confront readers trying to understand the main ideas in this literature.

Definitional Variation. A significant barrier to understanding when reading many studies on a particular topic is the variation in the way scholars will define key terms. For example, when I looked at the definitions for the term *media violence* in the published literature, I found quite a variety (see W. J. Potter, 1999). Some of these definitions included verbal acts, while most did not; some included accidents, while others required intentional acts; some had to be depicted on the screen, while others could be implied. It is likely that many other commonly used terms—such as *audience, message,* and *child*—also exhibit a wide variety of meanings across studies.

Another example of definitional confounding is with the term *flow.* Raymond Williams (1974) used *flow* to refer to how people experience a sequence of messages in a medium, such as television. He explained that television programs do not exist as discrete entities in the minds of viewers. Rather, a kind of flow across texts is the central experience of the medium (p. 95)—a fact that accounts for much of television's critical significance. This is when the audience member continues an exposure while having one message replace another and where a message is interrupted by other messages. Thus, to Williams, *flow* is an endless random juxtaposition of different texts. H. Newcomb and Hirsch (1984) picked up on this idea but referred to the elements as "viewing strips." In contrast, Csikszentmihalyi (1988) used the term *flow* to refer to a psychological state of being swept away by a task where the person loses a sense of time and place in the pursuit of a highly engrossing goal. Other scholars have referred to the same idea but use a different term, such as *transportation* (Bilandzic & Busselle, 2006; Green & Brock, 2000). These are all important scholars dealing with very interesting ideas; however, the definitional confounding substantially increases the costs to readers and serves to slow down the sharing of meaning.

Definitional variation is not limited to the few examples I illustrated in the above two paragraphs. There are many examples.

Little Synthesis. There are few published efforts at synthesizing parts of this very large literature. In our recent content analysis of the mass media effects literature (W. J. Potter & Riddle, 2006), we found only 47 articles out of the 936 we examined that could remotely be regarded as synthesis pieces. Most of these ($n = 36$) were standalone narrative reviews, many of which were fairly descriptive and did not ascend to the standard of synthesis. The other 11 published articles were meta-analyses, which provide the beginning steps of synthesis but often do not complete the synthesis task.

By *synthesis,* I mean that the literature on a topic is critically analyzed to reject faulty findings and bring forth credible findings into a second stage where those credible findings are organized into groups and the groups of findings calibrated by importance. In this step, it is important to realize that there is great definitional variation across studies using the same terms. Therefore, scholars need to be careful in grouping studies into like literatures without first conducting a careful critical analysis of definitions.

Then, once the literatures are grouped, we need a calibration of which literatures have produced not only the most insights about the phenomenon but also insights that are the most important in revealing the nature of the mass media. Finally, the synthesizer assembles the calibrated findings into a structure such as an outline, model, or graphic that presents a fresh construction that illuminates the structure of the findings as a mapping device—in this case, an explanation of "the how" or "the why" of some aspect of the mass media phenomenon.

As the mass media literature grows, it is crucial that careful syntheses be undertaken. Without this synthesis work, all findings—faulty and valid—will be regarded as equally important. The literature stays fragmented and fairly descriptive. There is little building of more probing insights into the nature of our phenomenon that is achieved in the synergies of juxtaposing various findings together in a system of explanation. Until we are able to organize our literatures into a unified system through synthesis, we will have to labor in a field with scattered findings, thus making it very difficult to choose the most important areas to work on and to access the full set of best thinking when conducting a literature review.

Little Programmatic Research. In *Milestones in Mass Communication Research*, Lowery and DeFleur (1988) argued that the "study of mass communication has been particularly unsystematic." They elaborated this point by saying that scholars "almost never coordinated their efforts or built upon the results of previous research" and that many of the questions guiding the research "were not theoretically significant" (p. 3). This condition persists today. Scholars who publish many studies typically will do a study or two on one topic and then move on to another topic, publish a few studies on that topic, and then move on to another topic. Few scholars identify themselves with a particular theory or programmatic line of research and are defined by it.

I think of this as a kind of "honeybee" approach to research, where scholars are busy bees whose attention is attracted by so many interesting topics (flowers in bloom). They flit from one topic to another as they make their way across the field of flowers. The positive aspect of this "honeybee" nature of the research is that many topics get explored. Also, the travels of the bees have an effect of cross-pollinating topics with ideas and methods from other topics.

However, there is a limitation to this honeybee approach. While flowers benefit from the cross-pollination and can grow on their own, research topics need scholars to stay in one place and build a system of explanation on each topic. To the extent that scholars spend time trying out lots of different topics, the field stays thin—that is, there are few places where scholars conduct programmatic research that builds depth. Now, after at least half a century of largely Generating-Findings research, it would seem to be time to begin concentrating our efforts in the areas that are the most important and start building depth of explanation through more extended lines of programmatic research.

Little Theory-Driven Research. A key characteristic of Generating-Findings research is a low level of theory in guiding the design of studies. Instead, most studies are question driven. This is understandable in new scholarly fields where there may not be many—or any—theories available to guide the design. Thus, using the inductive approach, scholars develop theories in their empirical work. Over time, a great many theories get developed, as can be seen with mass media study.

However, now that we have developed perhaps several hundred theories over the past six decades of research, a sizable proportion of our literatures continues to ignore these theories. Scholars who examine various aspects of our literatures frequently have observed that the use of theory is at a low level and that there needs to be a more explicit use of theory both in the generation of empirical research studies and in the interpretation of results (Shoemaker & Reese, 1990; Stevenson, 1992). Also, in their survey of major scholars in the field of mass communication, So and Chan (1991) reported that 63% of respondents thought that the theoretical development should be a lot better.

These opinions seem to be supported by a low level of theory use in the published literature. For example, in an analysis of published literature on mass communication from 1965 to 1989 in 8 competitive peer-reviewed journals, W. J. Potter, Cooper, and Dupagne (1993) found that only 8.1% of 1,326 articles were guided by a theory and provided a test of that theory; another 19.5% were tests of hypotheses, but these hypotheses were not derived from a theory. A similar pattern was found in an analysis of studies published in *Journalism & Mass Communication Quarterly,* when Riffe and Freitag (1997) reported that only 27.6% of the studies used an explicit theoretical framework, and there was no change in this percentage over the 25-year period they examined, from 1971 to 1995. Similar findings were reported by Kamhawi and Weaver (2003), who examined all articles published in 10 communication journals from 1980 to 1999 and found that only 30.5% specifically mentioned a theory. Likewise, our analysis of mass media effects articles published in 16 journals from 1993 to 2005 found that only 35.0% of coded articles featured a theory prominently (W. J. Potter & Riddle, 2007).

Many Theories. It is ironic that with so little theory-driven research, we still have a very large number of theories in the mass media literature. Table 1.1 lists in alphabetical order what I have found to be some of these theories in my perusal of media theory books and from my review of the past 5 years of the mass media published literature in eight journals. This list, which contains more than 150 theories, reveals a great variety of explanation. A few of these theories are widely known; others are relatively unknown either because they are new or because they have yet to be discovered by many scholars. Some are formal systems of explanations that have generated many hypothetic-deductive tests, while others have been generated from an inductive process in a single study. While most focus their explanations on a small piece of the overall mass media phenomenon, a few are broader and would qualify as middle-range theories (Merton, 1967). Some have been constructed by social scientists working in media studies or related fields (such as psychology, sociology, political science, economics, anthropology, business, or education), while others have been created by humanistic scholars working in fields such as film studies, comparative literature, linguistics, feminist studies, ethnic studies, and art. Some of these explanations display the term *theory* in their titles, while others are referred to as models, hypotheses, or effects. Of course, I am using a broad conception of theory. I have been willing to include in my list any systematic explanation based on ideas (concepts and constructions) that seek to organize, predict, or explain some aspect of a phenomenon.

Table 1.1   Theories Explaining Some Aspect of the Mass Media Phenomenon

ABX balance model (T. Newcomb, 1953)
Advertising and social change (Berman, 1981)
Affective aggression model (A. A. Anderson, Deuser, & DeNeve, 1995)
Affluent society (Galbraith, 1976)
Agenda building (G. E. Lang & Lang, 1983, 1981/1991)
Agenda setting (McCombs & Shaw, 1972, 1993)
Associative network model (J. R. Anderson, 1983)
Attitude construct approach (Fazio, 1990)
Audience as commodity (Jhally & Livant, 1986)
Audience flow (Eastman, 1993)
Audience polarization (Webster & Phalen, 1997)
Automatic activation model (Fazio, 1990)
Availability heuristic (Tversky & Kahneman, 1973)
Availability-valence model (Kisielius & Sternthal, 1984)

Buffering hypothesis (M. H. Davis & Kraus, 1989)

Capacity model (Fisch, 2000)
Catharsis (Aristotle; Freud, 1922; S. Feshbach, 1961)
Channel repertoire (Ferguson & Perse, 1993; Heeter, 1988)
Channel theory of publication (Coser, Kadushin, & Powell, 1982)
Character affiliation theory (Raney, 2004)
Civic engagement (Putnam, 2000)
Coalition model of agenda building (Protess et al., 1991)
Cognitive dissonance (Festinger, 1957)
Cognitive response theory (Greenwald, 1968)
Communication/persuasion matrix model (McGuire, 1986)
Conservative/moralist theory (Zillmann & Bryant, 1985)
Consumer culture theory (Ewen, 1976)
Cue theory (L. Berkowitz, 1965)
Cultivation (Gerbner, 1969; Gerbner & Gross, 1976)
Cultural imperialism (Boyd-Barrett, 1977; Schiller, 1969)
Culture of narcissism (Lasch, 1978)

Decision-making models (Ryan & Peterson, 1982)
Diffusion of innovations (Rogers, 1962, 1986; Rogers & Shoemaker, 1971)
Direct effects model (Lasswell, 1927)
Disinhibition effect (Bandura, 1994)
Disposition theory (Zillmann & Cantor, 1976)
Distribution of knowledge (McQuail & Windahl, 1993)
Double action model of gatekeeping (Bass, 1969)
Drench hypothesis (Greenberg, 1988)

Elaboration likelihood model (Petty & Cacioppo, 1981)
Elite pluralism theory (Berelson, Lazarsfeld, & McPhee, 1954; Key, 1961)
Empathy theory (Zillmann, 1996)

(Continued)

Table 1.1 (Continued)

Encoding-decoding model (S. Hall, 1980)
Exchange model of news (Sigal, 1973)
Exchange theory (Solomon, 1989)
Excitation transfer theory (Zillmann, 1983)
Exemplification theory (Zillmann, 1999; Zillmann & Brosius, 2000)
Expectancy value model (Palmgreen & Rayburn, 1985)

Fraction of selection (Schramm, 1954)
Frame analysis (Goffman, 1974, 1979)
Framing (Cappella & Jamieson, 1997; Scheufele, 1999)
Free market model of media (DeFleur, 1970)

Gatekeeping (White, 1950)
Genre theory (Kaminsky, 1974)
Global village (McLuhan, 1964)
Gratification seeking and audience activity model (Rubin & Perse, 1987)
Gravitation theory (W. J. Potter, 2005)

Hegemony theory (Gramsci, 1971)
Heuristic processing model of cultivation effects (Shrum, 2002)
Hidden persuaders (Packard, 1957)
Homogenization hypothesis (Bagdikian, 2000)

Imitation (N. E. Miller & Dollard, 1941)
Indirect effects model (Cartwright, 1949; Hyman & Sheatsley, 1947)
Information flow theory (D. K. Davis, 1990; Greenberg & Parker, 1965)
Information model of advertising (cited in Jeffres, 1997, pp. 279–281)
Information seeking (Donohew & Tipton, 1973)
Integrated model of media enjoyment (Vorderer, Klimmt, & Ritterfeld, 2004)
Integrated response model (R. E. Smith & Swinyard, 1982, 1988)
Interpretation by social class (Morley, 1980)
Interpretive resistance theory (Carragee, 1990)

Knowledge gap theory (Tichenor, Donohue, & Olien, 1970)

Law of double jeopardy (McPhee, 1963)
Least objectionable programming (Klein, 1971)
Levels of processing theory (Craik & Lockhart, 1972)
Limited-capacity model of mediated message processing (A. Lang, 2000)

Market power model of advertising (cited in Jeffres, 1997, pp. 279–281)
Marketplace model (Webster & Phalen, 1994)
Marxist theory (McQuail, 1987)
Mass audience (Blumer, 1946)
Media access (Westley & MacLean, 1957)
Media as culture industries (Hay, 1989; Jhally, 1987)

Media culture (Altheide & Snow, 1979, 1991)
Media enjoyment as attitude (Nabi & Krcmar, 2004)
Media entertainment theory (Mendelsohn, 1966)
Media flow theory (Csikszentmihalyi, 1988; Sherry, 2004)
Media-public relationships (McQuail & Windahl, 1981)
Media system dependency (DeFleur & Ball-Rokeach, 1975)
Medium is the message (McLuhan, 1962, 1964)
Medium theory (Meyrowitz, 1994)
Message construction (Shoemaker & Reese, 1990)
Mood management (Zillmann, 1988)
Motivated attention and motivated processing (Nabi, 1999)

Neo-associationistic model (L. Berkowitz, 1984)
Neo-mass audience (Webster & Phalen, 1997)
Network model of political priming (Price & Tewksbury, 1997)
News content theory (Shoemaker & Reese, 1996)
News diffusion (Greenberg, 1964)
News factory (Bantz, McCorkle, & Baade, 1980)
News frame theory (Tuchman, 1978)
News selection (Gans, 1979)
Newsworker socialization (Gans, 1979; Tuchman, 1978)

One-dimensional man (Marcuse, 1964)

Parasocial interaction (Horton & Wohl, 1956; Rosengren & Windahl, 1989; Rubin,
    Perse, & Powell, 1990)
Play theory (W. Stephenson, 1967)
Pluralistic ignorance (Allport, 1935)
Political socialization theory (Graber, 1988)
Politics of signification (S. Hall, 1982)
Polysemy theory (J. Fiske, 1986)
Power elite theory (Mills, 1957)
Priming (L. Berkowitz, 1984; Roskos-Ewoldsen, Roskos-Ewoldsen, & Carpentier, 2002)
Principled reasoning theory (J. M. McLeod, Sotirovic, Voakes, Guo, & Huang, 1998)
Profit-driven logic of safety theory
Program choice theory (Steiner, 1952)
Pseudo-events blur reality (Boorstin, 1961)
Psychodynamic model (DeFleur, 1970)
Psychological conditioning (Klapper, 1960; Skinner, 1974)

Rally effect (Coser, 1956)
Reasoned action theory (Fishbein & Ajzen, 1975)
Reception paradigm (E. Katz, 1987)
Resource dependency theory (Turow, 1984)
Revealed preferences (Mansfield, 1970)
Ritual model of communication (Turner, 1977)

(Continued)

Table 1.1 (Continued)

Selective exposure (Freedman & Sears, 1966; Lazarsfeld, Berelson, & Gaudet, 1944)
Selective gatekeeping model
Selective perception (Klapper, 1960)
Semiotic theory (Baudrillard, 1983)
Social cognitive theory of mass communication (Bandura, 2001)
Social construction of meaning (P. L. Berger & Luckmann, 1966; Lippmann, 1922; Mead, 1934)
Social construction of media technologies (Douglas, 1987)
Social identity (Meyrowitz, 1985)
Social learning theory (Bandura, 1973)
Social norms theory of enjoyment (Denham, 2004)
Sociological model of mass communication (Riley & Riley, 1959)
Sociology of news theory (Schudson, 2003)
Spiral of silence (Noelle-Neumann, 1974, 1991)
Star theory (Croteau & Hoynes, 2000)
Storage battery model (S. T. Fiske & Taylor, 1991)
Storage bin model (S. T. Fiske & Taylor, 1991)
Synapse model of priming (S. T. Fiske & Taylor, 1991)

Technological determinism (Fischer, 1992)
Technological drivers (Neuman, 1991)
Television trivialization of public life (Postman, 1985)
Third-person theory (Perloff, 2002)
Transactional model (Graber, 1988; J. M. McLeod & Becker, 1974)
Transmission model (Shannon & Weaver, 1949)
Transportation model (Carey, 1975a, 1975b)
Transportation theory (Green & Brock, 2000)
Two-step flow (E. Katz & Lazarsfeld, 1955)

Uses and dependency model (Rubin & Windahl, 1986)
Uses and gratifications (E. Katz, Blumler, & Gurevitch, 1974; Lasswell, 1948; Rosengren, 1974; Rosengren, Wenner, & Palmgreen, 1985; C. R. Wright, 1960)

Videomalaise (M. J. Robinson, 1976)

This points to a pattern of thin theory development—that is, few theories are introduced in a theory piece but then show up in multiple tests where they are shaped and refined. For example, Kamhawi and Weaver (2003) found that only three theories were mentioned in as many as 10% of their analyzed articles. These patterns led Kamhawi and Weaver to say that "theoretical development is probably the main consideration in evaluating the disciplinary status of the field. As our field grows in scope and complexity, the pressure for theoretical integration increases. It seems that scholars in the field should be developing and testing theories to explain the process and effects of mass communication" (p. 20). Also, in our study of mass media effects literature (W. J. Potter & Riddle, 2007), we found 144 theories in those published studies, but only 12 of these theories were mentioned in 5 or more studies in our sample of 936 published research articles. The remaining 132 theories were spread out over 168 articles.

Little Translation. There is little translation of ideas into mass media research from other fields. While importing ideas into a field can be a good thing—by expanding the pool of ideas to consider and tools to try—it can also be a problem if those ideas are not adapted well to the specific needs of the importing field. Media scholars are more likely to import ideas from other social sciences than to cite other media scholars in communication. To illustrate this point, Reeves and Borgman (1983) studied nine core communication journals. They reported that communication scholars are dependent on journals outside of communication, with communication journal articles exhibiting five cites of other journals for each cite they receive. In a subsequent bibliometric analysis and network analysis of citations in 20 communication journals from 1977 to 1985, Rice et al. (1988) found that for all communication journals, the average impact ratio was .43, which was the lowest impact ratio among 10 social science fields. A ratio of 1.0 means that the articles published in a journal received an average of one citation per year subsequent to their publication. So an impact ratio of .4 means that the articles a journal published this year will receive an average of one citation every 2.5 years. This indicates that compared with other social sciences, communication scholars are much less likely to cite the work of other scholars publishing in their journals. This pattern gives greater weight to the conclusion that the degree of programmatic research is lower in communication than in other fields.

I am *not* arguing that we need to invent all our own ideas, especially when contiguous fields offer so many great ideas that have usefulness for mass media scholars. However, I *am* arguing that when we import an idea, we typically need to transform it in some way to fit the purpose of explaining some aspect of the mass media, and this usually requires some translation. These translations serve to tailor the constructs for our own purposes. Over time, we need to cite more of our translations in proportion to the untranslated constructs from other fields. Also, over time, we will find that we have special needs for mapping arcs that are different from other fields, and therefore there are no constructs we can import. In these cases, we need to develop our own constructs. But doing this requires greater attention to our own special mapping arcs, and in order to do this, we need more programmatic research to develop greater sensitivity to our own special challenges.

In summary, it appears that the field of mass media research is fragmented for several reasons. There is an ever expanding literature, but because so little of it is programmatic or theory driven, there is great difficulty in synthesizing the major findings across studies. The low level of theory-driven research is especially troublesome because there are many theories available for media researchers to use. However, there is not a core set of theories that has had a strong impact on the development of the field. C. R. Berger (1991), writing about the field of communication research in general, said, "The traditionally high level of fragmentation manifested by the field seems to be increasing as the field expands. Although specialization is almost an inevitable consequence of growth, the fact that there is no particular theoretical paradigm or touchstone theory around which communication researchers might organize their efforts is a least one source of concern" (p. 101).

Critique of the Generating-Findings Perspective

The field of mass media scholarship has accomplished a great deal in its Generating-Findings phase. The scholars who have created the literature about the mass media and who have conducted empirical studies have laid down a good base for a scholarly field by identifying key concepts, arranging them in predictive relationships, and providing tests for many of those possible relationships. Much progress has been made.

My critique of the Generating-Findings perspective is not intended to denigrate any of that effort or any of the results of those many studies. Every bit of it contributes to our understanding of the mass media in its own way. My critique is based on the perception that this literature has reached a critical mass that allows us to move on to a more challenging stage of thinking and research. While some scholars have already moved onto this stage, the character of our literature remains largely in the Generating-Findings phase. If we continue with the methods, assumptions, and debates that have been so useful in the past, the marginal utility of these efforts will dwindle to a nonproductive point. We cannot continue to do the same things and expect to continue making progress. Furthermore, I argue that continuing to generate the same type of studies will further clutter our literature. We need to shift our perspective to overcome the problems that are increasingly crippling our efforts with fragmentation. We need to regard the concepts and methods from other scholarly fields more as tools that need to be translated into our purposes; in so doing, we will need to hybridize some of them in order to extend their usefulness to us. And perhaps most important, we need to shift from inductive processes to deductive processes that cluster around theories and provide rigorous programmatic tests of them that continually shape their mapping precision through falsification as well as support. This will orient us toward convergent thinking more so than wandering around in divergent topic seeking. Convergent thinking will foster a sense of shared purpose as we consolidate our scholarly resources to address our most pressing challenges of explanation. And when we work together with a common set of assumptions, definitions, and purpose, we will achieve the traction we need to make much more substantial progress.

The Generating-Findings activity has been an essential initial step in building a scholarly field. However, we have now produced a large number of ideas and findings; adding to that mass can only overwhelm new scholars and fragment existing scholars into smaller and smaller camps that find it harder and harder to understand what scholars in other camps are doing.

Mapping-Phenomenon Perspective on the Mass Media

It is time to shift away from a predominantly Generating-Findings perspective, where we spend most of our resources in generating more ideas, assumptions, definitions, and findings. We have reached a critical mass of thinking and research findings. It is time to shift toward a predominantly Mapping-Phenomenon perspective. While there are many examples of scholars who have been operating from much more of a Mapping-Phenomenon perspective for years, these scholars are a small minority. The dominant perspective has been Generating-Findings.

In this section, I will highlight five major characteristics of what I mean by a Mapping-Phenomenon perspective. These include shaping our findings into knowledge, getting past categorical thinking, focusing on depth over breadth, favoring convergence over divergence, and focusing on the big picture.

Shaping Findings Into Knowledge

The primary scholarly work in a Mapping-Phenomenon perspective is identifying the most important findings in our existing literature and organizing them in a way to extend their power of capturing the essence of our phenomenon. In this calibration process, we need to begin with an analysis of existing definitions for key terms, so we can weed out the less useful definitions and further explicate the more useful ones. We need to make a critical assessment of existing theories, so we can focus on deducing stronger tests from their key propositions, use the results of those empirical tests to pare away faulty predictions, and extend the theory's predictive power by synthesizing additional propositions. We need to background methods as tools that are useful only insofar as they can access various parts of our phenomenon of interest and foreground strong conceptualizations.

Getting Past Categorical Thinking

The diversity of worldviews, scholarly traditions, methods, and conceptualization of key ideas has been a strength—not a weakness—in the development of the field up to this point. The phenomenon of the mass media is complex, and the examination of that complex phenomenon benefits from the thinking from many different perspectives. I believe that our literature is stronger because it contains research from humanistic scholars as well as a full range of social scientific scholars.

The problem with the debates is not the diversity of thinking but the compartmentalization of that thinking. While the debates have offered the potential to expand the thinking of individual scholars, the debate format is limiting because of its polarizing effects. Debates tend either to turn off readers, who then fail to take the opportunity to learn, or to persuade readers to side with one position and thereby demonize other positions. If we are to take advantage of the full range of great ideas, we need to respect and understand all those ideas and then see if we can unify ourselves through a synthesis of the best ideas. In short, we need to get beyond the debates that foster categorical thinking.

Let's not debate whether the quantitative or the qualitative approach is better; both provide valuable and essential tools. There needs to be a confluence of ideas rather than a drawing of lines between camps. There is far more commonality in our thinking than we have been giving ourselves credit for. I made this point in my book *An Analysis of Thinking and Research About Qualitative Methods* (W. J. Potter,

1996), and I am not alone in this assessment. For example, in their book titled *Mediamaking: Mass Media in a Popular Culture,* Grossberg, Wartella, and Whitney (1998) laid out two fundamental models of communication: the transmission model and the cultural model. After contrasting the two models, they said, "Although many scholars assume that the transmission and cultural models of communication contradict each other—that they have to choose one model or the other—we disagree. We believe that each model has something important to say about the complexities of communication in the contemporary world; the usefulness of each model depends on our particular questions about communication. Thus we prefer to think of the two models as complementary perspectives" (p. 25). Gerbner (1983) concluded the "Ferment in the Field" issue of the *Journal of Communication* with a call for respect for all kinds of research. He argued that all are important. For example, he used the analogy of a three-legged stool, saying it is foolish to argue which of the three legs makes the stool stand up. "If the implication is that the other sections (or legs) are somehow less significant or even dispensable, the statement becomes misleading and harmful" (p. 357).

Rather than participate in the debate about whether the audience is active or passive, it would be far better to work for a synthesis (Livingstone, 1993; Power et al., 2002; Webster & Phalen, 1994). For example, Livingstone (1993) wrote about the danger of taking either side in this debate when she said, "If we see the media or life events as all-powerful creators of meaning, we neglect the role of audiences: if we see people as all-powerful creators of meaning, we neglect the structure of that which people interpret." There are times when audience members are active and other times when they are passive. The key to advancing our understanding of audiences is to get beyond the debate about which of these positions is more descriptive of the audiences and instead focus our resources on finding out why the audience is passive at certain times and active at other times.

Let's not debate whether media effects are powerful, weak, or nonexistent. They are all three, depending on the effect and the conditions. It is hard to believe that any scholar who reads a sizable portion of the media effects literature can seriously take a polar position on this long-standing debate about whether media effects exist. Let's not get trapped by categorical thinking but instead examine the full spectrum of effects.

The locus of meaning has been the topic of serious debate for decades. But again, it seems like there should be a range of options for considering where the locus of meaning lies, ranging from purely in the text to purely in the mind of the audience member. When we allow for a range of positions, we will most likely find that meaning typically emerges from the middle positions. The symbols in texts carry common meanings; if not, communication would not be possible. However, people have the ability to significantly alter the sender's intended meaning by translating the media messages through their own experiences.

Let's get beyond the jargon that separates scholars into differing camps. Let's get beyond the denial that both sides do not have limitations. And let's move from conflict that generates heat of argumentation to discussion that generates more light to illuminate the darker corners of our phenomenon. To the extent that the debates continue, they will limit our chances to progress as a scholarly field. Debates reinforce a fractiousness of scholars into camps who feel they must compete. The camps foster categorical thinking as a way of creating camp identity and loyalty. We need to get past the inclination in a Generating-Findings field to create camps and move to a higher level of thinking to pull the best from each camp and create a national identity around the idea of generating more powerful and insightful explanations about the phenomenon of the mass media.

Focusing on Depth Over Breadth

In shifting into the Mapping-Phenomenon phase, we need to focus our attention on a few topic areas and marshal our limited resources to make progress in deepening our explanations. We have identified a lot of the who, what, and where. Now we need to focus on addressing the questions of how and why. This will require much more analysis of the current literature than putting forth reasoned speculation about mapping mechanisms. The tests of these mechanisms need to conform to a set of definitions and shared meanings to build a genuine program of mapping research.

I am not arguing that we reduce the number of questions by ignoring many of them. Instead, I am arguing that we need to calibrate and organize. Calibrate the importance of questions in order to identify the most important ones. Then organize the other questions hierarchically as subsets of the most important questions. All questions that we have dealt with in the past are still important to examine, but not all questions are equally important. We need to organize our research efforts by first organizing our thinking about what is most important.

Favoring Convergence Over Divergence

To develop this depth, we need scholars who will build more on the work of others. This requires a focus on convergence of sharing definitions, assumptions, and procedures.

An effect of convergence is the bringing together of scholars into a more unified field. The more we share a common understanding of the nature of our phenomenon and how best to go about constructing explanations for it, the more we will share a sense of community and hence achieve a higher scholarly profile. Kuhn (1970a) provided a definition of a scientific community that can be applied usefully to any scholarly community: "Bound together by common elements of their education and apprenticeship, they see themselves and are seen by others as . . . responsible for the pursuit of a set of shared goals, including the training of their successors. Such communities are characterized by the relative fullness of communication within the group and by the relative unanimity of the group's judgment in professional matters" (p. 296). Community requires convergence.

Focusing on the Big Picture

Perhaps the most important characteristic of the Mapping-Phenomenon perspective is the focus on the big picture, that is, the nature of the mass media as our phenomenon of interest. Thus, we need more thinking at the broadest level. We need more macro-level theorizing.

I am not arguing that individual empirical studies are not important; to the contrary, the individual studies are essential. But when scholars design their individual studies and get down in the micro details of their one topic, their decisions will be much better if they keep in mind how their study fits into the map of the overall phenomenon. By carefully positioning their study in the design stage of the research, they can more clearly direct their eventual findings to the part of the overall Mapping-Phenomenon system where those findings will have the most impact. Without such positioning in the design, the findings easily can get lost in the clutter of a fragmented literature. This is why programmatic research is so important; each new study is clearly positioned along a developing path. This is why theory testing is so important; each test is clearly positioned as making a contribution in shaping a particular part of an identifiable system of explanation. This is why critical reviews of the literature are so important; they provide a map of a particular topic area. And at the most macro level, this is why a general framework is so important; it can provide the global map of the phenomenon.

Evolving

The question now becomes how to evolve from a predominantly Generating-Findings perspective to a more Mapping-Phenomenon perspective. The purpose of this book is to provide some guidelines for such an evolution. That is, in this book, I try to do more than point out the limitations of our current understanding about our phenomenon and criticize many of our current practices. I also show what could be done differently and highlight how those different practices (in defining terms, designing studies, and integrating findings) could greatly benefit the development of our scholarly field by substantially increasing our knowledge of the mass media, developing a greater sense of community among scholars, and giving our field a greater visibility among contiguous scholarly communities.

To be most useful in guiding a shift from a Generating-Findings perspective to a Mapping-Phenomenon perspective, we need a general framework that achieves three goals. First, it needs to guide the explication of definitions for key constructs. Almost every concept has a variety of definitions; we need to sort through the wisdom in those definitions, select the best elements, and synthesize those elements together into the most useful definition possible. Second, a general framework should provide a critical analysis of scholarly literatures on mass media so as to highlight the most useful findings. By this, I do not mean that the framework is an inventory of all the findings across those literatures. Instead, I mean that there needs to be a critical calibration of those findings such that the ones with the greatest conceptual leverage are foregrounded. Third, a general framework should offer a structure that serves to organize our understanding of the mass media phenomenon.

Beginning with the next chapter and extending through all the chapters in this book, I offer a general perspective that I call *lineation*. I believe this to be an apt label for this general framework because lineation means the marking with lines, a division into lines, or an arrangement or group of lines. Throughout this book, you will see many allusions to lines. The crafting of formal definitions is essentially about drawing lines, that is, establishing the perimeter of the concept. What should be included and what should be excluded? With the facet of media organizations, I talk about lines of thinking. Media content is expressed as narrative lines that are analytical devices that reveal the encoding conventions and decoding triggers in each mass media message. Audience experience is expressed in terms of exposure states that are separated by thresholds, which are lines dividing qualitatively different states. Effects are expressed in terms of baselines and fluctuation lines.

With this lineation general perspective, I attempt to achieve the goals I have laid out above. First, I attempt to bring greater clarity to our major constructs by synthesizing formal definitions. Second, the lineation general framework provides a critical analysis of scholarly literatures on mass media so as to highlight the most useful findings. Some of these findings that I regard as most important are highly salient in the literatures, but others are more obscure. These choices may prove controversial, but I was guided less by popularity of findings or size of literatures than by utility of ideas as contributing to a unified system of explanation.

Third, I have attempted to shape the configuration of research findings into large-scale knowledge structures that are relatively easy for readers to understand, whether those readers are students new to the study of the phenomenon or seasoned scholars entrenched in their own perspectives. This structure adapts the familiar organization scheme of Lasswell (1948), which is organized by the questions of who says what to whom in which channels to what effect. My adaptations include demoting channel as an important question because digitization has rendered channel a background idea. Also, I prefer to think of the other four (media organizations, audiences, messages, and effects) not as a linear process but as facets of the same thing, much like a diamond with its different facets that are integral to the stone itself. When we look at a diamond, we see the facet closest to us, but we also look through that facet and see the intersection of the other facets. I argue that we should think of our phenomenon in the same way—that is, when we think about the mass media, we focus on one facet primarily, but we must contextualize that one facet by considering the influence of the other facets on it.

Undoubtedly, some readers may ask, Is the lineation general framework a theory, a paradigm, or something else? I hesitate to label it as a theory or paradigm given the wide range of definitions of these (see Dervin et al., 1989, for illustrations of this point). It has elements that would make it look like a theory to some readers (a dictionary, explanatory propositions, axioms, some operational calculus); it may not look like a theory to other readers. It has elements that would make it look like a paradigm to some readers (attention to scholarly communities, widespread assumptions and practices); it may not look like a paradigm to other readers. I will resist such labels. However, if readers feel compelled to categorize it as a theory, paradigm, or something else, I ask that they do this as a background activity and in the foreground keep their focus on matters of building a scholarly field that more effectively and efficiently increases our understanding of the mass media phenomenon.

Conclusion

The mass media have become an extremely important phenomenon in our culture, and they will continue to be so. For more than six decades, this phenomenon has attracted the attention of a wide variety of scholars who have produced a great deal of scholarship about the mass media. This scholarship, which has largely been Generating-Findings in nature, has brought us to a point where we have a very large inventory of ideas as well as findings from individual research studies.

We seemed to have reached a plateau in our research and thinking about the mass media. Our scholarly practices and debates that have served us well in the past are losing their power in the face of new challenges. We continue to be too dependent on Generating-Findings research not driven by theory; by sporadic, nonprogrammatic research; and by importing many ideas rather than developing our own. Also, the debates that have helped us expand our vision of the phenomenon and stimulated lots of approaches to examining it have also fostered categorical thinking that now limits our ability to synthesize creative explanations. It is time to challenge many of our assumptions about theory, about research, and especially about the mass media phenomenon itself. This book presents a lineation general framework that is intended to guide an evolution away from a Generating-Findings perspective and toward a Mapping-Phenomenon perspective for approaching the study of the phenomenon of the mass media.

CHAPTER 2

Introduction to the General Framework

In the previous chapter, I critiqued the current state of mass media research as being stuck on a plateau where the further generation of research findings is beginning to contribute more to clutter than to knowledge. I argued for a shift in thinking and practices from a Generating-Findings perspective to a more Mapping-Phenomenon perspective. The purpose of this book is to provide a general framework to guide such an evolution. In this chapter, I take the first steps in addressing that purpose by presenting an overview of the lineation general framework.

In order to introduce this lineation general framework in as parsimonious a manner as possible, I use the metaphor of a bicycle wheel to illustrate the structure and function of scholarly fields. The three major components of a bicycle wheel are the central hub, the spokes radiating outward from the hub in all directions, and the rim. Each of these three is essential. The hub consists of a shared core set of ideas about what the phenomenon of scholarly interest is—in this case, the mass media. The spokes are the many lines of research that work off the hub. And the rim is a series of ideas that unify the entire enterprise into a whole. In this chapter, I will elaborate each of these features—the hub, the spokes, and the rim—of the wheel to introduce the main ideas of this general framework for mass media thinking and research.

The Hub

The hub is the set of shared axioms in a field. By the term *axiom*, I mean an assumption that must be accepted as a foundational premise. It cannot be tested to determine its ultimate truth in any objective manner. Instead, axioms are either accepted as beliefs or they are not. Scholarly communities are strong to the extent that scholars share a common set of beliefs about their phenomenon of interest.

One kind of axiom is definitional—that is, it is concerned with the meaning we attach to our terms and how widespread the acceptance of those meanings is. Another form of axiom is philosophical in nature; that is, it refers to matters of ontology (i.e., the nature of our phenomenon of interest) and epistemology (i.e., our abilities and limitations to perceive and understand that phenomenon).

Problems in the Hub

The mass media scholarly field exhibits two hub-type problems. First, there is a lack of clarity on the focal construct of *mass media*. Second, there is a fragmentation of worldviews. Each of these problems seriously undermines the formation of a scholarly community.

Focal Construct Problem. In new fields, scholars begin conducting research without a clear or a shared conceptualization of their focal phenomenon. They struggle to build this conceptualization in a hermeneutic process of trial and error. Each exploratory study adds a bit more understanding about which definitions seem to work better than others. Eventually, one definition emerges as being a more useful definition than others that have been tried. The more that scholars recognize the superior utility of this one definition, the more that the field can progress efficiently. A shared definition for the focal phenomenon more clearly directs future thinking and research as well as making it easier to integrate the insights from all that scholarly activity into a systematically growing knowledge base (for a discussion of the importance of explicating focal constructs, see Chaffee, 1991).

We are at a point where we need a clear, shared definition of mass media. However, there seem to be several terms used to characterize our phenomenon of interest, and scholars seem to operate as if there were a shared definition when there is not. This is a serious problem.

There appear to be several terms for the focal phenomenon—*mass communication, mass media,* and *media communication,* to name a few. Each of these terms is contested. To illustrate, the British sociologist John Thompson (1995) observed that "it has often been noted that 'mass communication' is an infelicitous phrase. The term 'mass' is especially misleading. It conjures up the image of a vast audience comprising many thousands, even millions of individuals. This may be an accurate image in the case of some media products, such as the most popular modern-day newspapers, films and television programmes; but it is hardly an accurate representation of the circumstance of most media products, past or present" (p. 24). Other scholars also struggle with addressing the criterion of audience size. For example, Webster and Phalen (1997) argued that in order to be a mass, the audience "must be of sufficient size that individual cases (e.g., the viewer, the family, the social network) recede in importance and the dynamic of a larger entity emerges" (p. 9). However, we are still left with the question of *how large* an audience needs to be in order for individual cases to recede, so we are still caught in the quantitative trap. Most scholars would agree that a PBS broadcasted documentary that reaches 5,000 households in a viewing market is an example of a mass media message, but it is likely that these same scholars would not consider the 10,000 fans at a stadium watching a high school football game as an example of a mass media message. Thompson concluded, "So if the term 'mass' is to be used, it should not be construed in narrowly quantitative terms" (p. 24).

The term *mass* has been used by sociologists to refer to a particular kind of society, which has implications for how communication from the media takes place. Here, *mass* refers more to the qualities of the audience than to the size of the audience. For example, Lowery and DeFleur (1988) defined mass communication not in terms of the size of the audience but in terms of the quality of the audience as being a "mass society" due to the influences of industrialization, urbanization, and modernization. Other sociologists have argued that people in the modern mass society were becoming both isolated and alienated from other members of society because increasing technology was making people into machines. Thus, a mass audience was one with no social organization, no body of custom and tradition, no established set of rules or rituals, no organized group of sentiments, and no structure or status roles (Blumer, 1946; McQuail, 2000). J. Thompson (1995) extended this idea by saying that mass "suggests that the recipients of media products constitute a vast sea of passive, undifferentiated individuals. This is an image associated with some earlier critiques of 'mass culture' and 'mass society,' critiques which generally assumed that the development of mass communication has had a largely negative impact on modern social life, creating a kind of bland and homogeneous culture" (p. 24).

But this conception of the audience was discredited as research revealed that audience members exhibit customs and rituals in media exposures and that they rely on social networks of opinion leaders to discuss issues they encounter in the media. People are interpretive beings, and not every person is affected by a particular media message (Cantril, 1940). Furthermore, it was later shown that the people who were affected were not all affected in the same manner, nor did they all react in the same way. Therefore, the term *mass,* which connotes a large-size audience or a particular kind of audience, is an adjective with ambiguous meaning. J. Thompson (1995) continued, "If the term 'mass' may be misleading in certain respects, the term 'communication' may be as well, since the kinds of communication generally involved in mass communication are quite different from those involved in ordinary conversation" (p. 25).

The term *mass media* also has an ambiguous meaning because it is typically defined in an ostensive manner by exemplification rather than through a formal statement that highlights the critical elements that are needed in such a classification scheme. For example, Traudt (2005) defined mass media as "the range of print, electronic, and filmic opportunities supported by multiple platforms for presentation and consumption" (pp. 5–6), although he acknowledged that such a definition is too simple. Also, Turow (1989) defined mass media as "the technological devices used in mass communication" and defined mass communication as "the industrialized production and multiple distribution of images through technological devices" (p. 454). And Janowitz's (1968) definition is "technological devices (press, radio, films, etc.) to disseminate symbolic content" (p. 41).

Defining mass media by channel has become an even more serious problem with the digitization of messages because the same message can move seamlessly through different channels, which raises the question about why a message would not be regarded as a mass media message if it is a DVD of a family's summer picnic but then does become a mass media message when shown on *America's Funniest Home Videos.* Clearly, there is more to the definition than channel. The problem of defining the mass media ostensively by channel is that the definition does not provide a decision rule that could be used to classify messages consistently as being either mass media or not mass media. This lack of a decision rule indicates that scholars do not agree on what is the critical essence of a mass medium—that is, what do all the ostensive examples have that other channels lack?

None of the above mentioned ideas has served as a clear classification element in defining a mass audience. There have been convincing criticisms to eliminate each one of them (for a good review of this criticism, see Webster & Phalen, 1997). Therefore, a definition cannot rely on channel or on audience type or size. Thus, we have a good idea now about what the mass media are not, but we as yet lack a clear articulation of critical characteristics of the mass media that captures their essence and can be used as a classification rule. Even so, the terms *mass communication* and *mass media* are commonly used by scholars.

Arguably, the best definition of the mass media to date has been provided by J. Thompson (1995), who defined it as "the institutionalized production and generalized diffusion of symbolic goods via the fixation and transmission of information or symbolic content" (p. 26). He said there are five key elements of this definition: "the technical and institutional means of production and diffusion; the commodification of symbolic forms; the structured break between production and reception; the extended availability of media products in time and space; and the public circulation of mediated symbolic forms" (p. 26). However, this definition is not without its problems. One problem is with the commodification of content. Of course, the mass media commodify their content, but so do non-mass images. One example is getting a family portrait at Sears. This photographic image is a commodity advertised and sold for a profit, but it is a private message, not one available to the masses. Another problem with Thompson's definition is the institutional means of production. There are many examples of entrepreneurs starting magazines, book publishing houses, and Internet software firms who had very few employees and a decidedly noninstitutional approach but who created messages that would be considered mass media. Perhaps Thompson regarded his list of five characteristics as each being nonnecessary—that is, none is necessary, but the more that these five characteristics are present in an example, the more that example is likely to be regarded as a mass medium. Perhaps, but he does not specify this.

Worldview Problem. By fragmentation of worldviews, I do not mean only that scholars are operating under different worldviews. By *fragmentation,* I mean that scholars are either fighting worldview battles or ignoring the differences. As could be seen in the previous chapter, both of these conditions persist. Ignoring the thinking of scholars who operate from a different worldview creates a low ceiling of understanding. And while fighting the battles over worldviews is better than ignoring worldviews, these debates usually take effort away from making more progress in explaining our phenomenon itself.

I am not arguing here that everyone should have the same worldview. Instead, I am arguing that scholars need to exhibit a broader base of cooperation. By this, I mean that we need to stop arguing about which worldview is best and learn to respect the full range of worldviews as being a strength in our field. We need to access the insights being developed by scholars across the range of worldviews with their many different methods and approaches. By rising above the worldview turf battles, we can gain a broader perspective on our phenomenon and learn useful things about our phenomenon from scholars working from different worldviews than our own.

Developing the Hub

The first step in evolving toward a Mapping-Phenomenon perspective requires a careful explication of the field's focal construct as well as its major constructs. Until this can be accomplished, the hub will be weak, and the lines of research that flow from the hub will serve more to increase clutter than to increase knowledge of our phenomenon.

Defining the Focal Phenomenon. The definition I propose for the mass media has two conditions, each of which is necessary but neither of which is sufficient. The first condition is the technological production of messages such that they can be made available to a large number of people at the same time. This reflects J. Thompson's (1995) definitional element of the mass media's ability to transmit a message simultaneously to a wide range of people over space and time. This definitional element is necessary to rule out face-to-face communication where immediate feedback is available from another human. My second definitional element is that the mass media are organizations (not necessarily institutions or commercial businesses, although they often are) that distribute their messages *with the purpose of creating and maintaining audiences.* The key idea here is that they are not interested in creating a one-time audience, such as what a concert promoter might do. Instead, their goal is more ambitious. Mass media have the clear intention of conditioning audiences for repeat exposures. To me, this is the key definitional element that has been missing in the literature thus far.

Thus it seems useful to define the mass media as *technological channels of distributing messages by organizations with the purpose of creating and maintaining audiences.* Notice that the definition of mass media is not keyed to the size of the audience or to particular channels, which are the key definitional elements that are used in everyday language. Nor is it keyed to the qualities of the audience, which were important to sociologists in the first half of the 20th century. Instead, the lineation definition is keyed to *how* the channel is used. The focus is on the sender. In order to be a mass medium, the sender must be an organization (and not an individual), and the sender's main intention is to condition audiences into a ritualistic mode of exposure—that is, the mass media are much less interested in coaxing people into one exposure than they are in trying to get people into a position where they will be exposed regularly to their messages. When an organization uses a technological channel of communication to create and *maintain* an audience, it is a mass medium. Thus, *mass* media are not interested in creating an audience for a one-time message exposure; *mass* media want to preserve their audiences so they can maintain their revenue streams and amortize their high initial costs of attracting the audience the first time over the course of repeated exposures.

Using the intention of the sender of a message is key because it sets up a line of thinking that has great explanatory power for all facets of the mass media phenomenon. It explains many of the strategies used by media organizations, why messages are constructed the way they are, the experience of the audience during exposures, and the eventual effects on the audience members.

Defining Four Facets. Now that we have the core, formal definition of mass media, we can elaborate this by considering the major components of the phenomenon. Lasswell (1948) provided a strong foundation for the consideration of components with his classic series of questions: Who says what to whom in which channels to what effect? The components suggested in these questions are very useful in categorizing the mass media research over the past six decades, and with one exception, they will continue to be useful into the future. That one exception, I would argue, is the component of channel. With cable TV, then with computers, and especially with digitization, the idea of channel has faded into a background issue at best.

The lineation general framework identifies four major facets—mass media organizations, mass media audiences, mass media messages, and the mass media effects. Notice that I do not refer to these four as categories or components of the phenomenon because those words imply parts such that the phenomenon can be taken apart and each part examined separately. Instead, I use the word *facets* to suggest the four are all sides of the same thing, much like a diamond has different facets. Of course, writing in a book is a linear format, so I must develop each of these four one at a time. But I am planting the idea early in this book that to understand this general framework's system of explanation, the mass media phenomenon needs to be regarded as multifaceted—that is, it has different sides, but those sides are really of the same essence. Those facets might initially appear different because each presents a different face. It is not quite accurate to say that the four components "work together" or that one component influences the others. It is more accurate to think of all four as being the same thing, simply a different perspective on the same thing.

In this section, I define the four facets in a particular way that makes them somewhat different from how other scholars have defined these terms. Because these definitions are different and because those differences are so important to this general framework, their definitions are carefully delineated in this section.

Media organizations are entities that compete for talent and other resources so as to construct audiences by providing messages with high perceived entertainment or informational value. A general framework purporting to explain the mass media must recognize the media organization as an integral facet of the phenomenon. Unfortunately, this facet is overlooked in much of our scholarship. Not only is the literature on the mass media organizations far smaller than the literatures on media audience, content, and effects, but the industry perspective rarely shows up in those other literatures. For example, the effects literature is largely critical of the media industries. This is not to say that media organizations should not be criticized. But there is a difference between reasoned criticism that builds from an understanding of an industry's goals and criticism that flows from the critic's personal preferences and lacks an understanding of the nature of the industry itself.

Media messages are developed using formulas to attract and hold the attention of the targeted audience members in a way to condition those audience members for repeat exposures. Media messages use standard formulas in the production of stories so as to make those stories easy to follow. Audience members use the formulas to tell them what the message will be about and how to process the information in that message.

Media audiences are collections of individuals who are exposed to particular media messages. Typically, an audience for a particular message is a niche, that is, composed of a set of individuals sharing a key characteristic that is tied to the message. Audience members look for value in messages—that is, they quickly and automatically make assessments of their costs compared with the benefits. Costs are money, time, and psychic energy. Benefits are primarily utility of information and emotional reactions.

Media effects are changes brought about by the media either in individuals or in larger social structures. On an individual level, a media effect is what an audience member experiences during exposure to a media message or as a consequence of that exposure. The experience can be the acquisition of some element from a media message, so the experience can add something new to the individual. The experience can also do something—trigger, alter, or condition something that already exists within the individual person. On a more macro level, a media effect can add or alter something in society, the public, or an institution.

Primitive Terms. There are many primitive terms that I am leaving undefined in the belief that scholars reading this would share the same meanings for these terms. These are terms where the everyday meaning, which is shared by most people, is the meaning that is used in this theory. Thus, there is no special—or technical—meaning for these terms when used in this theory.

There are too many primitive terms to list them all. The following list will provide some examples: newspapers, magazines, books, radio, news, fiction, advertising viewing, reading, listening, children, adolescents, adults, characters, perpetrators, victims, and weapons.

Audience-Defined Terms. There is a group of terms I label *audience-defined terms.* These are terms that are best not defined by researchers or theoreticians. These are terms that are often used in everyday language by all people. People have a clear, intuitively derived meaning for these terms, although sometimes it is difficult for them to articulate what that meaning is. But they know it when they see it.

It is also interesting to note that for each of these terms, there is likely to be a range of meanings in the general population. That is, not everyone defines the term precisely the same way. For example, think of the term *attractiveness.* Most people, whether they are social scientists or couch potatoes, know what this means to them. However, the meanings of attractiveness differ substantially across individuals. What a 14-year-old boy thinks is attractive is most likely something very different than what a 35-year-old woman thinks is attractive. Also, a Beverly Hills plastic surgeon, a 5-year-old girl hugging teddy bear, a gay Olympic gymnast, and a poor migrant worker from a Third World country are all familiar with the concept of attractiveness but are likely to have very different definitions for it.

What is important for this general framework is the recognition that this type of concept exists and that many examples of this concept are essential for the explanatory propositions presented in later chapters. Although these terms are important, I prefer that they be treated descriptively, not prescriptively—that is, I am arguing that we as researchers need to inventory the variety of meanings so we can understand how they are used in common, everyday language in the general population. Once those receiver definitions are described, those meanings should be related to the influence process outlined in Part V of this book. But rather than have these definitions imposed by me or any other media scholar, it would be much more useful for researchers to inventory the various meanings of each of these terms and then try to test that variety of meanings in the propositions where the term appears. This is one of the ways in which this general framework respects the interpretive nature of an individual's meaning making.

The Spokes

The spokes are the lines of scholarship, each spoke indicating a different topic area that extends knowledge about the mass media. The longer the spoke, the more thinking and research are building up on that topic.

Spokes are extended most efficiently when there is a system of explanation— like a theory—that is used to guide the design of empirical studies and the integration of the findings of those studies into a body of knowledge. Also, efficiency is gained when the research is programmatic—that is, when a scholar commits to a topic and carefully learns where a topic's frontier of knowledge is and then exerts his or her effort at that point where it will have the greatest pay-off in generating fresh insights by building efficiently from the strongest work on that topic while correcting the documented weaknesses. In contrast, when research is exploratory in nature, it is less like a metal spoke supporting a rim and more like a frayed piece of twine where tiny threads of studies sprout off in all directions and suddenly break off.

A spoke becomes stronger when there is a tight intertwining of theory and testing extended programmatically over time. The more scholars are concerned with testing a theory, the more convergent will be their research efforts and the greater the extension of a spoke. The value of a scholarly field to other scholarly fields and the public is usually traceable to the length and strength of its spokes, more so than the number of its spokes (i.e., lines of different research).

Problems With the Spokes

Many lines of mass media research have been started. In looking at the totality of this research, there appear to be two characteristics that have limited its usefulness. One is the lack of balance across lines of research, and the other is that some lines seem to be stuck in an exploratory phase.

Balance. Within the overall phenomenon of the mass media, certain topics have attracted more attention of scholars than have other topics. On the broad level, when we organize the phenomenon into four facets (mass media organizations, content, audiences, and effects), the facet of effects has received a great deal of attention. The facets of content and audiences have received a fair amount of attention, but the facet of the industry has received much less attention from scholars. So there is an imbalance of understanding across these four facets.

There is also an imbalance within facets. The effects literature is largely based on testing immediate effects. Also, it is focused on changes. Effects that take a long time to manifest themselves (such as 2 weeks or longer) as well as effects that manifest themselves as reinforcement of already existing cognitions, attitudes, and behaviors rarely are examined.

Within audiences, there has been a good deal of work on self-reported motives for exposure and on audience flow in television viewing. However, there has been much less research on exposure states and what attracts individuals into different exposure states, how individuals make exposure decisions in those states, and how people are affected in different states.

Within content, there has been a good deal of research looking at certain characteristics of news stories on television and in newspapers but not in other media. There has also been a good deal of research looking at sex, violence, and demographics (gender, ethnic background, occupations), but other characteristics of media content largely have been ignored. Also, there has been very little work on determining the storytelling formulas across media and genres.

This criticism of imbalance focuses concern less on past practices and more on the future. That is, it is understandable that a field with very limited research resources has not apportioned those resources in a balanced manner; instead, generating any kind of insight into the nature of the media has been likely to make a contribution. But if the field is to mature well, it needs synergies of explanation across facets, media, and topics. The more balanced the research is across these dimensions, the stronger can be the synergies of explanation.

Stuck in the Exploratory Phase. Recall from the previous chapter that the thesis underlying this book is that mass media scholarship needs to move out of an emphasis on the exploratory perspective and more into emphasizing an explanatory perspective. The way this translates into this spoke metaphor is that when scholars operate from an exploratory perspective, they keep trying to reinvent the wheel, and because their energy is limited, they continually invent a wheel inferior to the one that already exists. More literally, when a line of research already has a critical mass of studies, it is a far more efficient use of resources when scholars undertake the less difficult and more valuable work of fixing problems found in past empirical work than when thay start with a relatively blank page and try to design a study from scratch.

Developing the Spokes

The lineation general framework focuses attention on a series of "spoke tasks" to guide thinking and practices more toward a Mapping-Phenomenon perspective. Most primary among these tasks is for scholars to work from a common set of key constructs.

Another task is for designers to deduce empirical tests from theoretical propositions or from promising findings in the existing literatures. For reasons of efficiency in using our precious limited resources and effectiveness in getting the greatest increases in understanding out of our research efforts, we need to test theories and continually modify them as our primary guidance tools for building the spokes. For a good treatment of how to develop theories, see Shoemaker, Tankard, and Lasorsa (2004).

There needs to be more critical analysis of our growing research bases from time to time. This is why meta-analyses as well as narrative analyses of the literature are so important. We need to criticize the theory and research, force the theoreticians to alter their existing theories, and even construct additional theories to provide competing explanations. All of this activity contributes to the strengthening and lengthening of a spoke.

We also need to achieve more balance. That is, we need much more work in the understudied areas so as to build our understanding of the full nature of our phenomenon. When one area is not well understood, the context for understanding all other areas is limited.

The strength of our scholarly field lies in its spokes. Over the past six decades, scholars have begun many spokes. While the lines of research on many of these spokes are still at an exploratory stage and have not progressed very far, many spokes have moved into theory, attracting a lot of scholars who have provided critical analyses and additional testing. As that additional testing of theories progresses, we need to refine our theories and ask more of them. A theory that organizes thinking is a very useful tool in the exploratory phase of research. But as we develop each spoke more, we need to have more predictive theories that show relationships between two or more variables. Then we need more research with representative samples so we can move beyond examining *whether or not* X will occur and instead examine *how often* X will occur, how *powerful* X is compared with Y and Z, and how *widespread* X is. And eventually, we need to develop the explanatory features of theories to guide the testing of multiple factors in complex sets of relationships to address the questions of *how* and *why*. This will require thinking about larger sets of variables (Chaffee, 1977; Hyman, 1955) as well as the structure of how the variables work together (M. Rosenberg, 1968).

In summary, spokes will grow most efficiently and effectively when designers of research studies work from a common set of constructs and work from clear, conceptual definitions of key terms; when researchers use tried and tested measurement instruments; and when researchers are guided by a clear picture of what has been tested and what has not thus far in a research program. When researchers work off of common definitions, designs, and measurement instruments, their findings can be clearly positioned at the cutting edge where they will make a salient contribution to knowledge. Findings from exploratory studies have no such "cutting-edge" context—that is, they cannot be interpreted in the context of a program of research.

When there are many examples of programmatic research that have moved substantially beyond the initial exploratory stage, the longer and stronger are the spokes. And a field is more mature when the lines of research cover the entire span of the phenomenon. But to achieve a full set of lines of research, a field needs to have a group of committed scholars who work from a common conception of their focal phenomenon and who understand the broad context of findings across all the areas of research when they design their own research and write about the importance of their own findings.

The Rim

The rim serves three functions in this metaphor. First, the rim defines the perimeter of the field. This serves to give the field greater definition. Second, the rim provides a target point for lines of research. And third, the rim presents a series of ideas that are shared by scholars in the field. The rim displays high-profile ideas that are integrated into a set that gives coherence to the scholarly community, not just one line of research.

Each line of research feeds its important findings into the rim, and when those ideas are carefully assembled into a meaningful flow where each idea dovetails into the next, the set provides a solid context for each individual idea. For example, a line of research into a particular media effect is better guided when it is shaped by the knowledge gained about lines of research in other media effects. Also, this line of effects research becomes stronger when it is guided by findings about the media organizations, the formulas in the messages, and characteristics of audiences, all of which come from lines of research (spokes) in other areas of the wheel.

Problems With the Rim

The biggest limitation of the current research field, I believe, lies in an underdeveloped rim. That is, there is not enough integration of findings across lines of research. This serves to make the research appear idiosyncratic and fragmented rather than as converging into an integrated body of knowledge.

The nature of mass media scholarship has been fragmentary throughout its history. This is one of the reasons that I chose the metaphor of diverging spokes of a wheel to characterize it. The individual lines of research will always diverge; that is the nature of lines of research. They need to follow their own path because each has a different challenge than other lines of research. They will each have their own unique need for different methods and will follow a different path of speculation and testing. While each line of research needs to diverge from others, this does not necessarily mean that the field can never be more than a collection of fragmented scholarly areas. This fragmentary state of the field can be avoided if there is a sharing of findings and a use of those findings across all lines of research. Without this rim of sharing, it is difficult to see coherence in a field. For this reason, we have difficulty describing to other social scientists the big picture about our scholarly field. We also have difficulty describing to the public the map of our scholarly field or the list of most important research findings and speculations. Instead, when asked what our field is about, we typically describe the one piece about which we are most familiar, as if this one spoke were the entire wheel.

The phenomenon of the mass media is a complex system with many dynamic parts. The more we understand the interrelationships among the parts of the system, the more we can understand the value and function of each part. Of course, each of us needs to focus our attention most of the time on progressing with our one line of research. But to really understand the nature of our spoke, we need to compare and contrast it with other spokes. And even more important, we need to develop more of a sense of a scholarly community by considering more the nature of "wheelness."

We need to counterbalance the necessary movement toward specialization in developing a line of research with a movement toward seeking a broader understanding about our full phenomenon. Specialization is unavoidable as scholars build out their lines of research; in fact, progress in our understanding on a topic requires this. However, unless those studies are grounded in a context broader than one topic path, the findings from that line of research will not tie back into a larger system of understanding. Building such a larger system of understanding is the purpose of a scholarly community. The more we are able to build a common understanding of our focal phenomenon, the stronger our community will be to its members. Also, strong communities present a clear identity to others, thus making them attractive to the next generation of scholars as well as current scholars working in related fields.

Developing the Rim

What should be the rim ideas? These ideas should be the key tenets of the lines of research in each of the four areas, that is, the shared ideas of scholars working in a quadrant. However, they also need a unifying element—that is, they need to be linked strongly to the ideas in the other three areas. I mined the literatures for these ideas; I did not create them. However, in this lineation general framework, I do more than simply describe them. My intention is to synthesize a set of ideas. The challenge of synthesis lies in calibrating the importance of existing ideas, such that some of these ideas are brought into the foreground while others are moved to the background context, and the foregrounded ideas then work together as a set to explain the phenomenon of the mass media.

We also need to lengthen the arc of explanation. A great deal of the thinking about the mass media has a short arc. By this, I mean that theories, researchers, and even the public will fixate on a small piece of the overall mass media phenomenon, such as one type of effect, and attempt to link that effect to a particular media message or type of content. As for research design, individual studies usually need to have a short arc to make their designs manageable. But findings from these studies are building blocks that acquire more meaning when they are assembled into larger structures that bridge over a greater span of the phenomenon.

To explain media effects, we need to know more about media messages, not just the surface patterns of counts of characters (gender, ethnic background, or age) or acts (violence, sex), so that we can illuminate the formulas that structure messages for producers as well as for audiences. To explain messages, we need to know more about the mass media organizations. To explain the organizations, we need to know more about the audiences that are the markets for the organizations' messages. Thus, the more we know about one of these facets, the better able we are to understand the nature of the other facets. Therefore, it is useful to incorporate all facets into one system of explanation.

It is understandable why there is a short arc in the exploratory phase. We cannot sketch out the big picture until we have the pieces. Ultimately, we are forced to use a hermeneutic process that requires us to generate elements before we can look for patterns across elements, but to generate those elements, we need to be guided by the big picture. Which comes first, the recognition of pattern or the creation of elements? To do one, we really need the other to preexist. Thus, getting started in a new area of knowledge is very difficult. It is more useful in the early stages to generate elements, and thus the research has a shorter arc. Progress is slow at first, but it can speed up as there are more elements that can contribute to the recognition of consistent patterns. To make progress on this task, we need to move beyond a Generating-Findings perspective and into a Mapping-Phenomenon perspective.

We have reached a point in the exploratory phase where there are many elements available. Now we need to turn more of our attention toward looking at patterns across those elements, that is, to think with longer arcs. Thus, a broader framework for mass media scholarship can have great value. By articulating patterns across the full arc of the phenomenon, we can develop a more complete map of knowledge. And such a map will have great value in guiding the generation of particular research studies that would have the greatest ability to falsify (or confirm) the initially tentative reading of patterns.

The lineation general framework presents a line of thinking that reflects the main ideas from each of the four mass media facets and links them all together into a single thread that cycles back to the beginning (see Table 2.2). This is the rim. The ideas in this rim provide a "table of contents" of the major ideas that will be developed in the subsequent chapters of this book.

Table 2.1   Defining Terms

Focal Construct

Mass media—organizations that use technological channels to distribute messages
   for the purpose of creating and maintaining audiences.

Key Facets

Media organizations—entities that compete for talent and other resources so as
   to construct audiences by providing messages with high entertainment or
   informational value.

Media audiences—collections of individuals who are exposed to particular media
   messages; typically, an audience for a particular message is a niche (composed of
   a set of individuals sharing a key characteristic that is tied to the message).

Media content—messages that are developed using formulas to attract and hold the
   attention of the targeted audience members in a way to condition those
   audience members for repeat exposures.

Media effects—on an individual level, a media effect is any change in a human
   exposed to a media message. Change includes baseline alterations, fluctuations
   from the baseline, and reinforcing the baseline. On a macro level, a media effect
   is the change on a larger social structure such as culture or an institution.

Information—that which is sent from mass media organizations through the mass
   media channels to the audiences.

Media messages—the units of information.

Vehicle—that which delivers the media messages. For example, television is a
   medium, and programs (*Evening News, ER,* etc.) are the vehicles; newspaper is a
   medium and the *New York Times* is a vehicle.

Viewer-Defined Terms

Attractive
Bad/good
Consequences
Pain/harm
Successful/unsuccessful
Reward/punishment
Graphic/explicit
Hero/villain
Humorous
Justified
Negative/positive
Offensive
Real/fantasy

Table 2.2   Line of Thinking Defining the Rim

Mass media organizations are structures of people and other resources that perform aesthetic, sociological, and political functions. However, the most primary function is an economic one.

- Economic—at their foundation, all mass media organizations are economic, that is, they are primarily motivated to engage in resource exchanges to increase their value to their owners.

- Political—mass media organizations seek power to enhance their ability to control economic exchanges and keep the balance of power on their side in all negotiations.

- Sociological—mass media organizations structure the activities of people in certain ways so as to achieve their fundamental goal; they exhibit these values in the selection, training, and rewarding of individuals.

- Aesthetic—mass media organizations must construct messages of a certain type to attract and maintain audiences.

Mass media messages are tools constructed and used by mass media organizations to attract and maintain audiences.

- They attract and maintain audiences by maximizing the value of their messages.
- They maximize the value of their messages by increasing message benefits and decreasing message costs to potential audience members.

  - Benefit resources primarily include information (in the form of perceived satisfaction of increasing knowledge) and entertainment (in the form of emotional experiences), as well as the combination of the two.
  - Audience costs are the resources that individuals pay for the exposure to media messages. These costs are primarily money, time, and psychic energy.

- These messages follow certain narrative formulas that increase the probability that they will be successful in attracting and maintaining audiences.

  - When media messages are structured by simple, standard formulas, they are easier for audiences to follow, thus reducing the psychic costs for audience members.
  - However, designers of mass media content must also make small deviations from the storytelling formula, so as to generate surprise and suspense and thereby keep audiences interested in continuing with exposures.
  - Storytelling talent lies in knowing how to follow the standard formulas well enough to make processing simple for audiences AND at the same time knowing when (and how far) to deviate from the standard formulas to keep audiences intrigued.

- Each media message has a *narrative line*. This is the combination of elements in the message that signals to audience members how to make sense of that message. The narrative line contains elements about where the message is situated (in terms of genre, medium, vehicle, series, etc.), thus aiding audiences in matching meaning to those elements.

(Continued)

Table 2.2 (Continued)

- Meaning resides in both the messages and the audience member's interpretation. Both are constantly in play, hence the crucial distinction between meaning matching and meaning construction.

Mass media audiences are constructions of individuals into continuing exposure groups.

- During media exposure, audiences are both passive and active depending on exposure state. There are four qualitatively different exposure states:
  - Attentional state—individuals are cognitively aware of the flow of messages and consciously make choices about continuing the flow, ending the flow, or switching to another flow of messages.
  - Automatic state—individuals are not consciously aware of the flow of messages; the messages exert their influence on the person through peripheral routes. This state is governed by automatic algorithms, which are learned procedures stored in a person's mind and that run automatically when a person is not actively interacting with media messages. These states have triggers that recognize certain elements in media messages that trigger a person into the attentional state.
  - Transported state—individuals are pulled so strongly into the experience of a message that they lose awareness of their real-world surroundings and time; their attention is fully consumed by the flow of media messages.
  - Self-reflexive state—individuals are in a state of hyperawareness of both the flow of media messages and their own processing of those media messages; they are highly analytical and evaluative about the flow of messages.

- Audience members continually make assessments of message value. Value is conceptualized here in economic terms as the comparison of the cost to the benefits obtained—again as perceived by audience members.

- Audience members are constantly assessing the meaning of media messages through the dual processes of meaning matching and meaning construction.
  - Meaning matching is a competency that requires the recognition of referents in media messages and matching them to learned denoted meaning in the memory of audience members.
  - Meaning construction involves the application of skills (such as analysis, evaluation, grouping, induction, deduction, and synthesis) to create novel meanings.

Mass media effects are constantly occurring, although they might not manifest themselves.

- These effects can be manifest (observable in some way) or process (changes in the probabilities that a manifestation will occur).
  - These effects can manifest themselves as a behavior, a cognition, an attitude, a belief, an emotion, or something physiological.
  - These effects can be negative (harmful in some way to the individual), positive, or both.
  - These effects can be intentional or unintentional. Intention can be considered from two points of view: the mass media organizations and the individual audience member.

- Mass media are constantly exerting an influence on individuals and macro units both directly and indirectly.
  - Media shape individuals' baselines.
  - Media can trigger fluctuations from baselines, and these sudden fluctuations can last for a short or long period.
- Mass media are constantly exerting an influence on macro units, such as the public, society, institutions, and culture.

Conclusion

In the next four parts of this book, I lay out the details of the general framework, according to the four facets of the mass media phenomenon: organizations, audiences, messages, and effects. The ideas I cite in these chapters come from the literatures; that is, they do not originate with me. My contribution lies in how I have organized those ideas. As I described in the Preface, I used a hermeneutic process in which I employed the skills of analysis, classification, evaluation, induction, deduction, and synthesis.

In each of the next four parts, I begin with a chapter introducing the line of thinking about that part of the mass media phenomenon, where I present the key ideas and define the major terms. The subsequent chapters in each part elaborate and extend those ideas.

PART II

Explaining the Media Organizations Facet

CHAPTER 3

Mass Media Organizations Line of Thinking

The lineation general framework outlines a particular line of thinking about mass media organizations that helps us evolve from a Generating-Findings perspective to a Mapping-Phenomenon perspective. This mass media organization line of thinking does not include a critique of past research and a call for a different set of assumptions and research practices, as is the case with the other three facets of the mass media phenomenon. That is, I am not arguing that there are limitations in the media organization literature that need to be overcome; instead, I am arguing that the literature itself is very small compared with the literatures on the other four facets and that this literature is virtually ignored by scholars working primarily in the other facets. Therefore, my criticism is that all mass media scholars need to increase their understanding of this facet and use this increased understanding as a better context for the design of their particular research studies. To this end, I offer this mass media organizations line of thinking as a synthesis of the major ideas in that literature.

Definitions and Perspectives

Mass media organizations are the entities that control channels of communication to potentially large numbers of audience members. They produce the mass media messages and market them to their audiences with the intention of attracting their attention and conditioning repeated exposures.

The mass media are primarily *organizations*. They are composed of people working in a stable social structure where certain people are in leadership positions and others are in subordinate positions. Commonly shared goals and an established set of practices developed over time are used to achieve those goals consistently and efficiently. As new people are added to the organization, they must be socialized by those goals and practices so that they can function well in the organization. Mass media messages and audiences are never constructed by a single individual; instead, messages and audiences are always produced by organizations of individuals who each use their specialized skills in a cooperative manner to achieve the organizational goals.

Mass media are essentially *business* organizations. They are in the business of constructing audiences by attracting potential audience members and conditioning them for repeat exposures with the use of particular kinds of messages. To conduct this business, they must negotiate for resources in three types of markets. One market is a buyer's market for them, where they negotiate for talent, equipment, and materials to produce the messages. A second market is the audience market, where they compete with other media and other demands on potential audience members' attention to attract audience members and build audiences. A third market is the advertisers' market, where they negotiate with advertisers to allow them access to their constructed audiences. In each of these markets, they expect to be net winners—that is, they expect to acquire resources more valuable to them than the resources they give up. The more they are net winners, the more they are likely to stay in business and prosper.

To fulfill these business functions and to guide their negotiations, media organizations use three sets of strategies: business strategies, marketing strategies, and employment strategies. These are briefly introduced in this chapter and then developed in more detail in the following three chapters. Many of the techniques in these strategies are generic to all business organizations. We cannot ignore these strategies merely because they are general to all commercial businesses. Knowledge of business goals and strategies forms a basis for understanding the mass media organizations. However, we also need to focus on the characteristics that make the mass media organizations different from other businesses. There are two of these characteristics.

The first characteristic that makes the mass media businesses as an industry unique is their fundamental products, which are audiences. In their book titled *Audiencemaking: How the Media Create the Audience,* Ettema and Whitney (1994) placed the focus of the mass media on what they called "institutionally constituted audience" (p. 6), by which they meant that "audiences are seen to be the product of something like a manufacturing process" (p. 16). Of course, the public regards the messages as the most visible product because that is what the public encounters and buys with their time and money. Many employees of mass media companies also regard the primary product to be the message because they spend all their time manufacturing those messages. They get paid for manufacturing those messages. And professional recognition is tied to achieving one of the very visible awards for content—Oscars, Emmys, Grammys, National Book Awards, Nobel Prizes, Pulitzers, and Peabodys, to name a few of the more visible awards for media messages. But from the mass media organizations' point of view, messages are tools that are used to construct audiences, so audiences are the most fundamental product. If the mass media produced messages—even award-winning messages—but no audiences, they would not continue in business; in contrast, if the media could somehow construct audiences without first producing messages, they would continue in business. Therefore, their most essential products are audiences. Content has value only insofar as it can attract and maintain audiences. The ultimate value of a mass media business lies more in the audiences than it does in the content. Webster and Phalen (1997) reinforced this point when they said that the audience "is the foundation of the media's economic and cultural power. Without it, the entire enterprise has very little purpose" (p. 1).

The second characteristic that makes the mass media businesses as an industry unique is that they are often held to a higher standard than other industries. Critics argue that because the mass media control the flow of information, they have an enormous influence on shaping public knowledge, public attitudes, and culture itself. Thus, they should be held to a higher standard than businesses in other industries. Critics argue that the industries must be regulated to ensure a wide diversity in ownership of the businesses, which presumably will lead to a greater number of voices in the information flow. Thus, scholars have developed normative theories that explain why the mass media should be held to a different standard and what that standard should be (for a good overview of this, see McQuail, 2005, chap. 7).

Fundamental Goals

Mass media organizations follow a fundamental value goal as well as a fundamental operating goal. Unless we ground a system of explanation about the mass media in these goals, we will not be able to capture the essence of this phenomenon. These goals form the essential starting place for understanding the nature of the mass media organizations, their values, and their practices.

Value Goal

The most fundamental economic goal of mass media organizations is to maximize their value to their owners. There are several ways to conceptualize "value to owners," depending on who the owners are.

Most mass media organizations in the world, and especially in Western countries, are owned by people and organizations who buy shares in the company (Owers, Carveth, & Alexander, 1998). Individuals can participate in ownership by owning shares of the companies either directly (in their personal brokerage accounts) or indirectly (by owning shares of mutual funds or by being vested in pension funds that own shares of media companies). Because these mass media companies divide ownership up over many millions of shares, no one person can own a very large percentage of the company. With ownership spread over millions of owners, the motivation to own shares in a company is rarely to control the company or its operations. Instead, the motivation to own shares is to increase one's personal wealth. This is a purely financial goal. Owners want to receive larger and larger dividends on their shares each year, and they want the value of their shares to increase each year. Thus, shareholders benefit when the media company makes a profit that either is dispersed to the shareholders in the form of dividends or is reinvested in the company, thereby increasing the value of the company and each individual share. Also, when a company establishes a track record of profits over many quarters and especially when the company exceeds expectations for profit projections, the company is perceived as a good investment, and its share price grows.

Other mass media organizations are not owned by shareholders. These are owned by organizations with political, religious, educational, or cultural goals. For example, a political action group might start a magazine to reinforce the political opinions of the members of its organization. The members of the organization "own" the organization in the sense that they support it through their donations and expect something in return, such as a continual flow of messages to reinforce their political opinions. The more the organization achieves this expectation through its magazine, the more valuable the organization and the magazine are to the members and the more likely they will be to continue to be members and support the organization. Another example is a public university that runs a radio station. The radio station is supported by the university, which is supported by tax dollars; therefore, it is owned by the public and run to serve the public's need for educational services—that is, elevating public knowledge about key issues and important topics.

Even when mass media organizations are publically held corporations focused on seeking financial resources, they can also become concerned with achieving other goals besides purely financial ones. For example, media organizations often pursue the goal of gaining prestige and exercising influence or power in society (Tunstall, 1977). McQuail (2005) added that some media companies are run for "idealistic" social or cultural purposes such as to educate the public. This means that the value of a media organization to its owners is sometimes measured in nonfinancial terms, such as the prestige or satisfaction of owning a media business (Bates, 1998) or the influence that some media business is able to exert as an authority (Padioleau, 1985). Doyle (2002) pointed out that "most countries have a state-owned broadcasting entity which takes the form of a public corporation and which is dedicated to 'public service' television and radio broadcasting," and "their primary goal is to provide a universally available public broadcasting service rather than to make a profit" (p. 5).

There are many ways to define value of mass media organizations. Entities such as governments and institutions that start and maintain mass media organizations are oriented less toward drawing money from audiences than they are to drawing other resources such as audience time and attention. Their leger sheets define profit in terms of resources beyond money. And like the other mass media organizations, they are driven to construct and maintain audiences. While there are multiple value goals throughout the mass media industry, we must acknowledge that most mass media organizations—at least among the ones growing most powerful—have as their fundamental value goal the maximization of shareholder wealth.

Operating Goal

While there is a range of value goals depending on the media organization, there is only one operating goal—profit. This goal is monitored purely in financial terms where all resources are translated into dollar amounts. Profit is the difference between an organization's revenue and its expenses broadly construed.

At the core of the set of mass media organizations are the companies that are highly aggressive in maximizing profit. Moving outward from the core of aggressive profit-oriented businesses, we encounter organizations that are called "nonprofits" such as the broadcasting stations and book publishing houses owned and operated by universities. Although these nonprofits do not seek large returns on their investments, these organizations aggressively seek to avoid negative profits. That is, they must grow revenue to a point where their income covers their expenses. Once they reach that break-even point between revenues and expenses, their motivation to keep increasing revenues is reduced, unlike with profit-oriented media organizations. But they still need to meet their expenses. For example, of the 3,000 religious periodicals in this country, 58% of these are wholly supported by their owners; they generate no income from outside advertisers. Those religious periodicals that do generate some advertising support average only about 11.5% of their total revenue from advertising (Waters, 2001). Thus, religious publications do not generate a net income for their parent organizations, so their motivation is not financial gain. However, they must be creative and aggressive to generate enough revenue to avoid losing money year after year and thus putting themselves out of existence. Achieving at least a zero-profit point is required for a media organization to continue functioning.

The difference between profit and nonprofit media organizations is rather minor. Both types of organizations need to construct audiences and generate revenue. The difference lies in the point at which the organization can back off aggressive techniques in generating that revenue. Nonprofits can back off at the point where their revenues cover their expenses, but many nonprofits stay aggressive beyond this point so they can end the fiscal year with a surplus and use it as a buffer against unforseen problems in the next fiscal year. Also, mass media organizations—even highly commercial ones—can be motivated to fulfill goals beyond financial ones and also focus on political, cultural, and educational functions in society. However, the mass media must focus on meeting financial goals. Only when their operating goal is met can they shift their concern to other goals.

Strategies

The mass media organizations use three general strategies to achieve their goals. These are business, marketing, and employment strategies.

Introducing the Business Strategy

The business strategy addresses the challenge of meeting financial goals, that is, to generate at least enough revenue to cover expenses. And because most of the mass media organizations in the United States are highly commercial, the business strategy is used to generate revenues considerably beyond the mere covering of expenses such that profits are maximized.

The business strategy guides media organizations in maximizing revenue while minimizing expenses. They seek maximum revenue by increasing the number of revenue streams as well as the amount of revenue from each stream. To do this, they create audiences by providing content they believe will attract people to those audiences. At the same time, they seek to reduce expenses by using economies of scale and scope. Among their highest costs—and one with great elasticity—are the promotional costs of attracting audiences, so the mass media seek to reduce these promotional costs by conditioning existing audiences into repeated, habitual behaviors of exposure.

Introducing the Marketing Strategy

The mass media business organizations use a marketing strategy to attract and condition audience members. This strategy focuses on designing messages that audience members will believe have high value so they will feel satisfaction with the messages. When a series of messages continually satisfies audience expectations for value, audiences are conditioned for repeated exposures—that is, they are conditioned through the low-cost, pleasant experiences to seek out further messages in that series (such as a television series, a line of sequels in films, a series of articles on the same topic in newspapers and magazines, a recording artist's growing body of work, etc.). This conditioning makes audiences more familiar with the particular narrative line of the series, and this familiarity serves to drive down psychic costs even more. Over time, the conditioning leads to more automatic exposures from audience members, and the mass media can depend on the continuation of the audience, thus maintaining a dependable revenue stream while reducing the costs of promotions.

Audiences are created and maintained by perceptions of value in the minds of individual audience members. Value is conceptualized here in economic terms as the comparison of the cost to the benefits obtained—again as perceived by audience members. Audience costs are the resources that individuals pay for the exposure to media messages. These costs are primarily money, time, and psychic energy. Benefit resources primarily include information (in the form of perceived satisfaction of increasing knowledge) and entertainment (in the form of emotional experiences), as well as the combination of the two. Value is increased as benefits increase or costs decrease, especially when both of these occur simultaneously. The mass media are reluctant to reduce audience costs by asking for fewer financial or time resources. To the contrary, mass media want to increase audience expenditures of money and time because these increased expenditures contribute to the revenue of the mass media. Therefore, the mass media have a strong orientation to reduce psychic costs to audience members. The mass media that are successful at keeping psychic costs very low can provide audiences with a sense that their *overall* cost of exposures is low even when those audiences are paying higher costs in terms of money and time.

To reduce psychic costs to audiences, the mass media design content that follows simple formulas. When media messages are structured by simple, standard formulas, they are easier for audiences to follow, thus reducing the psychic costs for audience members. However, designers of mass media content must also make small deviations from the storytelling formula to generate surprise and suspense and thereby keep audiences interested in continuing with exposures. Storytelling talent lies in knowing how to follow the standard formulas well enough to make processing simple for audiences while knowing when (and how far) to deviate from the standard formulas to keep audiences intrigued.

Introducing the Employment Strategy

The mass media organizations use an employment strategy that focuses on people as talent resources. The mass media look for particular kinds of talent when making selections about who to hire. Those people who are hired and brought into the mass media organizations must be socialized in the goals and practices of those organizations. They must learn how to develop their particular talent and then use that talent in collaboration with others in creating messages as tools to construct particular kinds of audiences.

Criticism of the Economic Goal

In this book, I am taking a descriptive and explanatory approach to the mass media rather than a critical one, so I do not review criticism of the mass media. However, I need to make an exception here because I am building the explanation of mass media organizations so strongly on the fundamental idea of economics. The economically based strategies and the capitalistic structure of the mass media industries are one of the most criticized aspects of the media. Also, one characteristic that makes the mass media industry different from other industries is the belief among critics, scholars, and many in the public that the mass media need to be held to a different standard than other industries. Therefore, I need to acknowledge this, if even only briefly.

Main Themes

Many mass media organizations have been criticized for an aggressive pursuit of financial resources at the expense of the public interest. These criticisms have been generally organized into three categories by McQuail (2005). The first category consists of criticism that the mass media often behave in an irresponsible manner that has harmed society and individuals, such as through the marketing of antisocial messages of violence, sex, bad language, and so on. A second category of criticism deals with the mass media not operating in the public interest—that is, they do not support the democratic process or the maintaining of public order as they should.

McQuail's (2005) third category consists of criticism about how the media system is organized and allows for concentration of ownership that inevitably leads to a lessening of diversity in public voices, opinions, and cultural content. For example, Bettig and Hall (2003) provided such a critique in their book *Big Media, Big Money: Cultural Texts and Political Economics.* Using a public service model to guide their cultural critique of the mass media businesses, they argued that the media are not doing a good job of covering what they do in a balanced and accurate manner. But Bettig and Hall failed to address the issue of why—that is, do people really want balanced and accurate coverage of what the media themselves do? If so, where are the indicators for such demand outside of a few cultural critics? And if not, which is likely the case, then why does the public not demand this type of information? This needs to be the starting place for substantial criticism—an understanding of why the media and audiences behave the way they do; without such a basis of understanding, criticism that simply asks people to change what they do without giving them a compelling reason has no utility. Bettig and Hall concluded their book with a call for activists to demand "a seat at the table," presumably where negotiations will take place, but the authors did not explain what activists can bring to the table that would be of value to the media businesses.

Other scholars criticize the mass media's single-minded adherence to an economic goal as leading to concentration of ownership and consequently to fewer voices. For example, Bagdikian conducted an analysis of media ownership patterns in 1983 and found that the control of the media was essentially in the hands of 50 people—these were the CEOs of the largest media companies who, in combination, controlled more than half of the revenues and audiences in their media markets. Less than a decade later, Bagdikian (1992) found that the number had shrunk to 23 CEOs of corporations who controlled most of the business in the country's 25,000 media businesses.

Croteau and Hoynes (2001) argued that the public sphere model is an important alternative to the market model for understanding media businesses. They said that "the public sphere model suggests that society's needs cannot be met entirely through the market system. Because the market is based on consumer purchasing power, it behaves quite differently from the democratic ideal of 'one person, one vote.' In addition, the public sphere model argues that there are some societal needs that simply cannot be met via the market's supply and demand dynamic" (pp. 19–20). Of course that is true. But the media are primarily businesses, and they are not in business to meet all the needs of people in a democratic society. When our scholarly purpose is to understand how the media organizations operate, normative models fall out of bounds when they are used as a template to evaluate the performance of media organizations. However, they are useful at raising questions about why the media perform the way they do and not some other way. So when Croteau and Hoynes argue that the media businesses need to provide more diversity and substance in their messages, their argument is interesting because it raises the question about why the media do not present a greater variety of messages and more substance in those messages.

Analyzing the Criticism

It is useful to make a distinction between two types of criticism. One type of criticism is a structural one argued from a normative base. These are criticisms about the goals of the mass media organizations. For example, critics argue that the mass media should be owned by the government, not individuals, or that the mass media should not be profit seeking. While this type of criticism can help exorcize a critic's anger or frustration about the mass media, it has little chance of effecting change or even being considered seriously by those who control the mass media organizations because the criticism rejects the fundamental goals and general strategies that mass media have carefully developed through trial and error over years and that have been found to be most useful. This type of criticism calls for massive structural change. It is rather like criticizing a guard dog for barking at an intruder. That is the fundamental nature of guard dogs, and they should not be criticized for not being a cat or a chair. Likewise, it seems faulty to criticize the mass media simply because they act like businesses rather than governmental agencies or educational institutions. Given this country's political and economic system along with the history of the mass media, it is highly unrealistic to think that criticizing the fundamental goal will have any constructive effect on bringing about change.

A second type of criticism involves finding fault with the mass media for not fulfilling their stated functions better. Mass media organizations can be criticized for not using their resources better, for not constructing a wider array of target markets by producing a wider array of messages to attract those audiences, for misjudging the audience needs, and for crafting poor content.

It would seem far better to accept the nature of the mass media as they exist and judge their performance on their fundamental nature. For example, criticizing the mass media for presenting too much violence in their stories ignores the fact that there is a market for such stories and there has been for a very long time. Calling for governmental regulation of this type of content is not helpful because the government does not have the power to regulate speech such as violence in the media. However, consumers have the power to change the market, such that if the market for violent messages dwindles, the supply of such messages will also dwindle. Another way to attack the problem of violence in the media is through economic resources. Rather than ask the mass media to change their content in order to shift their goal away from an economic one and into a public service one, it is far better to stay within the economic realm and call for a shift in the market demand, as I have done in *Media Literacy* (W. J. Potter, 2005). Or one could criticize this type of content as having costs on society that are not borne by the sellers of this content, as Hamilton (1998) did when he showed through an economic analysis that the mass media are creating costs for society through negative externalities of their purveying of violence so frequently in their content. Also, I have argued in *The 11 Myths of Media Violence* (W. J. Potter, 2003) that perhaps we should regard media messages more as commercial products than as free speech, particularly when it comes to violent content. This keeps the problem purely within the economic realm and casts the negative consequences as product liability rather than a more amorphous call for a higher public interest. In short, let's treat the media for what they are—economic entities that reap huge economic benefits and must bear large economic costs. Therefore, key to understanding the mass media is for scholars, the public, and critics to increase economic knowledge about the mass media. Fortunately, other scholars have been making this point. For example, Gomery (1998) reminds us that "no research in mass communication can ignore questions of mass-media ownership and the economic implications of that control" (p. 45). He argued that "media economics should move into the center of communications study" (p. 45). But by studying control, it is not enough to list who owns the media; Gomery has argued that we need to explain "how a particular form of industrial structure leads to certain corporate conduct" (p. 46).

Conclusion

The beginning point of understanding the mass media phenomenon is to start with the fact that the mass media are primarily economic organizations with economic value goals and operational goals. To achieve these goals, the mass media organizations use three sets of strategies: business, marketing, and employment. Each of these three sets of strategies is developed in more detail in the following three chapters.

It is essential to begin the study of mass media organizations from an economic perspective, where the organizations focus on manufacturing audiences. This is the most fundamental perspective. There are of course other perspectives, but those are secondary to the economic perspective.

Table 3.1 Structured Glossary of Terms About Mass Media Organizations

Mass media organizations—groups of people with specialized sets of skills that work together to construct and distribute messages, so as to attract particular audiences and condition them for repeat exposures.

- Composed of people working in a stable social structure where certain people are in leadership positions and others are in subordinate positions.
- Commonly shared goals and an established set of practices developed over time that are used to achieve those goals consistently and efficiently.

Fundamental value goal—maximize value for owners.

- When owners are shareholders, value is defined primarily in financial terms—dividends paid per share and share price.
- When owners are institutions, value is defined by other resources such as public beliefs, knowledge, and behaviors.

Fundamental operational goal—increase revenues to at least cover expenses and, for most media organizations, to greatly exceed expenses.

Business strategy—a series of decisions used to achieve the goal of maximizing profit; these decisions are of two types: (1) maximizing revenue and (2) minimizing costs.

Marketing strategy—a series of decisions used to construct and maintain audiences.

Employment strategy—a series of decisions used to select, hire, train, and reward media workers.

Costs to audience members are primarily money, time, and psychic energy.

- Money—personal financial expenditures for media exposure (subscriptions to newspapers, magazines, Internet sites, cable TV, satellite radio; theater admissions; purchasing books; hardware and software; etc.).
- Time—hours spent in exposure to media messages, especially the time that is rented by advertisers.
- Psychic energy—cognitive and emotional expenditures that are reflected in the ease or difficulty in processing the message (getting attracted, getting into the message, staying in the continuation of the message).

Strategic management—focuses managers' attention on the ways in which organizations can enhance their performance in terms of financial measures.

Producers—the people who create media messages (novelists, screenwriters, songwriters, reporters, etc.).

Programmers—the people who make decisions about which messages get put through the mass media channels. Programmers are the gatekeepers of the media; they decide which content units get produced or disseminated in the media.

Table 3.2   Media Organizations Propositions

Organization 1: Mass media organizations strive to achieve the fundamental goal of maximizing their value to the owners.

With commercial mass media businesses, value is expressed in terms of financial resources. This means that media businesses need to be consistent net winners in the financial exchanges of resources.

With noncommercial mass media organizations, value is expressed in terms of a wide variety of resources, such as influences on public opinion, strengthening of institutions, the status quo, and so on.

Organization 2: When the fundamental goal is achieved, the organization may pursue other secondary goals.

Organization 3: Mass media organizations employ a *business strategy* where they try to maximize resources, reduce risk, orient to niche audiences, and increase their economic power in the marketplace.

3.1: The key to resource maximizing lies in consistently being a net winner in resource exchanges in the marketplace. This means negotiating deals of lowering costs and increasing revenues.

3.2: The key to reducing risk is to look for existing needs and to emulate messages that have been successful in the past in satisfying those existing needs.

3.3: Economic power in a marketplace is increased when a business uses economies of scale, consolidates ownership, moves up the pyramid of power, and establishes networks.

Economies of scope—reducing total costs of producing products when a company controls more than one function in the production process.

Consolidation—one media company buying another company.

Pyramid of power—moving from being one of a large number of small firms to become one of a few very powerful firms.

Networking—building ad hoc relationships with all kinds of organizations and people to help in the production process.

3.4: The fundamental product of mass media business activities is the audience. Mass media businesses also produce messages. However, messages are not the end product; they are tools to generate audiences.

Organization 4: To attract and maintain audiences, mass media organizations follow a four-stage *marketing strategy*.

Stage 1: Find out what needs exist in niche audiences.

Stage 2: Craft messages that will satisfy those designated needs in each potential audience.

(Continued)

Table 3.2 (Continued)

Stage 3: Put messages in channels that will physically expose potential audience members to the messages. Invest in initial promotions to get the attention of potential audience members.

Stage 4: Condition audience members for repeat exposures.

Organization 5: Mass media organizations follow *employment strategies* to select and socialize their workers.

5.1: Mass media organizations are more likely to select workers who have the values and talent levels needed to fit well into their organizations.

5.2: Like institutions, the mass media organizations socialize their workers and make structural changes to their practices to maintain their identity and ensure smooth functioning.

5.3: The more that people in media organizations share the same goals and practices, the better the organization is able to reach its goals.

Because mass media messages and audiences are never constructed by a single individual, workers must contribute specialized skills and work together cooperatively.

Business Strategies

The mass media industries are economically very strong. Combined, they account for about 3% of the gross domestic product (GDP) year after year (Owers et al., 1998). They have achieved this by consistently meeting their fundamental value goal by using a variety of business strategies.

To achieve the fundamental goal of maximizing owner value, mass media organizations primarily use three interrelated business strategies. The first of these business strategies is the maximization of resources. The second is reducing risk. And the third is increasing economic power in the media marketplace. These three business strategies come under the umbrella of a meta-type strategy known as strategic management, which has come to dominate thinking in corporate America. P. M. Hirsch and Thompson (1994) pointed out that over the years, CEOs of media companies have increasingly bought into the logic of strategic corporate management. "The logic of strategic management focuses managers' attention on the ways in which organizations can enhance their performance in terms of financial measures"

(p. 151). Thus, to understand the decisions that are made by media managers, we need to focus on how they acquire and use economic resources, especially financial ones.

Maximizing Resources

The mass media companies try to maximize resources because this makes them more powerful in the marketplace. In conducting their business, mass media companies are constantly negotiating exchanges of resources in a way to continually increase their value.

Value

Value can be viewed either at the macro level of the company or at the micro level of the individual exchange. As for the micro level, Bates (1998) said, "In the purest sense, the value of any thing is whatever someone is willing to give, or forego, in order to have it. It is a measure of desirability, of want" (p. 74). He explained that there are three economic theories for determining value—cost, exchange, and utility. The cost approach is summing the expenses of producing something, and thus it is the cost to the producer. Exchange value is what people are willing to give up to get something, and thus it is from the consumer's point of view. This negotiated value is traceable to the more fundamental judgment about utility of the thing. Thus, in exchanges, media organizations seek to have their trading partners perceive that what the media organizations are offering will have high value to them as they negotiate exchanges in two markets: resource markets and product markets.

In resource markets, media organizations exchange money for talent and the materials of production and distribution. That is, they are acquiring the raw materials to produce messages and attract audiences. Media organizations are buyers in resource markets. As buyers, they need to be convinced that the raw materials have the highest value to them. This is fairly easy to determine with tangible resources, such as newsprint, cameras, film stock, and transmission towers. However, it is much more difficult to make accurate assessments of the value of talent, and this makes talent exchanges much riskier (see section below).

Once media organizations transform raw materials into messages, they compete in a product market to negotiate exposures to audience members in return for their time and money. Also, this exchange creates audiences—another product— that is used in negotiations with advertisers (see Picard, 1989). In these product markets, media organizations are sellers of messages and audience access. In this role, media organizations must convince potential audience members of the value of their messages and then convince advertisers of the value of access to their constructed audiences.

Mass media scholars tend to focus on product exchanges rather than resource exchanges (Chan-Olmsted & Albarran, 1998). This is one example of a larger pattern in the scholarly literature for researchers to focus on outcomes (content analysis, audience compositions, effects on individuals) rather than inputs (how media organizations acquire resources and construct messages).

Increasing Revenue

Media companies follow a strategy of maximizing revenue in two ways. One way is to increase the number of revenue streams. The other way is to increase the revenue within a stream. Large mass media companies are large because they have aggressively pursued both of these and are successful at both.

First, they seek to produce a wide variety of vehicles, each with its own target audience, each with a special set of messages of high potential interest to that target audience, and each with its own revenue stream. The more revenue streams, the more total revenue is possible.

Second, they seek ways to maximize the availability of each vehicle to audiences. Thus, they develop means to disseminate their messages to everyone in their targeted niche. Not everyone in that niche may access the message at the same time, but it is available for access. Promotional costs are key to making everyone in the targeted niche aware of the availability of the message. The more a media business turns availability into exposures, the more it increases revenue from that target audience.

Decreasing Expenses

Keeping costs down is a major challenge. The media industries incur all kinds of expenses, but the major one is personnel. There are two categories of personnel— "above the line" and "below the line." The above-the-line personnel are regarded as talent—actors, television and radio personalities, recording artists, directors, producers, writers (screenwriters, songwriters, novelists, journalists), photographers, and graphic artists. With each of these, talent level is highly variable, with fewer people at the top levels than at the lower levels of talent. Above-the-line talent is in short supply relative to the demand, especially at the higher levels of talent. So the media businesses must compete aggressively for the pool of talent. This competition drives up costs, especially at the top end (such as actors for Hollywood movies and network television series, best-selling novelists, musical groups whose songs go platinum, etc.). Thus, the above-the-line costs are highly elastic.

The below-the-line personnel fill the more clerical and crafts positions. These below-the-line jobs include receptionist, secretary, ticket taker, bookkeeper, production assistant, sound technician, and the like. These costs are easier to keep low because the supply of these people exceeds the demand. These jobs require a relatively low level of talent, and this low talent level is widely dispersed in the general population. These are generally entry-level positions; people accept these jobs and are willing to be paid near the minimum wage for the opportunity to work in the media industries and to see if they have a degree of talent high enough to increase their value in the industry.

The above-the-line costs have escalated in the past few decades as the need for visual programming has increased with the number of cable TV and direct satellite distribution systems expanding. The above-the-line costs constitute about 50% of the cost of making a Hollywood movie, and these costs are skyrocketing because creative talent is in short supply (Wasko, 2003). The demand for production talent has increased much faster than the supply, so payments to production talent, especially those at the top of the pyramid in their ability to attract large audiences, have multiplied (Hoskins, McFadyen, & Finn, 2004).

Businesses are not only concerned about reducing total costs but are also interested in reducing unit costs. Thus, they use economies of scale. Economies of scale refer to the reduction of unit costs as more units are produced. With the mass media businesses, it is usually extremely expensive to produce the first copy of a message, but if those first copy costs can be spread out over many messages, the unit cost drops. For example, let's say the cost of producing one musical CD is $10,000. This cost includes studio rental time, studio musicians to back up the featured singer, audio engineers to mix the sound, graphic artists to design and produce the liner notes, and so on. If you print a CD at a cost of 20 cents, then your total costs for the production and copy is $10,000.20, and you must sell that single CD for at least $10,000.21 to cover costs and make a profit. But if you make 10,000 copies, then the cost to you of each of those is only $1.20, and you can sell each for a much lower price and still make a profit. The more copies you make, the lower the unit cost. Thus, the larger the scale of production, the greater the economic benefit of lower unit costs—hence the term *economies of scale.*

The mass media businesses are different from businesses in other industries because their first copy costs are usually very high in comparison to the production of additional copies, so there are huge economic incentives to increase the size of the audience. This is especially the case with television; one episode of a one-hour network drama costs about $1 million or more to produce (Hoskins et al., 2004), and once this show is broadcast or transmitted through cable, there is no additional cost of adding another member or two or three million to the audience, unless we consider the additional costs of promoting the drama to generate a larger audience. Promotion costs *are* high, but promotion costs are also subject to economies of scale. When we apply economies of scale across episodes over the run of a TV series, we see that it is very costly to build that audience initially, but the costs of promotion are greatly reduced once the audience is established and conditioned to view the shows habitually.

Economies of scale not only drive unit costs down but also motivate businesses to increase audience size as well as number of niche audiences, and these increases lead to greater revenues. They are also linked to the business strategies of reducing risks and increasing economic power through greater ownership and control of more and more media businesses.

Reducing Risk

Mass media companies each operate in highly competitive markets. I am using the term *highly competitive* in a broad sense. There are critics who say that with all the ownership consolidation over the past few decades, the degree of competition among media businesses is greatly reduced, and we are quickly moving to a monopolistic situation where there will be no competition among owners. While there has been a great deal of consolidation of ownership, there are many forms of competition apart from direct competition of similar vehicles for the same audience—although this is the focal point for most competition. For example, *Newsweek* magazine competes most directly with *Time* and *US News & World Report* for the audience interested in reading national weekly news magazines. But *Newsweek* magazine is also in competition with daily newspapers that deliver the news every day. Also, *Newsweek* magazine is in competition with television, radio, and Internet news services that deliver the news even faster. In a larger sense, *Newsweek* magazine is in competition with all the demands on news readers' time that seek to pull these people out of the news-reading audience and put them in all kinds of other audiences—for entertainment messages, as well as for real-world activities such as family duties, religious observances, civic participation, hobbies, and other leisure pursuits. Media vehicles must work hard to pull people away from these other activities to increase the size of their audiences, yet consolidation of ownership by itself does little to help in this task.

Costs have been increasing, and this adds to risk because media companies must now invest more money in creating messages while being uncertain about whether the investment will pay back their costs and earn a profit. For example, the cost of making and promoting a Hollywood film has grown from less than $8 million in 1975 to almost $90 million in 2002 (Wasko, 2003). Moviemaking is a very risky business. Only 1 in 10 films ever retrieves its investment from domestic exhibition (Motion Picture Association of America [MPAA], n.d.). To help reduce this risk somewhat, companies try to develop multiple outlets for a single message. With films, multiple revenue streams are needed to cut down on the risks. These additional revenue streams include foreign distribution, DVDs, cable TV, airline rentals, Internet viewing, and product placement within films. It is now estimated that 80% of a film's total revenue comes from the sale and rental of videos and DVDs as well as merchandising (Wasko, 2003). Foreign distribution is also important. Now 63% of a Hollywood film studio's annual revenue comes from overseas distribution ("Which Actress," 2007). U.S. films are shown in more than 150 countries, and American TV programs are broadcast in over 125 international markets (Wasko, 2003). Hollywood movies are becoming more commercial in terms of product placements sold in films as well as in the development of merchandise from movies (such as soundtracks, books, action figures, toys, games, costumes, etc.). Product placement in movies is now a common practice. For example, the James Bond movie *Die Another Day* featured more than 20 branded products; the producers sold more than $120 million in product placement and tie-ins to this one film (Wasko, 2003). But even with all revenue streams accounted for, only 6 in 10 films cover their expenses (MPAA, n.d.).

Each year, the commercial TV networks spend about $1 billion for the rights to show their prime-time series. They pay this money to producers who also share the risk, selling their rights for an average of about 80% of their production costs (Budd, Craig, & Steinman, 1999). Thus, producers of TV series lose money the first year and do not start making a profit on a series until they renegotiate their contracts for the second and subsequent years; however, most series do not get renewed for a second year.

Because rates of failure of all kinds of media messages are so high, mass media companies have gotten more careful in screening ideas and selecting only those ideas that have a very good chance for commercial success. For example, several decades ago, veteran screenwriter William Goldman (1983) said about Hollywood, "The business pays attention only to writers who write movies that are commercially viable" (p. 95). Since then, the industry has gotten even more competitive for writers. Now it is estimated that 99% of all scripts read by people in Hollywood are rejected (Wasko, 2003). Only 1% of ideas pitched to network television programmers make it to airing. Several decades ago, the major TV networks typically commissioned scripts for about 100 series each year, culling that down to about 30 for which they would commission pilots at a cost of about $40 million, and ending up scheduling about 10 new shows for prime time. Most of these new shows did not make it through the entire season before being canceled (Karlin, 1991). Now it is even more competitive.

The audience is fragmenting, and this too increases the challenge of identifying viable audience segments. This audience fragmentation is most clearly seen in changes in the audience of the most dominant mass medium of broadcast television during the past several decades. Webster (2005) pointed out that as recently as 1977, the three major commercial TV broadcasting networks accounted for more than 90% of the viewing audience, but by 2005, that figure had dropped to 29%. This fragmentation is also clear in the mass media of radio, recordings, magazines, and books.

Another key task in reducing risk is in predicting changes in audience tastes. Even if a mass media company is successful one year in attracting a large audience and maintaining that audience all year long, that company might find itself unsuccessful the next year because the audience has tired of those media messages or the audience's tastes have changed otherwise. Our culture is highly dynamic with changing preferences. This is why media content seems to follow a pack mentality, with spin-offs and new vehicles trying to copy the successful existing vehicles. For example, TV networks minimize their risks by "imitating what current or past program concepts pleased the audience rather than experimenting with new ideas or untested talent. Such financial incentives to copy were coupled with the oligopolistic structure of the industry and the desire to standardize practices in most areas of contact. The end result was even less of a desire to innovate or experiment with new program forms" (Litman, 1998, p. 143). Now about 50% of Hollywood films are adaptations—that is, they are not original stories. Instead, the film scripts are adaptations of published books and sequels to previous blockbusters. These adaptations are consistently rated among the highest grossing films (Wasko, 2003). However, every once in a while, a programmer takes a big risk with a new kind of message. Sometimes these risks pay off, such as with *All in the Family, Rowan and Martin's Laugh-In, Seinfeld,* or *The Sopranos,* to name a few innovative shows that were enormously successful. However, people who take big risks on trying new types of messages are usually those with less to lose, such as producers who are at low points in their careers or programmers experiencing low ratings (Turow, 1982).

Yet another way to increase the probability of success is to produce stories that are polysemic—that is, there is something to appeal to different types of audiences in a single story (S. R. Olson, 1999). Thus, a film can attract different audiences in America, but also the text is transparent enough to attract audiences in other countries and cultures. This is why action/adventure films export well; the use of violence is visual and therefore not language based. A comedy of manners with clever plays on words is much less exportable. Also on television, successful programs are those that have something to appeal to several different audiences. For example, *Ally McBeal* was found to trigger different reactions—a program favorable to women, a sexist program, and a humorous, harmless program. Many factors go into how a person interprets the program—personal view of women, feminist attitudes, relationship status, identification with the characters, and over-all liking of the program (E. L. Cohen, 2002).

Increasing Economic Power in the Marketplace

The mass media companies—like all businesses—seek to build greater economic power in their markets. The effect of increasing economic power is to provide economies of scope, which reduce expenses, and diversification, which reduces risks.

Economies of Scope

Economies of scope refer to the reduction of total costs of producing products when a company controls more than one function in the production process. Specifically, economies of scope exist when the total cost of producing two or more messages within the same business is less than producing them separately in two or more nonrelated businesses. Thus, if one company can publish a book, a newspaper, and a magazine at a lower total cost than what it would cost for three separate businesses (a book publisher only, a newspaper-only business, and a magazine-only business), then that company is experiencing economies of scope. Because there is considerable overlap in skills and talent needed to produce different types of media messages, there is great advantage to economies of scope within the mass media industries. Media businesses achieve these economies of scope through consolidation, such as mergers, acquisitions, and joint ventures.

Consolidation

Media businesses consolidate to increase their economic power in a marketplace. There are three different consolidation techniques. First, there is the horizontal merger. This is when one media company buys another media of the same type. An example is a newspaper chain buying another newspaper. This pattern was very popular during the 1980s when newspapers were being gobbled up by chains at the rate of 50 to 60 per year.

A second consolidation technique is the vertical merger. This is when one media company buys suppliers or distributors to create integration in the production and distribution of messages. An example is a book publisher buying a printing plant and some bookstores. This too increases economies of scope. One example of this is Viacom, which owns cable television services such as MTV, VH1, and Nickelodeon. In 1994, Viacom acquired Paramount Communications, Inc., which is a film and television production studio, for $9.6 billion. With this vertical consolidation, Viacom became a major player in both story production and distribution.

Third, there is the conglomerate merger. This is when a media company buys a combination of other media companies or companies in a nonmedia business. An example is a film studio that buys a newspaper, several radio stations, a talent agency, and a string of restaurants. At one time, Paramount Communications owned Paramount studios, which was one of the leading producers of motion pictures, television shows, and cable programming. It also owned Simon & Schuster—the world's largest book publishing company. It was a major maker of entertainment videocassettes, and it controled 1,100 movie screens in the United States and 11 foreign countries (Bagdikian, 1992). The conglomerate merger increases both economies of scale and diversification.

From the business point of view, cross-media ownership is very attractive because it achieves economies of scope, and it can reduce risk by diversifying across many different kinds of vehicles and audiences. But it also has the special advantage of allowing easy cross-promotion of messages. For example, when Paramount released its movie *The Brady Bunch,* Viacom put on several weeks of Brady TV reruns on its Nickelodeon cable channel as a way of promoting the movie.

For the reasons articulated above, the conglomeration of media ownership has been very popular over the past few decades. For example, one analysis of mergers and acquisitions in the media industries from 1981 to 1995 revealed that there was a total number of 3,391 deals (for a total of $340 billion), which computes to an average of 226 deals per year (Ozanich & Writh, 1998). Since then, the number of mergers has declined, but the value of the mergers increases as the big companies are being acquired by the very big companies.

Pyramid of Power

Throughout the mass media industries, there are pyramids of power where there are a small number of firms or people who exercise the greatest power. These few can be regarded as being at the top of the pyramid in an industry. Those companies at the top of the pyramid have more power because they control more resources. And because they control more resources, they are in a better financial position to earn even higher profits the next year and use those profits to acquire even more businesses, which in turn makes them even more powerful.

The companies at the top of the pyramid enhance their position by making it difficult for other companies to enter the marketplace. Porter (1980, 1985) explained that the economic attractiveness of an industry and the potential for profitability for an individual business can be assessed by analyzing five factors: ease of entry, threat of substitution, bargaining power of buyers, bargaining power of suppliers, and rivalry among current competitors. Businesses prosper by taking a defensive position that enables them to stave off threats from each of the five competitive forces and to earn a superior return on investment. Porter explains that during the 1980s and 1990s, newspapers lost attractiveness as an industry because of innovations in technologies that allowed easier entry for new players, as well as more competition. Therefore, the people in control of the companies at the top of the pyramid try to make it very unattractive for competitors to enter their markets, and this in turn makes it more attractive for their companies to continue doing business.

Mergers and acquisitions in the mass media industries have been taking place for a long time, but it was not until the 1970s that they began to profoundly affect the structure of the industries. For example, Powell (1982) observed that by the 1970s, it was clear that there was a two-tier structure to book publishing. Mergers just prior to 1970 had served to create a first tier of large and powerful media firms that owned multiple vehicles across several media. The rest of the book publishers dropped into a second tier of small independent firms that served small, highly specialized niche audience needs. Although Powell was specifically analyzing the book publishing industry, his observations are also a useful description of what has been occurring across all the mass media industries since that time. In 1983, Bagdikian conducted an analysis of media ownership patterns and found that the control of the media was essentially in the hands of 50 people—these were the CEOs of the largest media companies who in combination controlled over half of the revenues and audiences in their media markets. Less than a decade later, Bagdikian found that the number had shrunk to 23 CEOs of corporations who controlled most of the business in the country's 25,000 media businesses. The number of companies controlling most of the daily newspaper circulation was 11. In magazine publishing, a majority of the total annual industry revenues went to two firms. Five firms controlled over half of all book sales. Five media conglomerates shared 95% of the recordings market, with Warner and CBS alone controlling 65% of that market. Eight Hollywood studios accounted for 89% of U.S. feature film rentals. Three television networks earned over two thirds of the total U.S. television revenues (Bagdikian, 1992). Then in 2000, Bagdikian published an updated version of his analysis and concluded that "six firms dominate all American mass media" (Bagdikian, 2000, p. x). Each of these six companies (Bertelsmann, Disney, General Electric, News Corp., Time Warner, and Viacom) owned media vehicles in almost all of the mass media. Almost all of the media industries are oligopolies, especially film (Gomery, 1998), broadcast television (Litman, 1998), and recordings (Rothenbuhler & Streck, 1998).

As the media become more concentrated, so too does the advertising industry. The large, national agencies are becoming larger to deal better with the larger media companies. As ad agencies grow bigger, they become much less interested in local retailers and local markets, instead favoring the much larger national market where they can make bigger deals and more money. Thus, most advertising today is for national brands. For example, when most people think of hamburgers, they think of McDonald's, Burger King, and Wendy's—not some local restaurant run as a family business. So the trend toward concentration is not just within the media industries; it is also with retail stores and with advertising agencies. Through mergers and acquisitions, all of America's industries are becoming more concentrated. Whether the mass media businesses are leading this trend or following it is a matter for debate. However, there is no question that they are part of this trend.

Dynamic Nature

The mass media industries change as they pursue their fundamental goals and as they adapt their business strategies to achieve these goals. This section highlights the major changes in structures and business practices.

Changing Structures

Media scholars using the economic approach to study the mass media typically take a neoclassical approach (Wildman, 2006). Key assumptions of the neoclassical approach include a view of organizations making self-interested decisions based on the rational consideration of a full set of information; these decisions are made with current information and do not consider past or future events (Hollis & Nell, 1975). Furthermore, mass media scholars typically work only in one specific branch—industrial organization—of the neoclassical tradition. This branch of industrial organization (IO) is most concerned with investigations of structures of industries (Wildman, 2006). The typical structure found in mass media industries is an oligopoly, where there are a few interdependent firms operating in an industry with high barriers to entry (Chan-Olmsted & Albarran, 1998), and the mass media industries are getting more concentrated—fewer major firms and higher barriers to entry—over time (Albarran & Dimmick, 1996). Also, Gomery (1998) has said that the media industries exhibit an oligopoly structure where the major television networks, six major record labels, and six major Hollywood studios form oligopolies in their industries.

There is an alternative to the neoclassical tradition: a network approach that has been advocated in general by some organizational scholars (Castells, 1996; Fulk & DeSanctis, 1999; Nohria, 1992). Here the focus is placed more on the nature of economic exchanges at a more micro level than that of the firm or the industry. The focus is on people and their relationships with other people within and across firms. These scholars see economic action as being embedded in social relations more so than in impersonal economic exchanges (Granovetter, 1985). Also, importance is given to the role of collaboration in the exchange process and the need for reciprocity. Because networks are dynamic and constantly open to change, actors are constantly pulling information from the past and considering the future (Powell,

1990). Building trust in social relations is also important (Granovetter, 1992) because with many media products, we cannot know ahead of time how successful they will be.

While it is certainly the case that many of the mass media industries exhibit an oligopolistic structure, it does not automatically follow that all resource negotiations are controlled by a few companies—that is, the power to negotiate is dispersed through even the largest, most powerful companies. While these dispersed negotiations must take into consideration the most fundamental goals of the parent company, other considerations also enter into the negotiations. Thus, it is important to take a network perspective and examine what these other considerations are and the degree to which they exert power in the individual negotiations. It is too simple to equate the trend toward consolidation of ownership and a pattern of reduced diversity in messages, voices, and sharing of power. It may be the case that as the large media conglomerates increase their drive for profits, they will require their employees to increase the variety of messages and voices so as to create new and different audience configurations that can be turned into additional revenue streams.

Another macro-level change is occurring as media companies—and all companies in general—expand beyond their home borders and become more global. In his book *The World Is Flat,* Thomas Friedman (2007) argued that over the past few decades, a series of events have occurred that have leveled the playing field of economics and politics throughout the world. The old barriers that walled in certain economies and protected them from the rest of the world have been melting away as new technologies make information sharing more widespread. Now anyone anywhere on the planet has access to a great deal of information. There are many more opportunities for everyone, regardless of geography or social class. Friedman also argued that businesses have changed their structures and the way they perform their functions as the world becomes more flat through advances in information sharing. Companies have turned away from a strong, vertical central structure that plans all activities and governs all functions. Instead, companies are dispersing power to teams of collaborators focused on different functions. The team in the company collaborates with teams in other companies around the world to create the best products and services that are the most useful to consumer niches. Friedman argued, "The best companies are the best collaborators. In the flat world, more and more business will be done through collaborations within and between companies, for a very simple reason: The next layers of value creation—whether technology, marketing, biomedicine, or manufacturing—are becoming so complex that no single firm or department is going to be able to master them alone" (p. 457).

Changes in Business Practices

The drive for higher profits has changed some operating practices. For example, media corporations with news companies are promoting synergies between their editorial and business departments. D. Williams (2002) conducted a content analysis and found an increase in the quantity and quality of company-related materials mentioned on the news, especially in larger, more diversified and more integrated firms. Effects were found for total stories run and for tone.

Now newspaper managers examine every section of the newspaper for its revenue-generating potential. Newspapers have added sections for food, health, home decor, automobiles, and so on to provide some editorial content to attract readers to advertisers. Even the letters to the editor section of the newspaper has been examined. For example, Wahl-Jorgensen (2002) found that newspaper editors view the letters to the editor section as something that heightens the appeal of the newspaper and hence increases readership and financial rewards for the newspaper.

In their drive to reduce expenses, media businesses sometimes alter their messages. For example, Adams and Baldasty (2001) analyzed changes in the news content of the Scripps chain of newspapers and found that the news coverage in those newspapers revealed a heavy dependence on syndicated material and a lack of commitment to local issues. This had the effect of greatly reducing their costs, and it also resulted in the Scripps newspapers being in the last position in their markets as far as quality and readership. However, the Scripps chain of newspapers was the most profitable and largest newspaper operation in terms of number of newspapers owned at the beginning of the 21st century. This reminds us that profit is not keyed only to revenue or quality of product.

Another example of profit maximization can be seen in how television stations changed the content of their local news programs during the 1970s. During that decade, there was a growing realization that local news programs could generate a high profit, so many local TV stations began investing more heavily in their local newscasts as a way of increasing viewership and increasing profits. They did this by presenting an "action news" format with shorter and tighter stories, frequently featuring crime and violence.

These institutional changes have made companies more valuable. For example, Dominick, Sherman, and Messere (2000) showed how these practices were largely responsible for making local TV stations much more attractive to investors because they were seen as "cash cows," and many local TV stations were bought and sold for more than $500 million each. Thus, to understand the increase in the coverage of crime in local television newscasts, we need to follow the industry line of thinking all the way back to their fundamental goal of increasing the value of the business. Station managers believed that stories of violent crime would attract more viewers to their news programs, which in turn increased their advertising revenues from those programs, which in turn increased the overall profit margin of the television stations, which in turn made the stations more attractive to investors. This example illustrates the importance of examining decisions and changes in the context of strategies and goals. And even more important, this example illustrates the importance of looking at the businesses in the mass media industries as parts of a system of interrelated components, where a change in one component influences the functioning of all other components in the system.

Croteau and Hoynes (2001) argued that relaxing the regulatory rules on many media industries over the past decade has served to allow them to reorganize themselves in ways that reduce expenses, increase revenue, and hence increase profits. Now a large media conglomerate that makes a film can benefit from many revenue streams, including domestic box office, foreign distribution fees, rentals and then sales of videos and DVDs, sales of the soundtrack, sales of books and magazines related to the film, and merchandizing of apparel and items related to the film. Each of these not only brings in more revenue but also serves as cross-promotion for the other revenue streams. This helps to brand the film in many different ways and across many different niche markets. Cross-media promotion to increase revenue streams and amortize costs over many outlets is a trend that is continuing in the mass media industries.

Conclusion

The mass media organizations use three general business strategies to achieve their overall goal of maximizing the value of the organization for the owners. The first of these is to negotiate resource exchanges so as to be a net winner in those exchanges, that is, to end up with resources of more value than the resources given up. A second business strategy is to reduce risk. There are high degrees of risk associated with investing in the production and distribution of messages to attract the right kinds of audiences. The third business strategy is maximizing economic power. The mass media organizations do this by investing in other media (as well as nonmedia) companies. This serves to bring them economies of scope, which cuts their costs. It also reduces competition and thereby cuts their risk somewhat or at least spreads that risk out over media products produced by subsidiaries in many different media industries.

Marketing Strategies

The marketing challenge for mass media organizations lies in attracting and then holding on to a set of niche audiences. Mass media organizations use a sequence of four strategies to meet this challenge: delineating audiences, crafting messages, attracting audiences, and conditioning audiences.

These marketing strategies focus on the audience and not the messages. This reflects the shift in businesses over time from a sales strategy to a marketing strategy. With a sales strategy, the focus is on the product; the challenge is how to get people to buy the product. With a marketing strategy, the focus is on consumer needs; the challenge is how to develop messages that will satisfy those existing needs. For example, major book publishing houses used a sales strategy for years—that is, they looked for the highest quality literary authors. They had editors who would work with the author to develop the book to its highest literary quality. Then the publishers would try to sell those books to readers by trying to convince them that they should read literature. The locus of decision making in book publishing was with the editors, who decided what quality literature was. But over time, the segment of the population that bought these literary books remained relatively small. Publishers were under increasing pressure to grow their revenue so that they could reduce the high risk of commercial failures and show a steadily growing profit each year. Publishing businesses shifted into the marketing perspective, where publishers would break down the population of readers into segments as determined by their needs for books. Now we have segments for textbooks, religious books, self-help books, cooking books, genre fiction, and so on. Each of these audience segments has a different set of needs for books. These needs are carefully monitored by book publishers, who then look for books to satisfy those needs. This is what I mean by audience delineation—the breaking down of a general population into segments, each with its own recognizable set of needs for media messages. The key criterion in the audience delineation task is quality. By this, I do not mean an elite audience; instead, I mean the *kind* of audience as delineated by its particular needs for information and entertainment that can be satisfied by some type of media message.

Audience Delineation

There are many different ways to describe audiences—by demographics, by social class, by lifestyles, by psychographics, and so on. While these descriptors are useful in describing the types of people in the audience and helpful to media programmers and media buyers looking to place advertising in the appropriate media and vehicles, they are less helpful in explaining the types of audiences that mass media organizations want. Essentially, media organizations want to attract and maintain audiences that have three characteristics. First, media marketers want audiences that are the right niche. Therefore, they identify a population segment that has certain characteristics or qualities that are desirable to advertisers. Second, media marketers want to attract the largest number of people in that right niche. To do this, they invest resources to attract as many people as possible from that population segment. And third, media marketers attempt to condition that audience into habitually seeking out their messages. Thus, they try to build a high degree of loyalty. Once a media company has conditioned a large audience to loyalty exposure, the company can reduce its promotional expenses and thus grow its profit margin. This is why audience conditioning is such an important part of the process. For example, this is why magazines and newspapers depend on subscribers and are willing to give them a substantial reduction in price over the newsstand prices of their vehicles. Book publishers and recording companies want people to join their clubs so they can depend on their customers to continue purchasing their messages each month. And this is why movie and television companies brand their stars and franchises so that audiences will develop stronger attractions to certain actors and series.

The key with audience delineation is to look at the configuration of audiences in any market and then ask two questions of those audiences: (1) What audience needs exist that are not currently being met? and (2) What audience needs are currently being met but not as well as they could be?

Identifying Existing Needs

The generic needs for messages are entertainment and information that offer the biggest payoff for the lowest investment. Audience members are insatiable for new entertainment experiences and new information. Media businesses must build off this general need, but the satisfaction of needs lies in the specifics—that is, media businesses must find specific areas where they can meet a need not currently being met or where the business feels it can meet the existing needs better than competitors, which is the typical challenge with most media companies.

Finding existing needs that are not being met is the more difficult of the two questions to answer. An example of this would be a media company monitoring a wide range of organizations to find a new hobby that is growing in popularity. If the media company is a newspaper, the editors assign reporters to write a feature story on this topic. Over time, the newspaper might create a section that presents this type of information and surround it with ads from businesses that supply products to people engaged in this hobby. The media company might eventually create a magazine or a cable channel devoted to this hobby. The audience is delineated not in demographics of geography but by interest in this particular hobby.

More typically, media companies will look at where audiences are already spending their time and money to see where the existing needs are and where they are being met. The media company will then figure out a way that it can meet those existing needs in a better way and develop messages to do so. This is why film and television producers create spin-offs of successful shows. Book publishers will look for new authors whose writing is attractive to the readers in an existing niche as defined by a genre.

Not all identified needs are equally valuable to a media business. Three kinds of needs will be ranked low from an economic perspective. One kind of low-ranking need is held by only a few people. In this case, the media business will not want to devote considerable resources to satisfying this need, knowing that the payoff is small. Second, some existing needs might be strong among an economically weak group of people. For example, building an audience (even a very large group) of people who have almost no disposable income is not advantageous to a media business because that business will not be able to rent that audience out to many advertisers, and this will limit the company's return on its investment that was necessary to construct such an audience. And third, some existing needs might already be met by many competitors. Therefore, a media company will not be willing to make the investment in trying to construct its own audience by trying to pull people away from competitors' audiences. However, if the media business believes that the needs of the existing audience are being met only to a partial degree, that business may find the investment in going after that audience viable if it can either (1) more fully meet that audience's existing need or (2) meet that need at a lower cost to the audience. Lower costs can be defined in terms of either financial (like Amazon.com does with discounting books) or cognitive costs, such as degree of mental energy needed to follow an entertainment story or process a news story. Payoffs are usually emotional. For example, if a new television series has characters perceived as being more attractive or if plots are more suspenseful, they will attract audiences away from series where the characters are perceived as less attractive and the plots as delivering less of an emotional kick.

When a new medium comes along, it redefines the marketplace by giving audiences an opportunity to either (1) have their existing needs served at a lower cost or (2) have new needs met. When the new medium is able to do these things, the new medium consumes more and more resources that are usually taken away from the existing media. This was the case with the television medium, which took away the news and entertainment audiences from radio in the 1950s. Radio had to look for other existing needs to survive.

With the advent of the Internet, the existing mass media took quick action to avoid being replaced by a medium that offered more advantages to audiences. The existing media, especially cable channels, newspapers, and magazines, co-opted the Internet for their own purposes of promoting their existing services as well as creating Web sites to appeal to additional niche audiences. They typically used the Web to advertise their main business and thus maximize their institutional goals (Chan-Olmsted & Park, 2000; Lin & Jeffres, 2001). Over time, the Internet will become established as a channel of providing information on a par with the other existing media and become part of the status quo, which means it will follow the same patterns as the other more established mass media: pervasive commercialization, niche building and fractionation, less governmental regulation and oversight, and considerable economic concentration (Abrahamson, 1998). There is considerable evidence that these patterns are well under way with the Internet.

Niche Orientation

Another technique for managing the continual increases in competition is for mass media companies to abandon the practice of competing head-to-head with the largest, most powerful companies in trying to get the largest possible audiences for messages—a quantity-oriented strategy—and instead find smaller potential markets where the competition is not so strong—a niche-oriented strategy. This trend has showed up in all the media industries.

Within the newspaper industry, many companies lost a lot of their economic strength during the 1980s (Porter, 1980, 1985) and were faced with three options: a cost leadership strategy, a differentiation strategy, or a focus strategy. The cost leadership strategy requires a newspaper to lower its price and undersell all competitors and grow that way. The differentiation strategy requires newspapers to create a unique position in the audience mind. The focus strategy is to narrow the scope of the audience and become more niche oriented. Most newspapers have followed the third strategy.

Newspapers have moved away from a quantitative model, where the goal is to keep a high number of subscriptions; under this goal, the loss of subscribers represents an increase in risk. Now newspapers are more interested in niche audiences of high-quality consumers. For example, Picard (1998) pointed out that while newspaper circulation has been dropping for the past several decades, during that same time, newspaper profits have been increasing. Newspaper companies have accomplished this through a process of "profit engineering," where some newspapers in noncompetitive markets have sought to lower circulation to reduce some of their distribution costs into economically undesirable neighborhoods while trying to maximize circulation in upscale neighborhoods, thus constructing a more desirable audience for advertisers who are willing to pay a premium for the better audiences.

In the television industry, the broadcast network share of the U.S. audience shrank from more than 90% in the late 1970s to under 50% in late 1997, despite the increase of networks from three to six (Owers et al., 1998). The national TV audience was getting much more fragmented; it had already been fragmented for all other media. Thus, the broadcast TV companies gradually moved to a niche orientation to identify certain segments of the general TV viewing public and developed programming to attract only those types of viewers—a strategy that cable television had been using successfully for the past few decades. In its early days, cable television did not try to compete directly with the major commercial full-service television networks of ABC, CBS, and NBC. Instead, cable found niche audiences for sports, cooking, travel, home shopping, history, and so on and developed programming to attract, and then hold, audience members in those niches. This is why the homogeneity of audience members in an audience for cable channels is much greater than for the national broadcast channels (Barnes & Thomson, 1994).

The radio industry switched from a quantity strategy to a quality strategy in the 1950s when broadcast television took away its audience for entertainment and national news. Radio stations developed specialized formats to attract certain segments of the population.

As time goes by, the population continues to fragment in its many interests. The mass media organizations try to find those fragments and assemble them into audience segments. The newer media are all strongly oriented by the marketing perspective into finding niche audiences with specialized needs and then tailoring messages to attract people from those niches.

Differential Value

Not all audiences are of the same economic value to media businesses. Audiences that are harder to construct, as well as audiences with a more affluent composition, are more valuable. For example, advertisers usually want to reach audiences that are younger and more affluent, so they are willing to pay more for them. The most desirable age-group is 18 to 49, because these people buy the most products; also, their product loyalties and habits are less established than are older people's loyalties and habits.

The cost of reaching an audience for advertisers varies across media. For example, in 2001, the average CPM (cost per thousand audience members) of reaching men ages 18 to 34 was $77.35 for prime-time network TV, $52.05 in daily newspapers, $26.60 in weekly news magazines, and $10.70 for network radio (Napoli, 2003). Costs also vary by type of audience. Thus, some audiences are harder to reach and therefore more expensive than others.

Value entails more than cost; we also must consider benefits. Some audiences, such as older men with annual incomes over $200,000, are harder to find with media vehicles; when advertisers do find this audience, they must pay a premium to reach the audience. However, this audience is likely to spend a great deal of money on luxury cars, vacations, and high-tech toys, so advertisers are willing to spend large premiums to get their messages repeatedly to this audience. Therefore, media organizations find it worthwhile to attempt to construct such an audience.

Crafting Messages

Once the audience has been delineated, it is a much clearer task for the media company to select appropriate messages and to fashion those messages in ways to satisfy the particular needs of that audience. While the task is clearer, it is not simple. Producers must put salient characteristics into their messages to grab the audience members' attention and let them know that this message is satisfying some of their existing needs. This is very challenging.

Audiences gravitate to those messages with the highest value, meaning those messages with the lowest costs to them personally in comparison to payoffs. Therefore, in crafting messages, producers must include elements in their messages that signal to potential audience members that their specific needs will be met better than through other alternative messages and that these needs will be met at a lower cost to those people. Production talent lies in the ability to attract audiences with low costs and high benefits.

Placing Messages in Environments to Attract Audiences

Once a message has been developed for a market segment, the media company must make the people in that segment aware that the message exists. Then they must attract the audience. This is a relatively easy thing to do with active audiences, but it is much more difficult, although not impossible, with passive audiences. The key challenge here is to craft "triggers" in a message that will immediately and clearly signal to a potential audience member that the message fulfills a particular need. Individuals are bombarded with so many messages that a message outside of their normal exposure repertoire is usually ignored unless it has a salient characteristic that warrants attention.

An active audience is composed of people who are seeking the message the media company is providing. Thus, the media company need only announce the availability of the new message. For example, people in the movie theater are actively seeking movie entertainment, so presenting previews of new movies before the featured attraction is an announcement of the upcoming messages and when they will be available for viewing. But many people do not attend movies in theaters. To make these potential audience members aware of a movie, the media company must be more aggressive with its announcements, such as by putting an ad for the movie on television. People who watch television are not seeking information about new movies, so the media company must break through those people's filters and get their attention.

Sometimes marketers will have a media message that appears in one medium and want to attract people who do not usually expose themselves to that medium. In this case, the marketers need to go to the medium where their target does expose itself and promote to them there. A recent example of this is book publishers who create movie-like trailers on the Internet to attract readers for their books. Called book trailers, these often include dramatizations by actors and look just like trailers for movies. These book trailers have also been aired on television and in movie theaters (Soukup, 2006).

There are times when it is not possible to present a message in an environment that will attract an audience of the full size wanted. In this situation, the company must do cross-promotion. For example, a media company wants to start a sports magazine and build an audience for it. The company can buy lists of people who already subscribe to sports magazines and mail them promotional material. And the company can put its magazine on a rack of sports magazines in bookstores. But these techniques are not likely to generate a big enough audience for the new magazine. The company will also need to promote its magazine on sports cable channels and perhaps even at sports venues. Starting a new magazine (as with any new media vehicle) will usually require a high degree of investment to place a promotion for a particular new message in front of an existing audience. For example, a television network must create an audience for its new shows, so it will place a promo for the new program in an existing show. This means that the network forgoes selling that time to an advertiser. Or a book publisher will pay for an ad in a magazine. These promos and ads must be presented at a high frequency to break through the clutter, capture the attention of potential audience members, and motivate them to try the new message.

Cross–Web site promotions are important on the Internet because a person typically will access only a small number of sites (Webster & Lin, 2002). The most popular sites are usually run by traditional media companies, such as the TV networks of NBC, ESPN, CNN, and the like. So a site that is not one of the high-traffic sites must put promotions for its site in the high-traffic sites if it is to attract visitors.

Cross-vehicle promotion is made easier when a company is a large conglomerate that controls many different vehicles. It has become a common practice for these companies to do a lot of cross-vehicle promotion. For example, McAllister (2002) conducted a case study of how the last episode of *Seinfeld* was promoted and found that news organizations with connections to the show covered the last episode more extensively than those news shows without such connections.

Audience Conditioning

Mass media businesses attempt to condition audiences into habitual exposure patterns. Recall from the definition of the mass media that they are fundamentally in the business of creating and *maintaining* audiences. When they can maintain existing audiences they have already constructed, they achieve three major advantages. First, they reduce their overall risk by taking some of the pressure away from constructing new audiences. Second, they can amortize their high promotional costs associated with creating an audience over many exposures. And third, they can stabilize their pricing of audiences and thereby create a more predictable revenue flow.

As for this third advantage, Napoli (2003) explained that it is important that predicted audience, measured audience, and actual audience are all the same for good business. When the predicted audience is off from the measured audience, it affects the media adversely; they either underestimated the size of an audience and thus did not charge enough or could not deliver on what they had promised and must provide "make goods." Also, if advertisers think the actual audience is not as large as the measured audience, they will lose faith in audience measurement, which is the foundation of advertising pricing.

Programmers condition audiences for repeat exposures by gradually strengthening audience perceptions of value by (a) increasing perceptions of benefits through storytelling deviations to keep messages fresh and to promise further novelty while (b) decreasing audience perceptions of psychic costs while asking for more audience expenditure of financial and time resources. Notice that this is the general operating strategy for businesses translated into a smaller scale for individual audience members. The principle is the same for individuals as it is for businesses—that is, value is increased when benefits are increased and costs are decreased. Conditioning of audiences over the long term depends on strengthening (or at least maintaining) the audiences' perception of value.

The central challenge in conditioning audiences is to negotiate the conflicting goals of business that develop and provide the message with the audiences' needs. Specifically, audiences want higher production values, but to provide these increased benefits to audiences, businesses must incur greater costs. The same is true with using more talented production people (more famous personalities, movie stars, better writers, directors, news reporters, novelists, popular musical artists, etc.) who cost the businesses much more money. So the challenge for business managers is to know how much more to spend on talent in terms of significantly increasing benefits to the audiences. This challenge also cuts the other way with expenses. Specifically, the media businesses want to increase their revenue, and this typically increases the costs to audiences—that is, when audiences spend more for exposures, the media receive more revenue. However, many audience members might not want to continue in an audience if it costs them more to do so. Therefore, what the media businesses try to do is to decrease audience *perceptions* of overall costs through conditioning; this means making audiences feel they are giving up less of their own resources, even when they are spending more money and time with the media. By conditioning audiences to believe that their psychic costs are very low (messages are easy to process), the media can ask for more time and money from audiences while making those audiences believe their costs are going down. Thus, there is a huge premium among producers to create messages with very low psychic costs.

One example of audience conditioning at a general level is with crime and violence. "For more than 40 years, the Gallup Poll has found that Americans identify crime as either the first or second problem facing their local community" (Lipschultz & Hilt, 2002, p. 2). The mass media therefore see this as a need—that is, they present information about what the public thinks is a persistent problem. In this sense, they are merely satisfying an existing need. An analysis of the three big commercial TV network (ABC, CBS, and NBC) national newscasts from 1990 to 1996 found that crime was covered more often than any other type of story, even ahead of the economy and health issues (Hiebert & Gibbons, 2000). However, this continual coverage not only serves to satisfy a need but also conditions people to believe that crime is a major problem that creates a continuing need for information and reassurance on this topic.

The broadcast television industry has worked very hard to try to maintain its audiences by developing principles of programming to attract and hold audiences through an evening of viewing (Eastman, 1993). However, with each passing year, it becomes more difficult for broadcast television to hold their audiences. TV program loyalty, as measured by repeat viewing, is declining. In the early 1970s, repeat viewing for all TV series was about 55% (Goodhardt, Ehrenberg, & Collins, 1975). This means that of all audience members who watched a program one week, 55% watched the next episode either the next day or the next week. The nonrepeat viewers were not likely watching other TV programs; instead, they were usually not watching TV. So if a person was watching TV one evening, he or she was likely watching the same series he or she was watching the last time the episode was shown. However, by the late 1980s, repeat viewing had dropped to 25% (Ehrenberg & Wakshlag, 1987; Soong, 1988).

Within the area of audience behavior, there is something called the law of double jeopardy, which was introduced by McPhee (1963) as a label for an intriguing pattern of viewing he observed. It had been believed that large audiences contained many different kinds of people, and therefore there was not much program loyalty—that is, there were lots of different people watching a show at any given time. In contrast, small audiences were believed to be high on loyalty—that is, the same people would habitually watch a show. But McPhee found that repeat viewing was lower with low-rated shows than with high-rated shows. Thus, the term *double jeopardy* means that a low-rated show suffers not only because of a small audience but also because that audience is less loyal than audiences for highly rated programs. This effect has been found repeatedly (Barwise, Ehrenberg, & Goodhardt, 1982; Ehrenberg, Goodhardt, & Barwise, 1990). Thus, the prevailing explanation has been that popularity causes loyalty. But there is another explanation: Shows become popular by providing economic value, that is, a high payoff for little effort. There is a huge churn of viewers for TV, and those shows with the highest perceived value eventually attract the most viewers. The same characteristics that attracted them in the first place keep pulling them back—this is where conditioning comes in. Shows that do not attract well lack elements to pull people back.

It is likely that these principles and practices that have been developed with television audiences also apply to audiences for messages from other media. At base, the conditioning of repeat viewing of TV is likely to be the same as the conditioning for habitual exposure to certain radio stations, Internet sites, musical groups, magazines, or book authors and topics.

Conclusion

From the mass media organizations' point of view, the construction of audiences is their most important activity. They are guided by three strategies when engaged in this activity. First, they use the marketing perspective to identify potential audiences. Second, they attempt to attract those audiences by crafting certain kinds of messages and placing those messages in the information environment so that potential audience members will be exposed to them. Third, they condition people who are exposed to those messages so that those people will form the habit of continual exposure to those messages.

CHAPTER 6

Employment Strategies

To achieve the fundamental goal of maximizing owner value, mass media organizations use employment strategies in addition to the business and marketing strategies explained in the two previous chapters. Personnel is an important resource—perhaps the most important resource—for mass media organizations, so the selection and socialization of employees are crucial to the health of mass media organizations. You will notice in this chapter that there is less research on the topic of employment strategies than the other strategies or especially on other facets of the mass media. Also, the research that has been conducted on employment strategies is largely concentrated within journalistic organizations. In my treatment of these research findings, I will generalize their patterns, where appropriate, to all types of mass media organizations.

Selection of Workers

Managers in mass media organizations, like managers in all organizations, are careful to select people who have certain kinds of abilities and values.

Skills and Talent

There are many different skills required of people working in mass media organizations. Little research has been conducted in this area, presumably because the skills required for particular jobs are obvious. For example, journalists need to know how to write, news anchors need to know how to read, managers need to know how to manage, and so on. However, all employees need skill sets, that is, clusters of secondary skills to help them with their primary skills. For example, one thing journalists should have in their skill set is some mathematical reasoning ability to help them understand quantitative evidence from public opinion polls, economic indicators, and so forth. Maier (2003) found that while most journalists were competent in basic mathematical skills, one in six were still lacking.

The mass media organizations are constantly looking for a particular type of talent. But talent is defined less in terms of pure artistic ability and more in terms of ability to attract and hold audiences. Thus, talent is defined in terms of commercial appeal. When it comes to acting, it is not necessarily the person with the greatest acting skill who is regarded as being the most talented. Instead, people who look really interesting or attractive on camera can still attract large audiences even if they have a very modest level of acting ability.

The people who are able to attract the right kinds of audiences in the largest numbers are of the highest value to the mass media businesses. Therefore, those people are paid the most money, while people with less of this kind of talent are paid less—usually much less. Thus, there is a pyramid structure of workers in the talent guilds. For example, writers who have sold a script or story treatment to a film or a television production company are eligible to join the Writers Guild of America (WGA). The WGA has fewer than 9,000 members, so it is a fairly elite group to begin with. When we look at all writers of Hollywood movies, we see that they are arranged in a giant pyramid in terms of talent and compensation. At the bottom of the pyramid are the lower 25% of Hollywood writers, who each earns less than $30,000 a year. At the top of the pyramid are the top 5% of Hollywood film writers, and they each earn well over $560,000 per year. The very top writers are now selling film scripts for several million dollars each (Wasko, 2003).

The same pyramid structure is in the Screen Actors Guild. Peters and Cantor (1982) pointed out that in 1974, the Guild had 45,000 members, but less than 8% of them earned more than $10,000 a year from acting. The few actors at the top of the pyramid are not only paid a great deal of money but also have the power to alter films, stop production, and receive all kinds of perks. The actors at the bottom of the pyramid have no power and often receive no income.

In this rule-governed enterprise, creativity lies not so much in breaking rules or creating brand-new rules as it does in working off the rules in innovative ways. Producers who break the rules or try creating new rules will confuse the audience. However, producers who follow the rules of storytelling but then gradually pull away from those rules in a way that brings the audience along step by step will surprise and delight that audience.

Existing Values

What values are most important when media managers screen applicants? Hollifield, Kosicki, and Becker (2001) conducted a national survey of news directors at television stations and newspapers to determine the values in play behind their hiring practices. Specifically, they wanted to see if organizational or professional criteria were more important in hiring. They found that organizational criteria were more important, especially personality and work habits.

It is easier to hire people with values that contribute to the everyday workings of the organization than to try developing those values. So screening workers on values is important. However, once hired, the workers' values are shaped in the day-to-day work environment.

Demographics

While mass media managers carefully screen applicants for values, skills, and talent, there is evidence that screening also takes place on other characteristics, such as demographics. For example, Poindexter, Smith, and Heider (2003), who conducted a content analysis of local newscasts, found that Latinos, Asian Americans, and Native Americans were virtually invisible as anchors, reporters, sources, and subjects in the news. Although African Americans anchored and reported the news in some markets, overall there was segregation in story assignments. In his book, *Media Industries: The Production of News and Entertainment,* Turow (1984) also talked about the complex decisions that are made when producers hire ethnic minorities for roles in television series. Turow observed that social class is a key determinant in hiring journalists, with almost all journalists coming from the middle class.

Socialization of Workers

The mass media can be viewed as an institution (McQuail, 2005). As an institution, it has a bureaucratic organizational structure that seeks to instill professionalism, shape values, and prescribe routines for its members to foster an environment where the organizations can attain their goals. Also, during the 1970s, it became popular for sociologists to regard news organizations as factories where news was manufactured by news workers. For example, Whitney

(1982) argued that by the early 1980s, the idea that news reflected or mirrored real events had been supplanted in the scholarly literature by the idea that news was manufactured by news workers and that this change had been brought about by what he called interpretive sociologists using qualitative methods. While this model of analysis might be a bit too "industrial" for many scholars, the insights produced by these interpretive sociologists—particularly Altheide, Snow, Fishman, and Tuchman—have had a lasting impact on the way scholars view the journalistic process. Due to the influence of these scholars, we now think of the profound socialization influence on journalists—and to a larger extent all media workers—that the mass media organizations necessarily exert. Some of this influence comes from structural characteristics in the organizations, their resources, and their goals. But much of this influence also comes from the shaping of perceptions, behaviors, and values that accrue as media workers observe their colleagues and learn their professions on the job.

Tuchman (1978) defined socialization as the learning of norms or rules as a resource for the construction of meaning. "The use of rules is a creative, subjective, interpretive, and pretheoretic activity, not a mechanical response to their internalization" (p. 206). Turow (1984) built on this idea, saying, "As people move through social situations, including organizations, they get involved in activities. Through these activities, they and the people they work with negotiate rules explicitly and implicitly about their interdependent behaviors (their roles)" (p. 134).

Structural Characteristics

Some structural characteristics have to do with resources available to the organization. Parenti (1986) explained that some of the constraints on journalists are limitations of time to gather information and space to present the story, as well as budget limitations preventing them from covering certain stories as they would like. Other structural constraints have to do with the need to construct audiences, and this requires journalists to focus on sensationalized stories and the need to reduce complex events to simple stories.

Still other structural characteristics deal with the nature of working within an organization that requires collaboration. The production of media messages is a complex organizational process in which creativity of a producer is shaped by the constraints arising from the production routines and conflicts within the production organization. Successful producers must learn how to work in this culture (Ettema, 1982; H. Newcomb & Alley, 1982). Sociologists who study this process focus on the influence of factors such as organization structure, technology, and reward systems on the creative process. J. Ryan and Peterson (1982) illustrated this point in their case study of the production of country music songs. They showed that record companies have developed an institutional process of screening, shaping, producing, and then distributing their messages. Employees must learn the process and how to work within it if they are to be successful. The process is not arbitrary but has been developed over years of trial and error as a means of reaching the company's goal of maximizing sales to particular niche audiences. Each mass media industry has its own process where people with different talents collaboratively work on conceiving, producing, and then marketing their messages. While there are specific practices that are different from industry to industry, there is a general process that is common to book publishing (Powell, 1982), Hollywood film production (Peters & Cantor, 1982), commercial television (H. Newcomb & Alley, 1982), and even public television (Ettema, 1982). Scholars have also written about the manufacturing process with news content (Altheide, 1976; Fishman, 1980; Gitlin, 1980; Picard & Brody, 2000; Tuchman, 1978).

The socialization of mass media workers can be influenced by factors outside the mass media industry. Because people who work in the mass media businesses are in constant contact and negotiation with people in other businesses, there is a sharing of values across contiguous industries. For example, Fortunato (2005) explained that media workers are also influenced by external factors, such as advertisers, audiences, and resource providers (especially sources of information and governmental regulators). For example, Sallot, Steinfatt, and Salwen (1998) surveyed journalists and public relations practitioners and found that the two groups report similar news values, although the journalists are less aware of these similarities. Also, D. Berkowitz and TerKeurst (1999) argued that journalists and news sources together form interpretive communities where meaning is negotiated through the contextualization of events.

Part of socialization is training media workers to protect their industry and its practices. This is why journalists often feel threatened by movements such as the public journalism movement that seek to change how they select and tell their stories. When they feel pressured from outside their profession, journalists try to protect their professionalism and their independence from any one group trying to influence them. This dynamic serves to deflect criticism and reinforce existing practices (McDevitt, 2003). Also, the probability of an event or issue being covered as news is inversely proportional to the harm the information might cause to investors or sponsors. It is also inversely proportional to the cost of covering it and directly proportional to the expected breadth of appeal to audience that advertisers are willing to pay for (McManus, 1994).

While gender is an issue in hiring workers, it appears that socialization is more influential than gender in explaining how journalists cover their stories. Rodgers and Thorson (2003) investigated the news coverage of male and female reporters at three U.S. daily newspapers to determine whether gender difference resulted in reporting differences. They content analyzed news stories and found that there were gender differences in the stories. Female reporters drew upon a greater diversity of sources, stereotyped less, and wrote more positive stories than did male reporters. The authors then interviewed the reporters and concluded that socialization differences accounted for the differences in the stories.

Professionalism

Journalists view what they do as a profession. While prospective journalists can learn how to write, take pictures, and edit before they are hired by a news organization, they must learn the professional of journalism on the job.

Professionalism refers to the exercise of autonomy and the right of workers to control their own work. In news organizations, Tuchman (1978) said that editors cannot monitor all the actions of reporters, nor can publishers monitor the decisions of editors. Reporters and editors are given considerable latitude in doing their jobs. Thus, professionalism in an organization is related to flexibility. "News organizations maintain flexibility and save money by discouraging a more complex bureaucracy than already exists, and by encouraging professionalism among reporters. Among reporters, professionalism is knowing how to get a story that meets organizational needs and standards" (Tuchman, 1978, pp. 65–66).

Part of the news profession is developing news sources. "The higher the status of sources and the greater the scope of their positions, the higher the status of the reporters" (Tuchman, 1978, p. 69). A "star" reporter needs to have "star" news sources.

Another essential part of professionalism in news is building credibility in the minds of audience members. Part of this is learning about libel law so as to protect the news organization from lawsuits for libel. Another part is knowing how to get facts to give the story substance, and another part is verifying facts. Also, journalists must know how to tell their stories. This means knowing how to write for print journalists; for journalists using a visual medium, it also means knowing how to construct and sequence visual images.

Routines

The outcome of these socialization processes is a uniformity in how people do their work in mass media organizations. For example, J. Ryan and Peterson (1982) said that decisions in mass media organizations generally follow one of four frameworks. First, there is the assembly-line framework where all decisions are built into the machinery so that products can be manufactured efficiently and uniformly. Second, there is the craft and entrepreneurship framework, where media workers have technical skills but need managers to tell them what types of messages to produce. Third, there is the convention and formula framework, where news workers are socialized into a community of message producers. Fourth, there is the audience image and conflict framework, where all workers on a message production team argue their case about what will be best in the marketplace. Ryan and Peterson synthesized these four differing frameworks into something they called the commercial professional framework, where the focus is on developing professional technicians and artists to produce products that have high commercial value, that is, to appeal to audiences.

The way workers spend their time socializes them into a certain way of thinking and behaving. And the patterns in how people are rewarded for what they do reinforces certain behaviors and thus conditions them into certain behavioral patterns. Fortunato (2005) explained that the production of messages in media organizations is influenced by organizational routines (allocation of resources through budgeting, recruitment and socialization of workers, values in the organization), branding, and promotion.

Workers learn routines to get them through the day, especially through crisis or pressure situations. The routines bring order to chaos and keep workers on track to a satisfactory completion of a task (Tuchman, 1978; Turow, 1984). "Routines are patterned activities that people learn to use in carrying out certain tasks" (Turow, 1984, p. 151). These routines contain perceptions about the way the messages should be structured, called typifications. With journalists, an important formula or routine is "objectivity" or what it means to write an accurate story without bias.

Fishman (1980) said that "newsworkers do not invent new methods of reporting the world on every occasion they confront it. They employ methods that have been used in the past; they rely upon the standard operating procedures of their news organization and of their profession" (p. 14). He says that most stories are constructed with standard practices day after day. Part of the daily routine is making the rounds to "fountains of information" on a reporter's beat. The substance of what reporters gather on their rounds is information produced by daily routines in the organizations they are covering. This routine activity teaches reporters what sources to use, what is worth reporting, when things should be reported, what constitutes good information as well as suspicious information, and what constitutes controversial matters.

Shoemaker and Reese (1996) synthesized the research literature on influences on the construction of media content and the people who produce that content and found that socialization was a major influence in three ways. First, the more media workers follow the routines of their organizations, the more likely their content is to be used. Second, the more media workers learn the routines associated with their jobs, the more professional they are rated by coworkers. Third, the longer people work for a media organization, the more socialized they are to the policies—stated and unstated—of the organization.

Media Logic

Altheide and Snow (1979) said the media have a logic of their own: "Media logic consists of a form of communication; the process through which media present and transmit information" (p. 10). Media logic includes formats, which determine "how material is organized, the style in which it is presented, the focus or emphasis on particular characteristics of behavior, and the grammar of media communication. Format becomes a framework or a perspective that is used to present as well as interpret phenomena" (p. 10).

Altheide and Snow (1979) said that the elements of a media format include the grammar of the medium and the norms that are used to define content. "Grammar is defined as a set of rules governing the use, arrangement (syntax), and inflection of words" (p. 23). And "the significant features of electronic media grammar are: (1) the manner in which time is used, including compacting time, rhythm, and tempo (inflection); (2) the organization and scheduling of content such as the dialogue/action sequences and the scheduling of programs (syntax); and (3) special features of verbal and non-verbal communication, such as reliance on specific kinds of words and nonverbal gestures which represent words" (p. 23). They said that media format is the matching of media content with the culture of the audience and that radio understands the listener's daily routine and fits entertainment into that routine.

Audiences understand media logic and message formats. Altheide and Snow (1979) said, "For a major medium such as television, audiences have become so familiar with different formats that they automatically know when something on television is news, comedy, or fictional drama. In like manner, radio, newspaper, and magazine formats have become second nature to listeners and readers. Thus, the logic of media formats has become so taken for granted by both communicator and receiver that it has been overlooked as an important factor in understanding media" (p. 10).

People who work in a media organization need to learn this logic and how to use it when crafting messages. There are entertainment formats and news formats. Each specifies what topics qualify as a message and how to tell the story. With entertainment, media logic tells producers how to use actors and how to personalize performers. With news, the key elements of the logic tell journalists which news sources to use, how to write story angles and themes, and how to cover certain stories such as crime, politics, religion, and sports.

Learning Values

Once people are hired into an industry, they must be socialized in its values. This is why journalists share a common set of ethics; if there are variations in how they are applied, the variations are influenced by context (D. Berkowitz & Limor, 2003; Craig, 2003). Plaisance and Skewes (2003) conducted a survey and found that the 10 most highly ranked descriptors for journalists, in order, were honest, fair, responsible, capable, broadminded, just, aboveboard, intellectual, logical, and imaginative. However, there was considerable variation across the rank orderings by the surveyed journalists. This indicates that journalists have been socialized to hold the same values, but the rank ordering of those values might shift across situations. Underwood and Stamm (2001) conducted a nationwide survey of American and Canadian journalists to determine their religious beliefs. They found that journalists generally have a strong religious orientation, especially when it is viewed as a moral activism.

D. Weaver and Wilhoit (1996) found that there are some enduring values of journalists (getting information to the public quickly and accurately) while other values wax and wane (being critical of government and institutions by investigating and challenging their claims; tolerance on using deception and illegal means to get the facts).

Gans (1979, pp. 42–52) argued that there are eight values of journalists: (1) ethnocentrism (America values its own nation above all others), (2) altruistic democracy (politicians should follow a course based on the public interest), (3) responsible capitalism (optimistic faith that in the good society, businesses compete with each other to create increased prosperity for all people; that they will refrain from unreasonable profits and gross exploitation of workers or customers), (4) small-town pastoralism (news favors small towns; reflecting historical rural American values), (5) individualism (the freedom of individuals should be protected from the encroachments of nation and society), (6) moderatism (discourages excess or extremism in favor of middle ground), (7) social order (the desirability of a certain type of social order is favored in the news), and (8) national leadership (the need to maintain social order is rooted in the responsibility of our national leaders).

The news values then influence the criteria for what is news. Because those criteria must be inferred from looking across news stories, different scholars have different lists of news criteria. For example, M. Ryan and Tankard (1977) listed proximity, prominence, timeliness, impact, magnitude, conflict, and oddity. McManus (1994) listed timeliness, proximity, consequence, human interest, prominence, unusualness, conflict, visual quality, amusement, and topicality. McQuail (2000, p. 284) listed the key news selection factors as power and fame of individuals involved in events, personal contacts of reporters, location of events, location of power, predictability and routine, proximity to the audience of people and events in the news, recency and timeliness of events, and timing in relation to the news cycle.

Journalists see their roles as interpreter, disseminator, and adversary. The interpreter role involves analyzing and interpreting difficult issues for readers. The disseminator role involves getting information out quickly to the public. And the adversary role involves challenging government and business (D. Weaver & Wilhoit, 1996). Also, journalists have built a myth about localism to preserve their historic focus on local events. But as the commercial press gets more concentrated in ownership and sharing of messages, the idea of localism is more a myth than a reality (Pauly & Eckert, 2002).

Learning Processes

Media workers learn certain processes that structure how they do their jobs. Turow (1984) argued that the structures within the mass media industries and companies reflect power relations. People who work in the industries learn these power relations and tend to follow the examples of the people in power so as to benefit from resources. This increases the legitimacy of those in power and the cycle continues. People are socialized by watching other people and also by job switching and by interacting with others in their profession in professional associations. Most of the research on this point has been conducted with news workers, and the key processes are concerned with selection of stories to cover and news gathering.

Selection of Stories. Newspaper gatekeeping is influenced more by forces on the routine level of analysis than by individual staff writers' characteristics (Shoemaker, Eichholz, Kim, & Wrigley, 2001). Also, Gant and Dimmick (2000) demonstrated that TV news gatekeeping decisions were traceable primarily to resource constraints, visual potential, proximity, and novelty.

H. S. Kim (2002) surveyed journalists from major national networks and local television stations to find out how they make decisions about what international news to present. He found different values for national and local outlets. Network journalists manifested a global view, selecting international news with diverse themes; local television journalists were more influenced by local business pressures and audience demands, choosing international news with a local angle.

Newsmakers are typically White, male, and in positions of visible authority in government (elected officials) and the media (celebrities). For example, Larson and Baily (1998) analyzed 5 years of *ABC World News Tonight*'s Person of the Week segments and found the individuals typically worked in politics and entertainment; they were White, male, and famous.

News Gathering/Sources. News practices are influenced by how news workers adapt to information technologies. Garrison (2000) found that journalists' use of the Internet for research grew dramatically throughout the 1990s. However, journalists recognized there were problems with using online sources of information, especially regarding verification of facts, sites containing unreliable information, bad source information, and lack of source credibility. Also, Comrie (1999) examined sourcing patterns on prime-time news across a 12-year period in New Zealand and found that with deregulation, there was a switch to a more commercial news style. Sound bites decreased in length. News managers grew in their insistence to target news at ordinary people to increase viewership.

Shaping the News Formula

News formulas are human constructions. A lot of creative people's efforts have gone into the creation and alteration of these story formulas. Also, there have been strong macro influences on these story formulas.

Audience Influences. Audience needs for news are important. As needs change, so does the message construction. For example, Altheide (1985) argued that most people are not interested in issues but are instead concerned with personal problems. He said that people are most concerned about events that will affect them personally. Thus, this change in needs forced news workers to personalize stories.

Inside Industry Influences. Shoemaker and Reese (1996, pp. 262–271) synthesized the research literature on influences on the construction of media content in the area of news construction. Their findings include the following:

- A journalist's background and personal characteristics will affect media content in proportion to the amount of power the person holds within the media organization.

- Journalists' role conceptions affect content.

- Events that are congruent with media routines are more likely to be covered than discongruent events.

- Events are more likely to be covered than issues.

- The closer an event is to the media organization's routine definition of newsworthiness, the more likely it is to be covered.

- The more journalists cover an event, the more similar their coverage will be, and thus there is a pack mentality among journalists. Also, the more coverage the opinion-leading media give an issue or event, the more likely other media are to give subsequent coverage to the issue or event.

- The more powerful or successful people or groups are, the more negative news coverage of them will be.

- The larger and more complex a media organization is, the less influence professional routines will have on content and the more influence larger organizational forces will have.

- Television and radio are more sensitive to the need to make a profit than are newspapers and magazines.

- Media workers from organizations owned by chains form weaker attachments to the local community than do workers for independent organizations.

- News sources are more influential when they have more economic and political power and when they adapt to the news organization's routines.

- The more a media organization promotes itself within a target audience, the more its content will reflect the interests of that audience.

- Advertisers influence media content.

- The more deviant people or events are, the more likely they are to be included in media content.

- The more political, economic, or cultural significance one country has for another, the more the former will appear in the latter's mass media.

Society Influences. In general, media content is influenced by ideological positions that maintain the status quo. These are embodied in forces outside the media organizations as well as forces inside the media as media organizational routines (Shoemaker & Reese, 1996). McQuail (2000) said that this broad hegemonic value of maintaining the status quo works through several levels of social structures down to the individual journalists. The cultural value of the status quo influences social institutions and through those institutions influences media organizations and the routines of work there. Journalists engage in these routines and become socialized into a particular form of news working.

Medium Influences. The news formula used to be different across media—that is, there used to be a different way to tell a news story in a newspaper and on television, for example. But this difference is eroding with newer technologies. McManus (1994) wrote *Market-Driven Journalism,* in which he argued that technology would significantly alter the news environment and the news values that journalists bring to new media. Since that time, there has been a convergence of print, broadcast, and Internet technologies. McManus's predictions are coming true (E. L. Cohen, 2002). Technology increasingly drives journalism. Tuggle and Huffman (2001) analyzed TV newscasts and found that frequently, these newscasts will have live coverage of an event even when there is no apparent journalistic justification for going live. Chan-Olmsted and Ha (2003) found that television broadcasters use the Internet mainly to support the stations' broadcast products rather than to provide different products or services.

Geography. Differences by geography are also becoming less important to news values. For example, the differences between big-city and small-town newspapers are breaking down in terms of how they cover the news. It appears that journalism has gone global in the sense that there is a shared set of values around the globe concerning types of news sources, story topics, and types of storytelling (D. H. Weaver, 1998). Also, the same news formulas appear across countries. Natarajan and Hao (2003) analyzed news bulletins and found that CNA (Channel News Asia) stories differed little from CNN stories. Both focused on crises and conflicts in their news coverage of Asia.

Coulson, Riffe, Lacy, and St. Cyr (2001) conducted a survey of television journalists who cover city government in the 214 television markets in the United States. They found that more veteran reporters perceived diminishing commitment and quality of reporting of city hall over the past 5 years with fewer stories and less airtime. However, small market stations were seen as more committed to covering city hall.

Conclusion

Employment strategies focus on hiring the right people and then socializing them to perform their functions well in the mass media organizations. When hiring, managers look for certain values, skills, and talent, but other factors also seem to come into play. Employees are then socialized through everyday working practices and routines to develop particular values. Workers are also influenced by factors outside their organizations and from outside the mass media industry as well. The result of the socialization is to build an organization that further reinforces certain practices and values to fulfill its functions efficiently and effectively year after year.

PART III

Explaining the Media Audiences Facet

CHAPTER 7

Media Audience Line of Thinking

The lineation general framework suggests a particular line of thinking about mass media audiences that helps us evolve from a Generating-Findings perspective to a Mapping-Phenomenon perspective. This line of thinking is structured by a media exposure model that is based on two ideas. One of these ideas is that attention to media messages is best conceptualized as taking place in one of four qualitatively different exposure states. The second idea is that there are three fundamental tasks in which audience members engage when encountering media messages; these are the tasks of filtering, meaning matching, and meaning construction.

In this chapter, I develop the media exposure model and then elaborate it in the following four chapters. In the process of developing this media exposure model, I will first address the tasks of conceptualizing the audience, delineating the difference between exposure and attention, and then defining the fundamental tasks that people encounter when exposed to media messages.

Conceptualizing the Audience

Three Perspectives

When reading the literature on mass media audiences, we can see that the audience is viewed by scholars essentially through one of three perspectives. One of these is the perspective of the mass media organizations' point of view, where the audience is seen as a macro unit of aggregated individuals who are relatively passive. Audience behavior is shaped by structural factors about how messages are programmed (timing, sequencing of messages, packaging of messages) and structural factors about audiences (primarily demographics) (Webster & Phalen, 1997). Audiences are conditioned to habitual exposure patterns over the long term by media.

Mass media organizations are interested in attracting a particular kind of audience—one that has three characteristics. First, media organizations want to attract an audience that is composed of particular kinds of people, that is, the target niche people. Audience niches are usually defined with demographics (Nickelodeon aiming at children; Lifetime aiming at women) or personal interests (Fox Sports Network, History Channel, *Soldier of Fortune* magazine, books on how to build a boat). Second, media organizations want to attract as large a share of that target niche as they can. And third, media organizations want to condition the audience into habitually seeking out subsequent exposures. For purposes of ease, I'll use the anagram NSL (niche, share, loyalty) to refer to this type of audience. Typically, it is a target in the minds of programmers. For example, a media organization might start a magazine on a particular hobby to appeal to a niche of people who have that hobby; the organization wants to identify all those particular hobbyists and get them to subscribe to their new magazine. The media organization also will provide content and promote future issues in a manner to condition those hobbyists to continue to subscribe. Another example is a media organization that develops a video game to appeal to teenage boys. It will create in-store displays, Web sites, and blogs to attract the boys to buy and use the game, and then condition them to buy updates and manuals that will help them play better.

Thus, from the media organizations' point of view, NSL audiences are units that are composed of aggregates of individuals. Individuals themselves are not as important an entity as the audience unit is. For the sake of efficiency, the media organizations think of all individuals in an audience as being the same. By this

I do not mean that the media organizations think all humans are the same, only that they have constructed an audience on a particular characteristic that all members of the NSL audience have in common; so in a practical sense, it is possible to treat all members of the NSL audience the same within the bounds of that defining characteristic. Individuals are only important insofar as they contribute to the size of the audience and only insofar as they are able to represent the aggregate in terms of indicating certain characteristics that can be used to predict and control audience behavior. For more on this topic, see the 12 chapters in *Audiencemaking: How the Media Create the Audience,* edited by Ettema and Whitney (1994).

A second perspective that scholars have used to view the audience is from a sociological point of view, where the focus is on group affiliations. People are members of a social class group, and they also cluster together in interest groups (S. Hall, 1980; Morley, 1992). These groups each have their own culture or sets of values. People are socialized into a way of thinking about life by their groups. These socialization patterns then influence the media people use and how they interpret the meaning of those media messages.

A third perspective that scholars have used to view the audience is from a psychological point of view, where the focus is on the individual and his or her motivations for media exposures and his or her experience during those exposures. From this perspective, individuals are regarded as actively making decisions to satisfy their personal goals and desires. This conceptualization of the audience grows out of ideas from the fields of economics and psychology (Webster & Phalen, 1997; Zipf, 1949).

From an individual's point of view, people rarely think about joining an audience or becoming a member of a group of "others" doing the same thing. Instead, media exposure is typically more individualistic and personal—that is, people think primarily in terms of their own needs and seek out experiences to satisfy those needs. The exposure experience is often solitary. Reading a magazine, newspaper, or book is highly solitary, such that the presence of other people poses a threat of interrupting one's media exposure and thereby ending one's audience-ness. Other media, such as film, TV, radio, recordings, and the Internet, allow for some social interaction with a few other audience members during exposure. However, during these times, these audience members do not usually achieve an awareness of being part of a larger dispersed group of people having the same experience. Instead, they focus on having a personal experience with the few people around them and rarely think about the total audience that is experiencing the same message.

Big Questions

Because the conceptualization of the mass media audience is so different across these three perspectives, the questions of greatest interest to scholars vary by perspective. For example, from the mass media organizations' point of view, the dominant questions about audiences are practical ones that focus on business opportunities. What are the unmet message needs in the general population? Are there enough people who have an unmet need for a particular kind of message to make them a viable target audience? Can I create messages that would meet the needs of my targeted individuals? How can I attract the targets to my messages? Can I condition the attracted targets to expose themselves habitually to my messages so that I can depend on their continuing exposures? These questions are not particularly challenging conceptual ones and can be addressed using the ideas laid out in the previous set of chapters on mass media organizations.

The sociological question on mass media audiences poses several important questions. How are existing group memberships reinforced or altered by media exposure? To what extent do members of a particular group behave the same way in terms of seeking out the same media and messages? To what extent do members of a particular group interpret the meaning of a given media message the same? If there are differences in meaning interpretation across members of the same group, how can this be explained?

I argue that the psychological perspective has presented the most problematic part of the audience literature. Part of the reason for this is perhaps because the audience literature that has been conducted from a psychological perspective is larger than other literatures, and the size offers more opportunities for problems with definitional variation. But the larger part of the reason for the problem with this literature is the nonproductive tangent into motives—that is, much of this literature deals with motives for exposure, and I argue that most of this literature has low validity because it relies on self-report of motives and exposures (this criticism is developed in more detail in Chapter 9). When we take a broader view of exposure by considering four exposure states, we can see that for much media exposure, people do not encode their experiences to make them accessible in a way that would deliver valid responses to the way these data are generated in surveys of motives and exposures. From this psychological perspective, we need to generate better answers to three fundamental questions: (1) What is exposure? (2) What is attention? and (3) What are the essential cognitive tasks that audience members use when encountering media messages? The remainder of this chapter is devoted to answering these three questions.

Defining Exposure

Media Exposure Research

More than two decades ago, Webster and Wakshlag (1985) laid out the issues involved in determining what television exposure was and said there were three conceptualizations for exposure. Not much has changed up until today; that is, there are still the same issues, and those issues pertain not just to TV but to all media. First, there is exposure as choice. This focuses on what people expose themselves to when they are given many choices. Second, there is exposure as attention. This line of research focuses on what attracts people's attention in the messages and what people pay attention to during their exposure sessions. Third, there is exposure as preference. This research is focused on what people say are their general preferences and favorite messages.

Exposure as Choice. The media exposure as choice literature follows an economic approach to audience behavior. This was introduced by Steiner (1952) and has since been extended by Owen and Wildman (1992), Waterman (1992), and others. These scholars treat choices about media exposure the same as choices about consumer products. This approach assumes a rational model where people think about their goals and know their options and then make rational, well-informed choices to maximize the value of their resources.

Exposure as Attention. Several models of attention have been suggested by media scholars to delineate the different types. For example, Hawkins, Pingree, Bruce, and Tapper (1997) proposed a model of attention to media messages—specifically television—according to how long people gaze at a television screen. Their model includes four levels: monitoring, orienting, engaged, and staring. Monitors look for 1.5 seconds or less at a time, with the levels ranging upward to starers, who look for at least 16 seconds at a time. They found that only 11% of all looks were for as long as 16 seconds.

Another attention model was proposed by Comstock and Scharrer (1999), who argued that attention should be operationalized as three types: primary, secondary, and tertiary. Primary attention is when TV viewing is a sole and foremost activity. Secondary attention is when TV viewing is less primary than some other activity. And tertiary attention is when viewing is subordinate to other activities, such as viewing that is in the background during a conversation.

Geiger and Newhagen (1993) argued that there are two kinds of attention: controlled and automatic. "Controlled attention is synonymous with mental effort and is dictated by the goals of the individual processor. Automatic attention does not require the use of limited resources, and is determined by attributes of the information" (p. 44). Other cognitive psychologists explain that there is a range of consciousness about individual acts of cognition—that is, they fall along a continuum from automatic processing to controlled processing (Shiffrin, 1988). The positioning along this continuum is determined by the amount of cognitive resources required to execute it, which in turn is determined by the person's abilities and familiarity with a task (Pashler, 1998). Arousing content increases the resources required to process messages, thus making them less prone to automatic processing (A. Lang, Potter, & Bolls, 1999).

Exposure as Preference. This body of research has been strongly influenced by uses and gratifications theory, which posits that audience members are active in making choices based on their preferences for various media, genres, and messages. These preferences are governed by their motives, needs, and expectations for the exposures. The reasons for the seeking and the usage of messages are then designated as motives. These motives are compared with people's perceptions of how gratifying those exposures were. These scholars have generated a literature on motives that is quite extensive (this is presented in some detail in Chapter 9).

Exposure as Filtering

In this general perspective for explaining the mass media, I make a distinction between exposure and attention. Both are important, but exposure is more primary. I argue that for exposure to be achieved by an individual, three criteria must be met—that is, three hurdles must be cleared by a media message. These hurdles are physical, perceptual, and psychological. Let's examine each of these three hurdles in more detail.

Physical. It would seem that the most foundational criterion for exposure would be some sort of physical presence. A person must experience some proximity to a message in order for exposure to take place. Physical exposure means that the message and the person occupy the same physical space for some period of time. Thus, space and time must be regarded as barriers to exposure. If a magazine is lying faceup on a table in a room and Harry walks through that room, there is physical exposure to the message on the cover of the magazine but not to any of the messages inside the magazine unless Harry picks it up and flips through the pages. Also, if Harry does not walk through that room when the magazine is on the table, there is no physical exposure to the message on the cover of the magazine. Likewise, if radio program is playing in a room over the lunch hour, and then is turned off at 1 p.m., anyone who walks through that room after 1 p.m. is not physically exposed to that radio program.

Physical proximity is a necessary condition for media exposure, but it is not a sufficient condition. Another necessary condition is perceptual exposure.

Perceptual. The perceptual consideration refers to a human's sensory bandwidth or the ability to receive appropriate sensory input through the visual and auditory senses. There are limits to a human's sense organs. For example, human sensitivity to sound frequency extends from around 16 to 20,000 Hz, but sounds are heard best when they are between 1,000 and 4,000 Hz (Metallinos, 1996; Plack, 2005). A dog whistle is pitched at a frequency higher than 20,000 Hz, so humans cannot perceive that sound—that is, it is outside their range of sensitivity to sounds. With the human eye, people can see light, which travels at a certain frequency, but not sound, which travels at another frequency. Any auditory or visual signal that occurs outside of a person's sense organs' ability to perceive it is nonexposure.

The perceptual criterion, however, has a feature beyond simple bandwidth; we must also consider the sensory input/brain connection. There are instances when the sensory input gets to the brain, but when the brain transforms the raw stimuli, such that we cannot perceive the raw stimuli and therefore cannot be thought of as being exposed to the raw stimuli, we are exposed to the transformed stimuli. For example, when people watch a movie, they are exposed to individual static images projected at about 24 images per second. But humans cannot perceive 24 individual images in a given second because the brain transforms the raw stimuli (24 individual still images) into the perception of motion. Also with film projection, there is a brief time between each of those 24 individual images every second when the screen is blank, but the eye-brain connection is not quick enough to process the blanks, so people do not "see" them. If the projection rate of images slows down to under 10 images per second, people begin to see a flutter—that is, they begin to perceive the blanks—because the replacement of still images is slow enough for the eye-brain connection to begin processing them. The same limits are applied to watching television, where the screen appears to present motion pictures in a full range of color. But the television screen itself only has three colors, and the picture is really no more than 250,000 glowing dots (called pixels). Each pixel glows and fades

30 times each second as guided by an interlaced scan of every other line across a 525-line grid. Unless we put our nose on the screen, we cannot see the individual dots. Nor do we see the 525 individual lines of glowing dots. Nor do we see a full screen pattern of dots and lines. Instead, we perceive images and motion.

Stimuli that are outside the boundaries of human perception are called subliminal. Subliminal messages can leave no psychological trace because they cannot be physically perceived—that is, humans lack the sensory organs to take in stimuli or the hardwiring in the brain to be sensitive to them.

There is a widespread misconception that the mass media put people at risk for "subliminal communication." This belief is based on confusing *subliminal* with *unconscious*. The misuse of the term *subliminal* still occurs (e.g., see Erdelyi & Zizak, 2004). Subliminal messages cannot be perceived by humans because those messages consist of stimuli that are outside the ability of humans to perceive so the stimuli have no effect on humans. In contrast, many media messages can be perceived but a person does not pay conscious attention to them, so the stimuli work in an unconscious manner. For example, a radio might be playing a tune in our presence, but our attention is directed to other things and we do not notice the sounds. Later we find ourselves humming that tune and wonder where it came from. That is an unconscious exposure. If the tune were played on dog whistles, that tune would be subliminal, and we would not find ourselves humming it later because we never "heard" it.

In this general framework, subliminal refers to being outside a human's ability to sense or perceive, and thus it is always regarded as nonexposure. Once media stimuli cross over the subliminal line and are able to be sensed and perceived by humans, they are regarded as exposure. However, this does not mean that all exposure is conscious, and this brings us to the third criterion in our definition—psychological.

Psychological. In order for psychological exposure to occur, there must be some trace element created in a person's mind. This element can be an image, a sound, an emotion, a pattern, and so on. It can last for a brief time (several seconds in short-term memory, then cleared out) or a lifetime (when cataloged into long-term memory). It can enter the mind consciously through a central route where people are fully aware of the elements in the exposure, or it can enter the mind unconsciously through a peripheral route where people are unaware that elements are being entered into their minds (see Petty & Cacioppo, 1986). Thus, there is a great variety of elements that potentially can meet this criterion. The challenge then becomes organizing all these elements into meaningful sets and explaining how different kinds of elements are experienced by the individual and how they are processed as information. I begin this task with the next section on attention, where I argue that attention is not a single state but that there are several qualitatively different states of attention. These different states help explain the variety of experiences people have during media exposures.

Defining Attention

In everyday language, *exposure* is a term that is often used synonymously with the term *attention,* but in this lineation general framework, it is important to delineate the differences. Exposure refers to being in physical proximity to a media message that can make it through a human's perceptual bandwidth and leave a psychological trace in the human mind. Attention is a conscious awareness of the message. Thus, attention is encompassed within the idea of exposure—that is, a person cannot attend to a message without being exposed to it. However, exposure is broader than attention because people can be exposed to messages without attending to them.

Scholarly Literature

Attention has been conceptualized by scholars primarily as either a conscious state of awareness or as selectivity. For example, Csikszentmihalyi (1988) explained that "attention is the medium that makes information appear in consciousness" (p. 17). Attention leads to awareness, which interprets the information, and memory, which stores the information. Attention, like any cognitive nonreflex action, requires psychic energy to perform. As for selectivity, Bundesen and Habekost (2005) defined attention in the *Handbook of Cognition* as "a general term for selectivity in perception. The selectivity implies that at any instant a perceiving organism focuses on certain aspects of the stimulus situation to the exclusion of other aspects" (p. 105). Kruschke (2005) defined attention as "the selectivity of information usage in inference. People learn that out of the plethora of available information, only some aspects should be attended to in certain situations. Attention refers to both enhanced or amplified processing of some information and diminished or suppressed processing of other information" (pp. 192–193). S. T. Fiske and Taylor (1991) said that attention has two dimensions, direction and intensity. Direction refers to what is selected, and intensity refers to the amount of mental effort. This idea of intensity or mental effort is typical in definitions of attention (Kahneman, 1973; Norman, 1976; Posner, 1982).

Cognitive psychologists have built models of attention on the assumption that humans have a limited capacity for attention. The first modern explanation of attention was the filter theory of Broadbent (1958). Under this conception of attention, each sense organ provides information in parallel channels, which converge at a filter. The filter must choose which information gets through and what is screened out. The filter cannot let much information through because humans have a limited capacity, so the filter acts as a switch to let the information from only one of the parallel channels through at a time. The information that gets through the filter is attended to; the rest of the information is ignored. Treisman (1964) elaborated on Broadbent's model by saying that the filter is not an all-or-nothing switch but makes decisions about how much information to let through; he called this his attenuation theory. This set up a distinction between models of serial processing of information and parallel processing of information. Bundesen and Habekost (2005) explained the difference as follows: "a typical serial model assumes that attention focuses on one object in the visual field at a time, moving about at a high speed. In contrast, a typical parallel model assumes a broad distribution of processing resources over the visual field, shifting slowly, but comprising many objects simultaneously" (p. 112).

Research support has been found for both parallel and serial models. When it comes to the media, it is likely that the parallel models are in effect more often with audiovisual media because the stimulus fields are so active with film, television, and Internet. However, with print, it is likely that serial models are the better explanation because reading is such a linear process. Even more important, it appears that people have options for how they process information. Some of these options are favored with certain media and other options with other media. But most important, it is likely that the options are not keyed to type of media as much as to type of attention.

From the literature reviewed above, it is clear that attention typically is equated with awareness but that more is involved. There is a range of attention. This point is especially important to consider when we think about the everyday environment in which people typically encounter media messages.

Exposure States

There seems to be an assumption underlying the psychological literature on audiences that attention acts like a rheostat switch—that is, during exposure, it can be on or off, and if it is on, it can be on a little or a lot. There is a belief that attention is both a categorical variable (on and off) and also a continuous one that varies by degree. I argue that in the Generating-Findings perspective, it has been useful to generate many findings, but many of those findings are faulty. If we are truly to map our phenomenon, we need to elaborate attention more carefully so we can increase the validity of findings about audience experiences during exposures. I argue that there are four qualitatively different exposure states: automatic, attentional, transported, and self-reflexive. The exposure experience is very different across these four states for audience members. Until researchers can acknowledge these differences and build a sensitivity to these differences into their designs and measures, many of the findings of those studies will continue to be faulty. What audience members remember from each of these states and what they are able to tell researchers about their experiences greatly vary across these four states. Let's now examine what each of these four states is.

Automatic State. In the automatic state of exposure, people are in environments where they are exposed to media messages but are not aware of those messages— that is, their minds are on automatic pilot, screening out all the messages from conscious exposure. There is no conscious goal or strategy for seeking out messages, but screening out of messages still takes place. This screening out continues automatically with no effort until some element in a message breaks through people's default screen and captures their attention.

In the automatic processing state, message elements are physically perceived but processed automatically in an unconscious manner. This exposure state resides above the threshold of human sense perception but below the threshold of conscious awareness. The person is in a perceptual flow that continues until an interruption stops the exposure or "bumps" the person's perceptual processing into a different state of exposure or until the media message moves outside of a person's physical or perceptual ability to be exposed to it.

In the automatic state, people can look active to outside observers, but they are not thinking about what they are doing. People in the automatic state can be flipping through the pages of a magazine or clicking through the channels on a TV.

While there is evidence of behavior, this does not necessarily mean that people's minds are engaged and that they are "making" decisions. Rather, the decisions are happening to them automatically.

Exposure to much of the media, especially radio and television, is in the automatic state. People often have no conscious awareness of the exposure when it is taking place, nor do they have a recollection of the details of the experience later. Therefore, what happens in this exposure state cannot be measured on self-report questionnaires, such as viewing diaries.

This is one of the most overlooked conditions in all of media scholarship. For example, J. Thompson (1995) said that one of the shortcomings of mass media research has been the neglect of describing the mundane character of how people encounter media messages in their everyday life. He says that "the reception of media products is a routine, practical activity which individuals carry out as an integral part of their everyday lives. If we wish to understand the nature of reception, then we must develop an approach which is sensitive to the routine and practical aspects of receptive activity" (p. 38). He continued, "The reception of media products should be seen, furthermore, as a routine activity, in the sense that it is an integral part of the regularized activities that constitute everyday life" (p. 39).

Attentional State. Attentional exposure refers to people being aware of the messages and actively interacting with the elements in the messages. This does not mean they must have a high level of concentration, although that is possible. The key is conscious awareness of the messages during exposures.

Within the attentional state, there is a range of attention depending on how much of a person's mental resources one devotes to the exposure. The rheostat metaphor works in this exposure state. At minimum, the person must be aware of the message and consciously track it, but there is a fair degree of elasticity in the degree of concentration, which can range from partial to quite extensive processing depending on the number of elements handled and the depth of analysis employed.

Transported State. When people are in the attentional state but then are pulled into the message so strongly that they lose awareness of being apart from the message, they cross over into the transported state. In the transported state, audience members lose their sense of separateness from the message—that is, they are swept away with the message, enter the world of the message, and lose track of their own social world surroundings. For example, watching a movie in a theater, people can get so caught up in the action that they feel they are involved with the action. They experience the same intense emotions as the characters do. They lose the sense that they are in a theater. They lose track of real time and—in its place—experience the narrative's time. Their concentration level is so high that they lose touch with their real-world environment.

The transported state is similar to the idea of flow as expressed by Csikszentmihalyi (1988), who defined flow as a state of high concentration and internally generated pleasure. Most times, people are producing something during flow, such as an artist working on a painting, but there are other times when people are engaging in flow activities such as sports and games to avoid boredom. There is a distortion of time; hours can pass like minutes and, conversely, a few seconds can seem to last a long time. Also, the person temporarily loses the awareness of self that in normal life often intrudes in consciousness and causes psychic energy to be diverted from what needs to be done. According to Csikszentmihalyi, there are two key requirements for flow. First, there needs to be a challenge in a task so that it absorbs people, that is, it challenges their level of skill; thus, tic-tac-toe is a game of low complexity and has a low challenge and therefore is not likely to lead to flow, while chess is very complex and involving so it is much more likely to lead to flow. Second, there needs to be a set of rules known to the person. Ambiguous situations do not offer the potential for flow. The rules direct attention on the task and provide guideposts for satisfaction.

The transported state is similar but not identical to flow as expressed by Csikszentmihalyi (1988). It is similar in the sense that people are swept away by the experience and lose track of time as well as their real-world surroundings. It is different in the sense that the transported state is triggered and maintained by media messages that intensely resonate with the audience member, whereas flow is triggered and heightened by a challenge that slightly exceeds the person's skill level. In the transported state, people project themselves deeply into the media story; in flow, people project themselves into a challenge, and as they work hard, they are continually monitoring their progress in meeting that challenge.

The transported state is also similar to what various scholars have referred to as presence. However, presence has been used in a variety of ways. For example, Lombard and Ditton (1997) analyzed the literature and found that the term was used in six different ways, including the following:

social richness, the extent to which a medium is perceived as sociable, warm, sensitive, personal, or intimate when it is used to interact with other people;

realism, the degree to which a medium can produce seemingly accurate representations of objects, events, and people;

transportation, which includes three distinct types of transportation that can be identified: "You are there," in which the user is transported to another place; "It is here," in which another place and the objects within it are transported to the user; and "We are together," in which two (or more) communicators are transported together to a place that they share;

immersion, in which the senses are immersed in the virtual world;

social actor within medium, which includes parasocial interactions with characters in the medium; and

medium as social actor, in which the medium itself—like a computer—is regarded as being alive and having a personality.

K. M. Lee (2004) has also attempted an explication of presence, which she concluded is "a psychological state in which virtual objects are experienced as actual objects in either sensory or nonsensory ways" (p. 27).

Other scholars have used the term *transportation* in a different way than I am using it here. For example, Green, Garst, and Brock (2004) said a "transported individual is cognitively and emotionally involved in the story and may experience vivid mental images tied to the story's plot" (p. 168). They said that transportation may aid in suspension of disbelief, which reduces a person's motivation to counterargue the issues raised in the story. I argue that suspension of disbelief is a process that is required in order for the transportation state to be entered and maintained. To illustrate, a producer of a media message will meet audience members in their real-world experience in terms of settings, plots, and characters. Then gradually, step by step, the audience is pulled away from their world and transported into another experience by making the settings more attractive, glamorous, and intriguing; making the plot more vibrant, faster, and intense; and making the characters bigger than life. Audience members must accept each step away from their mundane, everyday real-world existence by willingly accepting each sweetened setting, plot point, and character alteration until they are transported into an experience.

The transported state is not regarded in this general framework as a neighborhood within the attentional state—that is, it is not simply the high end of the attentional state. Instead, the transported state is qualitatively different from the attentional state. While attention is very high in the transported state, the attention is also very narrow; that is, people have tunnel vision and focus on the media message in a way that eliminates the barrier between them and the message. People are swept away and "enter" the message. In this sense, it is the opposite of the automatic state, where people stay grounded in their social world and are unaware of the media messages in their perceptual environment; in the transported exposure state, people enter the media message and lose track of their social world.

Self-Reflexive State. In the self-reflexive state, people are hyperaware of the message *and of their processing of the message.* It is as if they are sitting on their shoulder and monitoring their own reactions as they experience the message.

In the self-reflexive state, people are not only consciously aware of the elements in the message but also aware of their processing of those elements—that is, they experience their own processing. This represents the fullest degree of awareness: People are aware of the media message, their own social world, and their position in the social world while they process the media message. In the self-reflexive exposure state, the viewer exercises the greatest control over perceptions by reflecting on questions such as the following: Why am I exposing myself to this message? What am I getting out of this exposure and why? Why am I making these interpretations of meaning? Not only is there analysis, but there is also meta-analysis. While the self-reflexive and transported states might appear similar in that they are characterized by high involvement by audience members, the two exposure states are very different. In the transported state, people are highly involved emotionally and lose themselves in the action. In contrast, the self-reflexive state is characterized by people being highly involved cognitively and very much aware of themselves as they analytically process the exposure messages.

Importance of Considering Exposure States

Why is it important to consider a set of alternative exposure states? I argue that there are two reasons, each of which helps in the evolution from a Generating-Findings to a Mapping-Phenomenon perspective. One reason is that it helps us get past the debate over whether the audience is active or passive. People are often active but are also often passive. This set of exposure states provides a way of understanding the experience of being passive (in the automatic state that occurs most of the time) and the different experiences of being active (attentional, transported, and self-reflexive).

A second reason why it is so important to consider a set of alternative exposure states is because researchers need specific guidance to increase the precision of their measures. If we are to do a better job of mapping the audience facet of the mass media phenomenon, we need to be more careful in considering what our research participants can tell us about the experience of their media exposures. It is likely that the validity of the data generated by the typically used measures of time spent with various media will be much higher from attentional and especially self-reflexive exposures than with automatic and transported exposures. If we do not make this distinction in our measurement designs, then we will continue to average valid responses with wild guesses, and this will trap us in a Generating-Findings perspective.

Information-Processing Tasks

By this point in reviewing the literature on audience exposure and attention, it should be clear that scholars have identified many things that people do during media exposures. This general framework attempts to organize that scholarly thinking by proposing that there are three fundamental tasks that people continually engage in during any media exposure to process the information from those messages. These three information-processing tasks are filtering, meaning matching, and meaning construction (see Table 7.1). Audience members are constantly confronted with exposure choices, so an essential ongoing exposure task is filtering. When information is encountered during any exposure, audiences must continually assess meaning through meaning matching or through meaning construction.

The important questions governing the filtering task are as follows: How can we make good decisions about filtering messages in a way that helps us take advantage of the positive effects but protects us from the negative effects of being overwhelmed or from having our minds shaped by forces outside our control? And furthermore, how can we achieve this in a relatively efficient manner?

Once we have filtered in messages, we need to determine their meaning. I break this meaning assessment task into two separate processes of meaning matching and meaning construction. This distinction is based partially on the idea of closed codes and open codes as expressed by S. Hall (1980), who pointed out that designers of messages have a choice of using closed or open codes when encoding meaning in their messages. This encoding can be done in a denotative fashion where "the televisual sign is fixed by certain, very complex (but limited or 'closed') codes" as well as in a connotative fashion, which "is more open, subject to more active transformations" (p. 134). As for the decoding of the meaning by individuals, Hall said that messages are open to more than one meaning—that is, the codes in media messages are polysemic. However, he did not believe the codes are "pluralistic"; in order for a code to be pluralistic, all readings must be given equal status. Hall said that there is one dominant reading of a code; this is usually the reading that is preferred by the encoder of the message. There are also oppositional and negotiated readings possible. An

Table 7.1   Summary of Three Tasks of Information Processing

Filtering Message

Task: To make decisions about which messages to filter out (ignore) and which to filter in (pay attention to)

Goal: To attend to only those messages that have the highest utility and avoid all others

Focus: Messages in the environment

Type of problem: Frequently partially specified because the criterion of utility is constantly changing

Meaning Matching

Task: To use basic competencies to recognize symbols and locate definitions for each

Goal: To access previously learned meanings efficiently

Focus: Referents in messages

Type of problem: Frequently fully specified

Meaning Construction

Task: To use skills in order to move beyond meaning matching and construct meaning for one's self to get more personal value out of a message

Goal: To interpret messages from more than one perspective as a means of identifying the range of meaning options, and then choose one or synthesize across several

Focus: One's own knowledge structures

Type of problem: Almost always partially specified

oppositional reading is one in contrast to the dominant one, and a negotiated reading is one that is created when a reader constructs a new interpretation somewhere between the writer's intention and the reader's natural position. Hall said that when audiences decode messages, they need to know the codes or meaning system. People in a given culture share the same meanings for particular codes. Thus, communicators use the codes to design messages, and receivers use the codes to decode them.

In this general framework, I build off of S. Hall's (1980) initial ideas and elaborate them in the distinction between the information-processing tasks of meaning matching and meaning construction. With meaning matching, meaning is assumed to reside outside the person in an authority, such as a teacher, an expert, a dictionary, a textbook, or the like. The task for the person is to find those meanings and memorize them. Thus, parents and educational institutions are primarily responsible for housing the authoritative information and passing it on to the next generation. The media are also a major source of information, and for many people, the media have attained the status of an authoritative source, so people accept the meanings presented there. Thus, the meaning-matching task involves working with closed codes.

While meaning matching is essentially a task composed of fully specified problems, meaning construction, in contrast, is composed of partially specified problems, and this makes it a much more challenging task because it requires reasoning, and reasoning is a process that requires some insight (Evans, 1998;

Evans, Legrenzi, & Firotto, 1999). Some steps in the process of meaning construction may deal with closed codes, but there is more to it. Because the process is only partially specified, accessing one's memory for denoted meanings will not completely meet the challenge posed by meaning construction tasks.

Meaning construction is a process wherein people transform messages they take in and create meaning for themselves. Many meanings can be constructed from any media message; furthermore, there are many ways to go about constructing that meaning. Thus, people cannot learn a complete set of rules to accomplish this; instead, they need to be guided by their own information goals and use well-developed skills to creatively construct a path to reach their goals.

The two processes of meaning matching and meaning construction are not discrete; they are intertwined. To construct meaning, a person has to first recognize key elements in media messages and understand the sense in which those elements are being used in the message. Thus, the meaning-matching process is more fundamental because the product of the meaning-matching process then is imported into the meaning construction process.

The Media Exposure Model

Now that I have laid out many of the fundamental ideas involved with mass media audiences, exposure, and attention, I want to synthesize what I regard as the most useful of those ideas in terms of explaining how audience members experience media messages. To this end, I am proposing a media exposure model that is essentially a matrix of exposure states crossed by information-processing tasks (see Table 7.2). It reminds us to consider that qualitatively different experiences have been amalgamated under the term *exposure* and that to understand how people process information from the media, we need to deal with the exposure states separately.

Table 7.2   Media Exposure Model

Exposure States	Information-Processing Tasks		
	Filtering	*Meaning Matching*	*Meaning Construction*
Automatic	Screening	Highly automatic	Highly automatic
Attentional	Searching	Automatic	Typical construction
Transported	Swept	Personal and highly automatic	Highly emotional construction
Self-reflexive	Deep analysis	Sorting through learned meanings	Highly personalized construction

The model does not rely on motives. Of course, motives can be plugged into certain cells of this matrix to help explain exposures, but researchers are cautioned to consider the degree to which their participants are aware of their motives. Also, researchers need to consider the level of generality of the motives. Notice that the information in the cells of the model refers to cognitive processes. These will be explained in the following four chapters.

The purpose of this model is to highlight the importance of the interaction of exposure states with information-processing tasks. It is hoped that this model will enhance researchers' ability to explain what happens during exposures. To illustrate this point, I'll show how one published research study could have expanded its explanatory power by using the media exposure model. Pool, Koolstra, and van der Voort (2003) conducted an experiment to find out if background use of media influenced adolescents' performance on homework. They found that music in the background left homework performance unaffected. Also, there was no indication that background media influenced the amount of time spent to complete homework assignments. However, watching soap operas during homework reduced student performance. These are interesting results, but they appear equivocal. Also, they do not explain why exposure to one type of media message could reduce homework performance while another form of message would leave it unaffected. In their results, the focus is on type of message or medium. However, if we used the media exposure model, we would shift the focus of explanation to the experience of the audience member during the exposure, and this could help explain the pattern of results. It is likely that background music was experienced by most students in the automatic exposure state where they did not need to expend any mental energy, saving their full cognitive capacity for the homework. In contrast, it is likely that many, but not all, students watching soap operas were in a transported exposure state, thus having no cognitive resources left over for studying during that time. Furthermore, it is likely that students who were in a transported exposure state in both soap operas and music had the lowest performance on homework. Therefore, exposure state would seem to be a much better predictor of audience cognitive allocations than would genre of media message.

The power of the media exposure model is that it allows for rational, conscious models of information selection and processing but does not require them. For example, there are many of these rational models where audience members make a series of decisions, consciously taking into consideration their motives and gratifications (Palmgreen & Rayburn, 1985; Rosengren, 1974), reality of messages and consequences of exposure (Comstock, Chaffee, Katzman, McCombs, & Roberts, 1978), how news is processed (Graber, 1988), or consistency considerations (Donohew & Tipton, 1973). For example, Donohew and Tipton (1973) created a model to explain information seeking, avoiding, and processing. This model includes five decision points of consistency of message, whether to reject it or not, what action to take if one does not reject it, closure, and whether sources are broad or narrow. Each of these is a cognitive decision that requires some evaluation and thought. I am not arguing against the usefulness of such rational models; however, I am arguing that there are a variety of exposure states and that rational models are not likely to be able to explain what occurs in either the automatic or transported states.

Conclusion

In this lineation general framework, exposure to mass media messages is defined as a sequence of criteria—physical, perceptual, and psychological. Once exposure is achieved, it occurs in one of four exposure states: automatic, attentional, transported, or self-reflexive. These states offer qualitatively different experiences to audiences across the three information-processing tasks of filtering, meaning matching, and meaning construction. A media exposure model is developed from these two ideas of a set of four exposure states and a sequence of three information-processing tasks.

If we try to explain the audience facet of the mass media phenomenon based on an assumption that audience members are largely active and thus typically aware of their exposures and their processing of media content, we will be able to explain only a small fraction of audience activity and experiences. In contrast, a general framework that tries to explain the phenomenon of the mass media in an information-saturated culture cannot be based on such an assumption. We must recognize that there are times when people seek out particular messages in the mass media and are therefore engaged in processing the messages and actively constructing meaning from them. But there are other times when people are not consciously seeking exposure, and their minds are on an "automatic pilot" as they navigate through their day while concentrating on nonmedia matters. However, there are media messages bombarding people while they are functioning on automatic pilot, and it is likely that these unconscious exposures have effects on people. Furthermore, it is likely that most of mass media exposure is in this state of automatic processing. Most media exposures do not take place in an attentional state—that is, people are not consciously processing messages. But even when people are actively processing media messages, they are not always in the attentional state; sometimes they are in a transported or a self-reflexive state of exposure.

Table 7.3   Assumptions About Mass Media Audiences

Assumption 1: People are interpretive beings. This means at any time, they *can* construct their own special meaning from any media message.

   1.1: At times, individuals are actively engaged in constructing meaning. At these times, they are typically rational, calculating, economically minded, utilitarian, and benefit-maximizing beings.

   1.2: At times, individuals are governed by a goal of efficiency and are only partially engaged in constructing meaning.

   1.3: At times, individuals operate on automatic pilot where preprogrammed mental processes govern habits with a very high degree of efficiency, that is, requiring almost no effort from the individual.

Assumption 2: The locus of meaning resides in the individual.

   2.1: Sometimes, meaning is accessed through a matching process where cues in media messages trigger memory recall of elements in memory.

   2.2: Other times, novel meanings are created through a process of meaning construction where people use their cognitive skills to perceive patterns, infer connections, deduce conclusions, make evaluative judgments, and assemble message elements in unique syntheses.

Table 7.4   Structured Glossary of Terms About Mass Media Audiences

Exposure—requires the clearing of three hurdles: physical, perceptual, and psychological.

Physical—proximity to the media message in terms of space and time.

Perceptual—message is within the capacity of human sense organs and brain functioning.

Psychological—messages leave a trace in the mind, no matter how brief.

Subliminal—outside a human's ability to perceive the message.

Exposure states—the kind of attention and experience a person has when encountering media messages. There are four exposure states: automatic, attentional, transported, and self-reflexive. These are qualitatively different states that are separated by a liminal threshold (line of perception).

> In the automatic state, audience members are not consciously aware of the exposure. Messages are processed but not consciously or in the immediate control of the audience member.

> In the attentional state, audience members process message elements consciously. They actively interact with the elements in the messages and can exercise some control over the processing, which can range from partial to quite extensive processing, depending on the number of elements handled and the depth of analysis employed.

> In the transported state, audience members experience "tunnel vision" with a very high level of concentration focused on the message to the point where the barrier between the message and the audience members disappears; all stimuli outside of this focus are ignored.

> In the self-reflexive state, audience members are not only consciously aware of the elements in the message but are also aware of their processing of those elements. This requires the highest awareness and concentration of the perceptual channels.

Perceptual flow—the uninterrupted continuation in a perceptual channel during an exposure session. There is an inertia to the flow; the longer people stay in a perceptual flow, the harder it will be to interrupt that flow.

Information-processing tasks—the three information-processing tasks are filtering, meaning matching, and meaning construction. These tasks are ordered in a sequence of information processing.

Filtering—decisions about whether to seek out exposures, selecting exposure states, changing exposure states, and changing messages in the exposure.

Meaning matching—accessing denoted meaning.

Meaning construction—creating novel meanings of an individual nature.

Algorithms—templates (or sequences of mental codes) that people use to (a) guide their perceptions during exposures and (b) interpret the meaning of messages in their exposures. Algorithms are accessed when a person is exposed to a content unit, searches the content for a few salient characteristics, and then matches those content characteristics to various scripts to pick the most appropriate one to make meaning of the current content unit. Algorithms are constructions by individuals and are the product of their experiences filtered through their mental processes of sorting and meaning making; they are also programmed by the mass media.

> The filtering task is governed by algorithms that are programmed by both the individual and the mass media.

> The algorithms used in the meaning-matching task are largely definitional and have been provided by authorities and internalized by the person so their use is automatic. They require basic competencies to perform well.

> The algorithms used in the meaning construction task are largely suggestive guides because meaning construction is always a partially specified problem. They require the use of higher order skills to perform well.

(Continued)

Table 7.4 (Continued)

Value of exposure—the comparison of costs with benefits. When the comparison is favorable (benefits exceed costs), the message is perceived to have value.

> Resources invested by audience members include money, time, and psychic energy.

> Return on investment is in terms of value of information and emotional impact of entertainment.

Triggers—elements occurring in the media messages or in the environment during exposure that activate attention in a person.

Simple associational networks—the pattern of simple connections among ideas and images in a person's mind.

Construct accessibility—during exposure to media messages, people will attempt to employ scripts as guides; in finding a useful script, viewers will find something salient in the portrayal they are viewing; the construct (character, plot point, setting, etc.) they have most recently been using is likely to be the criterion for selecting a script.

Scripts—while schemas are static frames, such as classification rules that draw boundaries for us, scripts are sequences of frames that tell us how action should progress.

Script relineation—altering an existing script by making it more general (leveling) so that a portrayal discrepant with the script can be made to fit or elaborating an existing script (sharpening) by adding more detail so that it becomes a more useful guide in making finer discriminations among portrayals.

NSL audience—most desired type of audience for media organizations to construct and maintain; refers to right niche, large share, and high loyalty.

Table 7.5   Media Audience Propositions

Predictive Propositions

Audience 1: Audience members will stay in a particular exposure state (and hence continue the perceptual flow) as long as they perceive continuing value in that state and as long as there is no triggering element to pull them into another exposure state.

Audience 2: The most powerful general motive for exposure is economic efficiency, where value is determined through a comparison of resources expended during an exposure to a media message with benefits expected.

Audience 3: The greater the perceived benefits from the exposure in comparison to perceived costs, the stronger the conditioned drive to seek additional exposures of this message type.

Audience 4: Audience members will generally access the easiest algorithm to guide any information-processing task.

CHAPTER 8

Audience Cognitive Algorithms

This chapter builds on the ideas structuring the media exposure model developed in the previous chapter. Specifically, this chapter is concerned with addressing the following question: Given the information-processing tasks and the different exposure states, what cognitive processes guide people through these tasks? My answer to this question is algorithms. But before I explain what an algorithm is and how it works, I first need to lay a foundation by overviewing some essential ideas about how the human mind is organized, what we know about its processes, and types of learning. Although brief, these overviews reveal a great many ideas that can appear to be overwhelming in their variety, abstractness, and complexity. However, without such an overview, it will be very difficult to appreciate the idea of algorithm.

Organization of the Human Mind

Cognitive psychologists have proposed numerous theories and models for how the human memory is organized. One thing these propositions all have in common is the structure of associations—that is, all present some variant of an associative network. In this section, I will first review those structures and then review the conceptions of the units of those structures.

General Structure

How are bits of memory organized? S. T. Fiske and Taylor (1991) pointed out that the basic model of memory used by cognitive psychologists is the associative network. The role of connections in the human mind has been recognized for a long time (Hume, 1739/1969; James, 1890; Mill, 1843). William James (1890) said, "When two elementary brain processes have been active together or in immediate succession, one of them, on re-occurring, tends to propagate its excitement to the other" (p. 566). Thus, associations are constantly made among ideas stored in a person's memory.

Associative Network. Associative network theories date back to Tulving and Pearlstone (1966), who theorized that elements in a person's memory can be independent, minimally connected units. For this form of organization, the simple associative network (SAN) is a useful explanation. SANs are networks of nodes and pointers. The nodes are referents and definitions. The pointers are the links between the nodes. Some links are short—that is, the nodes are close to one another and thereby conceptually linked tightly.

Collins and Loftus (1975), who presented a spreading activation model of memory. They believed that ideas are stored in nodes and that there are associations among the nodes that are represented by pathways. When a person thinks about an idea, the node where that idea is stored is activated, and psychic energy spreads from that node to other nodes along the pathways connecting them.

The structure of associative networks is open-ended, organic, and constantly changing. New nodes are added when new thoughts are experienced and remembered. The arrangement of nodes is determined by the person's frequency of accessing those various nodes. For example, the more often two elements are thought of at the same time, the stronger the association between them becomes. Also, associations are explained in terms of recency and frequency. The most recently accessed idea is likely to retain some residual excitation, so it is likely to be accessed first. Frequency relates to how often an idea is accessed; those ideas that are accessed the most are most prominent in the associative network and are therefore likely to be accessed first in subsequent recalls.

During the 1990s, memory research was primarily concerned with the debate over whether memory is better conceptualized as a set of independent systems (associative networks) or as a set of interrelated processes (Foster & Jelicic, 1999; Neath & Surprenant, 2005). This was essentially a debate over whether SANs were sufficient to explain the workings of the human mind or whether some more complex structure was needed. So some scholars began working with more complex conceptualizations; however, these newer conceptualizations still relied on the idea of individual units of memory organized in associative networks. These additional conceptualizations can be loosely categorized under the term *hierarchical models.*

Schema. Arguably the one term that has been used most often to refer to these associative networks is *schema,* which was introduced by Bartlett (1932). He defined schema as an "active organization of past reactions, or of past experiences, which must always be supposed to be operating in any well-adapted organic response" (p. 201). Since that time, the term *schema* has been used by many scholars in many different ways. For example, Rumelhart (1984) conceptualized a schema as a large unit of organized information used for representing concepts, situations, events, and actions in memory. The purpose of a schema is to help with encoding information, retrieval from memory, inference, and evaluation (S. T. Fiske & Taylor, 1991). Schemas are networks or groupings of concepts (Graesser & Nakamura, 1982), or associative structures "formed by connecting nodes representing individual objects or concepts with links" (E. R. Smith, 1999, p. 252).

Schema theories reject the associative network theories' belief that different pieces of knowledge are discrete and are stored at different memory locations.

Instead, schema theories (Brewer & Nakamura, 1984; Rumelhart, 1984) posit that many memory structures are organized schematically—that is, they are configured in sets of interrelated features. Schemas are more than categories where all elements are stored; instead, they are "schematic representations whose features are interrelated according to a set of rules that can be specified a priori" (Wyer & Albarracin, 2005). The rules set of relations can be spatial, temporal, or logical. For example, a spatially organized schema is a human face where the features are remembered not only individually but also in relation to one another in space. Temporal schemas are scripts, such as the sequence of events that typically happens in a restaurant.

Hierarchical Models. Cognitive psychologists have speculated that there are more sophisticated organizational patterns beyond a simple associative network, such as a hierarchy (Collins & Loftus, 1975), or in thematically and chronologically structured histories or streams (Barsalou, 1992). For example, Rips, Shoben, and Smith (1973) set up a test of the claim by Collins and Quillian (1969) by reasoning that a pig is a mammal and that mammals are animals; therefore, the link between pig and animal is longer (and has to go through an intermediate node of mammal), so when people are told to think about a pig, it would take longer for them to verify that a pig is an animal than that a pig is a mammal. But they found the opposite, and they concluded that the node of animal is closer to a pig than the node of mammal is to a pig.

Some cognitive psychologists view schemas as pyramidal structures "hierarchically organized with more abstract or general information at the top and categories of more specific information nested within the general categories" (Taylor & Crocker, 1981, p. 102). Thus, the structure is like an outline with ideas existing at different levels of generality, with the less general ideas subsumed under more general ideas. These models address the problem of how people are able to look at an image and recognize details at the micro level and also recognize the holistic nature of the image that is more than the sum of its parts (Kimchi, 1992).

Some of this variety in conceptualizing structures is attributable to different conceptions of human thinking and memory that have come about to try to explain the incredible range of mental tasks that people undertake each day. In cognitive psychology, "researchers have come to realize that modeling complex behaviors may require equally complex, multistage models involving various learning algorithms and a level of sophistication in building these models that requires considerable expertise and dedication" (M. E. Young & Wasserman, 2005, p. 162). This connectionist theorizing has helped psychologists recognize that associative learning is more than acquiring simple stimulus-response associations. The human mind is capable of making novel connections not learned, seeking patterns for itself, making inferences, using intuition, and ignoring associations altogether in favor of some other creative path.

Units

The units stored in memory are elements in the structure. What are those units? As I review the different kinds of units below, notice that there are a great many different ways to categorize these units, and therefore there are many different terms being used. Also, notice that the type of unit suggests a type of structure. I begin by making a distinction between simple units and more complex units, such as scripts, stories, histories, and implicit theories. Then I will describe the distinction between declarative and procedural knowledge.

Distinction Between Simple Units and More Complex Units. We cannot skip over a very large class of units that are fairly simple. These include a single word, idea, sound, image, or emotion. These things are stored as units, that is, monolithically. These units are simple because they contain little detail or complexity. They can be easily accessed and efficiently processed. These units almost always reside in larger structures. At times, accessing one of these units will trigger associations into a larger structure of a sequence of events or a laddered hierarchy of general principles, but they need not do so. They can stand alone as units. Examples include the recognition of a color (perceiving a hue and associating it with a name), a sound (perceiving a timbre and associating it with a musical instrument), a word (perceiving black lines on a page and being able to utter the sound of the word), or a face (perceiving the gestalt image in a photograph and associating it with the name of a person).

There are also more complex units; these involve more detail and complexity than simple units. These more complex units are usually referred to as event representations in memory. Wyer (2004) said that people perceive event representations in their everyday lives as narratives. These event representations take one of four forms as they are stored in memory and used in everyday life. These four forms are scripts, stories, histories, and implicit theories.

Scripts are prototypic sequences of events that occur in a particular situational context (Schank & Abelson, 1977). These can be routinized sequences of events that are specific to the person (turning on the TV and preparing dinner when one gets home from work), or they can be general social lessons (such as shaking hands when we meet someone new).

Stories are also composed of a sequence of events, but at least one element is unique. This unique element makes the story memorable in contrast to a more generic script. There is a deviation from normal expectations. The story elicits some emotion or affect (Brewer & Lichtenstein, 1981).

Histories are like stories in the sense that they consist "of a sequence of events that are specific to a particular person or group, and are localized in time and place," but they need not contain unexpected events or have emotional significance (Wyer, 2004, p. 20).

Implicit theories, like scripts, are composed of prototypic sequences of events. "However, the events are causally as well as temporally related. Moreover, the events are often defined more broadly. A theory is not localized in time, and, therefore, can be applied in many different circumstances" (Wyer, 2004, p. 20). "Theories play a very important role in processing new information about the world in which we live and making inferences on the basis of it. They are used both to explain events that have occurred in the past and to predict the future. Moreover, they can be used to fill in 'gaps' in a sequence of events about which one has incomplete information" (Wyer, 2004, p. 21). Implicit theories contain general principles about the world and are therefore useful in a deductive process. For example, people might have learned that lying is a useful tool in the short term to get out of a tough situation, but eventually the lie will be revealed, and the liar will be punished. This implicit theory has a causal claim and relates events over time. When the person gets in a tough situation, she may rely on her theory by lying to solve the immediate problem but then dread the expected upcoming consequences of getting caught in the lie and being punished.

Some scholars make a distinction between syntactic and semantic elements of television. For example, Bickham, Wright, and Huston (2001) talked about a difference between syntactic and semantic parts of a message where syntactic markers are the formal features of a message while semantic markers constitute the content part of the message. As examples of syntax, they cited the lag that dissolves between scenes, whereas scary music communicates the meaning of the movie. This lineation general framework does not make a distinction between syntactic and semantic referents; instead, this general framework regards all elements in media messages as having both a syntactic property (that serves as a signal) and a semantic property (that is an associated definition).

There is more language that scholars use to distinguish among types of units stored in memory. These terms include *episodic* versus *semantic memory* (Barsalou, 1992); *autobiographical memory,* which is memory for representations of personal events (Shum & Ripps, 1999); *declarative* versus *procedural knowledge; explicit* versus *implicit memory* (Schacter, & Tulving, 1994); *propositional, temporal, analog,* and *affect* (S. T. Fiske & Taylor, 1991); and *words* and *images* (Paivio, 1986).

Distinction Between Declarative and Procedural Knowledge. A frequent distinction in cognitive psychology is between declarative knowledge and procedural knowledge. Declarative knowledge concerns the referents of our everyday life experience (e.g., persons, objects, events, social issues that we read about, or ourselves). In contrast, procedural knowledge concerns the sequence of actions that we perform in pursuit of a particular goal (driving a car, using a word processor, etc.). Whereas declarative knowledge is reflected in the information we can recall about an entity or that we implicitly draw on in the course of attaining a particular objective, procedural knowledge is reflected in the sequence of cognitive or motor acts that are actually performed in the pursuit of this objective. People can of course have declarative knowledge about how to attain a particular objective, and might sometimes consult this knowledge for use as a behavioral guide. "Once the procedure is well learned, however, it may often be applied automatically, with little if any conscious cognitive mediation" (Wyer, 2004, p. 6). When a procedure is performed many times, it comes to be performed without consultation of one's declarative knowledge about the sequence of steps involved and thus becomes automatic, where it requires few if any cognitive resources (W. Schneider & Shiffrin, 1977).

J. O. Greene (1989) viewed procedural memory as "composed of a large number of modular elements termed 'procedural records.' Each procedural record comprises a number of symbolic primitives linked by associative relations. The symbolic primitives in each record are of three types: specifications of features of action, outcomes, and situations. In essence, each record specifies an action-outcome relation along with any situational features that have proven significant in mediating that relationship. The symbolic primitives composing procedural records may be defined at any of a number of levels of abstraction ranging from sensorimotor coders to abstract propositional representations" (p. 120).

Critique of Scholarship

A great deal of insight has been brought to the problem of explaining how the human mind is organized so that it can make decisions about processing information, storing it, and retrieving it at a later time. However, I want to point out two problems with this scholarship. One problem deals with the proliferation of terms and the other with the lack of attention to degree of interpretation.

As for the proliferation of terms problem, there are many examples where scholars will use different terms to refer to essentially the same idea. There are also examples where scholars will use the same term to refer to different ideas. This problem is in evidence most with the term *schema,* as well as with the use of other terms as synonyms for *schema.* Graber (1988) said about *schema,* "There is considerable disagreement about the precise definition. To make the confusion worse, schema have been called by various other names, such as social scripts, preliminary cognitive representations, prototypes, or constructs" (p. 104). However, Graber appeared to have underestimated the number of synonyms for schema; other alternative terms include *frames* (Minsky, 1975), *stereotypes* (Lippmann, 1922), *cognitive maps* (Rosch & Lloyd, 1978), *cognitive structure* (Graber, 1988), *propositional networks* (J. R. Anderson, 1976), *scripts* (Abelson, 1981), *social scripts* (Schank & Abelson, 1977), and *memory organization packets* or MOPs (Kellerman & Lim, 1989; Shank, 1982). While these terms have been used substantially as synonyms for *schema,* scholars have often altered the meaning a bit when using their particular term, and this also increases the definitional clutter. Graber herself called it a cognitive structure, which she said is a commonsense model of life situations.

Because of the variety of definitions of *schema*, cognitive psychologists are moving away from using the term. Also, because of the variety of synonyms for the term, there needs to be more definitional precision in theories to delineate how the concept is being used. One example is Shank (1982), who used the term *MOP* for memory organization packets, which are cognitive structures that organize behavioral sequences appropriate to a given situation in order to achieve one's goals. Shank used this term to distinguish them from scripts, which are cognitive structures providing conceptual representations of stereotyped event sequences. MOPs are not situation-specific, intact sequences but are open and flexible. Kellerman and Lim (1989) further defined MOPs as "knowledge structures that command how to organize scenes so that some higher-level goals might be accomplished. A scene, the key term in this new representation of action sequences, is a grouping of generalized actions with a shared instrumental goal. The scene describes how and where a particular set of actions take place" (p. 176).

It is very difficult to keep all these definitional distinctions salient and consistent. This is why I use the term *algorithm* in this general framework in order to provide an organizing idea to include the major ideas in the literature and organize them in a useful fashion (see the end of this chapter for more detail on this point).

A second criticism I have of the current literature is that it does not make a salient enough point about the objective-subjective continuum of knowledge. When this is made more salient, there is more of a focus on what is memorized and what is constructed—that is, we need to highlight much more the human interpretive processes and bring into the mainstream of cognitive thinking more of the ideas that are so important to interpretive scholars on the more qualitative side of the field.

Perhaps this distinction between objective and subjective knowledge appears as a confound with the distinction of external information and internal thought processes. Of course, information exists apart from and therefore is external to a person; furthermore, this information often gets transformed as a person internalizes it. That is, external occurrences are often altered in idiosyncratic ways as the person experiences them such that two people who encounter the same real-world experience at the same time might have two very different memories of it. I do not argue against this insight. However, the distinction is still important because external experiences have an objectivity to them that allows for a context of comparison, whereas internal processes do not. For example, let's say two people (June and Harry) watch a one-hour television program that is interrupted five times with commercial pods, each pod lasting 4 minutes and containing 12 ads. June may have a vivid recollection of the program and a fuzzy recollection that the show was interrupted a few times by ads; she can remember none of the ads but feels there were about 6 ads in the show. She judges the show to be excellent. Harry judges the show to be poor because he had his pleasure of the show destroyed by the constant interruptions. He believes there were five interruptions for commercials and at least 50 ads. We can conclude that June's recollection of the ads in the experience is less accurate than Harry's recollection because we have a standard for accuracy, that is, the actual number of interruptions and total number of ads. However, both people also evaluated the program, which is an internal process; we have no objective standard for evaluating the quality of the program itself.

Making a distinction between objective and subjective information would provide a context for examining the relative accuracy with which different audience members absorb and process information from the mass media. Of course, we could argue about whether any information is purely objective in an ontological sense or, even if there were "truth," whether we as humans are capable epistemologically of accessing it cleanly. I am not advocating that we engage in this philosophical debate that focuses attention on the poles of worldview positions. Instead, I am arguing that we need to recognize that there is a practical continuum of kinds of information and that we recognize the varieties of kinds in terms of degree of change in that information as it is processed by human perceivers.

Another key distinction that is important to make salient when studying the mass media is the distinction between factual information and social information. Factual information typically comes from formal learning. Thus, it is more carefully (rationally and consciously) processed than social information. Factual information is like semantic information, while social information is more like episodic memory, except that social information includes that which is learned either in real life or through exposure to the media. Either way, social information is autobiographical in the sense that it happened to the person either in social interactions with real people or in parasocial interactions with characters in the media.

Processes of the Human Mind

One set of explanatory constructs of cognitive science deals with mental processes as distinct from structures and content. While cognitive structure refers to "the form in which information is represented in the mental system" and content refers to the information itself, process refers to the "operations by which information is acquired, transformed, stored, and utilized. Examples of such processes would include categorization, memory retrieval, and inference-making" (J. O. Greene, 1989, pp. 118, 119).

The question is, Can we move beyond examples of the processes in the human mind and arrive at a conceptualization of the set of essential processes, at least concerning those processes audience members use when interacting with the mass media messages? I will attempt to move toward such a set by first reviewing the major processes that have been illuminated in the scholarly literature.

After reading over a great deal of the literature on the processes of human thinking, it appears that scholars are addressing this issue at two different levels. One level focuses attention on the broad general level of human thinking, talking about reasoning, inference, and decision making. The other level is more specific in focusing more on the skills used in the subprocesses of reasoning, inference, and decision making. These are the skills of deduction, induction, generalization, and categorization. In this section, I will display the nature of the description at the two different levels and argue that the description at the skills level is much more useful to providing explanations about how the human mind works.

General Processes

Cognitive psychologists talk about the process of human thinking in terms of reasoning, inference, and decision making. However, using terms at such a general level seems to have limited their ability to explain the process in detail.

Reasoning. "Human reasoning remains largely mysterious," said Chater, Heit, and Oaksford (2005). They acknowledged that laboratory experiments have produced a good deal of insight into human reasoning, but "deep puzzles over the nature of everyday human reasoning remain" (p. 314). They also argued that the study of human reasoning is so challenging because "everyday reasoning (in contrast to some artificial laboratory tasks) requires engaging arbitrary world knowledge. Consequently understanding reasoning would appear to be part of the broader project of understanding central cognitive processes and the knowledge they embody in full generality" (p. 308).

Inference. Chater et al. (2005) also said, "Almost every aspect of cognition can be viewed as involving inference. Perception involves inferring the structure of the environment from perceptual input; motor control involves inferring appropriate motor commands from proprioceptive and perceptual input, together with the demands of the motor task to be performed; learning from experience, in any domain, involves inferring general principles from specific examples; understanding a text or utterance typically requires inferences relating the linguistic input to an almost unlimited amount of general background knowledge" (p. 314).

Decision Making. Most things in life are uncertain, so humans must constantly estimate the probabilities of beliefs so they can go with the ones in which they have relatively high certainty. Everyday rationality is founded on uncertain rather than certain reasoning (Oaksford & Chater, 1991, 1998).

McKenzie (2005) argued that "the traditional view of making decisions in the face of uncertain outcomes is that people seek (or at least should seek) to maximize expected utility (or pleasure broadly construed). 'Expected' is key here. Expectations refer to degrees of belief on the part of the decision maker" (p. 321). A big part of the decision-making literature deals with the examination of how well people make inferences about the probability of outcomes.

There have been some significant changes in how scholars regard human decision making. In the 1960s, Peterson and Beach (1967) reviewed the literature on decision making and concluded that humans were "intuitive statisticians"—that is, people were able to solve abstract and unfamiliar problems in a fairly accurate manner. Then in the 1970s, the view shifted to the belief that people frequently made errors. Tversky and Kahneman (1974) showed that people frequently use shortcuts (heuristics) in the reasoning process and that these heuristics lead to systematic errors.

In the 1980s, the heuristics and biases approach was criticized as lacking specificity (see Gigerenzer & Murray, 1987) or for presenting too negative a view of human decision making (Phillips, 1983). Then in the 1990s, this heuristic explanation continued but was criticized for not considering the role of the environment. This means that experimenters fail to take into consideration the fact that behavior measured in the experiment is not new; people have a history, and they bring to the lab their biases that have worked well in the past in solving problems in their everyday environments (Klayman & Brown, 1993; McKenzie & Mikkelsen, 2000). People have adaptive behavior—that is, they might use strategies in the lab that work well in the natural environment, but experimenters might label those strategies as irrational. McKenzie (2005) argued that experimental psychologists will consider the role of environment much more in their designs in the coming years. Also, he speculated that the "conception of what it means to be rational will change" (p. 333). He said that a large literature on human cognition shows people making errors in decisions but that often those "purported errors have explanations that indicate strengths, not weaknesses, of human cognition" (p. 333).

More Specific Processes

Cognitive scholars write about four specific skills that are used in reasoning, inference, and decision making. These are the skills of deduction, induction, generalization, and categorization.

Deduction. Some cognitive scholars regard human reasoning as primarily following a process of deduction. For example, in their chapter on reasoning in the *Handbook of Cognition,* Chater et al. (2005) argue that "the cognitive science perspective on the mind views thought as information processing. More specifically, this information processing is not merely arbitrary computation; it typically involves deriving new information from existing information" through a process they refer to as inference (p. 297). But when they continue their argument by stating that "the given pieces of information on which the inference is based are the premises, and the resulting information derived in the inference is the conclusion" (p. 297), it is clear that they are talking about a particular kind of inference—one that relies on deduction.

The term *deduction* is often used as a synonym for a rational approach or logical thinking. But the two really are independent from one another. Logical thinking typically involves the deductive process where people begin with a general premise and a minor premise to reason syllogistically to a logical conclusion. However, there are other ways to reason systematically. Also, deduction is not always used in a logical or systematic manner. Often, people make mistakes in reasoning to a conclusion from a major and minor proposition (Chater et al., 2005). And frequently, people will not have a major premise to use to explain a minor premise. What made Sherlock Holmes such a great detective was not only that he was able to reason deductively but that he also possessed an amazing array of general premises. If a person has few general premises—or faulty general premises—then the logical reasoning process will result in faulty conclusions. So the question becomes, What do people do when they lack an appropriate general premise? Johnson-Laird began working on this question in the late 1970s and came up with what is regarded as a radically new theoretical perspective on reasoning (Chater et al., 2005). In his book *Mental Models,* Johnson-Laird (1983) argued that rationality does have a central place—that is, logical reasoning (deduction) is primarily used by people. What is considered innovative in this mental models theory is that it broke with the old belief held by Piaget and others, that reasoning required the direct application of logical rules in the mind. This is the general premise in deductive reasoning. In contrast, Johnson-Laird argued that when people go to a "general premise," it is not a logical rule; instead, people create models of circumstances. The mental model then is used as the general premise in a logical process of deductive reasoning. Also, people alter the deductive reasoning process by constructing alternative models one at a time and use each to reason to a conclusion. They select the conclusion that seems the most accurate. To test the validity of their conclusion, they search for a counterexample model and reason to a conclusion from that counterexample to see if the same conclusion occurs. If a counterexample model cannot be found, then the conclusion is assumed to be valid. This mental models explanation of human reasoning has been tested in a wide variety of reasoning situations and found to be a good explanation (for a review of this literature, see Chater et al., 2005).

Mental models theory says that often errors arise. There are several reasons for this. One reason is that people fail to construct relevant counterexample models. Another problem is that sometimes people need to use more than one mental model to get at a general premise; the more models needed, the more complex the task. Experimental research has found that people typically do not construct counterexamples spontaneously—that is, they typically construct a single model and reason to a conclusion from that one model (Chater et al., 2005). This is why people make errors in reasoning.

Beliefs can bias the process by influencing the construction of a mental model and then walling off the construction of counterexamples (Newstead & Evans, 1993).

Induction. While reasoning is usually considered to employ deduction, there are some scholars who also consider induction. "Inductive reasoning, in its broadest sense, concerns inference from specific premises to general statements or to other non-logically related specific statements" (Chater et al., 2005, pp. 310–311). "Inductive reasoning involves drawing conclusions that are probably true, given a set of premises. Inductive reasoning can thus be contrasted with deductive reasoning, in which the conclusion must necessarily follow from a set of premises" (p. 311). Unlike deductive reasoning, inductive reasoning produces conclusions that cannot be validated through a logical procedure; that is, their validity rests with not finding counterexamples.

Generalization. Humans' ability to generalize is very important. In trying to make sense of their world, people make observations of individual acts of human behavior. However, individual examples are much less interesting than are social patterns, norms, and rules. However, patterns and norms cannot be directly observed, so people infer them from the few examples they observe. M. E. Young and Wasserman (2005) pointed out that "our ability to generalize prior knowledge to novel situations both leverages prior knowledge and eases new learning. This process of generalization is rooted in similarity" (p. 167). Shepard (1987) has argued that similarity is a function of the distance between psychological representations. This has been called the "universal law of generalization" (M. E. Young & Wasserman, 2005). Thus, the more similar two psychological representations are, the more likely a person will generalize from one to the other.

Categorization. One way humans create order out of the chaos of the multiple stimuli to which they are exposed every day is to group like things together, so they can deal with a smaller number of things (in groups) instead of having to deal with each thing as unique. Categorical representations are groups of ideas that share some commonality. Once a memory is put into a category, it sits there in a pile with other ideas that exhibit no internal structure (Brewer & Lichtenstein, 1981). The person must give the mass structure by arranging the items into groups.

Kruschke (2005) said there are three kinds of methods that humans use to construct cognitive categories and use them: exemplar, prototype, and rule. One way to learn a category is to memorize its instances. Thus, a category is specified by the total set of all examples; the "specification of contents is not a global summary but is instead a collection of piecemeal information" (p. 186). With the prototype method, people learn examples but then—for the sake of efficiency—infer a summary, which is a prototype. The prototype can be a kind of average or central tendency that represents the typical example in the set. Another prototype is called the idealized caricature, which is the person's ideal model for what an example should be. The construction of a prototype allows efficiency because people can avoid having to memorize each example in the set. The rule method specifies conditions that must be met in order for something to be included in the category. Thus, it focuses on boundary conditions.

Types of Learning

In this section, I will delineate the distinction between explicit and implicit learning along with the distinction between active and passive learning. Then I will relate these types of learning to the idea of automaticity in a manner to show how essential automatic processes are when it comes to studying audience experiences with the mass media.

Explicit Versus Implicit Distinction

Cognitive psychologists make a distinction between explicit and implicit psychological processes. Explicit processes are deliberate and under the control and awareness of the person, while implicit processes are automatic and occur outside the consciousness of the person (Fazio, 1990). Implicit learning is generally characterized as "learning that proceeds both unintentionally and unconsciously" (Shanks, 2005, p. 202). Thus, learning can be dissociated from awareness.

Formal educational procedures focus on explicitly creating conditions to elicit learning of particular bodies of knowledge and skills. However, in everyday life, each of us learns a great deal in a nonexplicit manner; that is, the learning takes place even though we have no intention to learn, and the materials we learn were not created to elicit learning. The study of both types of learning is especially important when dealing with the mass media. "There can be little dispute that learning is possible even under conditions of reduced attention. Numerous studies demonstrate that people can become sensitive to informational structure even when they are not deliberately trying to learn that structure and when they are engaging in other simultaneous mental activities" (Shanks, 2005, p. 204).

Implicit learning has received much less attention by scholars compared with explicit learning, but this may be changing. Bassili and Brown (2005) pointed out that "by their very nature, implicit processes exert a subtle influence on the way we think and behave, and this very subtlety has kept them for long in the shadow of experimental research" (p. 543). However, research on implicit learning is becoming more popular in psychology. Shanks (2005) pointed out that in the 1980s, there were only 15 journal articles with this term in their title or abstract, but this number jumped to 253 during the 1990s. My search of the PsycInfo Index in the summer of 2007 revealed 765 published articles. It is important that we recognize that learning takes place, especially from media messages, when the media producers are not trying to teach a specific lesson and when the audience is not trying to learn.

Active and Passive Learning

In her book *Media Effects and Society,* Elizabeth Perse (2001) said there have been two approaches to learning. One includes a collection of active models of learning, and the other includes a collection of passive models of learning. She characterized active models as those that treat the audience as having goals for their media exposures and employing cognitive strategies to extract the needed information from those messages and integrating the new information with the information already stored in memory. In contrast, she characterized passive models as those that treat the audience as being unmotivated or unable to acquire new information, so the media actively pull people to exposures and, in so doing, give people information.

In Perse's (2001) view, three families of models explain active learning. These families are structures, processes, and schemas. Perse said that structure models view "learning as the movement of information through mental structures such as the sensory register, short-term memory, working memory, to long-term memory. These structures are sequential; information must move through them in the order specified in the model. The most complete learning is the result of the movement of information through all the structures to long-term memory" (p. 133). She saw process models as involving three steps in sequence, beginning with attention, then moving to recognition or categorizing, and then to elaboration, where the information is rehearsed and related to prior knowledge. Finally, the schema models rely first on existing associative networks to influence what is learned and then on the development of new associative networks when new information is learned.

As for passive learning, Perse (2001) seemed to indicate that this is explained more by the formal features, program attributes, and repetition of the content. "Formal features of a medium are the production techniques and elements that are used to convey meaning. In newspapers, for example, formal features involve headline size and placement, photographs or other graphic elements, the use of quotations, and so on" (p. 146).

Perse (2001) acknowledged that learning is likely to be explained by a combination of all of these, but she left it at that and did not try to work through the problems of when each model would be a better explanation or how the models work together in a synthesis. Nor did she explain the process of passive learning. These comments are not meant to be a criticism of Perse's treatment; instead, they are offered to illuminate the cutting edge of the research.

Essential Nature of Automatic Processes

While much of our activity with the mass media is active, there is also a large proportion that is not. That is, we are not in a state of awareness during much of our exposure to mass media messages, and yet we can function in this mode by making decisions unconsciously about filtering and meaning matching. This automatic state is not special to people's interactions with the mass media; instead, automaticity is a condition of much of a human's everyday life. The seminal figure on this topic in cognitive psychology is John Bargh (1997), who reminds us that "much of everyday life—thinking, feeling, and doing—is automatic in that it is driven by current features of the environment (i.e., people, objects, behaviors of others, settings, roles, norms, etc.). As mediated by automatic cognitive processing of those features, without any mediation by conscious choice or reflection" (p. 2). He said that "as research in areas of social cognition such as attribution, attitudes, and stereotyping progressed since the 1960s, evidence increasingly pointed to the relative automaticity of those phenomena" (p. 5), and "as the research has advanced, so the role of conscious processing has diminished" (p. 6). When certain triggering conditions occur, automatic processing takes place (J. R. Anderson, 1992). Bargh said the automatic process runs autonomously and independently of conscious guidance.

These processes are developed out of a person's frequent and consistent reactions to a set of environmental features (Shiffrin & Dumais, 1981), such as media messages. Initially, these reactions require some mental effort and conscious attention to process appropriately. But over time, as we encounter the same stimuli in our environment, the need for intention and attention diminishes to a point where they become automatic. If this were not the case, we could not get out of bed in the morning because we would be overwhelmed by the task of having to figure everything out from scratch each day (G. A. Miller, Galanter, & Pribram, 1960). With experience we become more efficient at living our daily lives. This also applies on a more macro level; the famed mathematician Whitehead (1911) said, "Civilization advances by extending the number of important operations which we can perform without thinking about them" (p. 143).

Preconscious and Postconscious Automaticity. There is a difference between preconscious and postconscious forms of automaticity. With preconscious automaticity, a specific state is triggered by things in the environment that occur without the person being aware of them. Given the mere presence of a triggering event, the process operates and runs to completion without conscious intention or awareness. In contrast, postconscious automaticity is goal dependent—that is, the person intends to perform certain mental functions; the processing then occurs immediately and autonomously, without any further conscious guidance or deliberation (E. R. Smith, 1994).

Preconscious automaticity engages emotions, behaviors, and cognitive processes, such as interpretations, categorizations, and evaluations. For example, there is considerable evidence for evaluations made in the automatic state, such as in forming social attitudes (Bargh, Chaiken, Raymond, & Hymes, 1996; Fazio, Sanbonmatsu, Powell, & Kardes, 1986) and face recognition (Murphy & Zajonc, 1993). Preconscious mental processes are similar to what computers do with agent programming. Many personal computers have personal agent programs that learn from the human user's actions and take over some functions automatically. These programs learn to screen e-mail, automatically respond to certain e-mails, schedule meetings, and select Web sites that the human user would be most interested in seeing (Negroponte, 1995).

Bargh (1997) has said that there are three kinds of preconscious systems or routes by which environmental stimuli automatically and nonconsciously produce social behavior. These are automatic social perception, automatic evaluation, and automatic goal activation.

The automatic social perception system deals with the link between perception and behavior that occurs automatically without any conscious intention. People quickly and unconsciously read other people, attribute personality characteristics to them, and then act accordingly (Srull & Wyer, 1979; Uleman, Newman, & Moskowitz, 1996). This is what happens with stereotyping (Bargh, 1994).

The automatic evaluation system follows two processes. One is emotional, where people read facial expressions of other people in an unconscious fashion

(Niedenthal, 1990). In the other process, attitudes are constructed without conscious reflection on the standards used for the evaluation (Chaiken, Wood, & Eagly, 1996). Bargh (1997) has said that typically, humans evaluate everything they encounter as good or bad within 0.25 seconds after encountering it.

The automatic goal activation system uses learned evaluations from the previous system (automatic evaluation) to trigger behavioral actions. This idea goes back to Lewin (1935), who said that "positive valence of an object in the field has attached to it an attraction motive or goal within the psychological situation, and negative valenced objects have avoidance motives attached to them" (p. 92).

Free Will? Bargh's (1997) position on automaticity seems to place much of human activity outside the realm of free will. If people are passive and unaware of much of their exposures to stimuli, then they are not in control of the exposure decisions. Also, if learning takes place in an implicit manner, then people are not guided by their intentions and are not in control of the learning process.

Many cognitive psychologists agree with Bargh. For example, Banaji, Blair, and Glaser (1997) felt that social psychology went too far in the direction of believing in an individual's free will as a reaction to the strict behaviorism of Skinner, who said that an organism is totally controlled by the environment. Banaji et al. argued that "humans do not and more accurately, cannot, choose their actions as freely as they or their observers expect. Rather, forces in the situation, of which they may be little aware, can have a determining influence on their actions, even those actions that have immense consequences for the well-being and survival of themselves and their fellow beings" (p. 64). They said that the public underestimates this environmental influence because the influence is not direct or immediate but rather indirect and acting over the long term. "When causes are removed in time or space from the effects they produce, namely, when causal action occurs at a distance, the relationship between the two may most naturally lie outside awareness" (p. 64).

L. Berkowitz (1997) agreed with Bargh that "it is not at all uncommon in social psychology to infer the operation of conscious processes without having any evidence that these processes did indeed occur" (p. 85). In communication research, Berkowitz said that we too often look at the immediate outcomes of experiments and focus on that immediate behavioral effect rather than look at how that experimental treatment exposure has strengthened some automatic process of interpreting the stimuli a certain way.

Baumeister and Sommer (1997) agreed with Bargh but also conceived that there is also conscious processing. "We propose that the role of consciousness is to override automatic, habitual, or standard responses on the infrequent occasions when such intervention is needed. Consciousness thus undermines the lawful, predictable nature of human behavior and produces a situation of relative indeterminacy" (p. 75). W. L. Gardner and Cacioppo (1997) also took the position that some social phenomena are not automatic; they preferred a multilevel perspective based on a neurophysiological perspective that focuses on "the neural systems underlying both conscious and unconscious mentation" (p. 138).

My own position is that, of course, people have free will; however, in the everyday mundane world where people are overwhelmed with media exposure choices and meaning interpretation choices, they typically default to a state of automaticity where automatic routines make filtering and meaning decisions for them. These automatic routines are a necessary part of human thinking. The essence of high intelligence is the careful creation of good routines, and then allowing those routines to run automatically to deliver accurate decisions quickly with almost no mental effort, thus saving the mental resources to create additional routines that make the mind work even more effectively and efficiently. Free will comes into play in the initial construction of the routines, which allows for human creativity. Free will is also a potential at any given second of every day, as a person can move out of the state of automaticity and into another exposure state, thus taking control of a decision-making process and going counter to previously learned routines.

This leads us to two fundamental questions about human thinking: (1) What governs the automatic thought processes—that is, how does the human mind know what steps and processes to follow when the person is not consciously guiding it? and (2) What guides a person's conscious thought processes? The answers to both these questions are algorithms.

Introducing the Construct of Algorithm

The key construct in explaining how people encounter media messages and process information from those messages is the algorithm. Up to this point in this chapter, we have reviewed many terms referring to how the human mind is organized and how it functions. The terms of *associative network, memory, schema, script, mental model,* and so on each have a substantial overlap with the idea to which I am referring. However, I use the term *algorithm* for two reasons. First, none of these terms as currently conceptualized captures my meaning fully. Furthermore, each of these terms has several slightly different meanings depending on which scholar you read. So to avoid this definitional wobble and to try to capture my conceptualization more accurately, I will refrain from using these existing terms. Second, I wanted to set this term off from the general flow of ideas in cognitive psychology and make it special for mass media messages. This is not to say that the term has no applicability to nonmedia information because it likely does. But I want to keep my focus on what is special about the mass media and people's exposures to those types of messages. Critics will complain that the introduction of another term increases clutter, which could increase the chance of misunderstanding. I typically agree with such arguments. But in this case, I believe that the use of an existing term would run the risk of greater misunderstanding than the introduction of the new term would.

Definition

I define *algorithm* as a set of codes that people use to make sense of media messages both consciously and unconsciously. People use algorithms consciously as guides in a thinking process to tell them where to start on a path of thinking; algorithms lay out the steps in a process along with the options at each decision point, provide direction down the path toward the goal, and indicate when the path is completed, that is, when a decision is reached. When people use a particular algorithm, it becomes familiar to them, and the mental effort needed to follow the guidance provided by the algorithm is reduced. In subsequent uses of that algorithm, people rely on decisions they made in previous uses of the algorithm, and this reduces the need for mental effort. Eventually, the use of an algorithm can become routine—that is, in a given situation, the algorithm is "loaded" automatically and runs to completion without the person needing to expend any mental effort because all the decisions are habitually made in the same way. Thus, when an algorithm is accessed in the same way repeatedly over a long period of time, it is what cognitive psychologists refer to as chronically accessible (Bargh, 1984).

Algorithms are composed of information of a cognitive, emotional, aesthetic, and moral nature; they include associations among facts, images, words, sounds, feelings, and judgments. And algorithms are organic; that is, they are continually in a state of change as people acquire new experiences and make adjustments to their existing algorithms to make them more useful and more efficient.

Essential Characteristics

Algorithms have three characteristics: type, structure, and degree of specificity. Each of these characteristics is developed in some detail in the following three sections.

Type of Algorithm. The first characteristic of algorithms is their type. This refers to the type of information included in their codes. At the most general level, there are two types of algorithms—declarative algorithms and procedural algorithms. Declarative algorithms hold associations of existing knowledge, while procedural algorithms hold processes that can be used to guide people in the acquisition, processing, and use of knowledge. Declarative "concerns the referents of our everyday life experience (e.g., persons, objects, events, social issues that we read about, or oneself). In contrast, procedural knowledge concerns the sequence of actions that one performs in pursuit of a particular goal (driving a car, using a word processor, etc.). Whereas declarative knowledge is reflected in the information we can recall about an entity or that we implicitly draw on in the course of attaining a particular objective, procedural knowledge is reflected in the sequence of cognitive or motor acts that are actually performed in the pursuit of this objective" (Wyer, 2004, p. 6).

Procedural algorithms present a problem-solving structure that is guided by the application of certain well-used skills. But the content is not included in the code, and thus the algorithm is general enough to solve any problem of a given type. The code specifies where decision points are and guides the person in how to make a decision, but it does not specify what the options are or how many there are or how the options should be weighted.

Structure. The second essential characteristic of algorithms is their structure. Some algorithms are very simple, consisting of two nodes linked together. Other algorithms are more complex, with many nodes arranged in a particular series. And the most complex structure is the hierarchy, where some nodes are nested within other organizing nodes. These are the three general types of structures: simple associative networks, series networks, and hierarchical networks.

What characterizes the simple associative network is not just the small number of nodes but also the way the nodes are tightly associated with one another. A good example of this type of structure is one's vocabulary. Building one's vocabulary is essential for the creation of a two-node simple structure for each word; one node is the referent for the word, and the second node is the denoted meaning. When a person sees a word—let's say *dog*—her dog SAN is accessed, and that word referent activates a network of nodes that include an image of a dog, sound of a dog, a few memories of dogs, and perhaps several emotions about a dog. The nodes are flexible; that is, a certain image of a dog might be accessed one day and not the next. This is due to which nodes have been accessed most recently—what cognitive psychologists refer to as the availability heuristic (Tversky & Kahneman, 1973).

A SAN can be regarded as a discrete network unit. Its boundary is defined by the dissipation of simple associations; that is, once a referent is accessed and immediate associations are accessed, the accessing of additional nodes ceases. The degree of accessing is finite and limited to only those nodes most closely associated with the referent. However, SANs are usually linked to other nodes in much larger structures; both series and hierarchical structures are composed of SANs as building blocks.

Series structure is also composed of nodes and connectors in a network like the SAN, but series algorithms have the additional characteristic of a logical structure. SANs can have a bunch of nodes connected, but the structure of connections is not important beyond what is next to what. With a series algorithm, the nodes follow a pattern of A-B-C-D and so on; that is, a person cannot go from A to C without going through B. Thus, B is an important interim step in a time sequence of events, or it is a logical step that requires the production of some element that is then the input into C. This is very abstract, so let me make it more concrete with an example. A typical series algorithm is the restaurant script. The general script for restaurant guides us through a sequence of entering the restaurant, being seated, reading the menu, and ordering food; the waitperson brings the food, we eat the food, the waitperson brings the bill, we pay the bill, and then we leave the restaurant. In this sequence, order is important—that is, we cannot be served food until we first order. An example of a logical series is an algorithm that guides us in constructing an opinion about a movie. This algorithm tells us to expose ourselves to the movie, access our standard for what a movie should be, and then compare the movie with our standard. We cannot get to the third step of making the comparison until we have completed the first two steps because the products of the first two steps are the essential raw materials required to undertake the third step.

The hierarchical structure is also composed of nodes and connectors in a network like the SAN, and it has a logical structure like a series, but it also needs to include several layers of generality nested in its structure. This additional structuring is what makes induction and deduction possible. To illustrate, if a person accesses one SAN (let's say an image from the news about an act of vandalism in one's neighborhood) and is bothered by it enough to want to think about it some more, she is likely to search beyond this one SAN to see if it is linked to other SANs of acts of vandalism. Let's say she finds three other instances (three other SANs linked up). Then she induces a pattern from these three examples to conclude the following: There is a lot of vandalism lately in my neighborhood. This induction is a construction of meaning that exists at a higher level of generality from the examples, so this induced pattern becomes the next layer up in the hierarchy. Let's say she is still curious and searches her memory for other criminal acts from her neighborhood recently and remembers several acts of thefts of public property, and so she induces the following conclusion: There has been a lot of crime in my neighborhood lately. She goes back to search her memory and finds no linked-up accounts of murders, muggings, rapes, or armed robberies. Now she constructs a more general conclusion through induction: There has been a lot of crime (not just vandalism, which is only one type of crime) lately in my neighborhood, but at least the crime in my neighborhood is not violent. With each construction of meaning through induction, she needed to access a wider range of SANs and also move up a meaning hierarchy. This task is much more involved than what is done in meaning matching; the extra steps require a greater expenditure of mental energy, but at the end of this process is a creation—that is, a construction of meaning that is new to the person.

Degree of Specificity. The third essential characteristic of algorithms is their degree of specificity. By this, I mean the degree to which the algorithm provides guidance in addressing the task at hand. Some algorithms are fully specified; that is, they present enough code to guide a person all the way through a process with no gaps. In contrast, other algorithms are only partially specified: There are gaps in the guidance, and while there may be a good deal of code to guide the decision, there is a significant degree of uncertainty at some point in the process. A good example of this is when the code is a reconstruction of a person's attitude, belief, or behavioral pattern that in the past has been accessed over and over with no problem. However, this time there is a counterexample or significant challenge to the habit, and the person must resolve the dissonance. The person cannot simply run the algorithm and arrive at a satisfying decision; he or she must devote some mental energy to bridging a gap in some way.

Origin of Algorithms

People are not born with algorithms but must acquire them or construct them for themselves as they experience life. Algorithms can be acquired from another person or the mass media where someone else did the construction and passed it along to another individual, or they can be constructed by the person himself or herself.

Acquisition. The acquisition can be through a conscious or an unconscious process. Conscious acquisition refers to when a person has an intention to learn something; usually the sender of the message has the intention to teach. People read a book, magazine, or newspaper or watch the evening news or a documentary with the intention of learning a particular fact or, more diffusely, picking up more information of a general nature about a topic in which they are interested.

Acquisition can also occur unconsciously. This is often referred to as unintentional learning, incidental learning, or implicit learning. When people expose themselves to entertainment messages, they are not trying to learn specific facts or social lessons; instead, they simply want to be entertained or to escape their day-to-day lives. However, they can pick up facts and social lessons unintentionally, that is, incidental to their main purpose.

Construction. When a person creates his or her own construction, the process is conscious, and it requires an expenditure of psychic energy; it is usually goal directed, but it need not be. The construction process usually involves skills that the person uses to transform the media message information in some way to make it fit better in his or her declarative algorithm.

Construction processes vary in terms of importance to the individual. When a construction process is of high importance, the process has a clear goal, the psychic energy expended is high, and the consequences of making a faulty construction are strong and negative. However, many construction processes are of low importance, so the person is governed by an ambiguous or emotionally felt but not clearly articulated goal, such as a drive to reduce uncertainty or dissonance. The degree of psychic energy expended is small so that the person can achieve efficiency, that is, a quick resolution with minimal expenditure of resources.

There is a wide latitude in mental effort used in the creation of these algorithms. Some of this latitude is covered by rational strategies, some by shortcuts, and some by irrational strategies (see Table 8.1). The difference across these three is as follows.

Rational strategies are governed by a clear goal, relatively high motivation to make an accurate decision, and the willingness to expend a relatively high degree of mental energy to achieve the goal accurately. People will use a rational strategy when the consequences of making a wrong decision are expensive in terms of finances or negative emotions. The high motivation is used to gather lots of factual information, evaluate the credibility and worth of that information, weigh the relative merits of counterinformation, and construct a solution that best conforms to the preponderance of the information and the rules of logic. Once the person has made the decision, he or she

Table 8.1   Creating Algorithms

Exposure States	Decision Making		
	Rational	*Shortcuts*	*Irrational*
Automatic	Screening	Highly automatic	Highly automatic
Attentional	Scanning	Automatic	Typical construction
Transported	Swept	Personal and highly automatic	Highly emotional construction
Self-reflexive	Searching actively	Sorting through learned meanings	Highly personalized construction

acts on it, and then monitors his or her feelings about it. If he or she feels good about the decisions (i.e., avoids buyer's remorse or second guessing), then the decision is reinforced by making it an algorithm to use as a model in future decisions.

Shortcut strategies are governed by a clear goal to make a simple decision, a relatively high motivation to achieve efficiency, and the willingness to expend only a low degree of mental energy to arrive at the decision as quickly as possible. People will use a shortcut strategy when the consequences of making a wrong decision are slight. People will use cognitive shortcuts such as heuristics (availability, representative, etc.) in lieu of gathering more information. Thus, the shortcut is usually a savings in energy and time achieved through reducing the amount of information in the base that will be used to make a decision. Thus, one info-bit might be enough rather than two or more. Once the person has made the shortcut decision, he or she moves on, not thinking about it much. The feeling is that he or she "got away with it," which is a rewarding feeling, and the algorithm is regarded as successful. The decision is reinforced by making it an algorithm to use as a model in future decisions. Shortcuts are not regarded as a form of irrational strategy; instead, shortcuts are thought to follow a rational model, but because they are governed by a goal of efficiency over accuracy, they are not as involved and as systematic as fully rational strategies.

Irrational strategies are usually governed by a desire to reach a particular decision that feels right. Gathering lots of factual information and using logical cognitive processing are less important than is arriving at the right conclusion, which is usually judged on an emotional basis. With irrational strategies, people would acknowledge that their decisions were wrong from a logical point of view, but they avoid evaluating their irrational strategies. Thus, with drug use, smoking, or other risky behaviors, people often make decisions that are not logically in their best interests. But if they shift the decision into an emotional arena, they can justify the decision in terms of what they feel like doing. They know there are likely to be negative consequences later but go ahead with the decision anyway. Irrational strategies can get translated into algorithms and stored in memory for continued use.

Once an algorithm has been stored in memory, the person loses track of how it was created, that is, whether it was created using a rational strategy, a shortcut strategy, or an irrational strategy. The algorithm is a tool that is available for use in solving future problems. The more an algorithm is used, the more habitual it becomes—that is, the more likely it will continue to be used. The more an algorithm is used in an automatic or transported state, the less likely it is going to be examined or altered; instead, the fact that it is used again is reinforcing. In the attentional state, the algorithm runs by taking a person from one decision point to the next. At each decision point, the algorithm presents the options but leaves the selection up to the person who is consciously making the decisions. In the self-reflexive state, the person confronts the algorithm as if it were a specimen on the dissecting table. The person is not using the algorithm online in a process of decision making; instead, the person is like a programmer analyzing the code. The person is not using the algorithm but is instead examining it.

The algorithm is a construction of the individual himself or herself and also of conditioning by the media and other experiences over time. Thus, the code in an algorithm is created and altered in conscious and unconscious ways. When people are in the attentional—and especially in the self-reflexive—exposure state, they are aware of their goals, the elements in the messages, and the processing of information; in this case, they are largely in control of additions to and alterations of their codes. When people are in the automatic—and often in the transported—exposure state, they are largely unaware of the conditioning influence of the media, and therefore additions to and alterations of their codes are not under their control.

Use of Algorithms

Algorithms are accessed by individuals during media exposure situations and are used to guide decisions, whether those decisions be conscious or unconscious. Sometimes people will consciously access an appropriate algorithm to help them process an unfolding narrative, such that when new characters appear, people can read a few cues in their appearance and use the algorithm to fill in other likely characteristics of the characters. Algorithms also provide guidance information about other message elements such as plot, setting, theme, and passage of time. However, at other times, algorithms will load automatically and "run in the background" as a person devotes mental energy to other tasks. Thus, algorithms can activate automatically and run without requiring mental effort so that the person can navigate many exposure decisions with greater efficiency.

The Set of Algorithms

Given all the analysis above in this chapter as well as in the previous chapter, I have synthesized a list of two dozen algorithms. They are outlined and briefly described in Table 8.2. They are more fully defined and described in the following three chapters, where their use is explained in particular tasks of filtering, meaning matching, and meaning construction.

Notice that the set of algorithms is organized by type and structure. Type makes a distinction between algorithms that contain declarative information (facts, images, sounds, experiences, emotions, etc., stored in memory) and algorithms that contain procedural guidance (rules, procedures, steps, etc., stored in memory). Structure makes a distinction between simple associative networks (i.e., several nodes linked in an associative network, all at the same level of generality and in no particular order), series (i.e., organized with nodes in a particular sequence), and hierarchies (i.e., organized with nodes clustered by level of generality). Also, each algorithm can vary by specificity, with simple ones usually—but not always—fully specified. Complex algorithms (those with many nodes in multiple patterns) tend to be partially specified; however, with repeated use over time, they move toward fuller specification as gaps are bridged over or ignored, certain pathways are habitually reinforced, and the mental energy required to use the algorithm is reduced to almost nothing as it becomes a tried-and-true routine and runs automatically.

One final note: This set of algorithms was developed primarily to explain information-processing tasks with the mass media, and most of the algorithms

Table 8.2   The Set of Algorithms

I. *Declarative Algorithms*

  A. Simple Associative Networks

   Referent/meaning pair—two nodes with one being a salient referent and the other the denoted meaning for the referent.

   Referent-cluster/single meaning—there are several referents attached to one denoted meaning (e.g., meaning of dog is associated with word *dog*, picture of a dog, and barking sound).

   Referent/meaning cluster—a salient referent is associated with more than one possible denoted meaning (e.g., the following words are referents, each with several meanings: *bad, cool, sweet;* picture of a person who has an identical twin).

  B. Series

   History—composed of a sequence of events, but at least one element is unique that keys it to a particular occurrence; story or memory of a particular show or happening; in contrast to a more generic algorithm or script.

   Story—same as a history in the sequence of happenings in a particular event; however, stories also have emotional significance or a lesson learned attached to them.

  C. Hierarchies

   Knowledge structure—a large-scale pyramidal network of simple associative networks (SANs) and series clustered by levels of generality on a topic.

II. *Procedural Algorithms*

  A. Simple Associative Networks

   Identifying frames—algorithm provides guidance in looking for salient elements in a message to indicate to the audience what the message is about and what it is not about.

   Identifying orienting nodes—algorithm provides guidance on moving from a story element to a person's SAN; tells the person which declarative algorithm to access and which node in that algorithm to access first.

   Directional pathing—algorithm provides guidance about how to move from the orienting node in a declarative algorithm and continue proceeding through the network of nodes.

   Monitoring value—algorithm provides guidance about how to continually make judgments about the value of the media exposure by making comparisons of message elements to personal expectations.

   Syntactic-semantic translations—syntactic markers are the formal features of a message, while semantic markers constitute the content part of the message; this algorithm guides audiences to recognize syntactic markers and associate them with meaning to be able to follow the story in the media message.

B. Series

Filtering Judgment

Screening—algorithm provides guidance about how to stay in the automatic state of screening out all messages until attention is triggered.

Scanning—algorithm provides guidance about how to monitor message field for general kinds of messages and then focus attention on those triggers.

Swept—algorithm provides guidance about how to stay inside a message experience and screen out all external stimuli.

Searching actively—algorithm provides guidance about strategies to use in locating certain kinds of messages.

Scripts—prototypic sequences of events that occur in a particular situational context; they guide people through a sequence by illuminating the series of steps.

Real-world scripts—steps in a routine that guide people through a series of events.

Media scripts—narrative formulas that guide audiences through a series of expected story plot points.

Implicit theories—are like scripts with prototypical sequences of events; unlike scripts, they contain general principles, such as moral precepts, themes, values, and beliefs about how the world operates. These general principles are useful in deduction, and they fill in the gaps in an otherwise partially specified sequence; they can be used to explain events that have occurred in the past and to predict the future.

Problem solving—algorithm provides guidance with a fully specified sequence of steps in a process to a convergent solution.

C. Hierarchies

Skill sequence process—how to use particular skills to perform mental tasks in partially specified problems.

Deduction—algorithm provides guidance about how to reason syllogistically to a conclusion when using a major and minor premise.

Induction—algorithm provides guidance about how to infer patterns across individual observations.

Generalization—algorithm provides guidance about how to leverage a conclusion about a specific message element or small set of message elements to apply to a larger set of elements.

Evaluation—algorithm provides guidance about how to compare an element in a media message against some standard.

Categorization—algorithm provides guidance about how to select a dimension of grouping and then arrange elements into groups along the dimension.

Decision making—algorithm provides guidance about how to work though the challenge of a partially specified novel problem that has many options and many ways of choosing among the many options.

presented focus on one of these tasks. However, often an algorithm might be developed using mass media information and then used in real-world situations, or a real-world algorithm might be used to make sense of mass media information. Therefore, some of the algorithms in the set are not purely mass media generated or limited to mass media information-processing tasks.

The meta-algorithm constantly running in the background of each human's mind is one that addresses the drive to simplify life by turning partially specified challenges into fully specified ones. Thus, people need to know how to use heuristics as shortcuts to bridge over gaps and get around difficult spots. The drive is to arrive quickly at solutions to problems and decisions that work, and then to routinize them so they can run automatically.

The first time people are confronted with a problem, they need to devote some mental energy to solving—or at least getting around—that problem. However, if they are continually presented with a particular problem in their everyday lives, people do not need to devote the same degree of mental energy in solving it, as if it were a new problem each time. Instead, people create an automatic routine—what I refer to as an algorithm. This algorithm can be created the first time they encounter the problem, solve it, and are satisfied with the solution. If they have an expectation of encountering the same problem again, they store the solution processing for use again later. Each time they encounter the problem, they load the appropriate algorithm and let it run with almost no mental energy required. Thus, the repeated addressing of a problem is accomplished in a very efficient manner and with a great deal of confidence that the outcome will continue to be successful. Everyday life is composed of a multitude of these kinds of mundane problems— getting up in the morning, driving to work, going to the grocery store, and so on. Media exposure is woven into the fabric of everyday life such that the thousands of decisions about filtering, meaning matching, and meaning construction are governed by these media algorithms.

Conclusion

This chapter laid out many important ideas in the scholarly literature concerning the organization and processes of the human mind. We examined how these organizational schemes and processes were used to predict and explain human learning. After sorting through all these ideas, the most useful ones for explaining learning from the mass media were reconfigured in a synthesis that focuses on the idea of algorithm. This focal idea of algorithm is further illustrated and developed in the next three chapters on audience tasks of filtering, meaning matching, and meaning construction.

CHAPTER 9

Audience

Filtering Media Messages

Throughout the Generating-Findings phase of mass media scholarship, the most asked question about the audience facet has been, "Why do people expose themselves to media messages?" There are several reasons why this has been so central to audience scholarship. One reason is that it is an important fundamental question; that is, if we knew why people expose themselves to particular messages, we would be in a stronger position to answer other important questions such as why certain types of messages are so popular while other types are not and why media content affects people the way it does. Another reason is that it is a relatively simple way to conduct research. That is, it is easy to generate a large database by simply asking people to fill out a survey and indicate the degree of various motives for exposures to channels, genres, dayparts, and messages.

In this chapter, we will examine the assumptions underlying this type of research and see that the utility of motives as an explanatory factor is very limited. I will argue for a more complete perspective on media exposure and then elaborate the media exposure model that was presented in Chapter 7 by focusing on the filtering task.

Use of Motives in Explaining Media Exposure

Arguably, the dominant theory used to explain audience exposure over the past four decades has been what is called "uses and gratifications." The uses and gratifications approach is based on what J. M. McLeod and Becker (1981) called five fundamental characteristics. First, audiences are active. Second, media use is goal directed. Third, media use fulfills a wide variety of needs. Fourth, people can articulate their reasons for using the media. And fifth, the gratifications have their origins in media content, exposure, and the social context in which exposure takes place.

With the uses and gratifications approach, researchers typically will measure either motives or satisfactions. Researchers who measure motives assume that users of media achieve acceptable satisfactions with their exposures or they would not continue with repeated exposures. Or researchers will measure satisfactions from exposures and reason backwards to infer what the motives must be. Using this approach, media scholars have generated a fairly large body of research that looks for patterns between what people say their motives are for media exposures, what people say they get out of those exposures, and what people report as their exposure patterns (Webster & Wakshlag, 1985). For a sampling of the more recent research on this topic, see Table 9.1.

Examining Assumptions

The key ideas in the uses and gratifications assumptions are that the audience is active in making choices and that the audience is rational in these choices; that is, audience members know their choices, know their needs, and strive to make the best choice to satisfy each need. While the active audience and rational choice assumptions hold in some media exposure decisions, they are inadequate to explain most of the filtering decisions that take place in a person's everyday experience in navigating through the message saturation in our culture. Let's examine each of these in some detail.

Audience Activity. One assumption is that media audiences are either active or passive (Biocca, 1988; Eastman, 1998; Himmelweit et al., 1958; Schramm et al., 1961;

Table 9.1   Selective Review of Motives for Mass Media Message Exposure

General Motives

McQuail (2000) wrote that there are four general motives for media exposure: (1) diversion, which is the escape from routine or problems, and emotional release; (2) personal relationships, such as the needs for companionship and social utility; (3) personal identity, which is self-reference, reality exploration, and value reinforcement; and (4) surveillance, which is a form of information seeking.

E. Katz, Gurevitch, and Haas (1973) said that there are five groups of needs: (1) cognitive needs such as the need to understand; (2) affective needs, strengthening aesthetic or emotional experience; (3) integrative needs, strengthening one's confidence, credibility, and stability; (4) needs related to strengthening contact with family, friends, and the world; and (5) needs related to escape or tension release.

Dobos and Dimmick (1988) saw five motives: (1) surveillance (to keep in touch with international, national, state, and local events), (2) knowledge (to get information about events, issues, the government, and things affecting one's family, to help make decisions), (3) escape/diversion (to fill time, for relief from boredom, to divert attention from personal problems), (4) excitement (for stimulation), and (5) interpersonal utility (for things to talk about and material to influence others).

McQuail, Blumler, and Brown (1972) said that there are six gratifications: (1) diversion (emotional release and escape from the daily routine and problems), (2) personal relationships (including parasocial companionship and social utility, which includes family viewing, viewing to meet the standards of a group, and viewing for ideas, topics, and things that feed into interpersonal conversations), (3) personal identity (such as self-evaluation), (4) reality exploration (for ideas about personal concerns), (5) value reinforcement, and (6) surveillance.

Corner (1999) wrote not about motives per se but about pleasures and provided a typology that includes the following:

> Visual pleasure—watching people/characters and being present at events
>
> Pleasures of parasociality—vicarious relationships with characters
>
> Dramatic pleasures—instantiating everyday experience and emotional life
>
> Pleasures of knowledge—acquiring broad and deep expertise
>
> Pleasures of comedy—laughter
>
> Pleasures of fantasy—stimulation through exposures to scenarios that are highly improbable in real life
>
> Pleasures of distraction, diversion, and routine

Edman (1939) argued that there are three functions of art: (1) the intensification of life's experiences by making them more vivid, exciting, and enjoyable; (2) clarification of what it means to be human and alive by exploring the full range of human experience and emotion; and (3) interpretation, giving people interesting and novel perspectives on common experiences.

(Continued)

Table 9.1 (Continued)

People use the media for cultural maintenance of their ethnicity (Rios & Gaines, 1998).

People use local media to ground themselves in the local culture and resist the erosion brought about by globalization (Sampedro, 1998). They ground themselves in symbolic environments. People use media ritualistically to secure their personal identity and create familiar formulations of cultural spaces.

Channel Motives

Television:

Abelman and Atkin (2000) segmented audiences of children viewing television and found three groups: medium-oriented viewers, network-oriented viewers, and station-oriented viewers.

Film Viewing:

S. D. Young (2000) found different motivations for film viewing.

Internet:

Papacharissi and Rubin (2000) found five motivations for Internet use that could be organized by instrumental and ritual use.

K. Wright (2000) found that senior citizens use the Internet for social support and becoming part of an online community.

Flanagin and Metzger (2001) found three primary motivations for using the Internet.

Kaye and Johnson (2002) found that users of the Internet had particular motives in getting political information: guidance in information seeking, entertainment, and social utility.

LaRose and Eastin (2004) reported that they found three predictors of Internet use: Internet self-efficacy, habitual behavior, and deficient self-regulation.

Electronic Media:

Ferguson and Perse (2000) found five motivations: entertainment, pastime, relaxation, social information, and information.

A variety of motivations were found for electronic media use, but these motivational patterns did not differ across three ethnic groups (European Americans, African Americans, and Hispanic Americans; Bickham et al., 2003).

Magazines:

A variety of motivations were found for women reading beauty and fashion magazines (Thomsen, McCoy, Gustafson, & Williams, 2002).

Video game playing:

K. Lucas and Sherry (2004) identified interpersonal needs for inclusion, affection, and control as motives. They also found gender differences in motivations and behaviors.

Music:

People use music to manage their moods. Knobloch and Zillmann (2002) ran an experiment where they manipulated participants' moods and then gave them a chance to listen to different types of music. They found that participants in a bad mood elected to listen to highly energetic and joyful music, and they were more decisive in exercising their musical preferences than participants in good or neutral moods. However, following the listening period, participants' moods did not appreciably differ across the experimental conditions.

Knobloch (2003) ran an experiment and found that participants use music to manage their moods. She made a distinction between mood management processes and mood adjustment processes.

Genre Motives

News:

Beaudoin and Thorson (2004) found three motives for exposure to news: surveillance, anticipated interaction, and guidance.

Talk Shows:

Rubin and Step (2000) found four motivations for exposure to talk radio.

Rubin, Haridakis, and Eyal (2003) found a wide range of uses and gratifications for talk shows, including dispositional factors (aggression, anger, attitudes toward women, and communication anxiety and reward) as well as television viewing factors (motivation, attitudes, topics, emotions, and parasocial interactions).

Reality Programs:

Nabi, Biely, Morgan, and Stitt (2003) conducted a survey to find out why people like reality-based programs. They found that regular viewers receive different and more varied gratifications from their viewing than do periodic viewers.

Vehicle Motives

Martha Stewart:

Mason and Meyers (2001) traced Martha Stewart fanship to three different motives: providing an escape from everyday life by encouraging the fantasy of an upper-class lifestyle of elegance and luxury, validation of women's interest in domesticity by making domestic work respectable and seem important, and fostering creativity and feelings of accomplishment and pride among those who complete projects and recipes.

Romance Novels:

Parameswaran (2002) found that women in south India have a variety of motives for reading romance novels: to learn about sexuality; to learn about being a cosmopolitan, global consumer; and to escape from the boundaries of preserving family honor.

Webster & Phalen, 1997). The uses and gratifications approach to audiences was itself a reaction to what the originators felt was an unexamined assumption that the audience was passive and that the media were the active agents in the exchange. During the 1960s and 1970s, when much of the uses and gratifications motives research was conducted, it was believed that audience members were conscious of their media needs and acted rationally to satisfy them (McQuail, 2005). But this is not the case. Often, people have no idea what their motives are or how much exposure they have experienced, so the research on uses and gratifications usually failed to find strong correlations between motives and exposures. The exceptions to this weak finding occurred only when people were asked about specific types of content, such as erotica (Perse, 1994), specific kinds of news (Levy, 1977), or specific kinds of political content (Blumler & McQuail, 1968).

This dichotomy between active and passive conceptions of the mass audience is faulty because audiences are active as well as passive. They switch back and forth continually. Hawkins and Pingree (1981) made this point several decades ago about television audiences. Also, Rubin (1984) approached this point with his distinction between instrumental and ritualistic motives. He said, "Ritualized television use appears to be habitual, frequent, and indicate a high regard for television as a medium. Instrumental television viewing appears to be purposeful, selective, and goal-directed" (p. 75). There is no longer any value in asking whether audiences are active or passive. Instead, we need to focus our attention on the question, Why are audience members active at certain times and passive at other times?

Rational Choices. Another assumption is that the audience is rational in its decision making. Key to this rational model of decision making is that people are aware of the elements that go into their decisions and that they logically use that information in the process of decision making. However, it appears that neither of these conditions holds for many of the decisions people make in their everyday lives about media exposures.

As for awareness of elements, the economic approach assumes people continually monitor the resources in the exposure exchange. The uses and gratifications approach assumes that audience members know their motives, moods, and needs and that they take all this information into consideration when making their exposure decisions. Of course, there are times when exposure decisions are very important and people do invest the effort into self-analysis before making the exposure decision. For example, a person might experience a strong drive to learn more about her investments after completing her taxes, so she goes to a bookstore and carefully looks through many of the personal investing books before choosing what to read.

It is likely that most filtering decisions are not rational; instead, most media exposure decisions are mundane and habitual. Mundane exposure decisions are so minor and occur so frequently that people do not put much if any effort into them. Habitual decisions are made when one's mind is on automatic pilot. With this type of decision, people do not understand—or care to understand—all that goes into those decisions, so they cannot provide good answers to detailed questions about their motives, moods, and gratifications. Instead, their brain automatically loads a routine that runs without any effort or conscious thought.

There is also a serious question about how logical people are, because engaging in a logical process of working through all the elements in a decision to arrive at the best selection often requires a significant investment of mental effort, as some gratification theoreticians believe. For example, Palmgreen and Rayburn (1985) created a mathematical model of decision making they called expectancy-value theory. This theory predicted that gratifications sought (GS) were equal to the sum of cross-products of $b * e$, where b is the subjective probability belief that a media message possesses some desired attribute, and e is the affective evaluation of the particular outcome or attribute. This model of decision making may hold under certain conditions, such as when people are forced to justify their ongoing behaviors or when the consequences of making a bad exposure decision are severe. However, it is likely that people only rarely would feel motivated to expend the higher degree of psychic energy required by this model.

The rational audience approach assumes a conscious state when making choices. If people are guided primarily by their expectations, then they need to have a continual awareness of what those expectations are. Also, people are assumed to be aware of exposure alternatives so they are able to match their expectations to the appropriate alternative. This requires a fair degree of mental effort, but there is reason to believe that much of media exposure is not consciously or logically driven. For example, Henning and Vorderer (2001) said that many individuals have a low need for cognition, and they are likely to expose themselves to TV because it reduces the need to think. Thus, escapism usage of TV is predicted by a person's need for cognition. Also, Heeter and Greenberg (1985) rejected the rational program selection models for TV viewing, saying that people do not assess all their options because they are not even aware of all their options. Writing at the time cable TV penetration had increased dramatically, they argued that "in a television environment where only three networks are available," rational models may apply, but "in cable television environments, as the number of program options increases vastly," those models are not plausible (p. 203). Now, more than two decades later, when there is so much more choice, it is even less likely that people consider all their options.

Critique of Motives Research

Now that I have laid out the key assumptions underlying the uses and gratifications perspective and critiqued them, I bring the focus back to motives. As long as we believe that audience members are aware of their needs and choices and rationally make selections, there is reason to believe that people understand their motives and remember them. As long as we assume that the audience is active and rational, it makes sense to measure motives. However, if we believe that media exposure is also habitual and ritualistic, then it is likely that audience members are not aware of their choices and not consciously processing these decisions. Instead, the decisions are made in a state of automaticity where the mind is running on automatic pilot, and there is likely to be no trace memory of the hundreds of filtering decisions people make every day.

While many media exposure scholars recognize that there are times when audience members are not aware of their exposures while they are happening, there is very little acknowledgment of the importance of this exposure state of automacity. It is not the case that media scholars argue that automaticity is an unimportant state; instead, many scholars simply ignore its prevalence and its importance. This is an important limitation of past research because much of the time, the human mind is running in a nonconscious state where information is still being processed and decisions are still being made (Petty & Cacioppo, 1986; Zajonc, 1968).

If much of exposure is habitual and characterized by lack of awareness of choices and expectations, then this raises serious doubts about the ability of many individuals to provide useful answers to questions about their motives. This is one of the reasons why researchers usually find little relationship between a person's attitudes and behaviors (Bower, 1985; Budd et al., 1999). For example, Budd et al. (1999) explained, "The gap between what people say and what they think or do is easily demonstrated, and the gap between what any of us feel and what language can capture is a commonplace of linguistics and psychoanalysis" (p. 173). This disconnect is largely ignored in the media exposure literature. Media researchers who survey audience members simply accept the numbers those respondents provide about their media exposures, motives, and satisfactions. These scholars run all their data, even data on those variables where there is a wide range in accuracy (due to self-awareness) among those respondents. It is not surprising that correlations among motives and exposures are fairly small. And although syndicated data services (such as the A. C. Nielsen Company and Arbitron) are aware of this problem, they ignore it when surveying audience members and simply report what audience members say their exposures are when they compile their reports.

While there are big challenges in figuring out how to measure human thought processes in the automatic state, this should not discourage us from recognizing that such a state exists. Furthermore, it is essential we address this measurement problem because it is likely that a very high proportion of media exposures take place in the state of automaticity.

Need for a More Complete Model of Media Exposure

Uses and gratifications theory has provided great utility in generating articulations of motives, needs, and satisfactions with media exposures when audience members are aware of their motives, needs, and satisfactions. But uses and gratifications thinking and research has not been so successful in explaining what happens when audience members are acting on habits outside of their awareness, when audience members are passive in their exposure choices and experiences, and when audience members have little if any memory of specific decisions or particular satisfactions. Therefore, uses and gratifications theory is fairly limited in what it can explain. Uses and gratifications researchers do generate data, but there is a serious question about the validity of many of their findings. Because most media exposure in everyday life is enacted through nonconscious habits, there is reason to conclude that people have no, or at best faulty, recollections of most of their exposure experiences when asked to recall them several days or weeks later.

What is needed is an exposure model that allows for the audience to be active at times and passive at others. It needs to allow for people to be systematic, rational, and logical at times, but it also must allow for people to be intuitive and irrational at other times. It needs to recognize that while audience members are sometimes aware of their motives and needs for media messages, much of their exposure is automatic and habitual. In short, the model needs to allow for a more complete set of media exposure experiences.

With this lineation general framework, exposure is not viewed through the perspective of motives; instead, exposure is viewed through the media exposure model. In this general framework, the focus is on a range of filtering decisions across exposure states where some decisions are made consciously but other exposure decisions are made unconsciously.

Filtering by Exposure State

Recall from Chapter 7 that the media exposure model is an attempt to provide a broad perspective on explaining why and how audience members expose themselves to media messages as well as the tasks they experience in meaning matching and meaning construction. In this section, the filtering task will be examined in more detail (see Table 9.2). This model recognizes the usefulness of motives at certain times, but it is much more focused on exposure states as the key idea in the explanation. The media exposure model includes all four exposure states and explains that there are profound differences across these four states in terms of the algorithms that guide the filtering decisions. Each state is governed primarily by a different filtering algorithm: screening, searching, swept, and deep analysis.

Automatic State

When people are in the state of automaticity, they employ a *screening algorithm*, which keeps them in the automatic state, filtering out all messages until a trigger interrupts the flow and they are bumped into an attentional state. This procedural algorithm runs as the default and thus requires almost no mental effort. There is no conscious goal or strategy. Messages are screened out automatically with no effort until some element in a message breaks through a person's default screen and captures his or her attention. The attention decision is triggered by the element in the message, not by the person. Thus, message designers are in control of the screening process.

The mode of screening is illustrated by Comstock and Scharrer (1999), who characterized typical television exposure as follows: "viewers most of the time are only passively involved in what they view" (p. 52). These authors cited studies that show that in large, representative national samples, when people are asked what they viewed the night before, few mention a specific program. Thus, they reasoned that many people expose themselves to television with no motive other than to monitor what is going on. To bolster this argument, they added that people typically attend to the screen only about 40% of the time, and this figure varies by type of content.

Table 9.2   Filtering in the Media Exposure Model

	Filtering	
Exposure States	*Algorithm*	*Nature of Algorithm*
Automatic	Screening	Automatic
Attentional	Searching	Triggers some questions
Transported	Swept	Personal and highly automatic
Self-reflexive	Deep analysis	Triggers many questions

If the content is formulaic, such as stereotypical characters acting out conventional-ized plots, then the percentage of time spent looking at the screen is even lower.

In our culture, it is likely that we spend much more time in the screening state than in the other three exposure states. Until about a century ago, there were very few media messages in the environment, so people did little screening. But today, when media messages are not just available but are aggressively competing to trigger our attention, the interaction with information has likely shifted from information seeking to information screening. Because our capacity for information processing has not changed over the past century, most of that screening is "screening out" or ignoring most of it. We are overwhelmed by the choices of messages. To protect ourselves, we establish a default of avoiding almost all messages. Instead of encountering each message and looking for reasons to ignore it, the opposite is the case. We ignore all messages unless there is some reason to pay attention to them. This puts us in the default condition of avoidance.

Attentional State

The *searching algorithm* governs filtering exposures in the attentional state. Searching is a process of information acquisition that begins when a person is aware of a particular need for a media message. This need then motivates a search of messages until the useful message (or combination of messages) is found to satisfy the need. This procedural algorithm guides the person through the searching process until it is resolved by locating a media message that satisfies the person's needs.

Sometimes this searching process is fairly short and requires a relatively low degree of mental effort. For example, in the morning, you turn on the TV or radio to find out what the traffic is like in preparation for your drive to work. Other times, this searching process can be fairly involved and requires a relatively high degree of mental effort. For example, you may be searching for some videotapes to entertain your 3-year-old daughter. You have a clear goal for what you regard as appropriate entertainment. You get on the Internet sites of companies selling videotapes and read dozens of descriptions of the tapes. But you are skeptical because those descriptions look more like ads than genuine reviews. So you search for Internet sites of organizations that care about children and where the tapes are reviewed by child psychologists. Then you rent a dozen tapes to check them out for yourself because the tapes recommended by psychologists look safe, but they may not interest your daughter.

The searching process is governed by an algorithm that suggests steps and options, but it leaves the decisions up to the person. It requires conscious choices. Therefore, this algorithm is more of a guide than a fully specified prescription that can run completely on its own with no conscious input from the person.

Transported State

When people are in the transported exposure state, the *swept algorithm* keeps them focused on the message and completely filters out everything else. This is the tunnel vision. The algorithm keeps the person propelled forward in the tunnel while ignoring everything else. Good movies are able to achieve this—that is, people get caught up in the story and forget that they are in a large room with many strangers. They are propelled forward in the story as the experiences in the story trigger personal emotional reactions in the viewers. People continue in this state either until the message is concluded or unless the message's power to keep them in the state erodes to a point where they switch into another state.

Self-Reflexive State

The filtering decision in the self-reflexive state is governed by the *deep analysis algorithm*. This algorithm puts people in a hyperconscious state by continually posing questions that require the person to evaluate options consciously. Audience members not only consider each media message option available by evaluating the utility of each in meeting their specific needs but also analyze the nature of those needs themselves.

Process of Filtering

There are four key issues when considering the process of filtering. These are attraction to a message flow, continuing with the flow, ending a message flow, and conditioning of filtering algorithms.

Attraction to a Message Flow

When a particular element in a media message connects with an element in a person's algorithm, triggering of attention occurs. For example, television programs will use changes in audio elements (switching of voices, music, sound effects, silence, etc.) and visual elements (switching among unusual or attractive characters, settings, motion, color, etc.) to appeal to viewers' needs for audiovisual stimulation. If a person does not have a need for such stimulation, then the triggers will not attract (switch a person from automaticity into an attentional state) or hold his or her attention.

The elements in the message interact with elements in a person's algorithm; if the connection is not made, then triggering does not occur. For example, people who are susceptible to attraction to the news are those people with a strong sense of civic duty to keep themselves informed (Poindexter & McCombs, 2001). News stories present triggers to capture audience attention, but audience members must have values in their personal algorithms that recognize and respond to these triggers. This is also illustrated with children in their developing cognitive abilities. Valkenburg and Vroone (2004) found that the attention of the youngest children was particularly attracted by salient auditory and visual features, such as applause and visual surprises. But as children aged past 2 years, they were also able to have their attention attracted by character action, numbers, and meaningful dialogue because their minds had developed to a point at which they became susceptible to these different types of triggers of attention. To further illustrate this point of increased mental development, Valkenburg and Vroone found that young children pay most attention to television content that is only moderately discrepant from their existing knowledge and capabilities; thus, children seek some discrepancy so as to increase their learning. Also with children, the most important predictor of Internet use is affinity with computers, followed by information and entertainment seeking (Valkenburg & Soeters, 2001); children who do not have a high need for entertainment and an affinity for computers will likely avoid Internet exposure even if all the message elements are attractive.

Attraction to the Internet is related to ethnic differences among people. In addition, Fredin and David (1998) argued that there is a dynamic to searching for information on the Internet and that this dynamic is characterized by shifting states of goals as people move through the dynamic. Also, self-efficacy helps in governing that movement. Self-efficacy is the sense or conviction that one can do what is required to accomplish a particular outcome. It is not just a mechanical knowledge of procedures or some mechanical amassing of past experience. It involves the sense that one can integrate knowledge, affect, and skills to devise goals and to meet challenges in changing, ambiguous, unpredictable situations.

Natural Perceptual Triggers. Elements in media messages can trigger audience members to switch attention to a new message or to cross a liminal line, that is, to switch from one exposure state to another while encountering a flow of media messages or within the flow of one media message. Typically, triggers will switch a person from the automatic exposure state to an attentional state, where the person begins to "pay attention" consciously to the message. However, a trigger could also switch a person from an attentional state to a transported state or a self-reflexive state. Triggers can also switch off a person from a state requiring a higher level of concentration to another state requiring a lower level, such as from an attentional state to an automatic state.

Some of these triggers are hardwired into a person's brain; that is, they are natural perceptual triggers. Humans are hardwired to monitor their environment automatically and attend to suddenly occurring and novel elements in their perceptual fields. The media make use of these naturally occurring connections to attract and hold audience members' attention. This is why the use of violence is so prevalent in media narratives, because audience members cannot help but perceive the threat and monitor its progress.

Researchers have identified many of these natural perceptual triggers of attention (see Table 9.3). To expand a bit on several of these elements, Lombard, Reich, Grabe, Bracken, and Ditton (2000) found that exposure to messages on a larger television screen resulted in people perceiving that the movement in the scenes was faster, experiencing a greater sense of physical movement, enjoying the movement to a greater extent, finding the viewing experience more exciting, and being more physiologically aroused. Also, Simons, Detenber, Cuthbert, Schwartz, and Reiss (2003) found a curvilinear relationship between ratings of emotional valence and alpha power; that is, there is more cortical activity with both positive and negative images, while neutral images require little cortical activity. They also found that attention is higher with moving images compared with still images, and this is independent of emotional valence. M. E. Smith and Gevins (2004) reported brainwave responses to media messages. Specifically, manipulations of a commercial's visual structure that result in rapid pacing or frequent scene changes can be engaging because they require a frequent redirection of visual attention. Manipulations of semantic content (humorous or anomalous elements) can elicit cognitive engagement. M. E. Smith and Gevins found a relationship between activity in different parts of the brain and different types of structural and semantic features of TV commercials.

Table 9.3   Natural Perceptual Triggers

- Arousing and positive elements
- Salient auditory and visual features, such as applause and visual surprises (Valkenburg & Vroone, 2004)
- Motion (Simons, Detenber, Cuthbert, Schwartz, & Reiss, 2003), such as pop-up ads and animation (A. Lang, Borse, Wise, & David, 2002) on Internet sites
- High imagery that engages audience imagination and cognitive resources
- Humor (Valkenburg & Janssen, 1999)
- Emotional valence (Simons et al., 2003)
- Novelty in photographs
- Comprehensibility and action (Valkenburg & Janssen, 1999)
- Prominence cues, such as story placement, headline size, story length, pictorial treatment, and frequent repetitions (Graber, 1988)
- Large size of message (Lombard, Reich, Grabe, Bracken, & Ditton, 2000)

Cognitive Triggers. While many triggers are hardwired into a person's brain, these natural perceptual triggers do not account for all triggering activity. There are also cognitive triggers—that is, algorithms that are learned or constructed by individuals to alert them to particular messages. Hawkins et al. (2002) made the point that biologic processes do not account for attentional inertia as much as cognitive strategies. We learn these strategies through repeated exposures until the sequence of techniques in these strategies is applied automatically.

Filtering algorithms consist of heuristics that allow people to seek out messages in the most efficient manner possible. These filtering algorithms are shaped by three factors: knowledge of the media, personality traits, and information-processing skills. A person with more awareness of media, vehicles, and messages will have more options. For example, if a person has a great deal of knowledge about books (i.e., how books organize knowledge and how books are organized in libraries), he or she will have more options in using libraries and books to seek out information-type messages. This message-seeking algorithm is also constrained by a person's personality traits, especially those most related to the message-seeking task, such as field independency, need for stimulation, and tolerance for uncertainty. For example, people who are field dependent, have a low need for stimulation, and have a low tolerance for uncertainty will generally exhibit a personality trait pattern that is weak on message seeking. And the message-seeking algorithm is constrained by the level of a person's message-processing skills, such as analysis, evaluation, grouping, induction, deduction, abstraction, and synthesis.

Continuing in an Exposure Flow

When people begin exposing themselves to a particular media message, they enter a flow. This is not the flow of being swept away by a message and losing all track of time and place. Instead, flow means the continuing experience of the message; thus, exposure flow begins with the exposure and ends when the exposure ends.

While people are in an exposure flow, they are continually monitoring the exposure for value. By value, I use Schramm's (1973) economic conception of expectation of reward divided by effort required. This task is performed with little mental effort and usually runs automatically. It is governed by the procedural algorithm I am calling *monitoring value.* The code in this procedural algorithm directs people to notice certain elements in the message and compare them with general expectations. Cast in economic terms, the running decision is about value, which is defined as a favorable comparison of resource expenditures with expected benefits. As long as the value is positive, the exposure flow continues. When value drops, the person feels dissonance and is likely to switch to another message exposure or terminate all media exposures.

Expected Benefits. Benefit expectations are highly variable and keyed to a person's individual perceptions. The benefits obtained refer to either informational or emotional returns.

When a person is seeking information, there is a satisfaction obtained from acquiring the particular facts sought. The intrinsic satisfaction is an expected benefit. There is also an extrinsic satisfaction when the person has an expectation to use the information in a conversation or written document that will impress another person.

As for entertainment, the expected benefit is pleasure, that is, a pleasurable emotional experience. Freud (1922) said that one of the primary things that governs human behavior is the pleasure principle. He argued that all psychological activity emanates from the ongoing need to reduce emotional tension, which is produced biologically. Pleasure is experienced in tension-reducing activities. But people do not automatically seek pleasure all the time; they learn to forestall immediate gratification so as to achieve even greater pleasure in the future. When humans do this, they are following the reality principle. However, the reality principle is weaker than the pleasure principle, and it is more vulnerable to breakdown. Freud also said that humans tend to reproduce previous emotional tensions over and over again; they like the repetition. Mendelsohn (1966) built on Freud's ideas and applied them to the mass media in his book *Mass Entertainment.* He said that when we watch fictional stories on TV or in films, we experience parasocial interactions, and this helps us relive and then reduce emotional tension. Also, laughter helps reduce tension.

It is this pleasure principle that is primal and that, as a narcotic, pulls people into continuing exposures so as to continue the flow of pleasure. Recall that pleasure in this sense is not intense orgasmic-like experiences; instead, it is the continual immediate gratification of the experience releasing tension from the worry of stressors in everyday life.

Resource Expenditures. The other key factor in the determination of value is the perception of expenditures of resources. When resource expenditure is primarily psychic energy, the key to the decision is the person's base of appreciation. This base of appreciation is the knowledge and skills one has developed to process the meaning of messages. For some people, the base is strong, and therefore the costs of processing otherwise difficult messages are low. Other people have a weak base of appreciation, and the costs are very high to process many kinds of messages. With very high costs, the chances are low that people will find value in processing those messages, so they do not expose themselves to those messages.

The most important key to understanding value in processing messages is the base of appreciation. To illustrate, let's take the example of a Shakespearean play. With such a play, the language, character development, and theme are much stronger than 99% of that of television series and commercial movies. So why don't Shakespearean plays get the highest ratings? The answer to that question is that the value is low to most people, not because the payoff is potentially high but because the costs are so high. If people have a strong base of appreciation, their costs are much lower, and the value equation is much more favorable.

The base of appreciation is not the same as age, although it is related to age—that is, people with stronger bases of appreciation are generally older. But not every adult has a base of appreciation superior to every child. Nor is the base of appreciation the same as education, although the two are related. The purpose of a high school education and especially higher education is to build a person's knowledge structures and skills. This is not to say that all college graduates have a wide base of appreciation; one college student might take a wide range of courses in a liberal education, while another student takes essentially the same course 40 times. Both graduate with a degree, but the former has created 40 really different knowledge structures that act kind of like 40 tent poles that hold up a very broad canvas of human knowledge.

Exposure Inertia. When people are experiencing a flow in a particular exposure state, they usually want that flow to continue because it is easier to continue in the same flow state than to make a switch. Thus, when people are filtering out media messages and paying attention to the events in their social world, they want to continue filtering out media messages. Likewise, when people are filtering in a particular message, they want this flow (same message, same exposure state) to continue. This is exposure inertia.

In the default filtering-out procedure, the flow is keyed to the exposure state. For example, people in the automatic exposure state experience the filtering out of all media messages and want to stay in this flow of ignoring all media messages. In the filtering-in procedure, the flow is keyed to both the particular media message and the exposure state. For example, a person watching a movie in a theater will want to continue watching that movie and remain in the transported state while doing so.

There is a range in the degree to which people want to protect an exposure flow. At the low end, people protect the flow because it is simply easier to continue with what one is doing than to make the effort (however small) to change. At the high end, people find the flow so pleasurable that they do not want it to stop or to be altered in any way.

Ending a Message Flow

Exposure flows can be ended through either triggering or erosion. With triggering, something in a new media message or social world experience connects with a salient element in a person's filtering algorithm (such as an existing need), and the person's attention is shifted to the message that triggers attention. Also, when people's emotions or cognitive elements dramatically change, they will quickly shift to a new message or exposure state. For example, people who are watching a horror movie on television in the attentional exposure state could experience sudden heightening of their emotions (such as through content cues of explicit or graphic violence) and quickly shift into the self-reflexive exposure state, where they are aware of their shock and see themselves arguing against the producers of the program who felt it necessary to show such a depiction. Or people might stay in the attentional state and switch channels to continue their exposure to television but with a less disturbing message. Also, people who are enjoying their favorite program and viewing it in the attentional channel might suddenly have that enjoyment interrupted by a break for commercials, and they shift down suddenly into the automatic perceptual channel throughout the string of ads.

Erosion can also account for the ending of an exposure flow. Audience members will become vulnerable to competing messages attracting them away from a particular flow when a message exposure degrades to a point where there is little or no value to continue. This perception of value is influenced by the perceived degree of payoff compared with the required costs associated with continuing the exposure. However, even when the message value degrades, exposure to that message can still continue if there are no attractive messages competing for the audience members' attention at that time.

Conditioning Algorithms

How do the media condition audiences for filtering decisions? The answer is that the media shape people's filtering algorithms. This is not to say that the media are the only influence; instead, people can shape their algorithms when they are aware of their motives, goals, and experiences.

The algorithms differ in terms of the degree to which they have been programmed by individuals and through media conditioning over time. Some algorithms are built by each individual through experience with message seeking. During these experiences, people learn how to seek messages and thereby favor certain techniques that they have found to work in the past and stay away from those techniques that they have found frustrating in the past. However, when people are in the default state of automaticity, the media exert a conditioning influence unchecked by the individual. The media shape a person's algorithms by reinforcing the use of certain triggers and by atrophying other elements through nonexposures.

The mass media have been increasing their conditioning and hence algorithm programming power with the development of newer forms of delivering messages. This can be seen in the way the newer media deliver their messages compared with the way the older media deliver messages. With print, which is the oldest of the mass media, consumers have had almost all the control over exposures. Books could not expose themselves to consumers; people have had to take the initiative to go out to a store or a library. Magazines and newspapers were a bit more intrusive because they were delivered to our doors, but we needed to subscribe in order for this to happen. Also, with all forms of print, we controlled the exposure sequencing and pace. We could begin reading a magazine with any story, read the stories in any order, and read the stories as fast or as slowly as we wanted. Thus, with the print media, we exerted a relatively high degree of control with all the important exposure decisions: whether to be exposed, which stories to read and in which order, the timing of the exposure, and the pace of the exposure.

With the arrival of electronic media, new forms of control were established that contrasted with print media. In the 1920s, radio was introduced, and people began to lose some of their control over media exposure. Of course, radio requires that someone turn on a radio receiver in order for information to flow, but once the audio is in the environment, everyone is exposed. In this way, radio is more intrusive than print. Also, radio controlled the timing, sequence, and pacing of the messages. If you wanted to listen to a particular show, you had to tune in when the program was broadcast. You had to listen to the messages in the order they were broadcast. Radio producers also gained control of the interruptions (for ads) and when to suspend the story (as in serialized stories). Of course, some magazines presented serialized stories, but an audience member could wait for all issues to be published and then read them all at once; this was not possible with serialized radio dramas. Radio, and then television, trained us to structure our lives around certain times when their shows were broadcast; they trained us to tolerate interruptions for commercial messages; and they trained us to develop weekly habits of exposure.

Over time, some technological innovations have been made available to give people the potential for more control over media exposures. For example, tape recorders and then MP3 players enable people to rearrange audio messages through editing; also, people can control the playback time. VCRs do the same for video. And computer software (Web browsers and search engines) seems to give people more control over searching for information. But in order to use these technologies, we have to expend more effort. We also have to scan more messages to make our decisions about what to record or use, and this serves to increase our exposures. Therefore, most people stay with their media-shaped habits of exposure most of the time. Also, these technologies have hidden features that serve to reduce our control while making it appear that they are increasing our control.

Table 9.4   Audience Filtering Propositions

Audience 1: Audience members will stay in a particular exposure state (and hence continue the perceptual flow) as long as they perceive continuing value in that state and as long as there is no triggering element to pull them into another exposure state.

  1.1: Audience members stay in the automatic state until a message element triggers them to cross the line into the attentional state.

  1.2: Audience members stay in the attentional state as long as they perceive value from continued exposure to the message. Value is an ongoing perceptual judgment made by the individual audience member.

  1.3: Audience members stay in the transported state as long as the message powerfully resonates with their experience.

  1.4: Audience members stay in a self-reflexive state as long as they perceive value from continued exposure to the message. Mental costs are highest in this state, so benefits must be perceived to be very high in order for people to perceive value from the exposure.

Audience 2: The most powerful general motive for exposure is economic efficiency, where value is determined through a comparison of resources expended during an exposure to a media message with benefits expected.

  2.1: Information is of greater benefit when

        It meets an existing need, either long-standing or acute.

        It can be easily incorporated into a person's existing knowledge structure on a topic and makes a useful extension to that existing knowledge or fills in an important gap.

        It is counter to a person's existing knowledge structure but can still be quickly incorporated into that structure; thus, this information is surprising, and its acquisition is deemed valuable as a correction to previously incorporated faulty information.

It puts the person in a position to do something he or she could not do without that information.

2.2: Entertainment is of greater benefit when

It provides the pleasure of continuing with a comfortable habit.

It provides an emotional jag with a positive valence.

It facilitates the achievement of a personal goal such as providing an emotional shock needed at the time to alter something dysfunctional or aversive in a person's life.

Audience 3: The greater the perceived benefits from the exposure in comparison to perceived costs, the stronger the conditioned drive to seek additional exposures of this message type.

Audience 4: The filtering task is governed by algorithms that are programmed by both the individual and the mass media.

4.1: Filtering task—the algorithm keeps the person in the state of automaticity and thus filtering out all messages from awareness until certain triggers are recognized in the flow of media messages. These triggers are programmed both by the mass media (through conditioning) and by the person (through conscious decision making).

People will remain in a state of automaticity with meaning-matching tasks as long as they can easily identify an orienting node in appropriate simple associative networks (SANs).

If they cannot identify an orienting node in an appropriate SAN, they will either go to an authority to learn the denoted meaning of the referent or give up the task.

The default state is the automatic state where a person stays in a filtering-out mode until attention is triggered. This exposure flow is governed by a filtering algorithm, which is a set of rules (or heuristics) programmed by the person as well as by the media.

- Person programming—learned through previous experience
- Media programming—conditioned habits by the media

4.2: Filtering task—in situations where efficiency is a dominant goal, people devote little psychic energy. They are not highly cognitively involved (analytical) and instead make filtering decisions emotionally (intuitively or based on what feels right). To the degree that accuracy is more important as a goal, people become more active cognitively and develop elaborate searching strategies.

For example, Internet Service Providers (ISPs) and search engines make people feel that they are in control of their Internet searches, but these devices constrain people's access. ISPs have links to favored Web sites while excluding others. Search engines cannot possibly access more than a small percentage of Web pages, so the decisions concerning which pages to access lie at least as much with the search engine company as with the user.

We are at a time when the number of messages bombarding us is at an all-time high, and it continues to grow. The providers of those messages are at a high point in being able to control our knowledge, our attitudes, and our behaviors. However, at the same time, we have more potential now than ever before to control our own exposures and their effects on us, but sadly, few people recognize this potential. Most people are too fatigued by the onslaught of messages to confront it consciously. Or people who do want to confront the problem and gain control for themselves are not sure about what to do.

Conclusion

Mass media researchers have focused primarily on motives in trying to explain why people expose themselves to media messages. This research has provided useful insights into exposure decisions that are primarily conscious, novel ones. However, over the long term, most exposures are governed by habits that were set in motion by the individual but were conditioned and shaped by the media. Thus, we require a different conceptualization of what governs exposures.

This chapter elaborates the media exposure model by focusing on the filtering task. Filtering decisions vary by exposure states. In each exposure state, there is a different dominant algorithm.

CHAPTER 10

Audience

Meaning Matching

Recall from Chapter 1 that there has been a considerable debate among communication scholars regarding the degree to which meaning resides in the message. The question is, do people learn denoted meanings for symbols (D. G. Ellis, 1995; J. Thompson, 1995), or do people construct their own meanings during media exposures (see, e.g., Barthes, 1975; Bochner, 1985; Deetz, 1973; Foucault, 1984; Grossberg, 1993; Shotter & Gergen, 1994). This debate in essence concerns how much of communication is meaning matching and how much is meaning construction. In the lineation general framework presented in this book, I argue that both are common and essential. In this chapter, the focus is on the first and more fundamental of the two—meaning matching.

This chapter illuminates the meaning-matching task by exploring four topics. First, it examines meaning matching as a process. Second, it explains how people acquire the authoritative meanings required in the meaning-matching task. Third, the chapter explains how algorithms are used in the meaning-matching task. And fourth, the chapter shows how meaning matching occurs in the four exposure states.

If media scholars are to shift from a Generating-Findings to a Mapping-Phenomenon perspective, we must delineate much more carefully in our research those information-processing challenges that involve meaning matching and meaning construction. We need to provide some sense of how much of the processing of media messages involves meaning matching and how much allows for—and more important, actually exhibits—meaning construction. And within the meaning-matching tasks, we need to understand much more about how we acquire our meaning-matching knowledge and apply it so automatically.

Process of Meaning Matching

Each act of meaning matching is composed of two phases. In the first phase, people encounter a message and must recognize a referent within it. In the second phase, people match the referent with the meaning they have stored in their memories. This second task is essentially one of recalling definitions as triggered by referents. Meaning matching is a relatively easy task when definitions for referents have already been acquired and when they are easily accessible.

Matching the meaning is rarely a single act of completing the two tasks; more typically, it is a process composed of a series of acts. Sometimes the process is long and involved, such as working with many referents of different kinds (i.e., auditory, visual, word, pictures, social situations, etc.). The longer the media message, the longer the meaning-matching process because each element in the message needs to be matched to its denoted meaning. Media researchers need to study this process to develop explanations for how the mass media expand referents and a common knowledge about referents.

Recognizing Referents

All media users must first go through a process of extracting elements from the chaos of raw stimuli that compose any message. This process is primarily perceptual because it requires a person to scan the perceptual field, usually visually or aurally or both. This process is also cognitive because the person needs to know what referents are and how to recognize them.

I am using the term *referent* as others might use the term *symbol* to refer to units in messages that signal meaning. I avoid using the term *symbol* because a great deal has been written about it, and much of that writing is peripheral to the focus I am trying to achieve here. So rather than use a term that will signal to many readers that they should expect a much broader and detailed treatment than I am presenting here, I use the term *referent* to keep attention focused on the idea of meaning matching alone.

Referents are any unit of signaled meaning in a message. For example, if I present the word *dog,* that should signal the same class of animals to all readers. If I present a picture of a four-legged creature about knee-high, wagging its tail, and being held by a leash, that picture is also a referent for the same meaning. Or if I played a tape of a bark, then that too would be a referent for the same meaning. Referents can be a word, a picture, a graphic, a drawing, movement, a sound, a touch—anything that signals an association with a denoted meaning stored in memory.

Sometimes this process is almost purely perceptual, such as making sense of the perceptual elements on a television screen. The stimuli elements on the television screen are really individual dots of one of three colors that blink off and on rapidly. However, what we perceive is moving pictures composed of the full spectrum of color.

Some referents are words, so we need to know what is a word compared with a letter, a sentence, a line of type, and so on. Some referents are elements in pictures, so we need to be able to recognize form, dimension, and perspective. Some referents are audio, so we need to be able to distinguish among voice, music, and sound effects. And some referents are movements on a screen; we need to be able to recognize a cut, dissolve, pan, zoom in, and so forth.

With newspapers, young children will look at the front page and will "see" the same thing as an adult but will not be able to extract many elements. Young children can recognize that certain things are pictures, but they will not be able to extract any of the words or graphics; that is, they will not be able to distinguish the boundaries of the referents there. They need to learn to recognize referents as units.

Children begin orienting to the TV screen as early as 6 months of age (Hollenbeck & Slaby, 1979). They are able to start recognizing referents and learning the meaning of those referents as young as 12 to 24 months (Meltzoff, 1988). Attention to the TV screen increases as they age, until about age 10 (D. R. Anderson, Lorch, Field, Collins, & Nathan, 1986). During this time, they are learning more referents and larger form referents. At age 10, they are well into the concrete operational stage (Piaget & Inhelder, 1969), so they have the cognitive capacity to handle referents of different sizes. Also, their experience has reached a point where they have developed competencies to process those messages in a relatively automatic manner.

Associating Referents With Meaning

After we have isolated a referent, we match the referent with a meaning that has been previously learned—that is, we automatically connect it with its denoted meaning. For example, we memorize the definitions of words and the conventions of grammar and expression to be able to read. From the experience of listening to radio, we know that certain sounds signal the lead-in to news, certain voices convey humor or seriousness, and certain sounds convey danger or silliness. With television and film, we learn the meaning of a flashback, an extreme close-up on a character's face, character stereotypes, and what to expect in the unfolding sequence of a detective show. We have learned to connect certain referents with certain meanings.

Once people recognize a referent in a message, they automatically access the relevant node in their relevant simple associative networks (SANs). This referent node is connected to a definition node and perhaps several other characteristics relevant to the referent, each with its own node. When the definition is closely linked to the referent, the path that connects the nodes is short and usually well traveled. The more a person makes an association (between referent node and definition node), the more traveled is the path that connects them.

Retrieval from memory begins with a referent that cues a path to a memory bit. We check the stored information and make an assessment of how closely the stored information matches the cue (probabilistic assessment). If there is a high probability of a match, then we think we have the memory. If the match is low probability, then we cycle through other paths to retrieval, sometimes having other cues triggered.

As an example, let's say people open the newspaper and read a sentence: "The President met with his cabinet today." The individual words *the, met, with,* and *his* have easy associations with one meaning. *President* requires a bit of context; the capitalization and the story itself would give readers enough to make the connection as the President of the United States and evoke that person's name and image. The word *today* requires a bit of context; readers need to look at the date on the paper to find out if it is today's newspaper, in which case today means today, but if this were yesterday's newspaper, the word *today* in text means yesterday. Finally, the word *cabinet* requires knowledge of how the executive branch of government is structured and that the word does not refer to a piece of furniture but instead to a set of high-level advisers who run the major departments in the executive branch. There are some demands on the reader to bring some context to the situation, but those demands are rather small, and the task of bringing some context is likely to be accomplished by all readers the same way, so this task remains within the domain of matching meaning because it requires very little interpretation or construction.

Acquiring Meaning-Matching Knowledge

By the time most people reach adulthood, they are able to speak, read, and write a language. Barsalou (1992) observed that "individuals typically know the meanings of over 50,000 words, and they know the characteristics for thousands of different kinds of things (e.g., of birds, cars, jungles, astronauts, weddings, complements)" (p. 148). How do we acquire this information?

Sources of Learning

The early part of life for all humans is occupied with the task of learning to recognize referents and learning what they mean. These referents are, essentially, sensory stimuli. Infants look at their hands and study the shape through the movement of color patterns on their retinas. They have to learn that the color and shape are a sensory stimuli representation of a part of their bodies. Infants also learn to recognize the pitch and tone of their parents' voices. They need to recognize that sometimes the voice is happy and sometimes it is anxious. Toddlers need to learn what is safe to touch and what is hot or sharp. There are thousands of sensory stimuli that youngsters must recognize as distinct referents and then learn their definitions, that is, their meanings as prescribed by authorities.

People learn these definitions by absorbing the associations. For example, a young child who touches a hot stove will quickly absorb the association of the stove with pain. Children learn to associate certain body movements with certain goals. Children absorb the association of certain expressions on the faces of their parents with certain feelings. Early childhood is consumed with the task of learning to recognize certain things as referents and absorb the association of those referents with their denoted meanings. Thus, the emphasis is not on constructing one's own unique meaning but rather on absorbing the associations that are naturally presented in the environment, that is, the presented meaning.

For millennia, parents and siblings were the primary conduits for teaching these referent-meaning connections to children. Then, several hundred years ago, with the spread of formal schooling to all children in most industrialized countries, the institution of education joined families with this role and expanded the range of learning to include many abstract referents (words and numbers) to develop basic competencies in reading and math. Children enter another layer of referent recognition when they enroll in school. The primary goal early in school is to help children learn how to look at lots of squiggly lines on paper and break them down into individual referents, such as words and numbers. These referents do not have natural connections to meanings (like between fire and pain upon touching), so children cannot absorb these on their own; instead, they need to develop the skill of memorizing the connections. Through memorization of the referent-meaning connection, people acquire enough authority-sanctioned meaning to make communication possible.

The institution of education also expanded to deal with the challenge of defining the physical world (referents in science) and the civic world (through history and government). It became a dominant authority that sanctioned the importance of certain referents (the words and pictures of certain people, places, times, and ideas) and provided the meaning of each of those referents. Becoming educated meant acquiring enough of those referent-meaning connections to be able to share the meaning with the educated public and continue to make broad-scale communication possible. Some scholars talk about "cultural illiteracy" (D'Souza, 1991; E. D. Hirsch, 1987), by which they mean either (a) that people have not acquired enough recognition of the common referents that constitute their culture or (b) that people cannot associate those referents with the authoritative meanings. When there is not much shared meaning across people in a culture, the culture is fragmented—that is, people do not share enough common meaning to converse with each other efficiently. So a person referring to ideas, people, and events would have to stop continually and explain to his or her listeners what those ideas, people, and events mean.

Over the past century or so (with the rise of film, then radio, and especially tele-vision), the mass media have grown in importance and have reached a point where they join (and perhaps even surpass) the institutions of family and education as a major authority on teaching referent-meaning connections.

Process of Routinizing

As a person learns the definitions for referents and practices the recognition of referents and accessing definitions, the process of meaning matching becomes more and more automatic. Eventually, certain referents will become very familiar, and the appearance of one of those referents will immediately evoke a definition with almost no mental effort. This means that the connection between a particular referent and its denoted meaning is so reinforced through use that the meaning is "taken for granted"—that is, people don't think to question where the denoted meaning came from. As this becomes more automatic, our speed at processing referents increases, as does our confidence in our ability to access the memorized meaning accurately. There is little chance we will get lost in this process, and there is little demand for creative activity or any kind of thought process that is not automatic.

When the meaning matching in a particular area is highly routinized, I refer to this as a competence. For example, when people can read a simple newspaper story, they have developed a basic-level reading competence. Most people are fairly competent at the meaning-matching task because it uses competencies that are learned at a rela-tively early age. Even young children understand story formulas and the meanings of many words. Once people have acquired the competencies of the task, meaning matching is usually accomplished with great efficiency because people can perform it automatically.

The task of meaning matching—much more than either the tasks of filtering or meaning construction—relies on competencies rather than skills. Competencies are contrasted with skills in the sense that competencies are dichotomous; that is, either they can be performed or they cannot. But the application of skills is not dichotomous: Skills are highly elastic and range over a wide continuum of ability. For example, we all exercise the skill of analysis, but some people are only able to exercise analysis at a very limited level, while other people are very powerful with the skill of analysis. Competencies require little practice to become learned, and once learned, they cannot be improved much if at all; also, they rarely atrophy. In contrast, skills—such as analysis, evaluation, classification, induction, deduction, abstraction, and synthesis—can each be performed at a very elementary level, but it takes considerable practice to improve to high levels of performance. Skills are tools that people develop through practice. The more skills are used, the stronger they become; when they are not used, they atrophy.

To illustrate this distinction between competency and skills, think of "reading" as it is taught in elementary school. Children learn to recognize written and auditory referents and then memorize their denoted meanings. They learn how to vocalize those symbols and how to fit those symbols together into sentences. These are com-petencies. By the time people have reached secondary grades, most of them have acquired a reading competency; this is what is meant by reading literacy. As reading is taught beyond the elementary grades, it is treated less as a competency and more as a skill. Students focus on how to get more meaning out of paragraphs and stories. For example, when teachers ask students to read aloud in elementary school, it is to check students' competencies at word recognition and pronunciation. But when teachers ask students to read aloud in high school, it is to check students' skill at reading for meaning and expression.

Role of Algorithms in Matching Meaning

Algorithms are essential in the meaning-matching task. To illustrate, let's consider a very simple meaning-matching task of being exposed to one word in a newspaper and matching meaning to it. If audience members are literate at reading, they are likely to be able to recognize almost all words in a typical newspaper and have a memorized denoted meaning stored in their memory. Thus, they have a SAN with the particular referent (the word) linked closely with the denoted meaning. This is the most simple and basic unit of declarative knowledge—a referent/meaning pair algorithm with its two-node simple associative network. However, the person needs more than this algorithm to accomplish the meaning-matching task, even one as simple as this one. The person needs guidance in recognizing what the referent is, and this task requires guidance from a procedural algorithm that guides him or her in the identification of referents; this is the task of unitizing.

Unitizing

Referent recognition is a fairly sophisticated task. It is essentially the challenge of unitizing. To very young children with no meaning-matching competencies, all messages are chaotic flows of stimuli. Breaking up a continuous narrative into referent units is a challenging task. As young children learn this task through trial and error, this information is stored in a procedural algorithm. People are able to "detect and process edges and other discontinuities in display, [and] they infer detailed world structures by extrapolating from partial views" (Pomerantz & Lockhead, 1991, p. 11). The *referent unitizing algorithm* helps people do this.

The task of recognizing a referent is essentially being able to delineate the perimeter of the referent, and this requires a sensitivity to what I will call level and span. Level refers to how general a referent is, and span refers to how long it continues in the flow of the message.

At what level is the referent? Some referents are micro (such as a letter or a word), while others are much more macro (such as a novel or an entire body of an author's work). For example, when you analyze a novel, you have lots of options for what a referent is. At the macro level is the entire story. Within this macro unit of the entire story, there are subunits or chapters, paragraphs, sentences, and words. There are also larger units than the message, such as the author (and his or her body of work), the vehicle setting (which includes the context of the medium and the vehicles in that medium), and the culture (history). The more levels one recognizes, the more options for analysis, and the more media literate the person.

Span is usually linked to level but not always. For example, in a newspaper story, a paragraph is longer than a sentence; the paragraph is also at a higher level of generality than a sentence because each sentence in a paragraph should address the same idea of the paragraph. However, span and generality need not be the same. For example, let's say a conversation between two characters in a movie continues for several minutes while they drive to a store, walk through the store, get back in the car, drive home, and continue the conversation at home. Viewers of this movie must determine what the unit of conversation is. On the surface, it appears to be one continuous conversation. But what about the scene changes? Perhaps the scene changes signal a substantial change in time, and the conversation depicted in 2 minutes of screen time represents 2 years in the characters' relationship. Or perhaps the conversation changes topics, in which case it is perhaps no longer the same conversation, even though the same two people are talking.

Associating

After a referent has been recognized, a procedural algorithm then directs the person to an orienting node in a declarative algorithm. If the declarative algorithm is a SAN with only two nodes, then the accessing of the orienting node (the referent in the media message) automatically leads to the second node (memorized denoted meaning). For example, you are introduced to the host of a party. You have a node with the person's image and another node with his or her name. Later when you see that person to say goodbye, it is easy to link up the face with the name. Of course, if you are like me, it takes several meetings for me to learn this link and be able to access that person's name when I see her or his face later.

There are times when the orienting node is associated with more than one other node, and the problem arises about which path to take, that is, which direction to go to find a node with the stored meaning that is appropriate for matching meaning in this situation. In this case, we need to access another procedural algorithm—referent/meaning cluster—that guides us by showing us which path to take from the orienting node through the network of other nodes. For example, if someone mentions the name of someone you know well (such as your mother, father, sibling, or best friend), you are likely to work out from that name node to many, many others, each with an image, a story, adjectives, emotions, and so on. Which path do you take? The procedural algorithm tells us to consider the context in which the name of the person was mentioned. For example, if someone mentions the name of your friend in a conversation about a personality trait—let's say trustworthiness—then the algorithm directs you to connections where memories of your friend exercising this trait reside.

With these associative networks, when people encounter a referent in their environment, they access that referent in memory and move out quickly to a node where the associated definition is stored. If they want more information on the referent, they move out through other links to the next set of most closely associated nodes. Thus, this model of thinking is called the spreading activation model. Because ideas are linked in networks, when people access one idea, they are able to make associations to other closely linked ideas. As they access each node, it is activated. When people want more information, they continue to activate other links to more and more nodes.

The more an algorithm is used, the easier it is to use. There are several reasons for this. One reason is that with use, the algorithm is more accessible; that is, it is easier to find and therefore requires less psychic energy to locate. Also, once the orienting node is accessed, the connections out from that node to other nodes are well established; the connections can be made automatically with little thinking involved. Thus, the more experience one has with particular kinds of media messages, the more knowledge one has about those messages (well-developed declarative algorithms) and the more facile is one in navigating those messages (well-developed procedural algorithms). Experience leads to efficiency and thus to the ability to stay in an automatic state during an exposure and thereby minimize the expenditure of cognitive resources.

Meaning Matching Across Exposure States

Recall from the media exposure model (Table 7.2) that meaning matching differs across the four exposure states. In the automatic state, meaning matching is routinized with a very high degree of efficiency. In the attentional state, meaning matching is still fairly standard and automatic, but it also includes meaning-matching tasks that require some decision making. This state also includes the learning of referent-meaning connections. In the transported state, meaning matching is again highly automatic but also very personal. And in the self-reflexive state, meaning matching requires a good deal more mental energy as people examine their existing referent-meaning connections, critically analyze them, and make alterations.

Automatic State

This is the most common form of meaning matching. If it were not, then the meaning-matching task would continually require a degree of effort that would make its use prohibitive to the degree it is used. For example, after a person learns to read a written language, the meaning-matching task of reading is largely automatic.

Meaning matching in this state is highly routinized, thus making it very efficient. Audience members rely on standard connections between referents and meanings. The referents are usually highly familiar and easy to recognize in media messages. The cognitive link between a referent and its prescribed definition is usually short and strong, and thus the association can be made easily. Also, the links are typically singular—that is, there is one and only one link to a definition, thereby keeping things simple. When the links are singular, short, and strong, the associations are made consistently, quickly, and habitually. The meaning-matching task is typically automatic.

Once the person has familiarity with the referent and its common definition, the meaning matching can be done with almost no effort or thought. The tasks of referent recognition and meaning matching are relatively automatic and therefore can be done in a parallel manner. This means that a person can do several automatic tasks at once. There is no bottleneck of information processing, such as what Broadbent (1958) proposed. Broadbent's bottleneck model says that a person's mental apparatus includes a central processing system that receives inputs from sensory channels and compares them with items stored in the memory system to determine their meaning. Overload of the central processor is prevented by means of a selective filter interposed between the central processor and the outside world that sifts incoming stimuli by letting through those that have certain properties and excluding others. For example, at a party where there is music and loud talking, a person will filter out everything but the sounds of the person he or she is talking to. If the person tries to monitor two conversations at the same time, a bottleneck occurs because the mind cannot shift back and forth between the two simultaneous conversations at once. But if a person is watching a familiar TV show and making small talk with a roommate, both can be accomplished at the same time through parallel processing because both processes are automatic. When a person is engaged in a process that is not automatic, the processing is serial—that is, it requires the person's full attention, and other tasks get bottlenecked, waiting for mental resources to become available.

Attentional State

In the attentional state, meaning matching is still fairly standard and automatic, but it also includes meaning-matching tasks that require some decision making, such as context-reliant meaning matching and deductive meaning matching. Both of these forms of meaning matching require more effort and concentration than is required in the automatic state.

With context-reliant meaning matching, the definition is not singular, so we must select among different definitions using the context of the message. For example, there are times when we will easily recognize a referent and look for an association with a definition but then find that the association is not singular; that is, there are several definitions associated with that particular referent. In this case, the process of meaning matching requires a bit of conscious reflection. In this conscious reflection, the person needs to make a decision about which association to sanction, that is, which is the proper definition for the referent *in this situation*. To make this decision, the person needs to consider the context of the referent.

Context-reliant meaning matching is more involved than automatic meaning matching. The person needs to concentrate not just on the focal referent but also on contiguous referents to make some sense of the context. With automatic meaning matching, the task is always regarded as being fully specified. However, there are situations when one can recognize the referents, but there may be several different definitions for those referents. Thus, the task is only partially specified. But the person can still solve the task on his or her own by looking at the context.

With context-reliant meaning matching, the person looks at the referents contiguous to the focal referent as context, and the context can be used to select the most appropriate definition for the referent in question. For example, when reading a book, a person might come across the word *bad*. This is likely to have more than one meaning. *Bad* can mean "not good," but it can also mean "very good." *Cool* can mean a "low temperature," "a chilly demeanor," "a laid-back attitude," or "very good." Which meaning do we match? It depends on the context of the sentence in which it is used.

Context is also important to consider with sets of referents. For example, the idea conveyed by a sentence often has more to it than the simple sum of the meaning of each word. The arrangement of words and the grammar as well as punctuation are important. For example, if two characters are kissing and one says, "Don't! Stop!!!" that conveys a very different meaning than if the character says, "Don't stop." And the way the sentences are arranged into paragraphs and stories conveys more meaning than the simple sum of the idea conveyed in each sentence. If you read about a mother saying "You are so smart" to her child, the meaning can change given the overall story. If the mother has just seen her child brag that he can take his bicycle apart and fix it but in the process he destroys it, the context indicates that the mother's comment is sarcastic. But if the mother has just looked at the child's report card and sees all excellent grades, the context indicates that the comment expresses sincerity and pride. In all of the examples above, the sense of the messages cannot be fully derived by making an association on only the focal referent because there are several potential meanings for the focal referent. To make sense of the focal referent, one must also consider the contiguous referents and factor the context into the selection of a definition. While it is more complex, it is still a fully specified task—that is, the person has enough information in the focal referent and the surrounding referents to derive one and only one sense from it. Also, while this requires more effort than a simple matching of meaning, it can still be accomplished in a relatively simple manner.

In accessing the context, there are times when a person will need to do more than consider the focal referent in the context of contiguous referents. Sometimes a person must try to infer patterns from the referents provided. The inference then becomes a meta-context. One way of doing this is to think about the sender of the message and see the message from his or her point of view. This is called local rationality (Woods & Cook, 1999). Every message sender has multiple goals, and sometimes the goals are in conflict with one another. Human problem solvers "possess finite capabilities. They cannot anticipate and consider all the possible alternatives and information that may be relevant in complex problems. This means that the rationality of finite resource problem solvers is local in the sense that it is exercised relative to the complexity of the environment in which they function" (Woods & Cook, 1999, p. 149).

The person sending the message is working from a particular perspective that supports the message. Understanding that person gives the receiver the ability to get inside the rational system that is the world of the sender. In this task, knowledge structures are more useful than associative networks. Knowledge structures include much more information that can help the receiver understand the world of the sender; this cannot be achieved with simple associative networks.

With context-reliant meaning matching, oftentimes people will take a shortcut and simply choose the first association they find and not bother to check to see if there are other definitions associated with the referent. In the condition where there are several definitions, one of those associations will usually occur to the person first.

Another meaning-matching challenge that requires an attentional state of exposure is deductive meaning matching. At times, the task of meaning matching relies on the skill of deduction. With deduction, people observe a specific occurrence and access a general principle to explain it. The general principle is the conventional definition rule. People perceive a set of referents that becomes a larger set referent, and then they look for a principle that could explain that larger set referent. This is more complex than looking for a simple referent and making a simple match. For example, when people are watching a new family situation comedy, they might access a principle that family sitcoms feature a father who is a buffoon; a mother who is the strong, rational family member; and kids who are quirky. This is the family sitcom formula; people who know this formula (general principle) are in a good position to quickly and efficiently construct the meaning of the show they are watching. But if they do not know this formula or do not have a general principle to use in order to deduce meaning, then they need to construct a general principle to help guide them in this task.

The more complex the meaning-matching task becomes, the more mental effort is required from the person, and the more likely the task is transformed from meaning matching to meaning construction. As the task moves away from automatically associating a referent in a media message with a previously learned meaning, more judgment is required from the individual. The higher the degree of judgment required by audience members, the more likely there will be a range of meaning found associated with the referent. And a variety of meanings across audience members is characteristic more of meaning construction processes.

Transported State

In the transported state, meaning matching is again highly automatic but also very personal. The meaning-matching task is very efficient as in the automatic exposure state, but the connections are much more of a personal nature. Thus, the meanings are personal memories, strong desires, and needs that are idiosyncratic to the individual. Also, they are much more emotional than cognitive. Thus, the meanings are less like definitions of referents and more like feelings triggered by the referents. The feelings resonate strongly with the person's past emotional experiences or with the person's fantasies.

Self-Reflexive State

In the self-reflexive state, referents are matched to their denoted, remembered meanings, but then these connections are examined critically. This state is usually triggered in an exposure flow when the message ceases making sense to the audience member or when the person feels that he or she is being lied to, exploited, or manipulated. This sense of discomfort or anger motivates the person to avoid taking the usual meanings for granted. The person sorts through his or her understanding of meanings and alters those meanings that are inconsistent.

Conclusion

Meaning matching is an essential step in processing information. When people encounter massages, they must recognize the referents in those messages and access the conventional definitions of those referents. These definitions are learned from authorities early in life and then stored in memory. When referents occur, these trigger an association with the remembered definition. Meaning matching relies on competencies that are learned early in life and then practiced automatically from that point forward.

Table 10.1   Propositions for Audience Meaning Matching

Audience 5: The formulas used in the meaning-matching task are largely definitional and have been provided by authorities and internalized by the person so their use is automatic. They require basic competencies to perform well.

  5.1: People automatically recognize referents and automatically associate the prescribed meanings they have learned and frequently applied in the past.

  5.2: People will remain in a state of automaticity with meaning-matching tasks as long as the orienting node is linked to one and only one definitional node.

   If the orienting node is linked to more than one node, but the information in each node is complementary with the information in all other nodes linked to the orienting node, people will stay in the state of automaticity and choose one node for meaning.

   If the orienting node is linked to more than one node, and the strength of the connection to one node is much stronger than the strength of connection to any of the other nodes, people will stay in the state of automaticity and choose the strongest linked node for meaning.

CHAPTER 11

Audience

Meaning Construction

Thtt he previous chapter laid out the meaning-matching task. Now in this chapter, we take up the related topic of meaning construction. Recall from the previous section that matching meaning is primarily decoding; that is, audience members recognize referents in the media messages and match those referents with their denoted meaning that has been memorized and resides in a person's set of associative networks. To be prepared for meaning-matching tasks, people acquire information from authorities outside themselves. This information can be learned in one exposure and, once learned, can be repeatedly accessed automatically with little effort.

With meaning construction, I draw from the ideas of Frank Parkin, Stuart Hall, and Dallas Smythe. To illustrate, sociologist Frank Parkin (1972) argued that meaning from messages is not uniform across all kinds of people but that people of different social strata construct different meanings of the same message. People bring their own experiences to bear on the construction of meaning. Stuart Hall (1980) built on this idea that the meaning of a message does not always reside exclusively within the message. Hall pointed out that producers encode meaning into messages, but the audience members must decode that meaning and, in so doing, create a received view. Dallas Smythe (1954) argued a transactional view of audiences (i.e., the media present messages), but "audience members act on the programme content. They take it and mold it in the image of their individual needs and values. In so doing they utilize not only the explicit layer of meaning in the content but also innumerable latent or contextual dimensions of meaning" (Smythe, 1954, p. 143).

In this lineation general framework, I argue that the meaning construction task does not simply invite people to construct a meaning for themselves; instead, the meaning construction task requires it. It is not the human condition of free will that accounts for this process; instead, it is the partially specified nature of many media messages that requires people to "fill in the gaps" and, in so doing, arrive at a construction that varies across people. It is not that the culture has only some highly creative, highly skilled people, strongly motivated by the exercise of free will, who construct meaning for themselves, while the rest of the population mindlessly defaults to accepting all the meanings they are presented. Everyone is confronted with meaning construction tasks every day.

When individuals construct meanings for themselves, typically there is variation in those meanings across individuals. The differences in those constructed meanings are attributable to the influence of three factors. One factor is the individual person's declarative algorithms. These contain information about past experiences with media messages and real life. Because these vary across individuals, the product of using them in meaning construction will vary across individuals. For example, highly political people will construct meanings with political shadings. People with a skeptical attitude and ironic sense of humor will typically construct meanings that are perverse. A second factor is the individual person's procedural algorithms that contain guides to addressing the meaning-matching task as well as skills that can be used to bridge gaps and create new information. Because skill levels and the detail in procedural algorithms vary across individuals, the product of using them in meaning construction will vary across individuals. A third factor is the individual person's motivation to address a particular meaning-matching task. Because motivational levels vary across individuals, the product of meaning construction will vary across individuals. When motivation is low, the meaning that is constructed is likely to be very similar to past constructions or to the same constructions that other people are making. However, when motivation is high, constructions can be more creative, more insightful, and more elaborately individual.

If media scholars want to evolve from a Generating-Findings perspective more to a Mapping-Phenomenon perspective, they need to treat meaning matching and meaning construction very differently and not confound the two. With meaning construction, scholars need to examine how the mass media allow for and even demand divergence of meaning across audience members. Scholars also need to examine the important issue of why many audience members do not make the effort—even a small effort—to construct meaning when messages allow for it but instead often default to meaning matching.

Problems in Meaning Construction

The meaning construction task is almost always less automatic than meaning matching because it is a partially specified task—that is, there are elements missing in the task that prevent it from being automatic. This means that people find themselves in one of four problem situations. One problem situation is that they do not have an existing algorithm to help them fully match meaning, so they must construct meaning on their own. Second, people have a declarative algorithm, but it is missing essential information that would help them fully match meaning so they must construct their own meaning to bridge over the missing informational gaps. Third, people have a procedural algorithm, but it is not precise enough to delineate all the steps involved in a prescriptive manner—that is, it allows freedom of choice of meaning options and paths—so people can only use the algorithm as a guide, not as a fully specified prescription. And fourth, the media message itself is ambiguous; that is, it does not fit with a person's existing algorithms, so the person does not know which algorithm to select as a guide.

When constructing meaning, people usually need a higher degree of motivation, which includes a drive to spend more mental energy along with a conscious goal that guides the path toward satisfying that drive. However, oftentimes people will not want to spend the additional mental energy to consider the array of options they may have available to them in bridging gaps, so they will drop back into a meaning-matching perspective and choose the easiest available meaning.

The Process of Meaning Construction

The meaning construction task is triggered when people realize that a meaning-matching process cannot be used to determine the meaning of a media message. People begin by picking out the salient elements of a message and try to find meanings for those referents stored in memory. However, either there are no stored meanings, or there is something missing in the message to guide a person to making simple associations with simple associative networks (SANs). The person realizes that gaps in the information provided by the message or by the person's background knowledge prevent the person from making simple associations and arriving at a satisfying determination of meaning. This realization creates a motivation to construct meaning. The next step is either to find more guidance in one's existing knowledge structure or to try to resolve discrepancies in the media message.

Assessing Information

The process of making good meaning constructions begins with assessing the amount of information one has to address the immediate task of meaning. Typically, meaning construction challenges are partially specified problems because the information a person has does not match the requirements of the task. Let's take a closer look at the nature of partially specified problems. Below we will examine three types: under-information challenges, over-information challenges, and barren-information challenges.

Under-Information Challenges. These problems are presented to us with information missing, so they clearly appear as partially specified problems. The challenge for solving this type of problem is to access more information, either from one's knowledge structures or from additional sources of information.

This "filling in of information" serves to render the problem fully specified. However, completing the information set does not also transform the task into one of meaning matching because it lacks the convergent solution. People are likely to bring different sets of information to the problem, and each information set bends the construction process in a different direction. Because people's knowledge differs substantially across individuals, the inputs into the process of solving partially specified problems substantially differ (E. R. Smith, 1999). Thus, people arrive at different meanings rather than all converge on the authority meaning. Each person may have a high value for his or her constructed meaning, so we cannot say that one solution is the correct one and the others are faulty.

Over-Information Challenges. Sometimes problems are presented to us with too much information. The amount of information may be overwhelming, and it might present us with a figure-ground problem where we get lost in all the trees and cannot find the forest. In this case, we must sort through the information and discard that which is irrelevant. We must also make the more difficult discriminations about which information is background to the more relevant foreground information. When an algorithm does not provide guidance to make these sorting decisions, the algorithm is missing something, and the problem is partially specified. We are confronted with examples of this type of problem every time we turn on the television. There are so many viewing options. Even if we decided we wanted to watch a movie, there are still at least half a dozen movies on at any given time.

Sometimes we are presented with a problem that offers multiple options and multiple criteria to select options. If we use criterion A, we will clearly select option X, but if we use criterion B, we will select option Y. Which criterion should we use? The algorithm does not specify a criterion, so all criteria are relevant, and the problem is therefore underspecified. Our first task in solving such a problem is to simplify by rejecting all but one of the possible criteria. For example, let's say we begin watching a movie and we are confronted with the problem of deciding whether it is good enough to continue watching or whether we should switch to another movie. What do we look for in the movie to solve the problem of deciding if the movie is worth watching? There are many criteria. Do we focus on the actors, the plot, the setting, the overall look of the movie, or the genre? We need to select a clear criterion, then use that criterion as a filter and reduce the information set down to a manageable size.

Barren-Information Challenges. Recall from above that there are under-information problems, and the task is first to get more information. But there are times when there is no way to access additional information that will fill in all the gaps to solve the problem in a systematic manner. These are barren-information problems.

The challenge for solving a barren-information problem is to engage in a reasoning process that allows one to bridge over the gaps in information rather than to be stopped by those gaps. This can be done with hypotheticals, where people can ask "What if?" questions and speculate what would happen if X were the case. In this way, people are plugging X into the gap as a bridge, and this allows them to move on down the path to decisions about the overall meaning of a message. Of course, it is important that people not lose sight of the nature of X, that it is speculation and not accurate information. Instead, people keep in mind that the bridge allows them to continue down a path to a solution that is only tentative.

Accessing More Information

With all three types of partially specified problems presented above, there is a need to check for more information. People cannot tell if a problem is an under-information type of problem or a barren-information type of problem until they try to find more information. Also, when people work on problems that are initially presented to them as being over-information and they pare away irrelevant information, they often end up finding that some crucial information may be missing, so they too need to search out more information. There are two places to look for more information to elaborate the problem at hand: outside sources and inside one's self.

Outside Sources. Additional information to solve partially specified problems can be gathered from sources outside the person. With outside sources, there are some obvious things to be concerned with, and these are—in order of how difficult they are to ascertain—credibility of the information source, the accuracy of the information, and the completeness of the range of sources.

The credibility of the information source is the easiest to ascertain. One needs to consider if the source, whether it be a vehicle or a person, is a reasonable conduit for the information. This means whether the person has access to the generation of the information. Therefore, a scientist who has made a discovery is likely to be a good source of information about that discovery. However, there are some people who are close to the generation of information but should not necessarily be regarded as credible. For example, if a political candidate makes a blunder, that candidate's press secretary is close to the candidate and hence close to the generation of the blunder, but the press secretary is not likely to be a credible source of information about why the candidate blundered; the press secretary's agenda is to spin the blunder to make it look planned and actually a brilliant move. So for a source to be credible, the source needs to know more than the accurate truth; he or she also must be trustworthy enough to transmit the truth.

The accuracy of the information is also an important consideration. To test this, people need to check the information against more than one source. If all sources provide the same information, then many people think the information must be accurate. However, accuracy is not determined by elections. People should give credibility to consensus information only when the various sources of that same information are each expert and trustworthy.

The completeness of the range of sources is the most difficult to test because it requires a constant search for more *types* of sources. By types, I mean sources that are likely to present a different perspective on an issue and hence present different information to support their perspectives. The mass media tend to simplify issues by reducing them to two sides. For example, in political races, the mass media typically limit their coverage to one candidate from the Republican Party and one candidate from the Democratic Party.

Inside Sources. When looking inside one's self, it is better to rely on well-organized knowledge structures than on informally derived SANs containing unconfirmed intuitive impressions cobbled together with heuristics. Good knowledge structures help people see the context of the problem more fully, and this helps in (a) focusing on the central essence of the problem and not getting lost in the details, (b) providing more information to fill in the gaps, and (c) selecting criteria to make good choices to proceed down a path to a useful solution.

Bridging Over Gaps

Frequently, people will not be able to find the information or guidance they need to bridge all the gaps and thereby turn a partially specified problem into a fully specified one. There comes a point when people must make a decision about continuing to try to find information, give up on the task, or take a shortcut that will get around the gap. Oftentimes, people will take shortcuts, which have been called heuristics (Kahneman & Tversky, 1973). These heuristics are very valuable in allowing people to get past gaps and proceed in the meaning construction task, but the use of heuristics often can lead to systematic errors (Tversky & Kahneman, 1974) and the construction of faulty meaning. Tversky and Kahneman (1974) highlighted three types of heuristics. One of these is the representative heuristic; this involves using similarity to make judgments. If we ask people how much X resembles Y, people will make a judgment based on the degree to which they believe X is a member of the Y class of objects. Fallacies arise with this heuristic because people fail to take into consideration base rates and sample sizes.

Another one is the availability heuristic, where people estimate probability or frequency based on the ease with which instances can be brought to mind. Of course, it is easier to think of instances from a large class of objects than from a small class of objects, so this shortcut often works. However, it is sensitive to the salience of instances.

The third heuristic is anchoring and adjustment, where people estimate an uncertain value by starting from some obvious value (anchor) and adjusting in the desired direction. The bias here is with the anchor; if people start with a faulty anchor, they will make bad decisions.

Heuristics are important, even with their obvious limitations. Without heuristics, people would often get stuck in the middle of meaning construction tasks and be unable to complete them.

Traps

Meta-memory judgments are the judgments about what information exists in one's memory. These judgments generally have been found to be accurate in the sense that people know whether they have some information on a topic. But much of the information they have is inaccurate (Payne, Klin, Lampinen, Neuschatz, & Lindsay, 1999). I will discuss four of these types of inaccurate or inaccessible information below. Each one is a trap that prevents people from constructing good (accurate and useful) meaning.

False Memories. Individuals are vulnerable to illusions of remembering. False memories may arise from external suggestive influences or when people mistake their internal thoughts (associations, fantasies, and dreams) for what actually happened. People are often very confident in false memories and sometimes claim to remember details of the episode in which the event supposedly occurred (Lampinen, Neuschatz, & Payne, 1998). One explanation for false memories is that sometimes people will store information from different kinds of experiences together. Then, when they go to access some of those memories, other closely stored memories are also recalled as being part of the same event (E. R. Smith, 1999). Also, "potential sources of inaccuracy in memory reports include not only the respondents locating and using the wrong representation in memory, but also defects in the perceiver's interpretive and constructive processes" (E. R. Smith, 1999, p. 252).

Confusing Media-World Knowledge With Real-World Knowledge. There are times when the information we bring to bear on a problem may be an accurate memory, but it was from the wrong "world of experience," thus making its applicability to this problem questionable. For example, sometimes we get disoriented and use a media narrative memory, which we have developed through media exposures, when we should be using an event memory, which we have developed through

exposures in our everyday social world. If we go to a party and ignore all of our previous experience we have had at real-world parties and instead expect to participate
in a party as it would take place in a Hollywood movie, this can get us into trouble
or embarrass us at the party or, at minimum, make us feel enormously disappointed when the party turns out not to be as glamorous or intense as we expected.

One of the problems with elements in memory and their organic growth of linkages is that media elements can get linked easily with real-world elements. When we
initially make an association between images and meanings, it is easy to remember
whether the image was from a media message or a real-world encounter. But over
time, the linkages can get rearranged, and we can confuse media- and real-world
images; thus, we might see a real-world image and trace its meaning back into a
media meaning. This is another reason why knowledge structures are better than
SANs, because the higher degree of construction that goes into fashioning knowledge structures makes it less likely that the two worlds will become confused later.

Inert Knowledge. When people are presented with a problem on a topic, they naturally go to the most relevant algorithm and seek out information to provide more
context for their meaning construction. But oftentimes, there will not be enough—
or any—information that will help with the current problem. In this case, people
need to seek out the information in other knowledge structures. This is relatively
easy if the knowledge structures are linked. But often they are not linked, and this
makes it difficult to find the relevant information when it is catalogued in a non-
linked knowledge structure. In this case, the knowledge is regarded as being inert
(Woods & Cook, 1999). This means that people may possess some knowledge and
be able to use it in one situation or with one type of problem, but they cannot
access it to solve another type of problem.

To avoid the situation of inert knowledge, people need a high degree of coupling.
Coupling is the degree to which the components in a system are linked. The more
the components are linked, the more the effect of a problem in one component can
cascade and influence other components (Woods & Cook, 1999). However, too
many linkages can create another problem. When every node is linked with every
other node, there is no efficient structure. The large number of links makes the
network very complex. Also, the activation of any one node will necessarily spread
out to all nodes, and this provides too much information. A better way to organize
nodes is through nestings where like ideas are nested together and fully linked within
a nest. Then the nests are linked together. This is rather like an outline. This form of
linking offers efficient access to all nodes in a branching pattern and thus eliminates
the possibility of accessing all nodes through spreading activation whenever one
node is accessed.

Assuming Shared Meaning. In all communication situations, people assume a high
level of shared meaning. Oftentimes, people will hold what is called *common ground*
(Clark & Marshall, 1981), that is, share the same mutual knowledge. In these situations, communication is accurate and efficient. But when the sender and receiver
do not share *common ground,* problems arise. In interpersonal communication,

people can monitor their conversations, and when they suspect a lack of common ground, they can clarify meanings, thus restoring the value of the communication.

Monitoring common ground is especially challenging with mediated communication. Senders know general things about their audiences (such as their demographics) in order to create their target audiences, but senders are largely ignorant about substantive characteristics. Also, there is no chance for feedback. This lack of true interaction raises three levels of problems: (1) The receiver knows he or she does not understand the sender's meaning but cannot ask about it, so he or she is frustrated; (2) the receiver thinks he or she may not be understanding the message as intended by the sender but cannot confirm this suspicion; or (3) the receiver believes he or she understands the sender but does not, so false impressions arise and are reinforced. The last problem is the most serious because the receiver does not know he or she is misunderstanding, so he or she cannot discount the message. The media are particularly good at creating this third problem because they make people believe that there is common ground by presenting message elements (images, characters, events, etc.) that look familiar and that are easily understandable to receivers. But often these message elements are highly complex. Because the media often do not deal with complexity, they mislead audiences.

Algorithms by Exposure States

Not all meaning construction tasks are equally important and warrant a high degree of mental effort. Some can be accomplished with a relatively small degree of effort and are guided by a criterion of efficiency, while other meaning construction tasks are much more important and are guided by a criterion of accuracy. The degree of effort put into the meaning construction task as well as the experience in undertaking these tasks differs across exposure states. Below, I will only sketch out the use of algorithms in the attentional, transported, and self-reflexive exposure states because these states require audience awareness and effort and so the process is more accessible. However, because the automatic state is so prevalent and operates largely at an unconscious level, I will examine the use of algorithms in more detail for this exposure state.

Attentional Exposure State

When a meaning construction task is very important and when people are in formal learning situations, they are willing to invest some mental energy into the meaning construction task. They are willing to think consciously about the gaps in information and in reasoning processes, and they are willing to spend some cognitive energy in searching for more information to bridge those gaps. Also, they are willing to be more formal in the use of skills and work through a more complete and more logical process in the construction of meaning.

Audience members are also likely to use heuristics in the attentional state. Although heuristics are regarded as shortcuts, their use does not always mean that people are unwilling to expend cognitive energy and are therefore in an automatic state of exposure.

Instead, there are times when a person continues in an attentional state and cannot find the particular information needed to bridge over a gap, so he or she will use a heuristic to allow him or her to continue making progress down a conscious path of meaning construction. Thus, heuristics can be more than shortcuts; they can be bridges over gaps in a meaning construction problem. It is too limiting to think of heuristics *only* as techniques for people in a hurry. It is better to think of them more broadly as alternatives to a formal logical process of problem solving. When a formal logic process is available, then heuristics are, of course, shortcuts. But there are times when a formal process is not available; in this case, heuristics are the only alternative. This is the case with most partially specified problems. Remember the problem $24 = X + Y$; solve for X and Y? No formal process is available to take you to one and only one accurate answer. So you use a heuristic to bridge over the gaps in information. In this case, we speculate that X is 1, for instance. This then allows us to solve for Y with certainty. A bridge heuristic is used when the problem-solving path has a gap—that is, there are elements missing that are not part of the problem, and thus the problem is partially specified. If you stop at the gap, you cannot proceed all the way to the end of the task. So you must use some kind of a heuristic to bridge over the gap.

Transported Exposure State

Meaning construction in the transported exposure state is similar to the attentional state except that the construction is much more personal and emotional. People continually construct meaning to keep themselves in this state of exposure; this is why the transported state involves them so strongly. The meaning that is constructed is a highly personal one where audience members continually factor themselves into the story so that they begin to feel that the action is happening to them.

Self-Reflexive Exposure State

Meaning construction in the self-reflexive exposure state is focused not only on the product of the process but on the process also. Thus, audience members undertake the careful relineation of their existing knowledge structures. Thus, they not only use their knowledge structures or add new detail to them, but are also likely to rearrange the structures themselves.

Sometimes these alterations of knowledge structures are done outside the person's awareness and control where the media rearrange meanings. The media influence on meaning construction is especially powerful when people are in the automatic state of exposure and are not aware of media message conditioning. Over time, knowledge structures are changed outside of the person's control or awareness by a process of accretion. That is, when the media continually present a certain message pattern that is outside of a viewer's perception, the mental formula gets shaped by the media—not the viewer. For example, when viewers watch television, they can recognize acts of violence, but over the long term of viewing, it is not possible for them to "recognize" an accurate percentage of violent perpetrators who are male. No one keeps a running count of all perpetrators categorized by demographics, so the processing of this type of information is outside of the perception of viewers. For example, television has been constant for the past 50 years in showing about 70% of all perpetrators being male. Over time, viewers "have become accustomed" to expect males to be the perpetrators.

Sometimes these alterations to a person's knowledge structures are done by the person himself or herself through the careful applications of skills in the service of trying to reach a certain goal. This is what is characteristic of higher level meaning construction and media literacy. Elsewhere, I argue that increasing media literacy requires people to spend more time in the self-reflexive state, where they are most careful to construct their own meanings and, furthermore, where they can deconstruct the meanings that the media have programmed into their memories while they were in the automatic state of exposure (see W. J. Potter, 2004).

Automatic State

Meaning construction can also take place in the attentional state. However, in this state, judgments about meaning are made very quickly and very intuitively. In his book *Blink: The Power of Thinking Without Thinking,* Malcolm Gladwell (2005) wrote about this phenomenon. Gladwell said that people typically make snap judgments about all kinds of things when they first encounter them—people, foods, music, talent, and so on. He called this the "theory of thin slices," where people notice a particular attribute about a person's face, for example, and make a quick intuitive judgment about that person's mood, character, or employability. Gladwell argued that these initial impressions are often as accurate as impressions that are made only after a great deal of research on a subject. Of course, people vary in their ability to make their snap judgments accurately, and there are times when people are wrong. But the point is that these snap judgments are right often enough to convince people that quickly jumping to conclusions is a worthy thing to do, especially when they consider the alternative of devoting major resources to investigate the phenomenon in more detail before making a judgment.

In the automatic state of media exposure, people are interested primarily in efficiency and therefore do not want to expend much mental effort in completing the partially specified tasks of meaning construction. They want to quickly resolve discrepancies and bridge gaps to arrive at meanings with as little effort as possible. They simply want to get some meaning quickly from a message and move on to the next one. They use techniques of bridging gaps with heuristics, quickly resolving discrepancies, and relaxing the expectation for logic.

One technique is to bridge gaps with heuristics. When people are motivated more by efficiency than by accuracy, they want to arrive at a solution to a problem as quickly as possible, so they take shortcuts, that is, use heuristics. Tversky (1972) introduced the idea of heuristics as rules of thumb or mental shortcuts that people use to reduce the amount of effort they need to expend in solving problems rationally. Heuristics are judgmental shortcuts that people use in times of uncertainty. Rather than gather more information systematically and reason carefully, they are more motivated by efficiency, so they want to take shortcuts to arrive at conclusions quickly and thus reduce their uncertainty. S. T. Fiske and Taylor (1991, p. 381) explained that heuristics are helpful especially when people seek efficiency, that is, a means to arrive at a reasonable solution as quickly as possible. To do this, people employ heuristics because of time constraints, complexity, volume of information, or uncertainty about the information.

The heuristics tend to keep people in SANs, where the effort required is much lower than in series or hierarchies. This simplifies the task, and people look for the closest associations in the simple networks. Thus, the advantage of using heuristics is efficiency. But there are risks to using heuristics because in the quest for efficiency, people typically sacrifice accuracy. If the heuristic is the only tool available, its use is good in the sense that it can reduce uncertainty, but if more powerful or systematic tools are available, then its use is usually a poor choice because the person could reduce uncertainty to a higher degree and much more accurately by using other tools and not using the heuristic as a shortcut. Thus, it is a mistake to oversimplify because it will result in distortions or misconceptions (Woods & Cook, 1999).

Sometimes a task is partially specified because the message presents conflicting information, and the person must decide which bits of information to accept and which to reject. Or a message presents consistent information throughout the message, but all that information is in conflict with the person's existing knowledge base. When there are discrepancies, people must resolve them. If they are governed by a goal of efficiency, then they are likely to use shortcut techniques of leveling and sharpening.

Leveling is the ignoring of differences. When people perceive a difference between what a message says and what they know about a topic, they tend to ignore these differences. For example, let's say people read a columnist they respect who says that something is a serious problem because of X. People have had experience with X in their own lives and do not see X as contributing much to a serious problem, so they erode the negativity out of what the columnist says about X so that the discrepancy about the columnist's perception of X and people's perception of X is eliminated.

Sharpening involves making elements in a message more salient so as to bring the message into conformance with a person's own view of things. For example, when people think of Z as a risky behavior and a movie portrays Z but does not show it as particularly risky, there is a discrepancy between what the person believes and what the movie portrays, so people will read into the movie some negative consequences for characters who do Z, thus sharpening that element in the movie and making it more salient than the producers intended.

These techniques, although sometimes applied in a relatively automatic manner, are regarded as meaning construction because people alter the elements in the message as they incorporate those elements into their existing knowledge structures, and this alteration changes the meaning to suit their purpose. This is relatively low-level meaning construction because it requires a low degree of mental effort and is motivated more by a desire for efficiency.

A third technique used to get through the meaning construction task as quickly as possible is to relax the expectation of formal logic. Solving a partially specified problem often requires a realization that a purely logical process is not possible. That is, the gaps in information required to be purely systematic prevent a step-by-step logical reasoning process. This is not to say that there is no chance to be logical at all. Instead, it requires that one understand that there are various challenges in the meaning construction task; some of the tools that are most useful for working on certain parts of the problem are logical, and some of the tools required for working on other parts are not.

To illustrate, let's consider how people use rules to categorize objects. A classic example of a partially specified problem that requires meaning construction is illustrated in a study where Hampton (1982) asked his participants, "Are typewriters office furniture?" Participants struggled with the logical inconsistency that typewriters were office furniture in many ways but not furniture in many other ways. People who use logic exclusively will not be able to provide a satisfying answer to this question because they have to reconcile different definitional rules. Instead, people must arbitrarily give more weight to one set of definitions over other sets, and then they can resolve the problem.

Cognitive psychologists have long recognized that the human mind is not only a machine-like calculating device; it can also take shortcuts, can reason intuitively, and is subject to emotion. If the mind could not do these things, we could not solve partially specified problems. This idea of nonrationality shows up quite prominently in cognitive psychology. For example, Hammond (1996) said that all judgments fall along a continuum ranging from analytic at one end to intuitive at the other, with quasi-rational in between. Barsalou (1992) said, "Many psychologists have concluded that human knowledge does not follow logical form closely. This is not to say that human knowledge is illogical, but only that other factors play more significant roles. In other words, human knowledge is generally non-logical" (p. 150). Simon (1957) argued that humans are neither rational nor irrational; instead, humans show a bounded rationality—that is, there is a range of reasoning processes that are relatively rational but not completely systematic. Simon created the idea of *satisficing,* which is a strategy that does not require us to consider all possible options and then carefully compute the relative merits of each as a means of maximizing our gains and minimizing our losses. Instead, we consider options one by one until we find one that satisfies our minimum level of acceptability and then go with that option. The advantage of this strategy is that it minimizes the number of options we must consider before making a decision.

Conclusion

Meaning construction requires people to solve partially specified problems. Too little information leaves gaps in the meaning construction process. Too much information can confuse people about what is most relevant to the task. Barren information is also a challenge because it requires people to find a way to bridge over gaps in the process when no information is possible. Additional information can come from either outside the person or inside the person from already existing knowledge structures.

Meaning construction takes place in all four states of exposure. However, the process of that construction, as well as the extent to which the person is in control of that process, is very different across the exposure states.

Table 11.1   Propositions for Audience Meaning Construction

Audience 6: The algorithms used in the meaning construction task are largely suggestive guides because meaning construction is always a partially specified problem. They require the use of skills to perform well.

6.1: The algorithms vary in stability/flexibility according to task and exposure state.

6.2: People will be more likely to construct meaning when their locus is strong, as characterized by one or both of the following conditions:

   a. They have a strong drive for control.

   b. They prefer mindfulness over automaticity during exposures.

6.3: People will be more likely to construct meaning (rather than accept the meaning in the messages) when the information-processing flow presents one of the following characteristics:

   a. People are faced with a strong skepticism about the meaning in a message.

   b. People are faced with an information task that has strong negative consequences if they act on faulty meaning.

PART IV

Explaining the Media Messages Facet

CHAPTER 12

Media Message Line
of Thinking

The lineation general framework suggests a particular line of thinking about mass media content that helps us evolve from a Generating-Findings perspective to a Mapping-Phenomenon perspective. The key explanatory construct for media messages is the "narrative line," which is introduced in this chapter and then elaborated in the following three chapters.

The narrative line is the key to understanding media messages. It is used by producers to construct their messages and by audience members to process the meaning of those messages. Media scholars need to analyze media messages for their narrative lines because the narrative line is a very useful construct that incorporates ideas from all four facets of the mass media phenomenon; therefore, it is an important contributor to the rim in the bicycle wheel metaphor introduced in Chapter 2.

Introducing Message Line of Thinking

Options Maze

People who construct messages are confronted with a very large number of decision points, and at each decision point, there are usually many options available. When a person selects a particular option at a decision point, the person goes off on that option's path and soon arrives at another decision point with its own set of options. To continue in the process of message design, the person must select one of the options at that decision point and then move down that option's path to the next decision point. The process of designing a message can be regarded as navigating through the maze of options. I refer to this as a maze because it is a complex of paths where the traveler must continually make decisions at forks in the road. Some paths are dead ends, and the person must retrace his or her steps and choose another path. Success lies in navigating one's way through the maze to the end. With media message producers, success lies in completing all the design decisions so that the message can be produced.

We can view this options maze as having the overall shape of a pyramid. All potential producers enter at the point where they are confronted with the most general decision, and the selection of an option branches those producers off into different paths that continue branching at each decision point until all producers reach a different place at the base of the pyramid, thus each designing a unique message. This is not to say that the messages do not also share many characteristics. They do share characteristics because producers follow many formulas and conventions.

Formulas and Conventions

Producers of media messages learn formulas that guide them through the options maze. The purpose of these formulas is to make their decision making more efficient as well as to make them more confident that their messages will be more successful. Producers also know that when they follow standard story formulas, they will be better able to appeal to potential audience members and make it easier to hold their attention throughout the message by reducing the psychic costs for those audience members. However, designers of mass media content must also make small deviations from the storytelling formula, so as to generate surprise and suspense and thereby keep audiences interested in continuing with exposures. Storytelling talent lies in knowing how to follow the standard formulas well enough to make processing simple for audiences *and* at the same time knowing when (and how far) to deviate from the standard formulas to keep audiences intrigued.

When media messages are structured by simple, standard formulas, they are easier for audiences to follow, thus reducing the psychic costs for audience members. Audience members use the story formulas as a way of guiding them efficiently through a story. They access their algorithms, where they have stored learned information about mass media stories, and follow the code in those algorithms to help them follow the story line. Some cognitive psychologists believe that virtually all the social knowledge we acquire is through stories (Schank & Abelson, 1995). Wyer (2004) said that narratives are also invoked in the course of understanding the causes or likely consequences of real and hypothetical social events. And Wyer even said that "life itself is in the form of a narrative, consisting of a sequence of temporally related events that we experience as either participants or observers. In short, narratives are fundamental to an understanding of ourselves and of the world in which we live" (p. 3).

When we look across many media messages, we can see certain conventions—that is, there are similar characteristics that keep appearing in those messages. These patterns indicate message conventions. These conventions are evidence in the messages that producers used formulas as guides in the design of those messages.

The Narrative Line

The narrative line is a path a producer took through the options maze. It is not the message itself or the sequence of occurrences in a plot. Each message has its own narrative line because the path each producer takes is slightly different, and therefore each message ends up looking slightly different from other messages. However, the content of many messages shares characteristics with other messages, so there is usually evidence of message conventions, which indicates a sharing of formulas that guided producers through the options maze. Thus, the narrative line is an articulation of the integrated set of formulas and conventions that went into the design of a mass media message. It is descriptive, elaborate, and often inferential.

Descriptive. The narrative line is descriptive in the sense that it provides a list of functional elements in the message. Functional elements are those that were consciously designed into the message to fulfill the purpose of attracting the attention of a particular niche audience, holding the attention of those audience members, and conditioning them for repeat, habitual exposures by stimulating a perception of high value. When an analysis of media messages focuses on these concerns, we maximize our chance of increasing our understanding of message construction. Also, these functional elements have a receiver perspective; that is, they can be viewed as functional to audience members. So we need to examine audiences for what attracts their attention (natural triggers and conditioned triggers), what kind of a build of elements holds their attention, and how they go about perceiving value (both consciously and unconsciously) in message exposures.

Elaborate. The narrative line is elaborate in the sense that it contains an articulation of all decision points along with the options available and the options selected. Thus, the narrative line of any mass media message contains a set of storytelling formulas that reflect producers' decision points, their options, and their selections. It places special emphasis on how the story attracts attention, holds attention, and creates a perception of value in the minds of audience members. The narrative line illuminates the interrelationship among different types of story formulas that include a fundamental story formula, a meta-genre formula, a genre formula, a medium formula, and often series and episode formulas.

Inferential. The narrative line is also inferential in that it requires insight to understand fully. Scholars can ask producers to articulate their decisions, and if producers are willing to spend the time being interviewed and are able to recall all the many decisions they made and why, then this method can generate useful information. However, it is more likely that scholars will analyze the messages themselves, and this will require them to induce patterns of conventions and then infer the formulas and values that were most influential with each decision.

Importance of the Narrative Line

The narrative line has great value as a tool to producers and audiences. For this reason, it is essential that scholars study mass media content in terms of the narrative line to understand why it is so important and how it has achieved its importance.

Producers

The training of producers of media messages is focused on their learning a complex structure of decision making. Producers need to envision the sequence of decisions they must make in the design of their messages and the options available to them at each decision point. And even more important, producers must learn how other producers—especially the most successful ones—typically navigate through all these branches. They learn this by analyzing the messages of other producers, that is, the paths that other producers take through this decision maze. Those paths are the narrative lines of those messages.

Success as a producer, therefore, is keyed to two things. First, the extent of success is tied to the extent to which a person has a complete picture of the options maze. Producers who understand the implications of each decision and where it takes them are in more control of the design process and more likely to create the messages they envision. Second, the extent of success is tied to the extent to which a person has an understanding of how successful producers have made their decisions, that is, an understanding of message formulas and conventions.

Audiences

The narrative line is also important to audiences. Audience members learn to spot particular message elements to signal to them how to go about understanding a media message. The more salient and recognizable story elements are to audience members at the very beginning of a message, the easier it will be for them to process those messages, that is, to locate the appropriate algorithm and to use an algorithm that offers a great deal of familiar guidance to the processing of the unfolding message. When this occurs well, the audience members can accomplish message processing with very low psychic costs. In contrast, when people encounter a message type for which they have no existing algorithm or when the algorithm they use to process the message has a lot of gaps, they experience a high psychic cost; in this case, they will typically terminate the exposure unless the message delivers a high degree of benefits, thus making the high cost worthwhile.

Typically, audience members focus on the *what* of messages and are unconcerned about *why* and *how* producers made their decisions. Keeping the focus solely on the *what* makes message processing much more efficient for audience members and allows them to process the messages in the state of automaticity. However, at times, people will want to conduct more analysis to try to understand more about why they liked a message so much or hated something about it. For example, a person who goes to a 2-hour film in an art theater might spend several hours thinking about the director's work and building a context for the film; then, during the film, he or she is very active in analyzing the elements on the screen, and after the film, he or she continues to construct a more elaborate understanding of the narrative line through conversations with other film buffs. Audience members then can use the narrative line automatically to match meaning or more analytically to construct meaning. This is what many scholars mean by media literacy (see Christ & Potter, 1998).

Scholarship and the Narrative Line

The options maze and the narrative line are essential tools for scholars who are interested in evolving to a Mapping-Phenomenon perspective. Research that elaborates the details and structure of the options maze will provide us with the generic map that illuminates how message design decisions are made. Furthermore, if we build a literature based on narrative lines, we will have a stronger means of comparing across messages and arriving at a clearer picture of the conventions and formulas used most often. This will lead us to a stronger focus on the *why* question, that is, why certain conventions are so prevalent and why producers make the design decisions they do.

Scholars need to consider three tasks when doing a full analysis of a message's narrative line: identifying the full set of formulas and elements in media messages, identifying producer decisions, and identifying audience sensitivities.

Identifying Formulas. This is the primary and central task of message analysis. It is primary because until it is completed well, the other two tasks cannot be undertaken. It is central because it focuses exclusively on the content.

Identifying Producer Decisions. This task links the patterns in a particular kind of message with the decisions producers made in constructing the message. The key analysis criteria are values and accuracy. Values are the motivators behind producers selecting the options they did over the options they rejected. Their decisions reflect their values. The criterion of accuracy raises the following question: Did the producer guess right? This means, did the producer's assumptions about which elements would attract and hold the audience members' attention prove accurate?

Identifying Audience Sensitivities. This task links the patterns in a particular kind of message with the typical audiences for those messages. The analysis looks at the elements, sequences of elements, and clusterings of elements in how they exercise power of attraction and holding audiences. This purpose is central to the mass media organizations' marketing strategy; the more that is known about the audience-building nature of the messages, the better we can understand the practices of the mass media organizations. Also, we need to understand message elements and structures because of two conditions. First, people live in an environment that is cluttered with messages, many of which aggressively compete for their resources, so people default to a screening-out procedure to protect themselves from the flood of messages. Second, mass media companies are in the business of constructing audiences. Therefore, it is extremely important that they attract and hold the attention of audiences, while they can rent their exposures to advertisers. If the media businesses do not meet the challenge well of attracting audience members and holding their attention, they cease to exist.

Conclusion

This chapter presented the narrative line as a guide to examining mass media messages. The term *narrative line* has appeared in the literature. For example, Budd et al. (1999) have used this term to refer to a series of questions and answers or problems and solutions. But a series of problems and solutions is really only the plot-line; the narrative line is much more. The narrative line is not the story itself but instead is *how* the story is told—that is, the decisions that were made in the telling of the story. As such, the narrative line is a set of decisions that confronted producers of the story. These decisions are usually made in sequences and governed by storytelling formulas.

The narrative line is a useful analytical device for scholars because it incorporates concerns inherent in all four facets of the mass media phenomenon. It is concerned with the decisions producers make in telling their stories. That is, what do they think is the right hook, the best pattern of presenting and then heightening conflict; what is the point of view to tell the story, the selection of characters and how they are introduced into the story; and how is the conflict resolved? These decisions are analyzed in the context of the producers' goals, which are to attract and maintain continuing audiences. These concerns are directly tied to the audience facet, with its focus on the needs that exist in cognitive algorithms that allow for triggering of attentional states. What are those needs, how are they arranged in algorithms, and what message elements work as triggers to those algorithms? This leads into the effects facet, where the focus is on alteration to audience members' lines of influence cognitively, emotionally, attitudinally, physiologically, and behaviorally. What message elements have more influence in shaping a person's baseline and why? Also, which factors have the most influence in explaining fluctuations off a person's baseline and why? The process of answering each of these important questions begins by mining the content—looking for patterns in a message and then comparing patterns across messages. While this process begins with a focus on the content, it is not limited to the content; it must follow lines of reasoning into the other three facets. The more carefully scholars follow these lines of reasoning through all four facets, the more useful will be their insights about why the content exists the way it does. I argue that the most useful guide to this process is to think about the narrative line because the narrative line is not limited to any one facet. It is also not limited to any one level of content. Micro units are important but only as elements in building patterns within messages. An inferred pattern in a message is important.

Table 12.1   Structured Glossary of Terms About Mass Media Content

Options maze—the full set of all storytelling decision points and options available to producers of media messages.

Narrative line—the path a producer takes through the options maze in constructing a particular media message. This is not the story itself but instead the series of decisions producers made in the process of creating the message.

Content units—a meaningful segment of media programming. With newspapers or magazines, it is the story (fiction or news). With radio and audio recordings, it is usually the song. With computers or the Internet, it is a screen. With television, the unit is the program; however, the program can be subdivided into more micro units of sequence, scene, or interaction.

Meta-genres of media messages—entertainment messages, information messages, and persuasion messages.

  News messages—the intention of the media is to evoke in audience members a sense that they are being informed.

  Entertainment messages—the intention of the media is to evoke in audience members a sense that they are having series of pleasant emotional experiences, particularly of laughter, character attraction, suspense, or vicarious fear.

  Persuasion messages—the intention of the media is to stimulate in companies paying for the advertising a sense that those ad messages are fulfilling those companies' goals of changing (or reinforcing) target audiences in terms of their cognitions, attitudes, or behaviors.

Simplified conflict formula—this is part of the general story formula that says that conflict that is simple is easier for audiences to follow. Thus, conflict is simple where there are only two adversaries and when they are portrayed as being polar opposites. It is also especially important to the news meta-genre formula, where the complexity of a current event is reduced to two people (or groups or ideas) in head-to-head conflict.

One-step remove-reality—this is a part of the general story formula that says that media messages must appear close to reality (in terms of settings, characters, action, etc.) to ensure that they will resonate with the audience members' own real-life experiences, but at the same time, media messages must "sweeten" that reality to appeal to the imaginations of audience members. This "sweetening" is done by making the characters, settings, and action more attractive.

Contextual characteristics—individual features about the way in which violence is portrayed that provide viewers with information about how to interpret the meaning of the portrayal. Contextual characteristics include features about the perpetrator (such as demographics, appearance, role, consequences), the victim, the environment (such as realism), the narrative (such as justification and appropriateness of the act), and the violent act itself (such as use of weapons and graphicness).

Contextual web—the pattern of contextual variables in a story that signals to audiences how the story should be interpreted.

Programming line—a norm of programming that is imagined by programmers, such that appeal is increased as high as possible without going so far as to offend audience members. Programmers push the line (relineation) by getting away from old, tired portrayals and presenting little surprises intended to pleasantly shock audience members and hold their attention.

Audience appeal—the primary tool used by programmers to attract the attention of as many people in an audience as possible. Programmers believe that appeal is created by arousing the viewers and triggering strong emotions in a pleasant way.

Creative bandwidth—the range of different variations on characters and narratives that programmers try. If programmers limit message elements to very minor deviations from the formula, then the creative bandwidth is very small.

Least objectionable programming (LOP)—selecting content units that have the lowest probability of offending (or challenging) viewers.

Least challenging programming (LCP)—selecting content units and structuring them so that they require the least amount of psychic costs from audience members.

Lowest common denominator (LCD)—programming for the lowest requirements of viewers; it is based on the belief that programs that are more efficient (that are easier to watch and deliver more emotional appeal without offending) will attract the lower tiers of viewers (lower socioeconomic status and lower IQ/education people) without losing the upper tiers (people who want more challenging programming).

Relineation of programming line—redrawing the programming line to keep up with what appeals most to society while avoiding criticism.

Table 12.2   Media Content Proposition

Content 1: The more formulaic a media message, the easier it was for producers to make and for audience members to follow.

CHAPTER 13

Message Formulas and Conventions—General

This chapter and the next build on the ideas of options maze and narrative line by examining message formulas and conventions. In this chapter, I will focus on those message formulas and conventions that are generic to all media messages, and then in the next chapter, I will elaborate on message formulas and conventions by delineating their differences across the meta-genres.

General Story Formula

At the most general level of storytelling, producers use a story formula that under-
lies messages across all media and all genres. Thus, there is a very fundamental
structure for all stories, whether the purpose of the storyteller is to inform, entertain, or persuade. In a sense, all stories are a mix of all three of these purposes and
rely on particular techniques to achieve all three.

Goal of General Story Formula

The way the mass media tell their stories relies on many formulas as old as human
storytelling. However, the mass media must fulfill a purpose that is different from
many storytellers, such as those who spin their yarns around a campfire or on the
back porch. Recall from Chapter 7 that the mass media organizations' primary purpose is to use messages as tools for attracting and maintaining NSL (niche, share,
loyalty) audiences. Therefore, the mass media must tell their stories in a way that will
attract people in a niche, to attract as many people as possible in that niche, and to
condition those people for habitual repeat exposures to subsequent versions of their
messages. To fulfill this purpose, the mass media follow formulas and conventions
that are sometimes different from the campfire storyteller—but oftentimes are
the same.

The goal of producers of mass media messages, therefore, is not just to tell a
story but to tell a story in such a way that audience members will want to continue
exposure to the very end *and* come back for subsequent stories. Thus, producers
must condition audiences into habitual exposures. They do this by continually
giving audience members the perception of maximum value. Audience members
experience value when the continuing benefits from exposure (in terms of satisfying needs for information and emotional experiences) are greater than the continuing costs of exposure (in terms of money, time, and mental energy). This is rarely
done in a conscious, attentional, or logical manner; instead, this continuing assessment typically is performed emotionally and intuitively in an automatic state. Let's
examine these ideas of payoffs and costs in a bit more detail.

To reduce the risk involved in conditioning audiences, producers try to create a
clearly promised payoff that the audience wants. This means that producers are
more likely to try to find existing needs rather than try to create new needs. At the
same time, producers try to minimize the cost to the audience. Cost in this sense
is not limited to financial considerations because the mass media usually want to
maximize the financial cost to the audience, which puts even more pressure on the
minimization of other types of costs, such as time and psychic energy. With time,
producers know that shorter, to-the-point messages are favored by audiences. For
example, if a newspaper reporter can write a story with high impact (information
and emotional kick) in 10 column inches rather than 20 column inches, the audience is more likely to perceive greater value with the shorter story. Also, most readers of popular fiction generally prefer shorter, easier-to-read novels, and most
students prefer shorter, easier-to-study-from textbooks. Popular music is dispensed

in units of about 2 to 3 minutes of song rather than symphony length; these songs feature a simple repeating chord structure. The more that producers follow the established formulas for telling stories, the less psychic costs they are requiring from audience members.

Producers of media messages are also sensitive to emotional costs, which is part of the psychic cost that audiences pay. Emotional costs are unwanted negative emotions generated by the media message. Sometimes, an audience member might want a media message to generate a negative emotion, such as fear or anger; in this sense, the negative emotion is more a payoff than a cost because audience members often seek out messages that will generate these emotions (e.g., horror films, revenge plots). However, there are times when a message will generate an unwanted negative emotion, such as frustration or anger about the message itself; in this sense, the negative emotion is purely a cost. To illustrate this distinction, audiences for horror movies expect to experience the emotion of fear. If the movie's action makes people feel the fear of the characters, then there is a strong emotional payoff, and the emotion is a desired payoff instead of a cost. But if the movie is too graphic and offends the viewers, they will become angry at the producers, and the emotion is more of a cost than a payoff because it takes away from the enjoyment of the media message. To reduce their risks of attracting and holding audiences, producers try to avoid triggering these negative emotional costs in their target audiences.

Designers of media messages must guess at what their audiences will regard as emotional costs and emotional benefits. When designers regard something as a cost to the likely audience, they will try to eliminate it. This is what Klein (1975) was referring to when he coined the term *least objectionable programming* to characterize mainstream television. Klein realized that TV viewing is inertial and that people will continue to view a program unless they have a reason to stop, that is, when the costs become too high and people object to the content, primarily because the content offends them in some way. But this concept can be expanded to cover anything to which an audience member might object, which would include anything that increases the cost of the exposure beyond the benefits experienced. Once producers have attracted an audience, they want to avoid giving the audience members a reason to stop their exposure, so producers seek to avoid offending audience members. Therefore, they try to reduce or eliminate all elements that are potentially objectionable. This consideration must be applied in the aggregate. By this, I mean that X might be an element to which some audience members might object because it violates their personal moral code, but other audience members might regard X as a benefit, such as sexual titillation, the arousal gained from violence, and so on. When producers feel that X will be regarded more as a cost than a benefit to more people in the potential audience, they are likely to exclude that element.

General Story Elements

All stories require certain elements. These elements typically include a hero who has a goal, a conflict that prevents the hero from reaching the goal, and a resolution.

There are always hero characters who are given a challenge to reach some goal early in the story. The goal can be physical (to acquire some possession or some geographical destination), psychological (to solve some puzzle), or emotional (to deal with feelings of love, anger, jealousy, vengeance, etc.). The hero sets off on a journey and encounters a series of obstacles along the path to the goal. Those obstacles can be fate, flaws within the hero, or obstacles created by other characters who are the villains and are working to prevent the hero from reaching the goal.

Conflict is essential in all stories (Barthes, 1975; Eco, 1966; J. Fiske, 1989; Levi-Strauss, 1968; Todorov, 1975, 1977). Stories begin in a state of harmony, and then something disrupts the equilibrium. Conflicts arise, and as the hero resolves each conflict, the conflicts become more challenging. Finally, the hero reaches the goal and is rewarded while the villains are punished. Audience members are motivated to follow the story to see how things will be resolved and how the harmony will be restored.

General Story Structure

The story elements must be assembled into a structure that audience members can follow. To do this, stories follow a logic that is constructed by the storyteller. "Without the spine of narrative logic and suspense, it (the novel) cannot be sufficiently organized to be understandable to the reader" (Smiley, 2005, p. 17). While Smiley was writing about the novel, a logical structure is inherent in all stories.

The general story formula can be traced back through human cultures to the oldest folktales. Folktales, regardless of the culture, can be reduced to a small number of functions and stock characters. In the classic book *Morphology of the Folk Tale,* originally published in 1928, Propp (1968) analyzed Russian folktales to identify their narrative structure. He argued that there were 31 functions or types of events that happen to characters in folktales. These include things such as situations in which a villain tries to deceive his victim, the hero leaves home, and the task is resolved. Propp's ideas have been picked up by scholars in all cultures who recognize the breadth and timelessness of his insights about story structure. To translate the general story structure most strongly into the mass media perspective, the general story formula is structured into three parts: the hook, the story line, and the resolution.

Hook. Message producers must set the hook that can attract as many people as possible of a certain type, thus creating the right kind of audience. The hook is what signals to the audience what the story will be about and why the audience should attend to the story. Therefore, the general message formula tells producers they must make decisions about the hook so that it will do three things simultaneously and well. First, the hook needs to attract the audience. To achieve this attraction, the producer needs to know what the audience members' existing triggers for attention are; then the producer must design the hook to send the proper signal to those prospective audience members to activate those triggers. Second, the hook must tell the audience what the story is about. Producers must convey this essence clearly in a few words or images, so that audience members can activate the appropriate algorithm that will allow them to process the message efficiently and not become confused. And third, the hook must present some compelling reason for the audience members to want to continue with the exposure and therefore continue to expend their limited resources to extend the exposure.

Story Line. Producers must build the story line by heightening conflict that involves the audience more deeply in the action as the message progresses. The building of a story line is a sequence of decisions that producers must make in constructing the middle of the message, which is almost always the largest part of the message. For example, in a half-hour television program, the middle is everything between the first minute and the final minute.

The challenge to producers is to sustain and heighten interest in the progression of the story. The producers must involve the audience members in the action by continually appealing to their emotions and moral sensibilities. The simplest way to do this is to contrast opposites. To illustrate, de Saussure (1966) argued that all stories are essentially the continual interplay of opposites; that is, the villain is what the hero is not. Thus, if the hero is on a quest, the villain is the barrier. All stories are about the friction in the interplay of opposites, such as good versus evil, right versus wrong, life versus death, and change versus tradition.

Satisfying Resolution. Producers must provide a satisfying resolution to that conflict. With entertainment messages, a satisfying resolution typically means that the conflict needs to be resolved with the heroes triumphing and the villains getting their appropriately justified consequences. The hero is the character with whom the audience has experienced the story and interpreted the action. With advertising messages, the resolution involves the use of the product advertised—that is, the product is shown solving a problem in a very satisfying manner.

Techniques

There are several fundamental techniques mass media storytellers use to reach their goals of attracting, holding, and maintaining audiences with their stories. Six of them are multiple appeals, creating presence, point of view, sequence of minor surprises, realism, and branding messages.

Multiple Appeal. Because producers of mass media messages have a strong niche orientation to audiences, they try to provide strong elements in their stories to appeal to the particular needs of a targeted group of people. Given this approach to constructing audiences, it is even better to construct stories with particular elements that would appeal to several niches at the same time. This helps to attract a larger overall audience. For example, producers of action adventure movies will build in a lot of action to appeal to young men, but they also put in a romantic love story to appeal to young women.

Scholars refer to the multiple appeal quality of media texts as polysemy. This means that many different meanings could be constructed from a single text (J. Fiske, 1989). Thus, several different niches can find high value in a single message because each niche "sees" something different of value in that message. There are media scholars (e.g., Butler, 2002; J. Fiske, 1989) who argue that all media texts, especially television messages, are polysemic. These scholars argue that while many different readings of any text are possible, there is usually one reading that is dominant among audience members. Certain meanings are more prevalent than are others; that is, "polysemic potential is neither boundless nor structureless; the text delineates the terrain within which meanings may be made or proffers some meanings more than others" (J. Fiske, 1989, p. 16). Butler (2002) adds, "There is a pattern or structure implicit in the meanings that are offered on television. That structure tends to support those who hold positions of economic and political power in a particular society, but there is always room for contrary meanings" (p. 7). Of course, this makes sense from a theoretical point of view. But from a practical point of view, producers want their messages to have a "dominant reading" for each intended niche audience—that is, there are a variety of meanings available, but all people in a given niche should be making the same reading of the message if the producers created the elements that would appeal to that one niche in a salient enough manner.

Creating Presence. Presence is a characteristic of the media message that moves audience members into the transported state of exposure. Producers want their audiences to get swept away with the media experience and cease to make the distinction between what is mediated and what is real. They want audiences to lose the distance they need to evaluate the message as something apart from them because when audience members become one with the message, they are not likely to stop their exposure (Lombard et al., 2000). Achieving this is a challenge; the ability to do this is a very valuable talent.

Point of View. Producers tell their stories from a particular point of view that will appeal to their audience members. They show the action through the eyes of one person or character. This reduces the emotional distance and personalizes the action for audience members. So when the focal character feels an emotion, the audience is likely to experience a sympathetic response. The stronger the response in audience feelings, the stronger the audience attraction to the message.

Sequence of Minor Surprises. If the message conforms too closely to existing story formulas, it will offer no surprise or suspense, and it risks the danger of boring audiences. So message producers must deviate from the story formulas, but they must be careful not to deviate too much because if they do, this will confuse audience members, thereby raising their costs to process the message, and increase the risk of losing them. Thus, producers must develop through experience the size of the creative bandwidth around formulas. Producing talent lies in knowing how far to push the creative bandwidth around a formula to attract audiences better without confusing or offending them. Typically, the creative bandwidth is fairly small because programmers are conservative, and they do not want to deviate much from a successful narrative line. Programmers usually limit message elements to very minor deviations from the narrative line.

Realism. Audience members are constantly making assessments of the realism in the media messages to which they are exposed. Effects research clearly shows that when audience members believe a message is realistic, it is usually likely to have more of an effect on them. Producers know they need to build in a degree of realism, even when their messages are fictional.

From a producer's point of view, all media stories need to have at least a veneer of realism. J. Ellis (1992) explained that a story "should have surface accuracy; it should conform to notions of what we expect to happen; it should explain itself adequately to us as audience; it should conform to particular notions of psychology and character motivation" (pp. 6–7). Storytellers can deviate significantly from accepted notions, but when they do so, they set up alternative rules for plot and characterization and get the audience to accept them; then those alternative rules must be followed so the audience can follow the different kind of action. There must be a coherent progression in the action where it is obvious what the motivation is for each action and decision; these motivations must come out of the character's psychology. "Realism is a regime of unified portrayal: every criterion of realism aims at the same objective, to combine all the elements of the representation at any one point into a harmonious whole" (J. Ellis, 1992, pp. 9–10).

Several scholars have written about techniques that enhance the reality of media messages. R. Williams (1977) said that drama has three characteristics that make it seem real. First, it has a contemporary setting. Second, it has a focus on secular action—that is, it is human action depicted in human terms. Third, it is what Williams called socially extended, where he meant that drama deals with the lives of ordinary people. J. Fiske (1989) argued that television entertainment is realistic "not because it reproduces reality, which it clearly does not, but because it reproduces the dominant sense of reality. We can thus call television an essentially realistic medium because of its ability to carry a socially convincing sense of the real" (p. 21).

Branding Messages. Branding messages makes them easier to find and helps develop audience loyalty to the message. Media businesses must brand their messages to create a constant presence in the market so audiences can find those messages repeatedly over time. An example of this is with television news. After analyzing national TV newscasts of cable and broadcast networks, Bae (2000) found strong evidence of product differentiation, which is an indicator of branding.

Part of branding messages is the use of stars in media messages. Stars are themselves people who have high brand recognition. Dyer (1998) explained that "stars were a guarantee or a promise, against loss on investment and even of profit" (p. 11) during the building of the film industry. Powdermaker (1950) said that the star system "provides a formula easy to understand and has made the production of movies seem more like just another business. . . . Here is a standardised product which they can understand, which can be advertised and sold, and which not only they, but also banks and exhibitors, regard as insurance for large profits" (pp. 228–229).

Story Formula by Medium

Stories are as old as human culture, but when the mass media came along, stories needed to be translated from the oral medium to a more technological form, such as print first, and then into the visual forms of film, television, and Internet. These translations follow what Altheide and Snow (1979) referred to as a "media logic"—that is, certain characteristics are emphasized and others left out in that translation. The key elements that are salient in the media logic, especially in the late 20th century and today, are fast pace, immediacy, brevity, conflict, dramatization, novelty, and a celebrity orientation. Thus, stories can work off of fundamental formulas developed over centuries of folktales, but when these stories are translated into mass media messages, they need to acquire these additional characteristics.

These translations from oral storytelling to mass media storytelling also must be sensitive to the particular medium that will carry the message. The different media are containers for conveying stories; the contours of those containers shape the messages in that medium. So while the basic story formula is the same, there are features added to the formula by the requirements of each medium. In this section, I will focus on medium changes by length of story and by medium conventions.

Length of Story

Each medium has standard lengths for stories, although some media are much more flexible than others with these standards. The media that are the most mass-like are the ones that have the most formulas for storytelling and are the least flexible with limits on space and time. For example, the broadcast media of radio and television are highly structured by time. With radio, news shows begin on the hour, and deejays work standard shifts, usually 3 hours. Within each shift, there are special times set aside for news and ad breaks. In fact, radio programmers construct a programming wheel that lays out by the second what content needs to be broadcast. With television, almost all shows are either 30 minutes or 60 minutes. They always begin at the top or the bottom of the hour and are separated by advertising pods.

Films are usually programmed in 2-hour blocks, but there is some flexibility here. However, Hollywood films, which are the most mass-like, are much less flexible with time than are independently produced films. The Hollywood film studios know that when a film begins to approach 3 hours or if it is under 80 minutes, its theatrical viability is severely limited. Also, musical recordings are usually 2 to 3 minutes, but as with film, there is some flexibility. Newspaper and magazine stories have a greater latitude of flexibility; however, the length in pages of a newspaper or magazine issue is usually very consistent from issue to issue. Producers of messages for a particular medium know that the medium has conditioned audiences over time for a particular limit on their attention span.

The media also have time-related formulas for the telling of stories. These are episode, continuing series, and episodic series. The episode is a stand-alone unit of time; message designers need to give the audience the background about the characters/people, tell the story, and resolve the action within the episode. The series is a sequence of messages; creators have already introduced characters/people, so they can assume the audience is familiar with them and their histories. However, the challenge lies in developing new actions for these characters without violating their personalities. The episodic series is a format that includes individual episodes where much of the action is resolved within the episode but where some of the action continues from episode to episode.

Medium Conventions

On the surface, the easy-to-recognize differences in story production across media are keyed to the human senses. All media but recordings and radio are visual. Recordings and radio are exclusively aural. Television, film, and the Internet are both visual and aural. Also, books are typically limited to words, but stories in magazines and newspapers use printed words and pictures, as do stories on the Internet, which can also include motion and aural elements.

When we get below these surface differences, other additional differences suggest opportunities and limitations in the way producers can tell their stories across the media. Arguably the most formulaic of all media is television because it is the most mass-like. Television producers must get the action started in the first minute or risk losing the audience. They must use easy-to-identify (stereotypical) characters and plots so that audiences need not pay much attention and can zone in and out throughout the story without losing the ability to follow the plot. TV producers must build action to a high point every few minutes and then break for a commercial message. Television producers have developed a language to describe some of the conventions they must follow. For example, they refer to the quick introduction of characters' backgrounds at the beginning of shows as "laying pipe." They know they must build the action to a high point before a commercial break to propel the action into the next scene and keep viewers from tuning out; they call this "top spin." Also, at the end of a scene in comedies, a character must deliver a joke; they call this a "button."

Television production is also concerned with what J. Fiske (1989) called "technical codes," which are production conventions such as decisions about camera placement and movement, lighting, editing, music, casting, setting, costumes, makeup, action, and dialogue. Each of these is an important tool in telling stories. For example, camera people know there is a 180-degree system, which means that a line is drawn to connect the two major characters in a scene, and the camera stays on one side of that line so as not to confuse audience members. Editors also use a standard formula of starting a scene with establishing shots in order to constitute the position of actors and physical location. Then they can move on to close-ups to show an intensification of the action. Editors know the importance of continuity. A break in continuity will confuse audience members and raise their psychic costs of processing the message (Budd et al., 1999). Actors are concerned with creating their characters through vocal (volume, pitch, timbre) sounds, facial expressions, gestures, and body movements. Camera operators are concerned with lighting, camera placement, camera movement, focus, color, and framing. Sound engineers are concerned with speech, music, and sound effects. Editors are concerned with continuity, pacing, length of shots, and sequencing.

Producing films is almost as rigidly formula driven as is television production. Writing for films is so formulaic that there are companies that will sell you script-writing software to put on your computer and tell you page by page what elements need to be there.

Conclusion

Producers of mass media messages rely on formulas and conventions when navigating through the options maze. Some of these formulas and conventions are general to all media messages, so producers encounter these decisions first. As they move along the design paths, they branch out into meta-genres, then genres, then decisions that are more and more specific to their particular stories. The next chapter lays out many of the formulas and conventions that become useful when producers move beyond the very general decisions.

Table 13.1   Message Production Propositions

Definitional Proposition

Message Production 1: Producers of media messages follow storytelling formulas so they can efficiently and effectively design content that will attract and maintain their desired audiences. These formulas provide producers with options about how to

- Increase audience appeal by planting appropriate attentional triggers at key places in the message, such as the beginning and other flow-in, flow-out places in the story
- Increase value in messages to potential audience members by

  Reducing costs to audience members, especially psychic costs, by closely following well-known and simple story formulas

  Increasing benefits to audience members by showing them how their existing needs are being better met by this message than by alternatives

Predictive Propositions

Message Production 2: Audience conditioning is more successful when producers can:

- Increase audience perceptions of benefits through storytelling deviations to keep messages fresh and to promise further novelty
- Decrease audience perceptions of psychic costs while asking for more audience expenditure of financial and time resources

Message Production 3: Audience attraction is predicted by how successfully producers negotiate the tension between needing to present messages that are highly formulaic (thus reducing audience members' psychic costs) and messages that are novel (thus potentially increasing payoff to audience members).

Message Production 4: Creativity is predicted by how well producers can deviate the right amount from story formulas.

Producers who do not understand story formulas cannot design successful narratives that attract and hold audiences.

Producers who stay too close to story formulas will design narratives that are too predictable and uninteresting.

CHAPTER 14

Message Formulas and Conventions by Genre

This chapter follows up on the exposition begun in the previous chapter concerning message formulas and conventions. The previous chapter laid out formulas and conventions at the most general level for all mass media and then highlighted differences keyed to medium. This chapter builds on those general formulas and conventions by showing how those guides get more specific by meta-genre and genre.

Meta-Genres and Genres

Genre analysis is important because it groups media messages and thereby helps make sense of an otherwise very large assortment of messages. The genres are, in essence, categories of messages. These categories are especially useful for this general framework because they can be constructed from story elements that attract and hold audience members' attention.

What are the genres of mass media stories? A good deal has been written about genres—especially entertainment genres—and there are many answers to this question. For example, Butler (2002) said there have been four types of what he called "principal narrative modes" on television (p. 13). They are theatrical film, the MOW (made-for-TV film or miniseries), the series program, and the serial program. Butler said that the theatrical film follows a classical paradigm that has seven basic components of classical narrative structure. First, there is the single protagonist who is the central character in the story. Viewers identify with this character. Second, there is exposition that introduces the viewer to the principal characters' personas and the space or environment the characters inhabit. Third, there is motivation, which is the driving force behind the protagonist's actions. Fourth, there is a narrative enigma, which is a question asked early in the narrative that pulls the action forward in the story. Fifth, there is a cause-effect chain that links together in a sequence all the scenes where the effect of the action in one scene is the cause of the action in the next scene. Sixth is the climax, where the narrative conflict culminates in a resolution; the enigma is solved. Seventh, there is the denouement, where there is a strong sense of closure. Butler said the MOW uses the same seven components as the theatrical film, but the MOW also includes small climaxes spaced throughout the narrative so the story can be interrupted. Butler said this presents weekly episodes with a defined set of recurring characters. The individual episodes do not build on one another. This type of program also follows the seven components. In contrast, the television continuing series uses multiple protagonists. On the television serial, the episodes build and expect the audience members to make connections across episodes. A serial has multiple protagonists, and the action really never resolves itself; instead, the effect of each episode is the cause for the conflict in the next episode.

A good deal has been written about genres of novels. In her book written primarily for local public librarians, *Genreflecting: A Guide to Popular Reading Interests,* Diana Herald (2006) laid out the most popular genres according to the public's interest in popular fiction. She said there are 10 genres: historical fiction (organized by time and geography), westerns, crime (including detective stories, suspense, and legal thrillers), adventure (spies, thrillers, survival, and military), romance (suspense, historical, paranormal, and ethnic), science fiction (shared worlds, time travel, technology, social structures, and future is bleak), fantasy (epics, myths, fairy tales, humorous), horror (monsters, supernatural, apocalypse, medical, psychological), Christian (romance, biblical, historical, speculative), and the newly emerging genre of women's fiction.

Rather than try to analyze all the ideas in the genre literature and synthesize the all-time best genre structure, I will be more practical and try to construct a useful structure of genres to help organize thinking about types of stories (see Table 14.1). This structure is a "first draft" of media genres. I expect scholars to revise it to fit their needs and as the media message landscape changes. The important point is that we have a useful set of categories to map types of media messages at a very general level (meta-genres), and more specific sets of subcategories within each meta-genre.

The genre organizational scheme divides all mass media messages into four meta-genres: entertainment, news/information, persuasion/advertising, and actualities. Entertainment stories are created by writers who put fictional characters in fictional situations to involve the emotions of audience members and thus entertain them. News/information stories are written by journalists who tell audiences about real people and their behavior in the real world so as to inform audience

Table 14.1   Genres of Mass Media Messages

I. Entertainment Meta-Genre

  A. Drama

    1. Action/Adventure—hero seeks to subdue an adversary.

- Police—heroes are police officers who solve crimes and fight criminals.
- Spy—adversary is a foreign country and its evil ways and minions.
- Military—characters are members of military organizations, and the plot features them carrying out their duties or rebelling against them. The adversary is a foreign country and its evil ways and soldiers.
- Western—heroes are rugged individuals who fight against outlaws or Indians.
- Political thriller—main characters are elected officials who use their power in an evil way to subvert the good of the people they represent or else use power in a good way to fight threats to the population.
- Financial intrigue/espionage—settings are in the world of international banking, oil cartels, and multinational corporations; focus on the crooked dealings of the rich and powerful; money is the prime factor in plots.
- Psychological thriller—a psychiatrist or psychologist tries to solve a puzzle of the mind, such as finding a mentally ill criminal.
- Detective story—this is a mystery tale involving detection to solve a problem and those who analyze the clues:

      Police detective

      Private detective

      Amateur detective (doctor, lawyer, journalist, academic, husband-wife team)

- Crime caper—adventure is seen through the eyes of the perpetrator. Focus on the planning and execution of the crime rather than finding the criminals and apprehending them.
- Personal adventure—focus is on a character and his or her setting out on a personal quest, such as to explore new lands, test his or her abilities (climb a mountain, go to the South Pole), or search for something of very high value.
- Disaster—adversary is a force in nature—predator, fire, earthquake, flood, meteor, disease; a catastrophe is the center of the plot; the catastrophe is either natural (nature or acts of God) or man-made (nuclear explosions, biological accidents, etc.).

    2. Romance—hero seeks a romantic relationship or life partner. Conflict arises from the search for the right person or in convincing a target person to engage in a romantic relationship with the hero.

- Continuing romance—soap operas.
- Melodrama—emotions and problems are highly exaggerated. Melodrama is a dramatic storyline of villainy, victimization, and retribution, in which characters' emotional states are exaggerated through grandiose facial expressions, vivid gestures, and stirring musical accompaniment; music is the "melos" of melodrama (Brooks, 1995).
- Historical romance—the setting is a time past brought to life.

    3. Family drama—hero seeks a stronger relationship with a family member; conflict is in the target family member resisting.

    4. Fantasy

- Science fiction—speculative treatment of the uses of science and how science will affect humankind. Usually, scientific advances are depicted as disrupting society or individuals' lives in a disastrous way. The plot then involves controlling the disaster and getting back to normal if possible.

(Continued)

Table 14.1 (Continued)

- Horror/gothic—supernatural horror and terror invade the seemingly innocent everyday world of the characters; the adversary is a monster either real or supernatural; the goal of the writer is to evoke in the audience true fright; it brings the supernatural into everyday life through ghosts, vampires, poltergeists, and monsters. It uses black magic, nightmares, hallucinations, ESP, and precognition.
- Fairytale—usually begins "once upon a time" and ends "and they lived happily ever after."

B. Comedy—hero is attractive in some way but also has foibles that are played for humor.

- Situation comedy—popular television subgenre; uses two-dimensional stereotypical characters in everyday situations played for humor; there is always a happy ending where all characters return to their beginning positions.
- Farce—begins with a fairly realistic setting, plot, and characters and then gradually moves step by step into the absurd as audience members willingly suspend disbelief for the sake of experiencing hilarity.
- Slapstick—humor is focused on physical comedy, especially harm from accidents, such as slipping on a banana peel.
- Comedy of manners—humor arises from the absurdity of polite conventions.
- Satire—humor arises when audiences feel "I can't believe they are saying or doing that!"

II. News/Information Meta-Genre

A. News

- Breaking news—events that are happening during the coverage.
- Hard news—what journalists believe are the most important events of the day about which the general population should be informed.
- Features/human interest—less time sensitive and less substantial information that is presented to appeal to the more positive emotions of audiences.

B. Talking heads

- Commentary—columnist interprets an event.
- Interview—journalist asks questions of a person of importance.
- Panel of experts—experts on a topic discuss an issue; offer context and opinions.

C. Documentaries

D. Education

- Formal education—structured presentations of subjects taught in schools
- Instructional for hobbyists—cooking, redecorating, golf lessons, etc.

III. Persuasive/Advertising Meta-Genre

A. Commercial ads

B. Political ads

C. Public service announcements

D. Promotions for media vehicles and messages

IV. Actuality Meta-Genre

A. Athletic sporting events

B. Game shows

C. Meetings

D. Live performances—concerts, award shows

E. Reality shows—real people, not actors portraying characters, in conflict situations, often competitive. Producers try to get audience members to identify with certain people on the show and thereby get caught up in the competition.

members of facts about events and issues those journalists think are important for people to know. Persuasion/advertising messages are written by copywriters who are trying to persuade audience members to pay attention to, develop a positive attitude about, buy, or use an advertiser's product, service, or idea. Notice that the primary intention of the creators of the messages is different across these first three meta-genres. Although the fourth meta-genre appears to be a kind of miscellaneous category, there is a coherence among the messages grouped here. To be in this actuality category, a media message must be something that occurs in the real world, so it is not fiction in the sense that actors are hired to deliver written lines that create a fictional made-up persona especially for the message. However, these programs usually have announcers, hosts, or emcees who deliver written lines to frame the actual action, which is usually unscripted in the form of a contest or a meeting. For example, a sporting event such as a football game is an example of an actuality. The game itself has rules, but it is not scripted in the sense that the contestants know how their actions will turn out. Announcers are hired to frame the contest in such a way as to get the audience involved in the action. This is not a news show because the coverage is occurring as the action itself unfolds, rather than after the action is over.

Entertainment Message Formulas

The entertainment story formula builds off the more fundamental general story formula. It does this by making some of the characteristics mentioned above more salient as well as adding some additional characteristics.

Goals of Entertainment Story Formula

The purpose of entertainment programming is not just to help audiences escape their lives and pass time. From a producer's point of view, the purpose is to build audiences. Pekurny (1982) has observed that the task of those who produce commercial television is, of course, to generate programming that can hold an audience for advertisers hour after hour, day after day, week after week. This task holds for all producers of entertainment messages. Therefore, story formulas need to guide producers in how to lower the costs to audiences while increasing the payoffs. The closer that producers follow established formulas for simple stories, the lower will be the psychic costs to audiences. Also, with entertainment messages, the payoff needs to be in terms of a strong emotional experience.

These story formulas are not new; they can be traced to premedia societies and their folktales that have been around for centuries and that still appeal to people. What attracts people to these basic story structures is the opportunity to learn something about their culture. The challenges that confront the characters and the way those characters confront the challenges tell listeners what their society values. Abercrombie (1996) said that narratives deal with how "societies see themselves. They are not simply stories; they deal with basic conflicts, events and relationships that characterize human societies" (p. 23).

Entertainment Story Structure

Set Hook. The industry is fond of high-concept movies, TV shows, and books. A high-concept story is one that can have its essence and appeal summarized in a single sentence that conveys the overall narrative development (Wyatt, 1994). High-concept stories put the emphasis on the narrative as the driving force. These stories also lend themselves to a clearer marketing message both in the initial pitch for the project and through the marketing pitch to the public.

Build Story Line. Conflict is essential. Producers must put characters in a conflict situation and then heighten the conflict step by step. There are several options for conflict. A character can experience conflict with another character (which is the most common in entertainment programs), with herself or himself, with an idea, or with some external force, such as fate, God, city hall, or a powerful institution. As each conflict is resolved, another larger one springs up; this is what keeps audiences following the story. Novelist Jane Smiley (2005) said the main character usually is in conflict with some group, and "the protagonist has only a few choices in his necessary relationship to the group—he can be subsumed, he can make a comfortable connection, he can make an uncomfortable accommodation, he can refuse to accommodate and remain apart, or he can be destroyed by the group" (p. 26).

Resolve Conflict. The resolution is evaluated by audiences primarily from an emotional perspective. Not only must the heroes be rewarded and the villains punished, but the rewards and punishments must be appropriate. Also, the payoff must be big enough to warrant the audience's expenditures of resources. If the message is a one-minute comedy skit on late-night TV, the payoff does not need to be nearly as big as if the message is a Hollywood movie in a theater.

Entertainment Techniques

To minimize cost and maximize payoff simultaneously, producers rely on several techniques: fast start, stereotypical characters, bending formulas, audience identification, quick build, simplified conflict formula, easy resolution, one-step remove-reality, transparency, and willing suspension of disbelief.

Fast Start. Action begins when the story begins—that is, there is very little warm-up. Sometimes producers start their story in the middle of some action. Thus, audiences feel anxious to "catch up" with what has been happening, and this pulls them into the story quickly.

Stereotypical Characters. Producers use types of people who are familiar to audience members. An image of a character with several obvious elements quickly shows audience members who this character is. For example, a pimply teenage male with a pocket protector, frizzy hair, and thick-frame glasses held together with tape and wearing ill-fitting, wrinkled clothes signals a nerd. The use of stereotypes reduces the psychic energy audiences need to follow the story.

Bending Formulas. Producers of entertainment messages know they must stay with the tried-and-true formulas of plot and characterizations, but if they stay too close to the formulas, audiences will get bored. So they typically bend the formulas here and there to introduce surprise. Recent examples of producers bending the formula on television are the featuring of gay characters (Battles & Hilton-Morrow, 2002; B. Cooper, 2002; Shugart, 2003), breaking with standard gender roles (Vavrus, 2002), and altering notions of morality (Grabe, 2002).

Audience Identification. Producers must get the audience to identify with a particular character. The more producers are able to do this, the more the audience members will be pulled into the story and stay with it until the end. One way to build audience identification is to tell the story from a particular character's point of view. With entertainment stories, producers try to show the action from the point of view of a sympathetic character with whom the audience can identify.

Another way to get the audience to identify with particular characters is to make the characters attractive in some way. There are several options for making characters attractive. Attractiveness can be achieved through physical means of an actor's natural beauty enhanced with makeup and costuming. But attractiveness can also be achieved by making characters similar to the audience demographically, for example in terms of age, gender, ethnicity, and social class. And yet another way is to give the character positive personality traits, such as wit and nobility.

If the story is part of a series (like on continuing television programs, a series of novels, a sequel to a film, etc.), producers want to try establishing a parasocial relationship between a character and audience members. This keeps audience members coming back to see what is happening to their special characters.

Quick Build. The events happen quickly and flow seamlessly into one another, giving the audience little opportunity to rest and thoughtfully evaluate whether to continue their exposure. Thus, once the producers have pushed their audience to identify with one character in the story, the producers subject that character to a series of events where the character gets in trouble. The plot unfolds as the character solves the problem but then finds that solution turning into another more serious problem. This escalates the conflict, which heightens the tension in the story and serves to involve the audience even more in the action and the travails of the character. As long as the audience continues to identify with the character, the audience will continue the exposure to find out what happens. However, good things must also happen to the character along the way to relieve the tension periodically and temporarily. This enables the audience to recover after each problem. Also, as the character solves the increasingly more serious problems, the audience builds confidence in the character's ability to deal effectively with the more serious problems that will need to be resolved later in the story.

Simplified Conflict Formula. The simplest form of strong conflict is to put two characters in a life-and-death competition for the same thing, such as money, freedom, or a love object. Both characters compete strongly for the same goal. Only one character can win. This is the underlying formula for action/adventure, westerns, and detective/crime stories.

Easy Resolution. The action in the story needs to leave people with a feeling that all the loose ends are neatly tied together, that all characters eventually got what was coming to them. To the extent that the story ends with ambiguities, audiences feel cheated, and their payoff is not as high as they would like it to be.

One-Step Remove-Reality. Producers select settings, characters, and events that are very similar to the places, people, and occurrences in the audience's everyday lives. This grounds their stories in reality. Then the producers "sweeten" those story elements by making them a little better than their mundane occurrence in real life. Characters are a little more attractive, are a little more wealthy and affluent, play with better toys, and so on. The problems are a little more dramatic and exciting. The settings are more gritty (if it is the mean streets of the city) or beautiful (if it is a beach or a hotel). Action happens at a faster pace, whether it is a car chase or career advancement from the mailroom to the CEO's office. The grounding in the trappings of reality makes it appear that the story is real or that it could happen, especially that it could happen to the audience member. The distortions to that reality "sweeten" the story and make it interesting, attractive, and appealing to the imagination.

Transparency. In *Hollywood Planet*, Scott Olson (1999) explained that American media products are so successful globally not because they show American culture but because they allow people in all different cultures to read their own cultures into the messages exported from America. He explained that people in many different cultures could watch the same episode of an American television series, but each person would "see" a different show. He said this is possible because each person brings "to their understanding of American television a completely different set of cognitive assumptions, taxonomies, and background narratives" (p. 3). The characteristic of the media messages that allows this to take place is what Olson called "transparency." He defined transparency as "any textual apparatus that allows audiences to project indigenous values, beliefs, rites, and rituals into imported media or the use of those devices. The transparency effect means that American cultural exports, such as cinema, television, and related merchandise, manifest narrative structures that easily blend into other cultures. Those cultures are able to project their own narratives, values, myths, and meanings into the American iconic media, making those texts resonate with the same meanings they might have if they were indigenous" (pp. 5–6).

While S. R. Olson (1999) used the term to explain why American media products are so successful in markets around the world where there are different languages and cultures, the idea of transparency would also seem to have great utility in explaining why American audience members expose themselves to media messages. America is a land of many different cultures. Therefore, if a media story is to attract people from different cultures and thus allow producers to build large audiences, that story must provide an attraction for many different types of people, and thus it must achieve transparency.

The term *transparency* is used by several other media scholars with several other meanings. Ang (1985) used it to refer to the media use of a style that makes it seem natural and gives viewers the illusion of reality, so that viewers can project themselves into the narrative. Baudrillard (1983) used the term *transparency* to refer to the experience of the audience where time disappears.

Thus, there are really two ideas behind this use of the term *transparency*. One is, as S. R. Olson (1999) defined it, a characteristic of the narrative that allows for audience members to put a great deal of themselves into the story interpretation. The other idea—as captured more by Ang (1985) and Baudrillard (1983)—is a characteristic of the narrative that invites audience members to lose themselves in the story. This relates to the idea behind the terms *flow* and *presence*. For example, K. M. Lee (2004) explicated the concept of presence and arrived at the following definition: "a psychological state in which virtual (para-authentic or artificial) objects are experienced as actual objects in either sensory or nonsensory ways" (p. 37). In essence, what he meant was that audience members get swept away in a media experience and cease to make the distinction between what is mediated and what is real. It is kind of an "out-of-body" experience (Rheingold, 1991). Both senses of the term are important to producers of media messages.

Willing Suspension of Disbelief. This idea was introduced by Coleridge (1847) to mean that writers of fiction need to get readers into a frame of mind where they will happily tolerate implausibilities in stories. Coleridge called this "poetic faith," and by this, he meant that readers would look past the supernatural characters in his poetry to find the truth about the nature of the human condition. He used the phrase to indicate when readers are willing to tolerate surface implausibilities to get to a deeper meaning.

The term has been borrowed by recent media scholars who have altered the meaning a bit (Laurel, 1993; Reeves & Nass, 1996; Wiley, 2000). In an attempt to explain why people get swept away by visual media such as films, television, and video games, these writers add the idea that audience members lose track of where the boundary is between themselves and the mediated messages. Recall that this idea is called *transported* in this book (see Chapter 7 on exposure states).

Entertainment Genres

A traditional starting place for categorizing entertainment stories is to divide them into the two broad categories of comedy and drama. This division is the most obvious because it separates stories along many dimensions, such as the emotions evoked in audiences, the types of characters used, the types of problems encountered, how those problems are heightened, and how the plot is resolved.

Comedy. With this genre, characters are divided into wits and buffoons who are in conflict with one another. The wits need to make humorous observations or deliver put-downs at frequent intervals. The buffoons are designated to be the butt of jokes; they have obvious shortcomings that make them easy to denigrate. The conflict itself is not the focus of the plot as much as it is the vehicle to deliver humor. All plot points need to have a humorous element. Also, characters never change—that is, they do not learn from their mistakes; they are the same at the end of the story as they were at the beginning, chapter after chapter or episode after episode.

There are several ways to subdivide the comedy genre into subgenres. For example, Kaminsky and Mahan (1985) wrote that there are four types of comedy: individual, courtship, family, and institutional. In individual comedy, the focus is on one character who has serious flaws that prevent him or her from growing or getting what he or she wants. In courtship comedy, the problem is finding a partner. In family comedy, the focus is on problems where family members are responsible for one another. In institutional comedy, a diverse group of people are thrown together in a setting like an office, a hospital, a school, or the military, and they must learn to get along with each other as they chafe under the rules and conventions of the institution. Humor arises from the antagonism among characters, especially between the heroes and the authority figures.

Each subgenre follows storytelling formulas. For example, a popular television subgenre is the situation comedy. Pekurny (1982) described the formula for Garry Marshall's situation comedies, which include *Laverne & Shirley, Mork and Mindy,* and *Happy Days.* He said, "First, the series are all meant to be viewed by children and adults together and so violence and other anti-social content is de-emphasized while pro-social content (such as borrowing books from the library) [is] played up. Second, the plots are simple for the benefit of young children. Third, each series has at least one key character who is the messenger of pro-social values. Fourth, there is some 'ticker,' heart, or warmth in each episode among the characters. Finally, there must be a joke or bit of business at work about every minute or so" (p. 140). He also said, "Each of the Marshall series is a variation of these general elements with its own specific formula of characters, typical plot lines, and standing jokes" (p. 140).

Drama. The drama is a serious narrative about the conflicts humans encounter as they try to attain their goals. Characters are divided into heroes and villains. The heroes have goals that can be financial, physical, and emotional, especially the building and maintaining of relationships. The plot points are primarily the encountering and resolving of conflicts between the heroes and the villains. Subgenres of drama can be distinguished by many different characteristics, such as goal of the main character (romantic relationship for romance), settings (western, political, military, financial, medical, legal), character (detective, crime caper, personal adventure), event (disaster), or degree of fantasy (fairytale, science fiction).

One popular subgenre of drama is the romance. Radway (1984) said that the romance narrative begins with the heroine becoming disturbed, through an antagonistic encounter with a more powerful or an aristocratic male. She separates from the male or fights with him as the conflict heightens. Finally, there is a resolution, which is a reconciliation with a sexual union, and the heroine regains her dignity and identity.

Soap operas are continuing romances that used to appear on radio and now are a staple of television. Each resolution of a problem plants the seeds of the next problem. Multiple plots unfold simultaneously. The space is usually confined to a small town, and all the action takes place there. Time is highly plastic. The events of a single afternoon can be portrayed over several weeks of broadcast; in contrast, young children can grow to adulthood in several years. The plots focus on human relationships—building them and betrayal. When characters get sick, it is usually exotic and very serious. Favorite mental illnesses are amnesia and split personality.

Themes explore taboo subjects of adultery, domestic abuse, homosexuality, and so on. The most often encountered problems are extramarital affairs where one spouse is unfaithful, family problems, difficulties at work, and physical disabilities (Katzman, 1972). Major causes of death include homicide (Cassata, Skill, & Boadu, 1979). With soap operas, it is especially important for producers to have a range of highly attractive characters so all audience members can bond strongly in a parasocial way with one character and follow his or her problems closely every day.

In mysteries, the narrative does not follow the chronological sequence of events; certain events are not revealed until the end so as to achieve mystery (Vorderer & Knobloch, 2000). Something occurs early in the story (or even before the story begins), and the hero characters go about solving the mystery by talking to people and encountering events. Bits of information are picked up along the way until the resolution, when the bits of information are finally assembled in the correct configuration and the mystery is solved.

The thriller has been characterized by B. Rosenberg and Herald (1991) primarily in terms of suspense, where "the characters and the reader are in a constant state of uneasy anticipation of the worst, which all too often happens" (p. 47). The thriller's suspense derives from the characters (their desires and personalities), the situations of hazard (physical and psychological), and the social or political setting. The type of problem to be solved separates the subgenres of detective, crime/caper, spy/espionage, financial intrigue/espionage, political intrigue/terrorism, disaster, and adventure.

In the police drama, the cops are usually middle-class people who chafe under the systems of rules and authoritarian bosses to catch criminals who do not follow such rules and even use the rules to hide their mischief. Stories begin with a crime. The audience is given more information about the crime or the criminals than are the police. The drama lies in how the police uncover this information and eventually catch the criminals. The primary tools of the police are the gun, the automobile, and clothes (either the uniform or undercover disguise) (Kaminsky & Mahan, 1985).

Westerns are another subgenre that used to be very popular in the early days of radio and television. B. Rosenberg and Herald (1991) claimed that the western is "essentially an adventure novel but is too large and diverse a kind to subsume under the adventure genre. Although action and adventure usually dominate the plot, they are secondary to the setting, a compound of scenery and history" (p. 15). They continued, "The story line derives from the entire westward movement in North America, beginning in the early nineteenth century with the traders, trappers, and explorers, and from the distinctive type of life continuing in the Far West in the United States in the twentieth century" (p. 15). They said, "the appeal of this genre is worldwide, based in a dream of freedom in a world of unspoiled nature, independent of the trammels of restraining society. The hero dominates the western: competent, self-reliant, and self-sufficient whether in conflict with nature or with man or himself" (p. 16). The conflicts are simple, between right and wrong. Steiner (1952) wrote about the formula used in the radio serial of the *Lone Ranger* in the late 1930s. This formula had eight steps that allowed the primary writer to produce 60,000 words of script per week: (1) establish a character, (2) give him a problem he can't solve because of a villain, (3) explain why he can't solve it, (4) the Lone

Ranger learns about the situation, (5) the antagonist learns that the Ranger is going to interfere, (6) the antagonist plots to kill the Ranger, (7) the Ranger outwits or outfights the crooks and survives, and (8) the Ranger solves the situation.

Fairytales also follow a standard formula (Bettelheim, 1975). The story begins with the hero at the mercy of those who think little of him as a person or of his abilities. People mistreat the hero and may even threaten his life. The hero is forced to depend on other people, animals, and magic creatures who help him. By the end of the story, the hero has overcome all obstacles and remained true to himself; he has gained the respect of others.

A difference between a novel and a melodrama is that "the characters in a melodrama speak in clichés because they don't have any thoughts of their own, while the characters in a novel may do or say evil things but they always have a logical point of view" (Smiley, 2005, p. 225).

News Message Formulas

This section looks at the goals of the news formula, its structure, the news construction process, and shaping the news formula.

Goal of News Formula

The media—even news programs—are less interested in educating people than in attracting and exciting them. If audiences want only information, the news formula can accommodate them, but usually audiences want information that is entertaining in some way, so the news formula must "sweeten" the information to make it more entertaining. This can be clearly seen in the way news organizations report disease and death. It would seem that there are few things more important to the general population than information about a person's risk of different diseases and death. However, "the media do not report on risks; they report on harms" (E. Singer & Endreny, 1987, p. 14), which means that the media are more interested in showing an individual being harmed, especially if it is very serious, than in presenting a bigger picture of risk for harm in the aggregate. Thus, the news story appeals to the emotions—fear in this case. This point was also made by Combs and Slovic (1979), who content analyzed newspaper stories and found that "although diseases claim almost 1,000 times as many lives as do homicides, there were about three times as many articles about homicides than about all diseases" (pp. 841–842).

This goal has led many scholars to criticize media news organizations for being focused more on building audiences than on educating them. For example, Croteau and Hoynes (2001), in their book *The Business of Media: Corporate Media and the Public Interest,* complained that the business perspective of the mass media hurt the public interest and that this harm shows up in some trends in the way content is produced and the patterns of that content. They said that there is a trend toward homogenization and imitation in messages, that is, the media use formulas so that all messages look and sound the same. This leads to a decline in localism and variety in messages. Also, Croteau and Hoynes complained that messages are becoming trivialized and sensationalized. Thus, shock value is achieved through violence, sexual titillation, scandal, and gossip. And the authors also complained about the disappearing line between journalism and commerce.

News Story Structures

Newspapers have always been in the business of telling a good story. Even in the frontier America days of the 1800s, newspapers in Nevada, Texas, Arizona, and California sprinkled fairytale-type stories into their hard news coverage, thus appealing to the imagination of readers who were living a hard life on the frontier (Kilmer, 2001). Thus, the news formula features information, but it also weaves in entertainment aspects.

The typical news formula is the inverted pyramid, where the producers present the most important information first and then present information less important in descending order. Producers check to make sure they have addressed the who, what, when, where, and why. An alternative formula is the entertainment narrative, where the producer presents the story as a sequence of events building to a resolution.

Recall from the discussion on the general story formula that all stories need a satisfying resolution. With news stories, resolution means something different. If the story is a human interest one, then there is likely to be a warmhearted resolution that makes the audience feel good about the people in the news story, about themselves, or about humankind in general. But with breaking news and ongoing news stories, the action in the story is not resolved in real life, so it cannot be resolved in the news story. With these types of news stories, resolution means something more general; that is, resolution means that the journalist has answered the main questions that were raised in the story—the who, what, when, where, and why—so that the audience members feel they have been given appropriate informational value in return for their exposure. When journalists cannot answer all the important questions raised by a story, they need to frame the story as a mystery so the audience expects a question to be left unanswered; furthermore, the journalists then need to leave the question unanswered in a way that gives the audience an emotional reaction. For example, when reporting a murder, it is likely that the journalist will not know who committed the murder, so the journalist frames the story as a murder mystery and gives the audience a fear reaction. When reporting a story about a missing child, it is likely that the journalist will not know where the child is, so the journalist must frame the story as a mystery and give the audience a reaction of hope or some other emotion to keep the audience interested in the story.

There are even formulas for advice columns in magazines aimed at young women. Garner, Sterk, and Adams (1998) analyzed advice columns in magazines popular among teenage women over a 20-year period and found that the advice has changed very little. They said the advice limits women's sociality and sexuality within narrowly defined heterosexual norms and practices. It encourages young women to be seen as objects and teaches them to subordinate themselves to others.

News Techniques

This section will highlight a few of the techniques journalists use in crafting their stories: appearance of objectivity, news frames, simplified conflict, hyperbole for dramatic effect, sensationalization, deviance, use of polls, branding, personalization, familiar faces, and context.

Appearance of Objectivity. News workers try to maintain the appearance of objectivity so as to achieve credibility. However, news producers must tell their stories with a point of view. Journalists like to create the appearance of an objective point of view. Of course, this can never be fully achieved because bias always filters into the news judgment of journalists. McQuail (2000) pointed out that there are many sources of news bias and that these can never be fully avoided. These sources of bias include the following: (a) Media news overrepresents the social "top" and official voices in its sources; (b) news attention is differentially bestowed on members of political and social elites; (c) the social values are usually consensual and supportive of the status quo; (d) foreign news concentrates on nearer, richer, and more powerful nations; (e) news has a nationalistic (patriotic) and ethnocentric bias in the choice of topics and opinions expressed and in the view of the world assumed or portrayed; (f) news reflects the values and power distribution of a male-dominated society; (g) minorities are differentially marginalized, ignored, or stigmatized; and (h) news about crime overrepresents violent and personal crime while neglecting many of the realities of risk in society.

Journalists can never present all sides equally well—unless the event being portrayed is very simple. Instead of trying to achieve the impossible goal of objectivity, journalists try to achieve the more modest goal of balance. D'Alessio and Allen (2000) conducted a meta-analysis of 59 quantitative studies containing data concerned with partisan media bias in presidential election campaigns since 1948. They found no bias in newspapers or magazines and only a small amount of coverage and statement bias with television network news. The types of bias examined were gatekeeping bias (the preference for selecting stories from one party or the other), coverage bias (the relative amounts of coverage each party receives), and statement bias (the favorability of coverage toward one party or the other).

News Frames. Semetko and Valkenburg (2000) content analyzed 2,601 newspaper stories and 1,522 television news stories in Amsterdam and attributed each to one of five news frames: attribution and responsibility, conflict, human interest, economic consequences, and morality. The most used frame was attribution and responsibility, followed by conflict, economic consequences, human interest, and morality frames. These varied by story and outlet. The most significant differences were not between media (television vs. the press) but between sensationalist and serious types of news outlets. Sober and serious newspapers and television news programs more often used the responsibility and conflict frames in the presentation of news, whereas sensationalist outlets more often used the human interest frame.

Simplified Conflict. News stories use a simplified conflict formula to make current events easy for audiences to understand and, at the same time, to dramatize the conflict in order to engage the emotions of the audience. Thus, complex social issues are reduced to two sides that are sharply contrasted. This presentation of ideas as categories that are far apart makes for a stronger conflict situation. But it deliberately ignores the real-world situation where most ideas and positions are in the shades of gray and where government officials must work through negotiation and compromise rather than confrontation and competition. For example, Fursich (2002) explained that the way U.S. newspapers covered the merger of automobile manufacturers Daimler-Benz and Chrysler misled the public by failing "to help readers understand the global relevance of this merger, the oligopolistic tendencies of the car industry, and the global dependencies of the world economy" (p. 353). Instead, the press covered the story with the simple ideas of marriage (two companies are joined) and birth (a new company comes to life).

Hyperbolize for Dramatic Effect. Adding entertainment elements to information can be accomplished by taking one informational element and exaggerating it to engage audience members' emotions more strongly. This is not a new development. For example, Soderlund (2002) analyzed how the *New York Times* covered the White slavery issue in the early 1900s. She says that at that time, there was a moral panic over White slavery, where women were kidnapped and sold into prostitution by organized bands of immigrants, often alleged to be conspiring with top city officials. She said that early on, journalists initially drew from a stock of sentimental narratives to describe the investigations.

Another example is the "runaway youth" story, which in the early 1960s was "unconstructed"—that is, it did not have a consistent discourse and consisted mainly of harmless adventures by boy runaways. Then in 1967, there was a moral panic associated with the hippie movement, which led to the runaway youth story becoming a socially constructed problem featuring teenage girl prostitutes. Thus, to attract the public that was experiencing moral panic, news workers altered their narratives (Staller, 2003).

Sensationalism. Related to hyperbole is sensationalism. Slattery, Doremus, and Marcus (2001) have analyzed public affairs reported on network evening news programs and found a trend toward more sensational reporting. Also, Semetko and Valkenburg (2000) found such a trend in newspaper as well as television news reporting in Amsterdam.

Deviance. Shoemaker and Reese (1996) explained that news stories focus on deviance: "The media give importance to some people and groups by portraying them frequently and in powerful positions, and marginalize others by ignoring them or presenting them less advantageously and outside the mainstream" (pp. 46–47).

Shoemaker and Reese (1996) said that the pattern of coverage on crime in the mass media represents a form of statistical deviance. This deviance comes about when certain things are considered more newsworthy by the mass media news organizations than the frequency of their occurrence in real life would warrant. A good example of this statistical deviance is the overcovering of violent crime in relation to other types of crimes and other types of activities. Another type of deviance is normative deviance, which is the presentation of ideas or events that break norms or laws.

Use of Polls. Reporters like to present the results of polls in their stories. Lipari (1999) argued that polls are used as rituals that affirm deeply held beliefs about community, democracy, and the vox populi. "Polling ritual enables the national congregation to affirm its unity in spite of difference" (p. 83).

Branding. Chan-Olmsted and Kim (2001) conducted a survey of general managers of commercial television stations and found that those managers perceived branding to be an "important tactical management function" (p. 75) with branding applications in areas most related to news and promotion. Branding practices were related to market size and news leadership.

Personalization. News readers on television try to come across as real people and establish a rapport with their audiences. News anchors on television simulate eye contact to make audience members feel the news anchor is talking directly to them (Budd et al., 1999).

Familiar Faces. Shoemaker and Reese (1996) pointed out that most news is about people who are already prominent. Also, most news comes from "official" (primarily governmental) channels, but journalists will use other sources when they are available. And in the United States, news coverage of a state is not related to its population. Minority characters and newscasters are generally underrepresented and portrayed stereotypically. In general, portrayals in media reflect the power relations of the general society.

Context. Barnhurst and Mutz (1997) argued that the traditional five Ws of journalism had become less dominant in determining what goes into news stories by the late 1900s. They found a trend more toward journalists now supplying context of social problems, interpretations, and themes. The authors say this trend springs from the workings of the news market.

Advertising Message Formulas

Goals of Ad Formula

The goal of advertising messages is to plant a connection in audience members' minds between their existing needs and the advertiser's product or service. Thus, audience attention during message exposure is not important. To the contrary, if advertisers can plant their connection while the audience members remain in an exposure state of automaticity, they can be most successful because audience members will not be discounting or critically evaluating their claims.

Advertising Formula Structures

With advertising messages, producers try to tell the story from the point of view of the target audience, so they cast actors who look and act like the target audience—or how the audience members in the target would like to look and act.

There are basically three story structures for ad messages. The first is the announcement. In this structure, the producers present key information about the product or service and make that information as salient as possible. This is the typical form of promotional ads for upcoming events or media messages. Walker and Eastman (2003) analyzed 4,469 promos for sports programs. They found that there was a wide range of announcement approaches for promos and that these approaches differed across genres and audiences.

A second type of ad story formula is the problem-solution. Producers of these ads give their characters problems that the target audience experience and show how the advertised product solves those problems. The focus is on one unique selling proposition (USP) that sets the producer's product apart from those of its competitors and makes it clearly superior.

The third type of ad story formula is the montage. In this story, multiple images and sounds are used as a mosaic to evoke a pleasant emotion in the audience. The product or service is then linked with that pleasant emotion. This type of structure is used to show a lifestyle of luxury or style with many images of successful people enjoying the good life in affluent surroundings. The montage is used frequently in television ads for luxury automobiles, perfumes, jewelry, and cruises.

Advertising messages also differ by format. Leiss, Kline, and Jhally (1988) said there are four basic formats for advertising messages. First, the *product information* format focuses on the product and its utility; the brand name and image of the product are prominent. Second, the *product image* format embeds the product in a symbolic context that conveys a meaning to the product beyond its actual composition or literal use. It depends on "narrative techniques like metaphor, implied use, allusion, allegory, story line, and simple juxtaposition to expand the symbolic dimension of the interpretation" (p. 190). Third, the *personalized* format focuses on the direct relationship between a product and the human personality; people are defined by their use of the product. And fourth, the *lifestyle* format interweaves the person, the product, and the setting. The product does not define the lifestyle or transform the person; instead, the product is shown as an integral part of the lifestyle.

Advertising messages can also differ by type of appeal. Butler (2002) listed eight types of appeals. First there is luxury, leisure, and conspicuous consumption. Second is individualism, which espouses the values of "self-fulfillment, self-reliance, self-expression, self-absorption, even simple selfishness" (p. 291). Third is the natural appeal, which associates products with wholesomeness, healthfulness, and purity. Fourth is folk culture and tradition, which espouses the values of traditional principles of "trustworthiness, simplicity, authenticity and raw patriotism" (p. 293). Fifth is novelty and progress, which is the opposite of tradition in its pushing for change as progress. Sixth is sexuality and romance, which is a popular appeal in ads for perfume, lingerie, shampoos, and cosmetics. Seventh is the alleviation of pain, fear/anxiety, and guilt. And eighth is utopia and escape from dystopia, which is the escape from boredom and moving into a life of abundance, energy, community, and intense, rewarding relationships.

Advertising Techniques

In this section, I will highlight four techniques used prevalently in the advertising formula. They are repetition, resonance, reality, and metaphor.

Repetition. Advertisers typically focus on one claim in an ad and repeat it over and over so that there is no way the audience can mistake the focal selling element. The key to designing such a message is to use repetition without boring the audience. So while the focal selling element is repeated, it must be altered slightly to keep it fresh with each repetition.

Resonance. The resonance technique instructs the producer of the ad to first clearly identify a need in the niche audience, and then present the advertised product as a way of amplifying that need and making the audience members crave the product. Schwartz (1974) explained that "the critical task is to design a package of stimuli (ads) so that it resonates with information already stored within an individual and thereby induces the desired learning or behavioral effect" (p. 25).

Reality. Advertisers frequently violate conventions of reality to attract attention. They hyperbolize in a humorous way so that audiences know that the claims are not meant to be true. This is a way of "sweetening" the ad by removing the portrayal a bit from everyday reality through the use of bending the facts in a humorous way or hyperbolizing problems or characters.

Metaphor. Advertisers frequently show that their products are like something else. Butler (2002) explained, "Perhaps the most common way that advertisers assert the desirability of their products is to associate them with activities, objects, or people that are themselves desirable" (p. 303). Using metaphors is a successful way for advertisers to appear to make claims about their products by saying that they are like other things that have many good qualities without actually claiming that their advertised product has all those good qualities; still the impression of the full set of good qualities is left in the mind of the audience member.

Actualities

This fourth meta-genre is rather new but, given its popularity and differences with other meta-genres, will be treated separately here, although in much less detail than the other meta-genres.

Goal of Actuality Formula

The purpose of actuality programming is positioned between the purposes of the entertainment and news meta-genres. Actualities try to entertain audiences but also provide them with some valuable information about themselves that they can use in their own lives. To be in this actuality category, a media message must be something that occurs in the real world, so it is not fiction in the sense that actors are hired to deliver written lines that create a fictional made-up persona especially for the message. Therefore, it is distinguished from entertainment messages. Several important characteristics of actuality messages distinguish them from news messages. One characteristic is that with actualities, the action is covered as it unfolds. With sports, the action is live. With game shows, the action is presented as if it were live. With news coverage, there is typically a feeling of past tense; that is, the news is the event that just happened, and the coverage reports the event after its occurrence. A second distinguishing characteristic is that news focuses on special people; that is, they are presented as newsworthy for some action. With actualities, the focus is typically (except for sports) on ordinary people. In the course of the actuality message, the ordinary people may end up doing something extraordinary, but they are not usually extraordinary to begin with.

Actuality Story Structures

The story structure is typically a real-life competition that involves real people who suffer real-life rewards and consequences. At times, the competitors have a high degree of talent and are highly trained, as is the case with sports. Other times, the people have no special skills or training, as in most game shows. The fact that these people have no extraordinary skills is what makes them so attractive to audiences who watch those people to see if they can do extraordinary things.

Actuality Techniques

Producers of actuality messages try to attract audiences with a resonance-type appeal. That is, audiences are told the people on the show are ordinary like them or that these people will be put in situations similar to ones the audience members have encountered—like playing a favorite sport. Thus, the experience is likely to resonate with the audience members' own experiences.

There is also an appeal to audience members' fantasies, such as learning to sing, to dance, to play a sport well, to experience romance with a hot partner, to appear smart, or to win a lot of money. The situation is set up so that audience members identify with a particular team or person—who becomes them in the game. Announcers tell the backstory to help audience members make their selections quickly. Audience members then experience the competition vicariously through their identified player. These characteristics are similar to entertainment messages; however, with actualities, the emotional involvement is greater because of the audience members' belief in the actual existence of not just the people but the action and outcomes.

Conclusion

Mass media messages follow story formulas and conventions that are keyed to meta-genres and genres. While some of these formulas are general and shared, the set of formulas for a meta-genre is unique to that one meta-genre. There are also similarities and differences across genres within the four meta-genres.

Knowledge of these formulas and conventions is what guides producers through the option maze in the design of their messages. Also, the more that media scholars understand these and other to-be-discovered formulas and conventions, the better they can construct the narrative line of a message.

CHAPTER 15

Critique of Media Message Scholarship

Now that I have laid out the lineation general framework line of thinking on mass media content in the previous three chapters, it is time to raise the following question: Given the current literature, how well have we been mapping the phenomenon of mass media content? My answer to this question is that the literature on media content is far less developed than the literatures on the other three mass media facets. This literature is the most scattered and exhibits the least conceptual leverage—that is, it is the most exploratory, question driven, and descriptive. Therefore, the biggest challenge in evolving from a Generating-Findings to a Mapping-Phenomenon perspective lies with altering our approach to designing research that examines the content facet of the mass media.

In this chapter, I will present my general broad-stroke critique of the literature on mass media content. Then I will conclude with some recommendations for a research agenda to increase our knowledge about mass media content.

Critique

My critique of the media message literature is composed of five areas. These areas are lack of overviews, breadth of content covered, methods used, manifest/latent content, and leveraging findings.

Lack of Overviews

If we are to evolve from a Generating-Findings to a Mapping-Phenomenon perspective, we need to assess where we are as a scholarly field in terms of understanding the general patterns of content that appear across all forms of the mass media. First, we need to know how large this literature on media content has grown and what topic areas are the most prevalent. Second, we need a critical analysis topic by topic to inventory the content patterns from the findings of all the individual studies. Once we have constructed this map of our literature, we will have the basis for identifying the crucial gaps in our understanding about our phenomenon, and this will help us most efficiently orient toward where we need to concentrate our content scholarship in order to construct a map of our phenomenon. This is the beginning point, and unfortunately, there are currently no general overviews or reviews by medium or topic to help us begin this task.

Over years of reading scholarly communication journals, I have noticed many published content analyses of various media messages, especially of violence, risky behaviors (such as drinking, smoking, drug use, etc.), demographics of characters, and types of news topics covered. However, there are very few general overviews of these studies, so it is difficult to know how large this content analysis literature is. One example of a content analysis of the published literature is a study by Riffe and Freitag (1997), who conducted an analysis of 25 years of published content analyses in *Journalism & Mass Communication Quarterly* and reported finding 486 content analysis studies in that one journal alone. This article is valuable in telling us how many content analysis studies were published in this one journal over 25 years, but there are no studies that give us a larger picture of the size of the literature over all communication journals or a longer span of years. Furthermore, there are few relatively broad reviews of content analysis literatures to synthesize the substance about what is known about topic area.

Lack of Breadth

There is also a lack of breath in research studies across the range of mass media content. Content in particular media are frequently examined while content in other media are ignored. Likewise, content in particular topics have attracted many researchers, while content on other topics has been virtually ignored.

By Medium. The coverage of mass media messages is limited to certain media. The coverage of messages in television and film has been more extensive than the coverage of messages on radio, in recordings, or in books. Magazine messages have received some attention but primarily ads. The Internet is starting to attract the attention of media scholars.

By Topic Area. The media message analysis literature appears to be concentrated in a few media and a few topic areas, such as minorities in mass media content (Greenberg, Mastro, & Brand, 2002) or violence in the media (W. J. Potter, 1999). For example, Shoemaker and Reese (1996) synthesized the content analysis literature into several general conclusions about media content and reported that television content (both news and entertainment) contains a high level of violence that is consistent over time; in media content, women and the aged appear less often than men and younger adults; and in general, portrayals in media reflect the power relations of the general society. Thus, three areas have been well examined in the mass media, at least on television. They are violence; the demographics of age, gender, and ethnicity; and the power relations among people or characters belonging to the different demographic groups.

The strength of this concentration is that there is a high degree of triangulation on those areas that are covered. These areas have a collection of different scholars using different samples, different coders, and often different codes to arrive at very similar findings. Thus, on these few topics, there is high convergence and therefore a high degree of confidence in the findings. However, the downside of this concentration of resources is that large areas are virtually unexamined as of yet.

It is understandable why the literature of mass media content is fragmentary. There are so many topics of interest compared with the number of mass media scholars that there are not enough resources to cover all topics. This is characteristic of the young nature of the field and is not meant to be a criticism of past research efforts. The task of covering the entire spectrum of mass media messages is enormous; we need to start somewhere. But as the field matures, we need to shift our resources around to achieve a more balanced coverage of all areas across the range of content. It is an irony that many mass media scholars are motivated to conduct their content analyses because of a perceived imbalance in news coverage topics or types of people; then, when they document these imbalances in their research findings, they strongly criticize the mass media for not being more balanced and presenting a wider range of coverage of topics and people to more accurately reflect the world they are covering. Yet by so doing, media scholars are creating a literature that is even more out of balance with the phenomenon they are trying to cover.

Method

Scholars who study mass media content use either a quantitative methodology of content analysis or a qualitative methodology, such as textual analysis. As for quantitative content analysis, the key to reaping its benefits lies in following the scientific rules well. The two problem areas are sampling and testing the consistency of coding decisions. As for sampling, the challenge is in constructing a sampling frame that represents the population. If this cannot be achieved well, random sampling from a flawed sampling frame will not allow the analyst to generalize to the population. Also, analysts must test for coding reliability, and this is not always reported. Furthermore, when it is reported, many of the tests do not correct for chance agreement, so the reliability figures are artificially high, leading readers to believe that the coders were more consistent in their decisions than was the actual case.

The social science literature built from content analyses does very little in the way of inferring patterns. Much of this literature is composed of studies that simply count the occurrence of particular elements, such as demographic characteristics or acts of violence. Some studies will make comparisons of counts across content groupings, such as medium (comparing counts from television to counts from newspapers), vehicles (comparing counts from the *New York Times* to counts from the *Washington Post*), content provider (ABC, CBS, Fox, and NBC), or genre (counts from comedy shows to counts from dramatic programs). These comparisons qualify as patterns, but this is a relatively weak form of patterning. A stronger form of patterning is looking for regularities among elements within messages. Some of this was done in the analyses presented by the *National Television Violence Study* (1997), where analysts looked for the co-occurrence of lack of harm to victims, lack of remorse from perpetrators, and lack of graphicness in the depiction of the violent act. The co-occurrence of these elements was an indication of the violence being sanitized. Coders did not code for degree of sanitization; instead, the analysts inferred a pattern of sanitized violence from several elements of content that were coded. There are not many examples of patterning in the social science content analysis literature, but over time, more content analysts are building this feature into their designs.

A nonquantitative literature has been generated by scholars taking a more humanistic approach, such as by using textual analysis, semiotics/semiology, narrative analysis, genre analysis, discourse analysis, dialogic analysis, Marxist analysis, feminist analysis, psychoanalytical analysis, postmodern analysis, and myth analysis. The intention of scholars using these methods is not to count the prevalence of elements in mass media content. Instead, these scholars are much more interested in identifying patterns qualitatively and in explaining those patterns by linking them to something outside the content itself. The number of qualitative content studies published is much smaller than the number of quantitative content studies.

Manifest and Latent Content

Oftentimes, analysts will design studies that require the coding of latent content rather than manifest content. This creates more of a challenge to achieve coder consistency. To help the coders, analysts will develop a codebook with many rules and guidelines and then subject coders to many detailed training sessions. Throughout this procedure, analysts will pilot test on coder consistency. When coder consistency is too low, analysts will add more rules and guidelines to the codebook as well as continue with coder training. Usually, this procedure will result in improvements in coder consistency until the reliability figures ascend to an acceptable level.

This procedure of adding coding rules and retraining coders, however, typically leads coders away from their natural meanings for media messages. The further away they are moved from their everyday meanings, the less their coding will resemble the way typical people understand media messages. For example, this has been a problem in media violence content analyses. In content analyses of violence, social scientists typically focus on acts that are intended to harm victims physically. These acts still get counted even when they are nongraphic, humorous, or fantasy, whereas the general public defines acts of violence primarily in terms of actions that tend to offend them, that is, actions that are high in graphicness, reality, and seriousness (see W. J. Potter, 2003 and 2008, for a more complete discussion of this point).

Leveraging Findings

In his classic 1969 methods book, *Content Analysis for the Social Sciences and Humanities,* Holsti said that content analysis is a method for "making inferences by objectively and systematically identifying specified characteristics of messages" (p. 14). Holsti argued that once the coding is finished and quantitatively analyzed, the researcher makes inferences about the results—either inferences about the causes of the communications analyzed or inferences about the effects of those messages. This idea has been supported by other scholars in their subsequent writings about the method of content analysis (Neuendorf, 2001; Riffe, Lacy, & Fico, 1998; Stempel, 1981).

A fair number of content analysts have attempted such linkages in their discussion sections. However, these linkages are usually to negative effects or negative practices. To illustrate, the mass media theories most often used for this purpose are cultivation, social learning theory, and agenda setting. With cultivation, content analysts expressly look for content patterns in the media world that are different from content patterns in the social world. Thus, the focus of these content analyses is to find patterns of deviation that will lead the population to false beliefs about the social world. Social learning theory is a popular theory used in content analyses of violence and sexual occurrences. Analysts will document risky patterns in the content portrayals and then use social learning theory to argue that these risky portrayals will lead audiences to learn faulty social information. And tests of agenda setting rely on content analyses of newscasts to identify the media agenda for news, and then analysts argue that the media present a narrow agenda rather than a more complete range of news stories.

Furthermore, when content analysts do not relate their inferred patterns to particular media theories, they still frequently relate them to a criticism of the media. Popular topics among researchers using scientifically based content analyses include violence, sexual portrayals, bad language, and misleading images of society (body images, health behaviors, degree of affluence, family interaction patterns, and bias in news stories). Of course, these are all relevant topics for content analyses. However, we need more of a balance that reveals patterns of messages that do not necessarily have a negative influence.

Research Agenda

The literature on media content is arguably the least developed across the four major facets of the mass media phenomenon. It is not that there are few published studies; rather, it is that this literature is very fragmented and descriptive. To make more substantial progress in developing a deeper understanding of mass media content, researchers should orient their efforts in three areas. First, at the descriptive level, we need to document patterns of media content in a more elaborate manner. Second, we need to link our elaborate content patterns more closely to the factors that have been found to have the strongest influence on audience members. And third, we need to trace the content patterns back to the media organizations and use them to try to parse the values and decisions made by producers.

More Elaborate Message Patterns

In developing our overall understanding of message patterns, we need to dig more deeply into the messages and construct more elaborate patterns. This requires a sensitivity to more factors in messages and to their organization.

Intramessage Examination. The humanistic approach has been better at meeting this challenge than has the social science method. Social scientists typically report counts, percentages, and rates of individual story elements. Rarely will they look for patterns across multiple elements. This is not to say that no content analyses code for many story characteristics; there are many such studies. What I am focusing on is the nature of the analysis and reporting of the results. Typically, content analyses will present the results of each story element in a univariate manner (such as a percentage of violent acts that are committed by heroes, that depict harm, that are justified, etc.) and sometimes in a bivariate manner (such as the percentage of violent acts that both are committed by heroes and are justified) but very rarely in a truly multivariate manner (for examples, see W. J. Potter & Smith, 2000; W. J. Potter & Ware, 1987, 1989), which is required for pattern construction.

We need a more elaborate intramessage examination. The intramessage examination needs to include more elements in the analysis so that patterns are elaborated. Scholars using the more humanistic approach are more likely to examine many elements in stories. However, their approach is usually guided by supporting a thesis, such as an ideological position. As such, the thesis serves as a filter that places the focus on certain story elements while ignoring others.

What is needed for more progress on intramessage patterning is an open-minded approach to examining as many story elements as possible. Then we need more examination into how all the story elements work together simultaneously in attracting and holding the attention of audience members.

Intermessage Examination. Often scholars are interested in not only the pattern of story elements in one message but also the breadth of that pattern throughout all mass media stories. The intermessage examination then takes the pattern found in the examination of one message and searches other messages to see if the same pattern exists. This is the concern with generalization—that is, how prevalent is a pattern that we find in one message? Is this finding special to the one message we analyzed, or is this pattern to be found in other messages, most messages, or all messages?

Here there has been a stark contrast in the accomplishments of the social scientific and humanistic approaches to analyzing media messages. Both approaches have been helpful but in different ways. Also, both have exhibited strong limitations, again in different ways. Social science is very much concerned with patterns across units and in generalizing findings from small samples to larger populations. With content analysis of messages, social sciences have done this well, but that which they generalize is usually not a pattern but a frequency of occurrence of a story element. In contrast, scholars using humanistic methods make a strong case for a story pattern in a single message or set of messages (like a TV series such as *Dallas* or a genre such as soap operas), but then they show no concern for generalizing those patterns to larger sets of messages.

Hierarchy of Contribution. To help clarify the most important issues in my critique of the content literatures, I have constructed a template that has five categories of contribution (see Figure 15.1). Category 1 is the lowest challenge and Category 5 the most ambitious. Each makes an important contribution, and research is needed in each category to fully develop the field. Category 1 includes those studies that provide counts of some element. Category 2 presents those counts in a contingent analysis; that is, counts are displayed in different categories of content. This type of study might present counts on more than one variable, but the reporting is done in a sequential manner; that is, the counts are done on one content variable at a time. Category 3 includes those studies that simultaneously consider the co-occurrence of a small set of characteristics of a message. Each message is examined for the co-occurrence pattern. Category 4 is similar to Category 3, but it draws on a greater number of content elements in constructing patterns. Finally, Category 5 is a multilevel analysis of media messages—that is, it looks for patterns in scenes, story lines, and overall messages.

The social scientific literature is composed of studies almost exclusively in the first two categories. Its strength is that it uses relatively large samples of messages, usually of randomly selected messages within a sampling frame, so it has a strong basis to generalize patterns found in the samples analyzed. The purpose of these analyses is to identify regularities across the coded micro units. The limitation is that it focuses primarily on manifest content of micro units and largely stays away from the more latent meanings found in more macro units. For example, with content analysis on violence, coders count micro acts (such as punches and gunshots) and rarely look at the broader contextual web to determine if the micro acts are likely to be interpreted as violence by audience members. Thus, with social science content analysis, the focus is on patterns across messages in samples; let's call these sample patterns.

In contrast, the humanistic literature typically focuses on meaning at the macro level. Scholars examine messages holistically and try to relate them to contexts outside the messages themselves, such as genres, discourses, and the body of work of the producers. The strength of this scholarship is that it focuses on larger structures that are closer to those likely used by audience members. However, the limitation is that these studies are based on very small samples, even as small as one TV show or

Category 1: Counting
Purpose: To count instances of manifest content
Focus of Reporting: Counts, percentages, rates (per vehicle, hour, page, etc.)
Examples: Character demographics, especially gender and ethnic background

Category 2: Landscaping
Purpose: To compare counts across groups of content units
Focus of Reporting: Counts, percentages, rates compared across content units, such as
> By medium (e.g., television counts vs. film counts)
> By vehicle (e.g., *Time* vs. *Newsweek* or *CSI Miami* vs. *Alias*)
> By content provider (e.g., ABC, CBS, Fox, and NBC or Virgin Records vs. Columbia)
> By genre (e.g., news vs. reality programming)

Category 3: Small Patterning
Purpose: To identify associations of a small set of content characteristics (about two to three) *within* content units, and then look across content units to see if the associations are prevalent and can be considered a pattern
Focus of Reporting: Pattern of association of content characteristics
Example: Across all television entertainment programming, males are more likely to be portrayed as being employed outside the household. In this example, the content units are television entertainment programs, and the content characteristics coded are characters' gender and place of employment.

Category 4: Contextual Patterning
Purpose: To identify patterns from multiple contextual features in media messages; limited to one level of analysis

> Step 1: Identify regularities among multiple content characteristics (three or more) *within* a media message.
> Step 2: Examine additional media messages to see if the same regularities are in evidence.
> Step 3: Infer a pattern.
> Step 4: Generalize the pattern to all media messages in the same population.

Focus of Reporting: Patterns of association of content characteristics that are on the same level of analysis
Example: Across portrayals of violence on television, seldom are victims portrayed as being harmed, seldom is the violence depicted in a graphic manner, seldom do perpetrators exhibit remorse, and seldom are perpetrators shown being punished.

Category 5: Narrative Line
Purpose: To account for the major decisions made by media message creators as well as the major decoding elements used by audiences; not limited to one level of analysis
Focus of Reporting: Fully detailed elaboration of the formulas used in media messages

Figure 15.1   Hierarchy of Media Content Analysis Challenges

one book. So the patterns they report are detailed descriptions about one message (or small set of messages), but they tell us very little about how far those patterns extend. Thus, with humanistic content scholarship, the focus is on patterns within a message; let's call these message patterns.

What is missing by level is a literature that focuses on larger meaning structures within messages (not limited to elements such as gender of characters or consequence of one act) and then analyzes many messages at this level to see if the message patterns hold across samples in sample patterns.

Understanding Effects of Patterns on Audiences

The important questions on this topic are as follows: What attracts audience members' attention the most, what structures of storytelling hold their attention the most, and what story resolutions are the most satisfying? How far can producers deviate from story formulas, and what deviations are optimal, that is, maximizing audience payoff with only minimal increases in psychic investment? We need to know more about how content formulas of different levels (meta-genre formulas, genre formulas, medium formulas, episode formulas, etc.) work together. We also need to look at how producers use techniques to attract audience members and hold their attention. Recall from Chapter 6 that there are many techniques that producers use. We need to study more carefully the specifics of how they use these techniques. For example, what do producers do specifically to create presence or to get audience members to suspend disbelief willingly in some messages but not others?

On the surface, this might sound like a call for more administrative research, that is, findings that could help producers and programmers working in the media industries. Granted, this information would help them, but this knowledge would also help scholars understand the values and practices in the industry better. There may be some beliefs operating in the industry that are false, and this research could show where producers' beliefs about what message elements work and which elements in messages perform the best may be different.

But more profoundly, this knowledge is needed to help us understand the dynamics of audience formation and the experiences people have in different exposure states. This knowledge is needed to help us understand movements on the line of influence (see the effects chapters) and how they alter effects levels over a lifetime of conditioning. And this knowledge is needed to help us understand the structure of mass media narratives in a more detailed and dynamic manner.

There are two ways this task can be approached. One way is to look at micro patterns and then test those micro patterns to see which are most effective in attracting and holding audience members' attention. This works best when audience members are in the automatic state of exposure and the content elements are regarded as triggers of attention. The other way is to look at more macro patterns, that is, to consider the simultaneous interaction of many story elements and assess how they work together to signal story meanings to audience members.

The social science method is focused on the more micro task of identifying story elements, providing clear operational definitions for those elements so coders can be trained to spot them systematically, and then having coders count the occurrence of those micro elements. Because social scientists focus on counts, percentages, and rates of individual story elements, their contribution involves providing story information that is likely to affect audience members when frequencies vary. This speaks more to the repetition of messages, the conditioning function of media exposure, and reinforcement effects, which typically occur in the state of automaticity. This also has more value with meaning-matching tasks than with meaning construction. Thus, when we are studying meaning-matching tasks and what occurs in the state of automaticity, the social science approach is likely to be much better than the humanistic approach. Social scientists have a large literature of experiments that show them which elements have the greatest chance of attracting attention and triggering particular reactions through the exposure session. Therefore, it is important to know *how frequently* these elements occur during typical exposures, and to generate this frequency information, researchers should use the content analysis method.

In contrast, when we are more interested in what happens when people are in an attentional state or especially in a self-reflexive state and are focused on constructing meaning, we need much more elaborated patterns about messages to understand how audience members are being affected. Thus, in these situations, the results of humanistic scholars' analyses of media messages are much more useful.

Understanding Producer Decisions

We need more examination about how story formulas are used by producers. This literature is rather small compared with other literatures. An example of this type of research is a study by Oliver and Kalyanaraman (2002), who examined violent and sexual portrayals in movie previews featured on video rentals. What is needed is more research that focuses on elements in media messages that were designed to attract and hold audience attention. This then could form a stronger foundation for research into how producers make their decisions.

When examining how producers think and how they make their decisions about constructing their stories, two issues are central: awareness and accuracy. As for awareness, the question is, How aware are producers of the patterns they create? That is, to what extent are producers in a kind of automatic state where they are following formulas without conscious knowledge of them? As for accuracy, the question is, How accurate are producers' guesses about what will attract and hold the attention of their intended audience members? This question, in essence, raises the issue of how much of media message production is craft (i.e., dependent on skills that can be learned) and how much is art (i.e., a creative vision). Unfortunately, scholars have not regarded these concerns as being particularly interesting. Social scientists almost totally ignore these issues, and humanistic scholars address these concerns obliquely when they regard producers as being influenced by ideologies.

At first glance, it might appear that the existing humanistic approaches would be useful to address this issue. For example, narrative structuralists such as Barthes (1977) focus on how narratives operate to structure meaning. But producers are not trying to structure meaning as much as they are trying to structure exposures; meaning is secondary. If a dozen audience members all interpret different meanings from a particular media message, the producer does not care as long as the dozen audience members continue with the exposure and are conditioned to come back for subsequent exposures. The same is the case with the audience members; to them, the specific meanings they derive from an exposure are less important than the fact that those exposures produce the perception of value. Scholars who shift the focus to speculating on meanings produced without grounding those insights in the producers' experiences or the mundane everyday exposures of the audience members are creating a scholarship on the periphery of the phenomenon itself.

Some critical/cultural scholars (Althusser, 1970; J. Fiske, 1989) argue that there are ideological codes embedded in any television message. These codes convey information about individualism, patriarchy, race, class, materialism, and capitalism. The codes are put there by television producers, and they are used automatically by readers of the messages. But this raises the question of why a producer would be primarily concerned about these themes. If producers are concerned about these themes and conveying messages, they are only concerned in a peripheral manner. Centrally, they are much more concerned with attracting and maintaining audiences. That is the core concern. Critical/cultural scholars point out that stories can be studied syntagmatically, which is a structural analysis that looks at the linear sequential ordering of story elements. The other way stories can be studied is paradigmatically, which is more speculative and deductive. This involves studying the deeper structure of stories where polar opposites conflict, such as life/death, male/female, good/evil, and so on. Levi-Strauss (1955) called for taking story elements out of the narrative flow. For him, the chain of events is a surface structure that is less important than the deep structure of the story. So characters, settings, and actions are analyzed from a meaning perspective.

This is the irony of narrative analysis. The worldview of scholars using narrative analysis is that humans are interpretive beings who construct meaning for themselves; that is, meaning is constructed by audiences, not in the text itself. It is one thing to do a syntagmatic analysis of manifest elements on the surface of a story and record them as they occur. It is quite another to do a deep structure analysis paradigmatically; scholars make interpretations, but those interpretations are their own, and we have no warrant to compare them with an objective base standard, so there is no way to judge the relative degrees of interpretive value. In a pluralistic worldview, the value is on the range of interpretation, and no one interpretation can be sanctioned as the only interpretation or as better than any others. This is a trap.

To avoid this trap, it is better to stay with the more syntagmatic analyses. But then after documenting the elements and their chronological appearances, they need to be linked to other things besides a range of interpretations by audience members. Instead, it would seem to be better to link them to decisions by producers and effectiveness in attracting and maintaining the attention of audiences.

Within this view is the assumption that when we use formal logic to understand communication, we get into trouble. Therefore, scholars should not give technical discourse a higher status than rhetorical or poetic discourse. Instead, scholars are asked to recognize that people use a more informal rationality in telling stories, so scholars should use a "narrative rationality" to understand communication. This narrative logic is based on the principles of coherence and fidelity. Coherence means the consistency of characters and actions (a kind of internal validity), while fidelity is a matter of truth (analogous to external validity; i.e., does the story ring true to the listener's own experiences in real life and provide a reliable guide to our own beliefs, attitudes, values, and actions?).

Sources of Information

What can scholars use as a source of information when constructing a narrative line for a media message? There are three sources: the message itself, producers of the message, and audience members.

Scholars can analyze the message itself and infer the set of decisions that faced producers, their values, their skills, and the ways they made selections among their options in constructing the message. The advantage of using the text as a source of this analysis is that scholars can sometimes see patterns in message content that producers did not plan intentionally. Thus, such an analysis can produce fresh insights. But to achieve this type of advantage, scholars need to be very skilled at analysis, pattern construction, and persuasive expression.

Scholars can go to producers and interview them about their design decisions. The advantage of using message producers as the source of a message analysis is that scholars can accurately document the intentions of the producers rather than having to infer them from the content. Scholars can ask producers why they chose to design a message within a particular meta-genre, genre, and subgenre; why they began the message the way they did; and why they sequenced elements as they did.

Scholars can also interview audience members about their experiences in decoding the message. The advantage of this form of analysis is in documenting what was received. However, the challenge in this analysis lies in being a skilled enough interviewer to access audience experiences. Often audience members will not be able to recall many details about processing a message after an exposure. And even during an exposure, audience members may not have the ability to recognize and articulate what occurs during highly routinized information processing. Audience members are likely to be able to articulate whether they were attracted to the message or not and why, if their attention waned throughout the message, and what they valued most in the message. But they are likely to be much less able to talk about genres and the differential conventions of those genres in any detail.

Each of the three sources outlined above has its inherent advantages and disadvantages that reflect the situation that each can provide only a partial perspective on the phenomenon of message design-appearance-interpretation. Therefore, it is a less interesting scholarly task to focus on only one than it is to use two—or all three—sources and contrast the results. For example, the results of an analysis of producers' intentions and practices can be contrasted with an analysis of the message to generate insights into the degree to which producers achieve their goals or the degree to which producers are aware of all the by-products of their decisions as exhibited in the message patterns.

Conclusion

This chapter presented a critique of both the quantitative and qualitative approaches to analyzing mass media messages. Following from this critique, the chapter presented a series of recommendations for moving scholarly thinking about media messages from a Generating-Findings to a more Mapping-Phenomenon perspective.

PART V

Explaining the Media Effects Facet

CHAPTER 16

Media Effects Line of Thinking

T he lineation general framework suggests a particular line of thinking about mass media effects that helps us evolve from a Generating-Findings perspective to a Mapping-Phenomenon perspective. In this chapter, I argue that the Generating-Findings perspective has been dominated by a set of assumptions about media effects and a set of practices for conducting media effects research that I call the Groups-Differences strategy. This Groups-Differences strategy has served us well by helping us explore the effects facet of the mass media, and it has helped us identify many examples of media-influenced effects. But it has limitations that are becoming more serious barriers as we confront new challenges. I argue that to evolve past the limitations in the Groups-Differences strategy, we need to consider a different strategy—one I call the Target-Degree strategy.

In this chapter, I also make one other argument that is sure to be very controversial. I will argue that almost all of what is regarded as the mass media effects literature fails to report on media effects. While I believe there is value in this literature, it cannot be used to make defensible claims about media effects. The Groups-Differences strategy, which dominates the formation of the mass media effects literature, has been built on particular assumptions and procedures that serve to divert the design of research studies away from testing effects and instead test only differences. Thus, scholars who report their findings of differences must finesse a claim that they have (or have not) found evidence of media effects.

This chapter is organized to address two strategies for thinking about mass media effects. First, I will describe and then critique the Groups-Differences strategy that has been so dominant up to this point. Second, I will introduce an alternative strategy—Target-Degree—and argue that this strategy is what is needed to help us evolve as a scholarly field and more effectively address the present and future challenges of explaining the effects of that mass media.

The Groups-Differences Strategy

By a Groups-Differences strategy, I mean that the media effects literature is focused less on effects directly and more on differences in means across groups, hence the name Groups-Differences. To explain what I mean by this research strategy and why it is limited, I need to begin with the idea of "comparison." Essentially, all research designs require comparison. Some designs compare current events with historical events; some compare particular facts with a standard; some compare certain characteristics across groups. With media effects studies, the effects means are never compared with some standard, and they are rarely compared with previous measures on the same research participants over time to develop a historical pattern. Instead, the typical mass media effects design compares effects means across groups where groups are determined by an experimental treatment or by some characteristic of the research participants, such as gender, age, and so on.

With the Groups-Differences strategy, the procedure is as follows: An "effects" measure is taken from all participants, means are computed for each group, and then those means are compared across groups. With experiments, groups are determined a priori as treatments, and participants are randomly assigned to the groups. If there are relatively large differences in means across groups, the researchers conclude that differences were generated by the differential treatments—usually a media message. With surveys, participants are grouped in the data analysis according to characteristics, such as age, gender, amount of media use, and so on. If there are relatively large differences in means across groups, the researchers conclude that differences are attributable to the grouping variables. Hence the name *Groups-Differences* for this strategy.

If the literature were directly focused on effects themselves, the empirical research would have to be designed differently to answer questions such as the following: Which research participants experienced the effect and which did not? Instead, these studies are designed to answer the following questions: In which group was there a greater mean on a particular effects measure? Were the differences in group means large enough for us to conclude that such a difference could not have occurred by chance alone? What is the degree of relationship between the distributions of two scores? Almost every study in the published literature can provide clear answers to these Groups-Differences questions, but those answers tell us nothing about how any one participant was affected, and they tell us very little about what that effect experience was.

The popularity of the Groups-Differences strategy can be attributed to its ability to provide a way around two problems: the category-continuum problem and the effect-criterion problem. Rather than working to solve either of these problems, the Groups-Differences strategy avoids them by shifting the focus to group averages and comparing those averages across groups. Thus, this strategy has provided great utility to researchers who are more anxious to generate some empirical findings than to work out some difficult conceptual issues first. Thus, the Groups-Differences strategy contributes much more to the Generating-Findings perspective than to the Mapping-Phenomenon perspective.

Category-Continuum Problem

One problem for researchers in documenting whether media effects occur is that most effects are not categorical. There are, of course, some effects that are truly categorical; that is, there is clear evidence that some people experience an effect, while other people clearly do not. For example, with a learning effect, a person has learned a particular fact from exposure to a particular media message and can recall that fact or cannot. Another example is an attitudinal effect where a person has changed his or her opinion about something or he or she has not. With these natural categorical effects, it is a simple matter to identify who exhibits an effect and who does not.

Mass media effects researchers, however, rarely examine effects in such a categorical manner because there are few natural categorical effects. Furthermore, many natural categorical effects are far more interesting to study when they are transformed into continua. To illustrate, let's say we show 12 children a violent cartoon and then put them in a room with a variety of toys (guns, knives, swords, building blocks, clay, crayons, etc.). We observe that 5 of those children choose to play with the violent toys while the remaining 7 children ignore the violent toys. In this case, we can clearly regard the 5 children who play with the violent toys as exhibiting an aggression effect and the other 7 children as not exhibiting such an effect. This example makes it appear that aggressive play is a categorical variable, but this is rarely the case in research studies. Typically, there are many behaviors exhibited that make it impractical to maintain the categorical nature of this variable. For example, what if some children play with the violent toys for 5 seconds while other children play with the violent toys for 10 minutes; should all these children be regarded as being in the same category of aggression? With most effects measures, researchers use continuous measures, and this opens the door for the next problem.

Effect-Criterion Problem

This is the challenge of determining what should be regarded as threshold evidence of an effect. Because social scientists typically use continuous measures for media-influenced effects, they end up with a distribution of effects scores and must decide at what point on the distribution they should establish a threshold, such that participants with higher scores are regarded as exhibiting the effect while participants with lower scores are regarded as not exhibiting the effect. To illustrate, let's say we conduct an experiment to test an aggressive effect from exposure to media messages, so we show our participants one of several movies (high violence, low violence, no violence) and then give them the chance to deliver shocks to an opponent in a game they play after the exposure. What if an experimental participant delivers only one shock; is that enough to conclude that he or she was behaving aggressively? What if there are participants who deliver 15, 40, and 100 shocks? We cannot select a point along the distribution of effect measures in a nonarbitrary manner and use it as a threshold, such that all scores on one side of that threshold represent participants who experienced the effect, while the scores on the other side of the threshold represent participants who did not experience the effect.

Social scientists have taken a shortcut around this effects-criterion problem by using a combination of two techniques. One technique is to divide research participants into groups so that the degree of evidence of an effect can be compared across groups. The second technique is to rely on statistical significance for differences. This is the Groups-Differences strategy. While this Groups-Differences strategy helps researchers get around the threshold problem, this practice fundamentally alters the research question. That is, researchers are no longer posing questions such as the following: Is there an effect? How many people experienced an effect? Did more people in one treatment experience an effect compared with the number of people experiencing the effect in another treatment? Instead, the question we really answer is this: Are the differences across group means on a continuous measure of an effect large enough for us to conclude those differences could not have occurred by chance alone?

Experiments by their very nature always set up group comparisons. Surveys also rely on group comparisons where group means are compared across respondent groups as constructed typically by their demographics, psychological characteristics, or media exposure patterns. With survey methods, researchers typically use continuous variables but then correlate scores across pairs of distributions rather than means across groups. But my point still holds. Survey researchers avoid the problem of identifying who in their samples experienced effects and instead report correlation coefficients that are interpreted in the context of probability; that is, the magnitudes of the coefficients are compared with probability tables to determine if they could have occurred by chance alone.

With qualitative methods, researchers observe people in interactions with the media and each other and then offer conclusions about whether certain people are affected by particular media experiences. To support their conclusions, they offer rich descriptions of patterns of behavior and patterns of thinking. This leaves the reader of this scholarship questioning whether other people exhibiting slightly different patterns of behavior would also have impressed the qualitative scholar enough to conclude that those people were also experiencing a media effect. The qualitative scholar writes about an X-ness that can be interpreted as evidence of a media effect. But the reader is left wondering about the perimeters of X-ness—that is, how far can people deviate from those patterns of behaving as described by the qualitative scholar before losing the essence of X-ness? In short, what is the threshold of the effect?

The Groups-Differences strategy has generated a very large literature. This literature has high value in suggesting where there may be effects, but it cannot be used to make direct and defensible claims about whether there are effects. Please do not take my claim out of context; I do believe the mass media exert influences that lead to effects. In fact, as you will see in the next chapter, I believe there are many more effects than have been claimed thus far in the mass media literature. My argument here is that mass media researchers, by following a Groups-Differences strategy, have not been generating the kind of evidence needed to support directly their claims for media effects.

Critique of the Groups-Differences Strategy

This Groups-Differences strategy has allowed us to produce a great many research studies that suggest effects. We have learned that many characteristics of media messages are associated with variation on effects measures. We have also learned a great deal about the characteristics of people and the exposure situations that are associated with effects measures. However, there are limitations in using this strategy. In the past, these limitations have been worth tolerating to reap the benefits provided by this strategy. But now that we have a good base of research that suggests where effects are, we need to move on to the greater challenge of documenting the strength and prevalence of those effects and of attaining greater precision in calibrating the mass media's role in shaping those effects. In this section, I will highlight eight of those limitations in the areas of conceptualizations, design, and reporting findings.

Conceptual Limitations

Lack of Definition for Effect. One of the most limiting characteristics of this literature on mass media effects is a lack of a conceptual articulation of what an effect is. There are no formal general conceptual definitions of mass media effects. By formal definition, I mean a definition with classification rules that can be used to determine clearly whether something is an example of an effect. Formal definitions are essential for mapping. If we are to map the media effects literature, we need a formal definition with clear classification rules so we know what examples should be included and which should be excluded. Also, the classification rules establish the perimeter of the concept such that we can see the full territory, and with this full territory as background, we can organize the examples and thus illustrate areas where there is concentration of thinking and research and areas that have been ignored. Without a formal definition, mapping can only be done in a partial and suggestive manner.

Scholars typically finesse this point and instead treat effects in an ostensive manner (pointing to certain things as effects), an operational manner, or a primitive manner (assuming we all know what an effect is).

To illustrate the ostensive finesse, scholars who publish reviews of the mass media effects literature will point to what empirical studies report as effects (Basil, 1992; J. Bryant & Zillmann, 2002; Grossberg et al., 1998; Harris, 2004; Hovland, 1954; Iyengar, 1997; Jeffres, 1997; Lazarsfeld, 1948; Littlejohn, 1999; Lowery & DeFleur, 1988; McDonald, 2004; McGuire, 1986; J. M. McLeod & Reeves, 1980; McQuail, 2005; Perse, 2001; D. F. Roberts & Maccoby, 1985; Severin & Tankard, 2001; Sparks, 2006; Weiss, 1969). I am not denigrating the value of these reviews; they are all written by respected communication scholars, and each provides a valuable service in attempting to organize the literature. However, it is interesting to note that none of these reviews provides a formal definition of a mass media effect. Even in their classic essay "On the Nature of Media Effects," J. M. McLeod and Reeves (1980) failed to provide a definition of effects. The closest the literature comes to providing a general formal definition of media effects comes in *Mass Media Effects* by Leo Jeffres (1997) with his section on "Defining Media Effects" (pp. 3–5). Jeffres argued that before defining effects, he needed to first define mass media, communication, encoding, channel, and decoding process—all of which he did define. But then he ended this section by saying, "The issue of what constitutes effects is difficult to resolve because it means different things to different people. 'Effects' may refer to the relationship between encoding and decoding activities within mass communication. . . . 'Effects' may link mass communication processes with other systems and the larger society. . . . Media effects may refer to the impact of media 'as a whole'" (pp. 4–5).

The operational finesse is typical with empirical studies. However, this practice leads to definitional confounding and clutter. A prime area in which to see the definitional confounding is in the literature on the topic of effects of exposure to violence in the media. The term *learning* has been used to mean learning lessons about violence, learning the details of how to commit a particular violent act, triggering behavior, literally imitating the violent act viewed, or becoming disinhibited so that aggressive behavior is later more likely to be exhibited. Also, the term *aggressive behavior effect* has been used to denote at least two very different processes. One of these processes regards the media as creating cognitive associations through priming certain nodes in a person's memory scheme. Later, when people see a portrayal of violence similar to what they have stored in a highly accessible associative network, they are ready to behave violently (Jo & Berkowitz, 1994). But there is also a social learning explanation where the media present lots of portrayals of violence where perpetrators are rewarded and where victims do not show many harmful consequences. This leads to audience members perceiving a pattern that violence is often a good thing. There is also a generalization effect, where people then take this pattern and accept it as a lesson that is valued in their social world. Then later, when people see an act of violence in an experimental setting, it triggers their aggressive behavior (Bandura, 1973). Thus, this disinhibition explanation has the media exerting several different influences—on inferring a pattern, generalizing the pattern, and triggering a behavior. For more on this definitional confounding in mass media effects research on violence, see W. J. Potter (1999). However, this confounding is not limited to violence research.

The primitive finesse is to talk about a presumption of media effects where people just assume they exist. This historical format is popular with this type of definition; that is, the authors keep the focus on changes in beliefs about effects and assumptions underlying the research over time rather than on conceptualizing what an effect is.

Ostensive, operational, and primitive forms of defining effects are all unsatisfying because they leave the reader with the fuzzy feeling that there may (or may not) be other effects. It is rather like planning a vacation to see the United States and someone hands you a pile of brochures where some of these brochures are about states, some about cities, some about national parks, and some about amusement parks. While each brochure may be very well written and highly descriptive of its topic, you are left with a feeling that there may be other attractive states, cities, and parks that are not included in your pile. You have the feeling that the brochures are a haphazard collection rather than a complete set from which you can make the best choices. Also, you probably would like a map that would show where all the attractions are so that you could plan the sequence of your trip.

Maps are essential organizing devices. But to construct a good map of a scholarly area, we need a formal definition with clear classification rules. With the media effects literature, we need a map to show the full set of effects, show the boundaries of what media-influenced effects are, and provide a structure to show the relative positions of each effect.

Ignoring Attentional States. Another limiting part of the way the Groups-Differences strategy regards the nature of media effects is that it assumes conscious attentional processing over automatic processing. However, this is not how most media exposure takes place; most exposure is in the automatic state. Thus, we need to take much more of a history of a person's media exposure over time.

We also need to rethink how we measure the participants' experiences during experiments. And in surveys, we need to think about what respondents are able to tell us so that we do not end up creating attitudes, beliefs, and false recollections during the data gathering.

Misplaced Locus of Meaning. With the Groups-Differences strategy, meaning is assumed to lie much more within the message than in the individual. This is especially the case with experiments where researchers will design different treatments. When researchers find within-group variation in reactions to the treatment, they regard this as error variation. I believe it is a waste of an opportunity to ignore this variation as error. Instead, researchers can significantly increase our understanding of the effects process when they take the time to measure participants' individual reactions to the stimulus materials and build those reactions in as explanatory variables. In my own research, I have found that these individual-differences interpretation variables can explain much more of the variation than can treatment group differences (see W. J. Potter & Tomasello, 2003).

Focus on Immediate Over Long-Term Effects. Another limitation with the Groups-Differences strategy is its view about the nature of media effects. The Groups-Differences strategy focuses on immediate over long-term influence, change over reinforcement, and conscious attentional processing over automatic processing. Experiments typically take a measure of effects during the exposure or immediately after. A few studies also measure for the stability of the effect over time, usually days or weeks. Even with a 2-week postmeasure, the assessment is still relatively proximate to the treatment. To illustrate this point, a 20-year-old research participant is likely to have experienced more than 900 weeks of media exposures at the time of the experiment, so a 2-week period accounts for only 0.2% in his or her exposure history—the other 99.8% is ignored. Thus, the focus is on the blips of change over long-term shaping of the reactions. This conditioning in terms of continual reinforcement of existing attitudes, beliefs, thought patterns, emotional reactions, and behavioral habits is largely ignored. Some of these characteristics are measured, but typically they are considered as peripheral factors in the analysis, not a featured part of the explanation. This would not be a serious limitation if we assumed that all people were conditioned the same and therefore operate from the same base. However, this is not likely to be the case; instead, the very nature of individual differences lies in the differences in long-term conditioning. Thus, when people enter an experiment, some are much more likely to exhibit a particular effect than are others. Even if we believe that random assignment of people to treatment groups will adequately balance out these differences across treatment groups, it seems a tremendous waste of opportunity to ignore these differences. Of course, ignoring these differences is an efficient thing to do when the focus is simply on mean differences across experimenter-created treatment groups. But if the focus is on increasing our understanding about the nature of media effects, then a great deal of this opportunity for increasing our understanding lies in the patterns of individual differences.

Design Limitations

Overreliance on Categorical Attribute Variables in Grouping. It is understandable why researchers using the Groups-Differences strategy would use grouping variables with values that appear nominal. It is easy to group people into male and female values on gender or children into grade level. The categories exist and do not have to be constructed by researchers who must encounter the problem of determining and then defending cut points. But these categorical variables are often attributes that are used as surrogates for more active factors of influence. For example, biological gender (male, female) is almost always less important in media effects research than socialized gender (which is a continuous distribution); also, age level is really a surrogate for either degree of experience with the media or cognitive developmental level, which has been shown to be only loosely related to biological age (P. E. Bryant & Kopytynska, 1976; Donaldson, 1978; H. Gardner, 1983; Hashway & Duke, 1992; P. M. King, 1986; McGarrigle & Donaldson, 1975; Moore & Fry, 1986), compared with what early stage theorists such as Piaget theorized (e.g., see Piaget & Inhelder, 1969).

Shifting from attribute variables to active variables would increase the pressure on dividing continuous distributions, which are characteristic of active variables, into categories so group differences could be tested. But this pressure to divide the continuous distributions produced by active variables would be eliminated if we focused more on relationships than on group differences.

Random Assignment of Participants. Researchers designing experiments carefully craft their treatments around differences they build into media messages, so that when mean differences across treatment groups are found, the researchers can attribute those differences to specific characteristics in the media messages. However, when experimental researchers examine their data, they always find variation within treatment groups, but this variation is typically assumed to be error. Of course, if we press experimenters, they will acknowledge that some of this within-treatment variation is not actually error but is systematic variation that could be explained by other variables that were not included in their design and therefore cannot be partitioned in their particular study. To factor out the influence of this variation that cannot be attributed to the variables in the design of the experiment, researchers randomly assign participants to conditions. This serves to give experimenters peace of mind as they assume this technique of random assignment of participants to conditions has balanced out the influence of all unmeasured variables across conditions.

Is this peace of mind warranted? Let's examine the usefulness of this strategy in the context of media effects research, where there are likely to be dozens of interacting influences. For example, let's imagine conducting a two-group experiment that will test people's reaction to political ads. We randomly assign 100 participants to Group 1, where they see one set of ads, and another 100 participants to Group 2, where they see another set of ads that differ on some key characteristic Y. We want to test if Y makes a difference in the way the groups react to the ads. We run a post hoc analysis on participant demographics and determine that the gender split does not differ significantly across the two groups; also, the mean age and the mean GPA are the same across the two groups. However, can we really use these three demographics to talk ourselves into a feeling of confidence that the two groups are equivalent? The groups may be equivalent on these three variables, but to what extent are these three variables really reflective of the active factors that will be brought into play in interpreting the stimulus materials? Not much. It is far more likely that political orientation (conservative, moderate, and liberal) is important. Also, general reaction to the political system as well as political campaigns would be important. It would be easy to think of at least 10 such attitudes or beliefs that would likely be brought into play when reacting to the political ads. For the sake of simplicity, let's say each of these 10 variables has only three positions; that would make 3^{10} or 59,049 unique clusters of attitudes and beliefs about the political system that these 200 participants could hold. To be fair, let's say that about two thirds of those clusters might be logically impossible (i.e., if a person is politically liberal, she or he is not likely to have a positive attitude about a particular conservative candidate), which would leave us with about 20,000 different attitude/belief combinations. The probability that any one of the 100 participants randomly assigned to Group 1 matches the same attitude/belief cluster as any one of the 100 participants randomly assigned to Group 2 is tiny, and the probability that all 100 in Group 1 have an exact counterpart in Group 2 is absurdly small. Of course, there could be balanced proportions on *individual* attitudes (i.e., the same proportion of conservative, neutral, and liberal participants in each group). But these attitudes are not independent from one another; instead, they are likely to be tightly networked into attitude/belief clusters, and the unit of comparison should be the cluster configuration. It is likely that the differences in these clusters can explain the differences in interpretations of Y, but we will never know unless we build this type of analysis into our designs.

Even if we were able to accept the assumption that random assignment of participants to conditions would balance out the influence of all the individual-difference factors, it is still a weak practice for explanatory research because it ignores the opportunity for stronger explanation. By measuring a greater number of potential explanatory factors and building them into the analyses, researchers greatly expand their ability to explain the nature of media effects above and beyond what the traditional experiment and analysis of variance (ANOVA) allow.

It is not possible, of course, to measure all the potential individual-difference factors that might be active in an explanation, but increasing the number of these factors beyond what is built into the independent variables design of an experiment is a very useful thing. In selecting these additional factors, I suggest that the most useful ones are individuals' personal interpretations of the elements in the media messages. No matter how carefully an experimenter designs treatment materials, individuals always bring their interpretive histories to the experiment. When 20 participants are exposed to the same media message as a treatment, it is highly unlikely that all 20 will "see" the same thing, and what each participant "sees" is a much better explanation of the subsequent effect on each participant than is what the experimenter built into the design.

Reporting of Findings Limitations

Misleading Reporting of Findings. Researchers often report their findings in a categorical manner, even when they have generated continuous distributions of effects measures. Such reporting simplifies things to help with reader comprehension, but such simplicity is almost always misleading. For example, experimental researchers typically will report their findings in the following form: We found an X effect in the first treatment, a Y effect in the second treatment, and no effect in the control group. In such an experiment, the researchers are likely to have observed a wide variation in each of their three experimental groups. It is likely that there were participants exhibiting an X effect and a Y effect in all three groups; it is also likely that there were participants exhibiting no X or Y effect in all three groups. Designers of such experiments do not care much about the differences in effects experienced by individuals *within* a treatment group; they care more about the *average* score on an effect within a group, and they care most that the average effect score for each group is statistically different from the average effect scores in all other groups. This is what I mean by categorical focus of experimental researchers—that is, the focus is not on effects scores themselves and how they change across time for individuals. Instead, the focus is on an average effect score for each group. Thus, the group is the primary unit of analysis, not the individual or the individual's effect scores.

This shift in unit is not limited to experiments; survey researchers follow the same practice. Let's say that researchers gather data to test the degree to which beliefs about gender are related to media exposure. When analyzing the data, the researchers are likely to construct demographically defined categories and test the relationships across them. So, for example, they might test the relationship between beliefs and media exposure first for males and then for females. In the male group, there are likely to be people who are strongly influenced by the media, weakly influenced by the media, and not influenced by the media. A similar distribution of influence is likely among respondents in the female group. However, what the surveyors are most interested in is the strength of the relationship in the male group compared with the strength of the relationship in the female group. The strength of the relationships is captured in correlation coefficients that use the measures from individuals but then shift the focus to patterns in the groups.

Overreliance on Statistical Significance. In social science research, we use the tool of statistical analysis as a way of *apparently* setting a threshold for effects. For example, when we run an experiment, we use ANOVA to tell us if the differences in means across our experimental groups are large enough to conclude that they could have occurred by chance alone. If the answer is yes—it is large enough—then there is a statistically significant difference, and we conclude that we "got results" worthy of reporting. But what we have documented is that a particular effect (dependent variable) is influenced by how we constructed our experimental groups (independent variable[s]), and thus this reflects a Groups-Differences finding. But it does not tell us how many of the participants experienced the effect or what the threshold of evidence for the effect is. This statistical procedure focuses our attention on comparisons of differences on an effects measure, thus allowing researchers to avoid the need to identify a threshold level that must be crossed to conclude that an effect has occurred. However, when researchers talk about their results and make claims that they have observed effects, the implication is sometimes made that the participants in the group with the significantly higher score experienced the effect while the participants in the other groups did not. To illustrate, consider a survey where the researchers are looking at the correlation between amount of watching television and number of aggressive thoughts, and they want to compare males and females. Let's say they find that the correlation among males is $r = .29$ $(p < .05)$, and the correlation among females is $r = .17$ $(p = .25)$. With these figures, researchers would typically conclude that they found a fairly strong relationship among males and no relationship among females. While such reporting about the male group is accurate, the reporting of the female group is a bit misleading. The researchers did not find no relationship among the females; instead, the probability figure of .25 indicates that they have little confidence that the r value of .17 could not have occurred by chance alone. This does not indicate no relationship; it indicates a lack of confidence in the *r* statistic.

Relying on statistical significance for interpreting results also tends to ignore the strength of the effects measures while keeping the focus on the differences in groups. To illustrate this problem, let's say we are testing for an effect called Y, and we design an experiment with two conditions. Condition 1 is a treatment condition containing a series of media messages we expect to evoke a Y effect, and Condition 2 is a control condition containing a series of media messages that are expected *not* to evoke a Y effect. Our dependent measure is designed to capture the degree of Y, and it ranges from 1 (not much Y at all) to 10 (a great deal of Y). Let's say we find a mean score of 8.2 for the treatment group and a mean score of 6.8 for the control group on Y, and thus there is a difference of 1.4 between the two means. The ANOVA statistical test will analyze the within-group variance, the between-group variance, and the total variance to determine the probability that a mean difference of 1.4 could have occurred by chance alone. If the power of the test is high, the ANOVA statistical procedure will tell us that the probability of achieving a mean difference of 1.4 or larger by chance alone is highly unlikely—perhaps less than one chance in 100, or $p < .01$. Thus, we conclude that the media messages in the treatment group produced a Y effect.

Now let's examine the meaning that making such a conclusion conveys to people who do not understand statistics and probability. The average layperson is likely to interpret this conclusion in a categorical manner—that is, the treatment messages stimulated a Y effect in the treatment participants, and the absence of such messages in the control condition resulted in a lack of a Y effect among those participants. This is a faulty interpretation because both means are rather high, and it is likely that many people in both groups experienced a Y effect. Furthermore, there was a distribution of Y scores in both groups, and a fairly sizable proportion (maybe as high as one third) of the control condition participants had Y scores above the mean of the treatment condition distribution of scores, so it is likely that many people in the control group experienced a stronger Y effect than many people in the treatment group. Also, to illustrate the faulty nature of such interpretations even more, let's say the results of the experiment were that the treatment group mean was 2.7 and the control group mean was 1.3. Again we get the 1.4 difference in means and the conclusion that the treatment group exhibited more Y than did the control group. But can we conclude that the treatment messages stimulated much Y effect? No. The Y effect was rare in both groups, although it was slightly less rare in the treatment group.

Statistical significance is an important thing to test, especially where we have no history of documenting effect sizes in a particular line of research. However, statistical significance is sensitive to effect size, number of participants, and complexity of design—three factors that deflect attention away from absolute levels of effects. My point is not to belabor the difference between statistical and substantive significance. Instead, my point is that tests of statistical significance require variation and hence continuous distributions; they focus on relative comparisons across groups and are not designed to provide help in establishing criteria that could be used for thresholds of effects. ANOVA tests report effect sizes, but these are not helpful in determining thresholds because effect sizes for tests of differences are expressed in terms of standard deviation units across group means, not as a threshold score on the effects measure.

Given the widespread use of the Groups-Differences strategy, the analysis of the existing literature on media effects is limited to differences across groups rather than levels of effect. For example, in her book *Media Effects and Society,* Elizabeth Perse (2001) has a section in which she wrote about the strength of media impact. In this section, she reviewed the findings of several meta-analyses of media effects and showed that the standard measure of strength is a *d* statistic, which expresses the standardized difference between experimental group means. She said that "an effect size of .30, then, indicates that the groups differ by .30 of a standard deviation" (p. 6). Thus, effect sizes again reflect group differences, not the strength of an effect itself.

Little Calibration of Influences. Another problem with the current state of the mass media effects literature is that there is little highlighting of differences in the degree of influence of factors on media effects. There is very little sense of calibration, that is, a recognition that some influences are much stronger than others (i.e., very few meta-analyses). Furthermore, there is almost no explication of a calculus about how the factors in the list of influences interact to bring about their effect. With any given effect, its list of factors can be put together in a predictive equation in a variety of ways, and it makes a difference (for an illustration of this, see W. J. Potter, 1997).

We need to move beyond the reporting of whether a particular media message can be linked to a particular effect; we already have a good deal of information of this nature. Our challenge now is to examine *how strongly* particular patterns of media exposure are related to each particular effect within a constellation of simultaneously interacting factors. We need to develop more understanding about how powerful the media influence is relative to other everyday influences such as a person's traits, cognitive abilities, lifestyle, social situation, and many other factors.

Another facet of calibrating influence is the issue of prevalence, that is, how many people experience an influence (prevalence in population) and how often people experience the influence (prevalence in time). Until we can determine this well, we will not have much ability to focus the attention of the public on their risks of media exposures. As of now, we have identified a long list of effects that have been linked with various kinds of media exposure—that is, our list of "yes" effects is very long. If we simply present this to the public, we will scare many people with the length of the list and turn off others with the apparent range of effects. It is rather like the health community giving us a list of harms to our health that includes not taking a vitamin, smoking, having unprotected sex with someone who is HIV positive, and getting too little sleep once in a while. We need to develop more of a sense of the range of degrees of media influence across the entire range of effects. Until we can do this, we cannot target our policy and educational efforts well.

Summary of Critique

Our research field has developed a long list of effects that have been linked to media exposures. Also, we have generated an inventory of particular factors about the media messages, audience members, and situations that have been found related to those effects. While there are likely more effects and more factors of influence yet to be identified, we are reaching a ceiling on the value of continuing this type of research.

The shortcomings in the Groups-Differences strategy become more salient and more limiting as the size of the literature grows. We need to move past the conceptual limitations of the lack of a formal conceptual definition for media effects, ignoring attentional states, misplacing the locus of meaning, and favoring immediate over long-term effects. We need to move past our design limitations with an overreliance on categorical attribute variables in grouping and random assignment of participants to treatment conditions. And we need to move past the limitations in reporting our findings that mislead readers about the nature of effects through shifts in units, overreliance on statistical significance, and lack of calibration of factors of influence.

We have produced enough of a base of information to position ourselves to consider a higher challenge. We need to start shifting our limited resources out of a predominantly generating phase of research with its focus on description—that is, inventorying effects and their associated factors of influence. We need to orient ourselves to a higher challenge of mapping, and this will require a different strategy.

The Target-Degree Strategy for Designing Media Effects Studies

If we are to evolve from a Generating-Findings perspective to a Mapping-Phenomenon perspective, then we need to get past the limitations in the Groups-Differences strategy. In this section, I argue for such an evolution into what I refer to as a Target-Degree strategy. I label this strategy as *Target-Degree* because it begins with the identification of the target of the media influence. This target is usually individuals, but it can also be aggregates of individuals such as organizations, institutions, or the public in general. The target is that which experiences the media effect. By using the word *target,* I do not mean that the mass media organizations have intended every effect that targets end up experiencing; some effects that are experienced by a target are unintentional. A key element in this strategy is that the target is both the unit of measurement and also the unit of analysis. Also, the focus is on the degree to which targets experience the effect. This degree can be relatively large or be indicated by no change at all (zero degree).

This is not a call for a shift in worldview or paradigm. It is not an argument to reject either quantitative methods or qualitative methods. It is not a radical departure from the Groups-Differences strategy. This is an evolutionary shift in the way we conceptualize mass media influence, the way we make decisions in designing effects studies, and the way we report our findings.

When designing any study, hundreds of decisions need to be made about the research focus, variables, measurement, analysis, and so on. The shift I am calling for focuses on four of these decisions. In this section, I will outline the types of options available for each of these four design decisions, indicate the options typically selected by researchers following a Groups-Differences strategy, and then show how the selection of another option on each of these four decisions would lead to much more interesting and useful results. These four decisions are the basis for the study, the unit of analysis, the warrant for an effect, and the examination of media influence (see Table 16.1).

Basis for the Study

Empirical studies generally can be motivated by one of three things: curiosity, empirical literature, or theory. To this list, I add a fourth option of conceptual addressing. The mass media effects literature has been largely motivated by the first two and about a third motivated by theory. The choice of one of these three options is characteristic of the Groups-Differences strategy. That is to say, it has been acceptable to base a study on curiosity. A researcher can notice what he or she thinks is an anomaly or something interesting in the way people behave, then pose some questions about what might be responsible for this, and test the possible influence of the mass media. As long as the methodological design is strong, scholars will regard the study as having high quality. Or a researcher could replicate a study in the published literature by running a test using a different media message as a stimulus, different measures, or a different group of participants. Third, a researcher could take a mass media effects theory (of which there are many), operationalize a test of some facet

Table 16.1   Key Design Decisions for Media Effects Studies

1. Basis for the Study

    a. Curiosity
    b. Empirical literature
    c. Theory
    d. Conceptual addressing

2. Unit of Analysis

    a. Constructed groups
    b. Natural groups
    c. Individual over time
    d. Nonhuman entity

3. Warrant for an Effect

    a. Statistically significant difference
    b. Substantive difference
    c. Substantive constant

4. Examination of Media Influence

    a. Categorical
    b. Degree of influence of all predictors of an effect
    c. Unique degree of influence of media
    d. Unique dynamic degree of influence

of that theory, and run an empirical test. Each of these sources of motivation is valuable from the point of view of generating a large literature. However, each of these has its shortcomings from the point of view of generating a study that will maximize its potential for contributing to a unified knowledge base about the phenomenon. Curiosity is so open-ended and does not build from a clear context. With replications, it is not always clear which design elements were kept constant across studies. With theory, there are so many theories, and so few of them have well-developed dictionaries, calculus, or traditions of testing that the findings of the operationalized tests are difficult to leverage beyond reflecting on the particular theory itself.

To move to a Target-Degree strategy, one must focus on a motivation for the study that is most concerned with positioning the eventual findings within a map of mass media effects. And to do this, we first need a map of mass media effects. I attempt to provide such a map in the next chapter.

Unit of Analysis

Mass media effects studies have four options for a unit of analysis: constructed groups, natural groups, the individual over time, and a nonhuman entity. The weakest of these options is the constructed group, which is the preferred option of the Groups-Differences strategy. The natural group is a better option because it avoids the arbitrary nature of constructing groups. But the best option for designing research into how individuals are influenced by the media is to monitor changes in their effects levels as they experience different influences. This is the central characteristic of the Target-Degree strategy.

The fourth option is the nonhuman entity, which is usually a macro unit such as society, the public, or an institution. This is the functioning of institutions or human constructions that have an existence of their own apart from humans. With this type of unit, the interviewing of individual people is less "on the mark" than is the examination of records, rituals, and functions of those macro units themselves. These need to be studied over time to look for patterns and then attribute those patterns to media influence.

Warrant for an Effect

Social scientists make a distinction between statistical significance and substantive significance. I will not belabor this obvious distinction except to say that in practice, researchers often stop their analyses after showing that their results are statistically significant. In the reporting of results of empirical studies, there is little discussion of the magnitude of the effects, how they compare with the findings of similar studies, and what these numbers mean for making a case for the influence of the mass media on particular effects.

To these two options outlined above, I would like to add the warrant of *substantive constant*. What I mean by this is that the media influence should be tested in different ways and that the more stable the finding is, the stronger belief we can have in the validity of the finding. I do not merely mean robustness, although this is a part of substantive constant. If a particular degree of media influence is found repeatedly across different measures, different types of samples, and different stimulus materials, then the finding is fairly robust. But substantive constant also refers to the same degree of influence showing up across many different types of tests. As for tests of differences, the degree of influence should remain the same whether it is tested as a main effect, as an interaction, or after covarying the influence of other variables on the effect. As for tests of association, the degree of influence should remain the same whether it is a zero-order or partial correlation and regardless of where it is entered into a multiple regression computation. The essence of substantive constancy is that the media element is found to exercise an influence to a particular degree that is stable over many operationalizations and that its influence is unique, even in the constellation of other influences. When mass media effects researchers focus on this warrant for their findings, they are orienting themselves to the ways in which media exert their strongest, most persistent influence.

Examination of Media Influence

When examining media influence on particular effects, there are four options for focal areas. The simplest option is to examine whether there was a difference across groups on a media treatment. This is a categorical focus; that is, either there is a difference or there is not. A second option is to examine the degree of influence of all predictors of an effect. This is better because it contextualizes the media influence in the constellation of other influences. Better yet is to examine the unique degree of influence of media; thus, after considering a variety of influences, it is important to parse out the unique contribution of the media variable. The best of the four options, as far as increasing our knowledge about mass media effects is concerned, is to examine the unique dynamic degree of influence. This is the same as the third option, but it also considers how media influence may change in degree over time as it interacts with other influences.

In summary, there are many options available for designers of mass media effects studies. To evolve from the Groups-Differences strategy to a Target-Degree strategy, research designers need to focus attention most on four decisions: the basis for the study, the unit of analysis, the warrant for an effect, and the examination of media influence. This focus will enable researchers to select particular options that will incrementally increase the value of their findings. Also, this will enable research to be much more programmatic, achieve much more conceptual leverage, make stronger progress in constructing stronger explanations of media influence, and help organize the field in a way that makes it much more useful to scholars and the findings much more understandable to outsiders.

Conclusion

Our current challenge is to do a better job of organizing our thinking about media effects. This starts with the development of a formal definition that can be used for classifying examples and mapping our efforts. Such a definition and a map can guide the design of studies and more efficiently integrate the findings from those empirical tests. They are also an essential first step in providing a means to more effectively inventory our knowledge.

To evolve from a Generating-Findings perspective to a Mapping-Phenomenon perspective, we need to pay more attention to the big picture. Such a big picture is necessary to give our field more unity and to guide future research studies to position their findings much more effectively and efficiently. But to evolve in this way, we need to shift our assumptions and practices into what I call a Target-Degree strategy. I introduced this strategy in this chapter, and I will elaborate it more in the next chapter, where I will also present a formal definition of mass media effects and a matrix for mapping those effects. Then, in Chapter 18, I will continue to elaborate the Target-Degree strategy by providing some recommendations to use when designing empirical studies, both qualitative and quantitative.

Table 16.2   Structured Glossary of Terms About Mass Media Content

Groups-differences strategy—a set of assumptions about media effects and research practices that have dominated the media effects research literature up to this point. It relies on putting research participants into groups and then comparing mean differences across groups.

- It finesses the lack of a formal definition for effects by focusing on mean differences across groups.
- While the unit of measurement is usually the individual, the unit of analysis is the group or the sample.
- Rather than focus on thresholds of an effect, the focus is on thresholds of statistical significance.
- Meaning is typically thought to reside in the media messages as treatment stimuli.

Target-degree strategy—a set of assumptions about media effects and research practices that are recommended to replace the Groups-Differences strategy and help bring about an evolution from a Generating-Findings perspective to a Mapping-Phenomenon perspective.

- It builds tests of various effects from a formal definition and designs studies so the findings can be positioned clearly within a map of mass media effects.
- Both the unit of measurement and the unit of analysis is the individual. Changes (and nonchanges) are plotted over time as the individual experiences media messages.
- Statistical significance is still regarded with importance, but it is not a substitute for an effect threshold.
- Meaning is regarded as residing both in the media messages and in the interpretations constructed by audience members.

CHAPTER 17

Conceptualizing Media Influence and Media Effects

n the previous chapter, I argued that mass media effects researchers have produced a great many empirical findings but that those findings have been very difficult to organize for several reasons. One reason is because there is no formal
general definition of a mass media effect, so there are no clear classification rules
that can be used to determine what should be included. Another reason is that there
is no commonly accepted structure or map that could be used to organize the great
variety of things that are regarded as effects. It is the purpose of this chapter to
develop both a formal definition and an organizing map.

Conceptualization of Mass Media Influence

When we think about how the mass media exert their influence, there are three
essential issues to consider. These issues are timing of influence (immediate vs.
long term), change (difference vs. no difference), and manifestation (observable
vs. latent). Let's consider these three issues and then put those ideas together into
some fundamental patterns of influence. Then I will present a formal definition of
mass media effects.

Foundational Issues

We begin with three foundational issues. The first issue is timing. This includes
how long it takes for an effect to show up. Some effects are immediate and others
are long term; that is, they do not manifest themselves during an exposure situation, but as exposures accumulate, the effect begins to emerge. Duration refers to
the time the effect lasts. For example, an effect can last only during an exposure
session (such as increased heart rate) and then disappear shortly after. Or an
effect can last for a very long period of time, even over the course of a person's
lifetime, such as remembering an image from a movie. Given the research on
mass media effects, there is reason to consider both immediate and long-term
effects. Also, we need to consider effects that are short-lived and those effects that
last a long time.

The second issue is change. This raises the question about whether an effect
needs to be evidenced by a change or whether a nonchange of something in a person's life can be regarded as an effect. The research literature is focused on changes
on effects measures such as behaviors or attitudes. Almost all experiments conclude
there was no effect when there was no difference in means across groups. But conceptually, it would seem that nonchange could be evidence of important effects.
When we consider that the mass media have the intention of reinforcing exposure
behaviors and habitual product usage of advertised brands, we cannot overlook a
reinforcement effect, which is typically evidenced by no change on behavioral and
attitudinal measures.

The third issue is manifestation. This raises the question about what to consider evidence of an effect. Must there be an observable manifestation? Or should we also consider that some influences from the media are so subtle and gradual that it would take a very long time for a manifestation to occur, but in this case, we should conclude that the effect happened only on the day the manifestation occurred and that nothing happened on all the days of media exposure that led up to that magic day of manifestation? Clearly, it is an underestimation of media influence to ignore all the influence that gradually shapes a person's cognitions or beliefs until a manifestation occurs.

Patterns of Influence

Let's put together the ideas discussed above, beginning with timing and duration. These three issues suggest that at the most fundamental level of thinking, the mass media can exert only four patterns of influence: gradual long-term change, gradual long-term nonchange (reinforcement), immediate shift, and short-term fluctuation change. All mass media effects follow one of these four patterns.

With a long-term change type of effect, the messages from the mass media gradually alter a person's baseline. Figure 17.1a illustrates this pattern. The line in the figure represents a person's baseline on a particular effect. Over time, there is a slow, gradual upward slope that indicates an increasing degree of the effect. An example of this would be a cultivation effect where, over time, a person is more likely to believe the world is a mean and violent place. In contrast with a long-term reinforcement type of effect, the media influence serves to maintain the status quo with the particular effect (see Figure 17.1b). There is no slope to the baseline—it is flat. An example of this would be when a person continually exposes himself or herself to the same political point of view through magazines, newspapers, television, and the Internet. His or her political attitude experiences greater and greater reinforcement; that is, it becomes more and more fixed and hence much more difficult to change.

With an immediate shift type of effect, the media influence serves to alter something in a person during an exposure or shortly after a particular exposure and that alteration lasts for a very long time (see Figure 17.1c). That alteration may be relatively minor. However, there are times when the degree of change might be relatively dramatic. An example of a dramatic immediate change effect might be when a young person watches a movie about an attractive person in a particular career— say a heart surgeon—and the person decides to become a heart surgeon, talks about this career choice continually, and alters her or his study habits to earn the grades necessary to go to college and medical school.

With a short-term fluctuation change type of effect, the media trigger a fluctuation off the baseline during the exposure or shortly after. The change is short-lived, and the person returns to the baseline level quickly (see Figure 17.1d). This is a fairly prevalent finding in a lot of studies of public information/attitude campaigns. Researchers find a spike in knowledge, attitude change, or behavioral intention as a result of exposure to some media material, but this

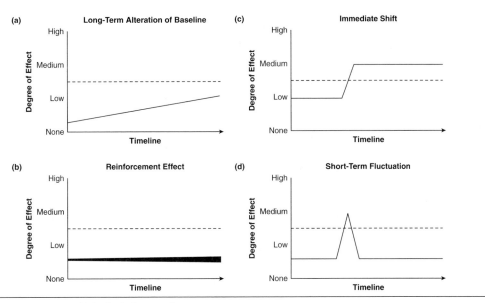

Figure 17.1   Types of Media Influence Patterns

change is not observed in subsequent measurement periods beyond a few days after the exposure.

Baselines differ in terms of slope and elasticity. Slope refers to angle (an upward slope indicates a generally increasing level of an effect, while a downward slope indicates a generally decreasing level of an effect) and degree (a sharp angle reflects a relatively large degree of change in effects level, while a flat slope reflects a continuing level in the baseline). Elasticity reflects how entrenched the baseline is. Over time, a baseline that has been reinforced continually by the same kind of media messages will become highly entrenched, making it less and less likely that there will be fluctuations off the baseline, and when there are fluctuations, those fluctuations are smaller and smaller over time.

The baseline is the best estimate of a person's degree of effect at any given time. It is formed over the long term by the constant interaction of three types of factors: psychological traits of the person, sociological experiences of the person, and media exposure patterns. This is likely to be the most important aspect of media effects.

Fluctuations have three characteristics: duration, magnitude, and direction. The duration refers to how long the fluctuation lasts before returning to the baseline. Magnitude refers to how far the fluctuation deviates from the baseline. And direction refers to whether the fluctuation moves upward (thus representing an increase in the level) or downward (thus representing a decrease in the level).

Notice the dotted line in all four graphs in Figure 17.1. These dotted lines represent the manifestation level. In the first graph (a), notice that the baseline stays below the manifestation level. This indicates that the degree of the effect has not reached a level where there are spontaneous observables. By this I mean that the research participants exhibit something that clearly indicates a change that can be attributed to media influence. In two of the other three graphics, there are examples of the baseline breaking above the manifestation level; with those three patterns, we have clear manifestations of a media-influenced effect.

Should we limit our conceptualization of media effects to only those effects where manifestations occur? I would answer no; we should also be sensitive to what occurs below the manifestation level. Returning to graph (a), notice that the baseline has a positive slope, which indicates a gradual long-term change. The line does not move above the manifestation level, but something is happening that indicates media influence. For example, let's say a young girl exposes herself to lots of print messages on a particular topic. Over time, these exposures gradually increase her reading skills and increase her interest in that topic as her knowledge base grows. Her baseline moves close to the manifestation level. Then one day, she picks up an article on the topic and begins telling all her friends about what she has just learned (this activity takes place above the manifestation level because it is spontaneous and easy to observe her knowledge, attitudes, and emotions as she exhibits them to her friends). However, is it accurate to conclude that this manifestation was caused by the one exposure to the article alone? No, of course not. We must account for the long-term media influence that allowed her to practice her reading skills and grow her interest in this topic. The magnitude of the manifestation level is a combination of the initial level on the baseline and the magnitude of the fluctuation itself. Contrast this with a young boy who did not have this pattern of practicing his reading skills or growing his interest in this topic; his baseline would be far below the manifestation level. If he were to read the same article, he would not be likely to manifest the same indicators as did the girl; however, the boy could still have been influenced by his exposure to the article (change in level), although he did not manifest that effect.

Limiting the conceptualization of mass media effects to manifestations greatly reduces our understanding of the phenomenon. We need to make a distinction between manifest and process effects. It is likely that most of mass media influence is in the form of process effects rather than manifest effects. If we do not pay attention to process effects, we will greatly limit our ability to understand media influence. Process effects are more difficult to measure and make stronger cases for their validity than are manifest effects. This challenge parallels the challenge of social scientists who wanted to break through the limits imposed by behaviorism; it was much more difficult to measure attitudes, cognitive states, and other internal hypothetical constructs and make strong cases for their validity compared with behaviors. We are indeed fortunate that social scientists continually rise to this challenge. It is time to rise to the challenge of more clearly documenting process effects in addition to manifest effects.

With this conceptualization of media influence, the mass media are regarded as exerting an ongoing influence. Their influence is not limited to certain kinds of messages; instead, their influence is constant and continuing. Some of this influence is direct—that is, it occurs with exposure to media messages. This media influence also occurs indirectly as people encounter other people and institutions that have themselves been influenced by the media and pass that influence along in conversations and in institutional practices. Also, media influence is indirect when people think about media messages and continue to process that information and make meaning from it long after a media exposure is over.

The media exert their influence in a constellation of other factors of influence. Some of these factors have to do with the person who is being exposed to the messages—factors such as traits, states, habits, memories, goals, and so on. Some of these factors have to do with the situation—whether a person is being exposed alone or with others who talk about the exposure, societal supports and sanctions, and so forth. Also, the media are not monolithic—that is, there are many different types of media factors; some of these factors are medium characteristics, some are genre characteristics (news messages have different characteristics than entertainment or advertising messages), and some are characteristics about the message itself (characters, plots, production elements, etc.).

To illustrate these patterns, let's consider a disinhibition effect, which is a lowering of people's inhibitions that prevent them from behaving aggressively. Let's say Leo is a 12-year-old boy who has been raised to be highly aggressive and who has low trait empathy, while Julie is a 35-year-old mother who was raised by the golden rule and who has high trait empathy. Leo's disinhibition effect baseline is likely to be higher than Julie's. Let's say that Leo is continually exposed to many media messages of violence (in movies, television shows, and video games), where the consequences to the victims are sanitized, while Julie avoids all such messages. Adding these elements to the prediction, we can say that there will be a relatively large difference between the levels of Harry's and Julie's disinhibition baselines. This example is supported by research; Haridakis (2002) found that aggression (physical, verbal, anger, and hostility) were all predicted by trait variables such as gender, locus of control, and long-term experience variables such as experience with crime and television viewing. Furthermore, over time, Leo's baseline is likely to have an upward slope while Julie's is likely to have a downward slope.

Now let's say that Leo and Julie watch a Dirty Harry movie where a great deal of violence is perpetrated by a rogue police officer who is glamorized, humorous, and successful in his use of violence. Perhaps Leo is highly attracted and entertained by Harry; he strongly identifies with Harry and wants to be like him. Leo is likely to show a sharp fluctuation increasing his level on a disinhibition effect. In contrast, Julie is horrified by Harry and finds his actions reprehensible and insulting to her. Julie is likely to show a sharp fluctuation decreasing her level on a disinhibition effect. Although the media message presented is the same for both Leo and Julie, the experience for each is very different because of what the two people bring to the exposure situation. This history is captured in their baseline.

Let's say that Julie watches a lot of crime drama where criminals' violent acts are always punished and where the suffering of victims is continually shown (such as on the *Law & Order* TV series). This is likely to condition Julie's disinhibition baseline at a low level and keep it there. If she were to see a violent portrayal where the perpetrator was glamorized and the violence sanitized, she would likely not experience much of a fluctuation effect because her baseline has been so strongly reinforced. A reinforcement pattern is one where the position of the baseline is entrenched; that is, the baseline continues at its current level, and its elasticity is reduced, rendering fluctuations more rare. If the elasticity of the baseline is narrow, then the long-term stable factors (traits and typical story formula) are dominant, but if the elasticity is wide, then the immediate factors (dispositions and idiosyncratic factors in the portrayals) are dominant. Reinforcement narrows the elasticity.

Definition of Mass Media Effect

Given the analysis of mass media influence above, I propose the following formal definition of a mass media effect: A mass media effect is the occurrence of one of four patterns, when the shape of that pattern can be attributed to mass media influence. The four patterns are (1) gradual alteration of a baseline, (2) reinforcement of baseline, (3) sudden alteration of the baseline, and (4) sudden fluctuation from the baseline with a return to the baseline. Notice that this definition has two necessary conditions. One of these conditions is that the set of four patterns is necessary—that is, there must be one of four patterns, but any one of these four patterns would satisfy this condition. The second necessary condition is that the pattern must be attributable to mass media influence. Implied in this general definition are other elements of defining mass media effects; however, those other elements are not used as inclusion rules because those elements are too broad. To illustrate, one of these elements is timing. Implied in this definition is that a mass media effect can occur immediately or take a long time to occur, so timing is too broad to be used as an inclusion rule. However, timing is still an important characteristic that can be used to organize different kinds of mass media effects once they have been included by the formal definition.

The processes and products of mass media influence act directly on targets (such as individuals as well as macro units of society and institutions) as well as indirectly on targets through other units. They can be intentional or nonintentional on the part of both the media senders and the target receivers. They can be manifested or hidden from natural observation. They are constant and ongoing. And they are shaped not just by the media influence; their shaping occurs in a constellation of other factors that act in concert with the media influence.

Notice that this definition captures most of the elements that scholars have used to talk about mass media effects, but these elements are useful only as dimensions of kinds of effects, not as inclusion rules. The reason for this is because the definition I proposed above is a broad one and accepts all values along these dimensions. For example, implied in the lineation formal definition is both intentional and nonintentional, both manifest and latent, both process and products, both direct and indirect influence from the media, and both micro level (effects on individuals) and macro level (effects on the public, society, institutions, and culture).

Organizing Mass Media Effects

Now moving beyond the general idea of mass media effect to more specific effects, we are confronted with the following question: How many media-influenced effects are there? If we look at the literature, we can see the names for a great many of them—agenda setting, cultivation, disinhibition, learning, displacement, priming, persuasion, identification, third person, parasocial interaction, socialization, social learning, cue, and the list goes on and on. Some of these names cover more than one effect, and other names are used by different scholars to mean very different things. Also, some of these effects are very micro and others are macro and themselves include several other types of effects. We need a way to organize all of these effects so that we can take stock of what we have documented thus far and position future research studies more efficiently.

In this section, I will develop an organizational scheme that I will refer to as a Media Effects Template (MET), which is like a periodic table of mass media effects. On the path to that end, I first need to review the literature where scholars have attempted this task of organizing mass media effects. This literature highlights many dimensions that can be used to structure such an organizational scheme. After sorting through this list of dimensions, I will highlight the dimensions of type of effect and media-influenced functions.

Dimensions of Organizing Mass Media Effects

In the 1954 review "Effects of the Mass Media of Communication," published in the *Handbook of Social Psychology,* Hovland wrote that "there is at present no adequate conceptual framework within which to classify the diverse types of effects reported" (p. 1090). Hovland acknowledged that scholars frequently made some distinctions among effects, such as long term and short term; manifest and latent; intentional and nonintentional; activation, reinforcement, and conversion; and psychological, political, economic, and sociological. Hovland went so far as to argue that "one cannot talk about the effects, but only about particular sets of responses selected for study" (p. 1090). This hard-core empirical position appeared to have been shared by many subsequent scholars. In the second edition of the *Handbook of Social Psychology,* Weiss (1969) updated Hovland's review and argued that a media effects category scheme would have "considerable heuristic value that a sound accounting system has. For it not only reveals gaps in research but imposes a rational order on diverse kinds of research. By so doing, salient differences and similarities are more sharply illuminated and restraint is placed on loose discussion of what the mass media can and cannot do. Furthermore, the resulting collation can be of use in testing theory and suggesting theory" (p. 80). However, Weiss concluded that Hovland's observation in 1954 still held in 1969 and that there existed no theoretically derived template available for categorizing media effects. Weiss declined to develop a classification scheme but organized his review around several of the dimensions suggested by Hovland and added another dimension of type of effect (cognitive, attitudinal, overt behavior, etc.). A decade later, J. M. McLeod and Reeves (1980) attributed the "confusion of evaluating mass media impact" (p. 27) to the diversity of potential effects. Then, in 1985, D. F. Roberts and Maccoby updated the work of Hovland and Weiss and again concluded that there was no single set of dimensions to organize mass media effects. By default, they used the dimensions of timing, type (attitudes, cognitions, and behaviors), acquisition versus performance, and the relation of effect to specific content (direct to diffuse).

Organizing the mass media effects literature by effects has always been difficult. As the literature grows, scholars suggest more dimensions that can be used. Early in this literature, Lazarsfeld (1948) suggested a core set of dimensions that are still recognized today. Lazarsfeld said that "mass media can affect knowledge, attitudes, opinions and behavior of individuals. These effects can be immediate or delayed, of short duration or long-lasting. Effects upon individuals might slowly become transformed into institutional changes. They can come about in simple reactions or complicated chains" (p. 249). J. M. McLeod and Reeves (1980) said that mass media effects vary by macro versus micro, direct versus conditional, content specific versus diffuse-general, attitudinal versus behavioral versus cognitive, alteration versus stabilization, and "many other ways in which the various alleged effects of the mass media might be classified" (p. 26). Jeffres (1997) argued, "We can categorize effects by levels, by domains, by duration (short term or long term), by intentionality (deliberate or not), by medium, by method of investigation, by the nature of the effect, by what aspect of media creates the effect, and so forth" (p. 9). Basil (1992) suggested that there are five dimensions: level of analysis, type, nature, intention, and whether effects are influenced by message content or form of medium. Perse (2001) also listed five dimensions of micro and macro, intentionality, content dependent versus content irrelevant, timing, and reinforcement versus change. Grossberg et al. (1998) laid out six dimensions of cognitive/affective/conative, manifest/latent, change/reinforcement, intentionality, level, and timing.

Each of these dimensions appears useful, but the large number of suggested dimensions is unwieldy. J. M. McLeod and Reeves (1980) pointed out that if a plot were to use their five dimensions and each of these dimensions included only two categories, it would require 32 nested categories to capture this full organizational scheme. Obviously, we cannot use all five (or more) dimensions in a single scheme where we simultaneously showcase each. So what can we do? There seem to be three options. One option is to select a small number of these dimensions and ignore the rest. This is what McQuail (2005) did when he selected only the two dimensions of intentionality (planned effects to unplanned effects) and time (short term to long term). He used these two dimensions to plot 20 types of effects (e.g., propaganda, framing, agenda setting, news diffusion, socialization). While this is helpful, it is also a tease because it makes the reader wonder how the plottings would look if other dimensions (such as reinforcement vs. change, micro vs. macro, or cognitive-affective-behavioral) were also included.

A second option is to try to incorporate all dimensions but only in a partial way, thus avoiding the need to cross each dimension with all others. This is what most scholars do when trying to provide a book-length organizational scheme of chapters (J. Bryant & Zillmann, 2002; Harris, 2004; Iyengar, 1997; Perse, 2001; Sparks, 2006), organization over several chapters (such as Baran & Davis, 2000; Grossberg et al., 1998; Littlejohn, 1999; McQuail, 2005), or a within-chapter organizational scheme (Severin & Tankard, 2001). They typically mix dimensions of types of content, types of effects, different media, and names of theories. So there will be chapters on effects of violence, sex, stereotypes, persuasion, priming, agenda setting, socialization, and so on. While these individual chapters and sections may each provide a complete description of their subliterature, the set leaves the reader with questions about what is missing. This too is a serious shortcoming. While it creates a vehicle to deliver a great deal of information, it neglects the context that would be conveyed by a map. So readers are given the double challenge of absorbing a great deal of information without being presented with a strong, complete framework to anchor their knowledge acquisition.

A third option is to attempt to use all dimensions but not to afford each one equal status. This serves to avoid the problem of having to fully cross all values of all dimensions, thus calling for a matrix with many dimensions and a very, very large number of cells. Instead, some dimensions are nested within other dimensions. This is the option I will follow in developing an MET. The two dimensions that are the most important in this development are type of effect and media-influenced functions.

Type of Effect

Scholars who write about dimensions to organize effects typically lay out three types (cognitive, affective, and behavioral), as I illustrated in the previous chapter. I will augment this list to include six types: cognitive, attitudinal, belief, affective, physiological, and behavioral. Although attitude is typically regarded as a cognition, I treat it as a special type because it can be delineated clearly from other cognitions and also because its literature of media effects is so large. I added physiology, not because its literature is large, which it is not, but because it is very different from the other types and warrants its own category.

These six refer to the character of the experience of the effect within an individual. While one or more of these terms is used in just about every mass media effect study, these terms are often used in an ambiguous way; that is, some terms are used as synonyms for one another (especially attitudes and beliefs) or as subordinate to others (e.g., effects require a physiological stimulus and cognitive labeling). In this section, I will delineate each of these in enough detail to make them distinct from one another.

Cognitive Effect. A cognitive media effect is conceptualized as media exposure exercising an influence on an individual's mental processes or the product of those mental processes. The easiest-to-document cognitive effect is the acquisition of factual information from media messages, particularly news stories and educational programming. The acquisition of facts requires the mental process of memorization. But the human mind can do more than simply acquire message elements through memorization; it can also create new information when stimulated by media exposures. This new information can be in the form of inferring patterns, deducing conclusions, and synthesizing novel perceptions.

Attitudinal Effect. Attitudes are a very important part of social science. In fact, Gordon Allport (1935) claimed that the concept of attitudes is the essence of all of social psychology. To illustrate this point, a recent search of the American Psychological Association's comprehensive index to psychological and related literature (PsycINFO) yielded 180,910 references for the use of the term *attitude* (cited in Albarracin, Johnson, & Zanna, 2005).

As important as attitudes have been to social science over the years, they have also presented some significant challenges. Perhaps the biggest problem with attitudes is that different scholars conceptualize them in different ways because they are hypothetical constructs, and therefore different scholars construct different definitions for them. Albarracin, Zanna, et al. (2005) pointed out that there are hundreds of definitions of attitudes in the research literature. For example, M. J. Rosenberg and Hovland (1960) argued that attitudes cannot be measured directly, so their existence must be inferred through the use of indirect measures, such as affective, cognitive, and behavioral measures. Also, Albarracin, Zanna, et al. (2005) pointed out that there are scholars who have defined attitudes as having the components of affect, beliefs, and behaviors but prefer to define each as being a separate yet related construct. However, this is problematic because affects and cognitions are also hypothetical constructs that cannot be directly measured. They continued, "Cognitions include perceptions, concepts, and beliefs about the attitude object" (p. 4) and said that attitudes have been inferred most often through affective measures, which include verbal statements of an evaluative nature, such as feelings for or against something. This conceptualization is based on a correspondence between attitudes, affects, cognitions, and behaviors. But over the years, researchers have clearly shown that there are often not correspondences. For example, Budd et al. (1999) explained, "The gap between what people say and what they think or do is easily demonstrated, and the gap between what any of us feel and what language can capture is a commonplace of linguistics and psychoanalysis" (p. 173).

Let's set aside these operational challenges for the time being and focus on conceptualizations. However, this too is a considerable challenge. Virtually all of the authors of the 18 chapters in *The Handbook of Attitudes* wrestled with this challenge of how to define attitudes and illustrated that the construct has had a wide variety of definitions in the past (Albarracin, Zanna, et al., 2005). For example, Krosnick, Judd, and Wittenbrink (2005) pointed out that because of the multiplicity of definitions, attitudes came to mean "whatever internal sets of predispositions motivated social behavior" (p. 22). However, Albarracin, Zanna, et al. (2005) pointed out that the most often used contemporary definition is that of Eagly and Chaiken (1993), who focused on the evaluative nature of attitudes. This evaluative element is widespread in definitions of attitudes (Borardus, 1931; Fishbein & Ajzen, 1975; Hovland, Janis, & Kelley, 1953; D. Katz, 1960; Osgood, Suci, & Tannenbaum, 1957; Petty & Cacioppo, 1981, 1986; Petty & Wegener, 1998; Sherif & Hovland, 1961; Thurstone, 1928).

In my definition of attitudes, I therefore put the primary focus on the idea of the evaluative nature of attitudes. When people are exposed to media messages, they compare those messages (or elements within those messages) to their standards, thus making value judgments of those elements. Those value judgments are their attitudes. Thus, standards are essential to the evaluation; that is, there needs to be a standard in play, or there cannot be an evaluation. The standard can be explicit—obvious and consciously applied by the person—or implicit—unconsciously applied.

Belief Effect. Beliefs have been defined as cognitions about the probability that an object or event is associated with a given attribute (Fishbein & Ajzen, 1975). There are times when scholars use the terms *beliefs* and *attitudes* as synonyms, and there are scholars who argue that beliefs are a type of attitude. Beliefs and attitudes can be highly interrelated, as Albarracin, Zanna, Johnson, and Kumkale (2005) pointed out, but this does not mean they are the same thing.

The key difference between an attitude and a belief is that an attitude is clearly an evaluation, and thus it is the comparison of something against a standard, and the variation on a measurement of an attitude is in terms of valence—strongly negative through neutral and toward strongly positive. In contrast, a belief is a construction about the probability that an object or event is associated with a given attribute (Fishbein & Ajzen, 1975). Beliefs are in essence estimates of the likelihood that the knowledge one has acquired about a referent is correct or that something will occur (Eagly & Chaiken, 1998; Wyer & Albarracin, 2005). The variation on a measurement of a belief reflects how confident a person is in the probability of something occurring, and this confidence is related to how much knowledge the person has to support the belief.

Beliefs are easier to verify than attitudes; that is, beliefs can be verified or falsified with objective criteria external to the person (Eagly & Chaiken, 1993). In contrast, attitudes require an understanding of a person's standards, which are often idiosyncratic to the person, intuitive, and difficult to discern apart from the judgments the person makes. Also, attitudes rely on an internal process of comparing an element to the person's standard, and it is difficult to verify this process because it might be complex and beyond the ability of the person to articulate. To illustrate this, consider a conversation you have with your daughter after you find out she has a very positive attitude about a boy named Buster. You point out that Buster has tattoos covering almost all parts of his visible body and that your daughter has never liked guys with tattoos; your daughter agrees. You point out that Buster is short, bald, and runty, while your daughter usually prefers guys who are tall, blonde, and athletic; your daughter agrees. You point out that Buster dresses like he is in prison, while your daughter usually prefers guys who are preppy and neat; your daughter agrees. In frustration you plead, "Then why do you like Buster so much?" and your daughter replies, "I don't know, but he is so cool." Your daughter clearly has a strongly held positive attitude about Buster, but she cannot articulate her standard or the process she used in arriving at her evaluation. Therefore, your attempt to get her to analyze her attitude and show her its faulty nature falls woefully short of being convincing.

Affective Effect. This involves the feelings that people experience and may or may not concern a particular object or event (Albarracin, Zanna, et al., 2005;

L. Berkowitz, 2000). Affect can be conscious, where the person is aware of feelings, or unconscious, where the person is not (Schimmack & Crites, 2005). Writing about the structure of affect, Schimmack and Crites (2005) argued that there are three types of affective experiences: emotions, moods, and sensory reactions. Like attitudes, affect has valence (positive and negative) and intensity. But unlike attitudes, the characteristics of frequency and duration are also important.

Emotions have long been considered as having a physiological component. Our current conceptualizations of emotion go back to James (1894), who argued that emotional stimuli trigger bodily responses, and feedback of these bodily responses produces the emotional experience. Thus, there is a physiological component and the cognitive labeling. The physiological reaction is what makes it possible for us to tell the difference between anger and fear—they feel different physiologically. The James-Lange theory (James, 1894) regarded the differences in emotions (such as the difference between anger and fear) as being due to different patterns of physiological activity. However, after a century of research testing this theory, researchers have been able to find very little evidence of physiological differences across emotions (Eagly & Chaiken, 1993).

Now it is believed that emotions are composed of a combination of physiological and cognitive components (e.g., see Frijda & Zeelenberg, 2001). This point is emphasized in Schachter and Singer's (1962) two-factor theory of emotions, which says that the physiological arousal is responsible for the intensity of the emotion, and cognitions are responsible for the labeling of the feeling into qualitatively different states. Cognitions are required to label the emotional experience to differentiate among different emotions. Cognitions also set up expectations for emotional experiences and can help determine the intensity of the experience.

While emotions are reactions to a particular object, moods are generalized states of feeling. Emotions are typically more intense affects that are directed at objects and have a known cause. Examples of emotions are the feelings of hate, jealousy, love, pity, terror, outrage, disgust, and anger. In contrast, moods have lower intensity and are not directed at an object. Examples of moods are optimism, nostalgia, indifference, restlessness, grouchiness, boredom, fatigue, alertness, relaxation, and tension. Moods require bodily monitoring, as of mental and physical energy levels. They are often related to neurological states, as is the case with depression or anxiety.

Sensory affects are reactions to sensory stimulation (Reisenzein, 2001). Some of these reactions are innate and part of the human condition to ensure survival. Taste of foods tells us which foods are dangerous substances. We exhibit fear in response to certain physical threats. Some sensory affects are learned through classical conditioning, where an artificial symbol is linked with an affective reaction.

Affect is often a powerful basis for attitudes, but affects are not attitudes themselves (Wyer & Srull, 1989). For something to be an attitude, there needs to be an evaluation of an object; emotion can be a part of the evaluation, but it is not the evaluation itself. For example, a person might watch a trashy love story on a TV show and feel lust, which is an affect generated by the characters and the story. But the person might form the attitude that the show is bad because it does not come up to his or her standard of what he or she should be watching.

Physiological Effect. A physiological effect is one that triggers an automatic bodily response. The bodily response can be either purely automatic (such as pupil dilation, blood pressure, galvanic skin response) or quasi-automatic (heart rate, sexual responses).

Behavioral Effect. Behaviors are typically and simply defined as the overt actions of an individual (Albarracin, Zanna, et al., 2005). This is a term that is used often in mass media effects research. However, many references to behavior in the empirical research may not be regarded as actual behavior. Much of the "behavior" measured is through self-report of one's own behavior or of another person's behavior, such as children's behavior being measured by parents' or teachers' reports. Thus, there is a wide range of confidence we can have across the different types of measures as reflecting actual behavior. With some measures of behavior, we can have a high degree of confidence, as when actions are observed by trained coders or recorded on electronic devices. Less confidence should be attributed to measures of self-report, especially self-reports of mundane behaviors or behaviors occurring in the distant past. Also, some reports of self-behaviors are influenced by the need for privacy and not revealing actual behavior or by the need to appear socially desirable. There is likely a long continuum of so-called behavioral measures with credible observations on one pole and with constructed recollections on the other. Those constructed recollections are largely a product of cognitive processes and should be regarded more in the cognitive category than in the behavioral category.

Media-Influenced Functions

When considering the definitions and thinking of each of the six types of effects and when looking across the research topics examined under each of the six categories, there appear to be four things that the media can do to bring about an effect. These four things, which I am calling media-influenced functions, generally span across all six types of effects. They are functions in the sense that they refer to distinct actions that influence and shape the character of an effect differently in each of the six categories of type.

These four media-influenced functions are acquiring, triggering, altering, and conditioning. The first two of these are immediate effects that would show up as fluctuations either during the exposure or immediately after. The fourth is a long-term effect that would show up as a baseline effect. Altering has features that can show up immediately during exposure as a fluctuation effect, but it also has other features that may take longer to manifest themselves. Let's examine each of these in some detail, and then we will construct a template based on them.

Acquiring Function. The mass media provide messages composed of elements, and during exposures to these messages, individuals acquire and retain some of these elements. During a media exposure, a person could acquire a fact, a belief and attitude, affective information, or a behavioral sequence (although this might be regarded by some scholars more as a cognitive effect). These are things that are simply accepted from the media; they require no alteration or cognitive construction. The acquiring function shows up in all types of effects except for physiology, where media messages have no power to *create* a physiological element in an individual. Individuals acquire information and store it in their memory structures. People can also acquire beliefs, attitudes, affective information, and behavioral sequences in the same manner through the use of the skill of memorization. With all of these subcategories, the media are creating something in a person's mind that was not there before the exposure. It is possible to argue that all of these effects are essentially cognitive because they all require the use of the cognitive skill of memorization and the retention of information in the individual's memory. And that is a valid point. However, while the process and the skill used may be the same across categories, the nature of what is retained is very different. Thus, the function remains the same, but the effect itself is different and requires different categories for type.

Triggering Function. During media exposures, the media can activate something that already exists in the individual. The triggering function would seem to be applicable for all six types of effects. A media message could activate the recall of previously learned information, an existing belief or attitude, an emotion, a physiological reaction, or a previously learned behavioral sequence.

The media can also trigger a cognitive process. For example, when people read some news coverage about a political candidate that they have never heard about before, they have no existing attitude about that candidate. During exposure to this news coverage, people can take the information from the news story and compare it with their standard for political candidates and create an attitude. This is different than simple acquisition because the person is not memorizing someone else's attitude presented in the media but instead goes through a construction process in the creation of his or her own attitude.

Altering Function. During an exposure, the media can alter something that is already present in the individual. The altering effect would seem to be applicable to work with all types of effects except physiological ones. Media messages can alter a person's knowledge structures with the addition of new facts. A belief can be altered when the mass media present a fact revealing that an individual's existing belief was faulty. The media can alter individuals' standards for use in constructing attitudes. By shifting content, the media can alter a person's mood. Finally, learned behavioral sequences can be altered through vicarious learning, where people watch media stories and alter their learned behavioral sequences according to what is punished and what is rewarded.

The alteration shows up immediately, that is, during or immediately after the exposure to the media message. The alteration can be temporary, in which case it is a fluctuation effect, or it can last a long time, in which case its influence works on shaping the baseline.

Conditioning Function. Through repeated exposures, the media gradually and continually change the individual's experience with the media. The conditioning function is not simply the altering function over the long term. With the alteration function, there is a change that occurs suddenly, and that change persists over time; in contrast, conditioning is constant change over time, although the increments of change are very small at any given exposure. This change is so slight during each exposure that it cannot be recognized in the short term; however, over a long period of media exposures, its evidence is stronger. The change can be a decrement to the baseline (such as with a gradual loss in intensity of emotional reactions to horror films over time), an increase in the baseline (such as gradually and constantly rewarding a person's exposure to a particular program, thus increasing his or her habitual viewing of that program over time), or a reinforcement of the baseline (such as a steady stream of a particular kind of media message contributing greater and greater weight to a person's attitude about a political issue, thus making it much more difficult over time to convert that attitude to a different one).

The conditioning effect would seem to be applicable to all six types of effects. Conditioning by media messages can influence the way individuals process information, steer individuals to want to construct attitudes on particular topics while ignoring other topics, narcoticize emotional responses, build tolerance for physiological responses, and habituate behavioral patterns. Conditioning strengthens the key skills of each type of effect. It also can strengthen physiological connections. For example, video and computer games strengthen hand-eye coordination and reduce reaction times to stimuli.

The Media Effects Template for Individuals

By using type of effect and media influence functions, we can create a matrix that could serve as a way of mapping the full range of mass media effects. This can be done for effects on individuals as well as effects on macro units.

This MET for individuals is displayed in Table 17.1. For more detail about how the existing mass media effects research fits into particular cells of the MET, refer to Tables 17.2 through 17.6. These tables, of course, are not comprehensive displays of the research; rather, they are illustrations of the utility of the template as an organizing device.

For this template to be useful, the definitions of the six types of effects and the four media-influenced functions need to be accepted. To the extent that there is definitional fuzziness, the categories lose their value. Using these definitions will lead to a new placement of some effects. This will especially be the case with self-reported behavioral measures, which generally have been regarded as behavior. Some of these measures appear to be accurate reflections of actual behavior, and thus there is little concern about them being classified as behavioral measures. One example of this would be this question: Did you watch television so far today? However, many measures of "behavior" could be considered less accurate at reflecting behaviors and more accurate at reflecting a person's ability to recall, where a person draws the line at privacy, or a desire to be consistent with beliefs or attitudes. Thus, many but not all self-report behavioral measures should be categorized in a type of effect that is not behavior. For example, a frequently used measure of a child's behavior is asking the child's parents and teachers about his or her behavior. These measures have a behavioral exemplar in the respondents' minds, but the self-report measurement requires cognitive processes sometimes so substantial that it is hard to justify them as being more of a behavioral rather than a cognitive measure.

Another example of category fuzziness is with the category of emotion. For example, some scholars regard emotion as an attitude, some as a cognitive labeling of a physiological state, some as a recollection of a cognition, and so on. Also,

(*Text continues on page 282*)

Table 17.1   Media Effects Template: Individual Unit Effects

Type of Effect	Media Influence Functions			
	Acquiring	Triggering	Altering	Conditioning
Cognitive	Memorize message element	Recall information	Memory structure	Strengthen skills
		Construct pattern		Reinforce connections
Belief	Memorize belief	Recall belief	Belief change	Strengthen generalizations
		Construct belief		
Attitudes	Accept attitude	Recall attitude	Attitude change	Strengthen evaluation
		Construct new attitudes		Reinforce attitudes
		Need for new attitudes		
Affects	Learn emotional information	Recall emotion	Mood change	Strengthen emotional connections
				Reinforce mood
				Emotional sensitivity
Physiology		Automatic response		Improve reactions
Behavior	Learn behaviors	Recall behavior	Behavioral change	Reinforce habits
		Imitation behavior		
		Novel behavior		

Table 17.2   Cognitive Effects

Acquiring

- Acquiring specific facts:
  - Current events (Greenberg & Brand, 1993; C. J. Lucas & Schmitz, 1988)
  - Political candidates and campaigns (S. E. Bennett, 1989; Garramone & Atkin, 1986; Graber, 1988; Valentino, Hutchings, & Williams, 2004)
  - Science (Pifer, 1991; Ressmeyer & Wallen, 1991)
  - Health and nutrition (Juanillo & Scherer, 1991)

- Acquiring faulty beliefs about one's own risk of being affected in comparison with the risk of other people being affected; third-person effect (Davison, 1983)
  - Influence of television violence (Hoffner et al., 2001; Hoffner & Buchanan, 2002; Salwen & Dupagne, 2001; Scharrer, 2002)
  - Problems from Y2K (Salwen & Dupagne, 2003; Tewksbury, Moy, & Weis, 2004)
  - Influence of the mass media (Gunther & Storey, 2003; D. M. McLeod, Detenber, & Eveland, 2001; Peiser & Peter, 2000, 2001)
  - Body image effects (David, Morrison, Johnson, & Ross, 2002)
  - Direct-to-consumer prescription drug advertising (Huh, Delorme, & Reid, 2004)
  - Political ads (Meirick, 2004)
  - Internet pornography (Lo & Wei, 2002)

Triggering

- Constructing patterns from media examples and generalizing those patterns to the real world in terms of
  - Prevalence of crime and violence in society (Gerbner, Gross, Signorielli, Morgan, & Jackson-Beeck, 1979; Hawkins & Pingree, 1981; Nabi & Sullivan, 2001; W. J. Potter, 1991; Romer, Jamieson, & Aday, 2003)
  - Use of violence as an effective solution to conflict (Liebert, Neale, & Davidson, 1973; Tan, 1981; Zillmann & Weaver, 1997)
  - Personal risk (Gibson & Zillmann, 2000; Griffin, Neuwirth, Dunwoody, & Giese, 2004; Rimal, 2001; Rimal & Real, 2003)
  - Degree of materialism in society (Kwak, Zinkhan, & Dominick, 2002)
  - Race of criminal suspects in news stories
  - Number and personality of certain types of people, such as medical doctors (Chory-Assad & Tamborini, 2003), public relations practitioners (Sallot, 2002), criminals (Appiah, 2002; Oliver, 1999; Oliver & Fonash, 2002), homosexuals (Rossler & Brosius, 2001), and welfare recipients (Sotirovic, 2001a, 2001b)
  - Values in a culture
  - Motherhood (Ex, Janssens, & Korzilius, 2002)
  - Body image (Botta, 2000; David et al., 2002; Holmstrom, 2004; Thomsen, McCoy, Gustafson, & Williams, 2002)
  - Frequency of deviant behaviors (S. Davis & Mares, 1998)

(Continued)

Table 17.2 (Continued)

- – General social lessons
- – Social secrets and backstage behaviors
- Constructing beliefs about what issues are most important in the real world (Althaus & Tewksbury, 2002; S. Davis & Mares, 1998; Golan & Wanta, 2001; Gross & Aday, 2003; Iyengar, 1991; Iyengar & Kinder, 1987; S.-H. Kim, Scheufele, & Shanahan, 2002; Ku, Kaid, & Pfau, 2003; McCombs & Shaw, 1972; Noelle-Neumann, 1984, 1991; M. Roberts, Wanta, & Dzwo, 2002; Tewksbury, Jones, Peske, Raymond, & Vig, 2000; Tsfati, 2003)
- Misjudging media influence in areas of
  - – Public opinion (Gunther & Chia, 2001)
  - – Television violence (Hoffner et al., 2001; Hoffner & Buchanan, 2002; Salwen & Dupagne, 2001; Scharrer, 2002)
  - – Problems from Y2K (Salwen & Dupagne, 2003; Tewksbury et al., 2004)
  - – Direct-to-consumer prescription drug advertising (Huh et al., 2004)
  - – Political ads (Meirick, 2004)
  - – Internet pornography (Lo & Wei, 2002)
  - – General influence of the mass media (Gunther & Storey, 2003; D. M. McLeod et al., 2001; Peiser & Peter, 2000, 2001)

Altering

- Becoming aware of the importance of certain issues, such as environmental issues
- Altering and weighting beliefs (Fishbein & Ajzen, 1975)

Conditioning

- Intense video/computer game playing shifts cognitive strategies from sequential to parallel (Healy, 1999)
- Conditioning how people acquire beliefs (Cappella & Jamieson, 1997; Cartwright, 1949; Hyman & Sheatsley, 1947; E. Katz & Lazarsfeld, 1955; Lasswell, 1927; Scheufele, 1999)

Table 17.3   Attitudinal Effects

Acquiring

- Acquiring attitudes about
  - – Advertised products (Andsager, Austin, & Pinkleton, 2002; Buijzen & Valkenburg, 2000; Nabi, 2003; Pfau et al., 2001; Pfau et al., 2004; Pfau, Holbert, Zubric, Pasha, & Lin, 2000)
  - – Civic engagement of other people (Putnam, 2000)
  - – Social responsibility of businesses (Lind & Rockler, 2001)
  - – Social issues

Women's rights (Holbert, Shah, & Kwak, 2003)

Social trust (Moy & Scheufele, 2000)

– Political matters

Candidates and campaigns (Cwalina, Falkowski, & Kaid, 2000; S.-H. Kim, Scheufele, & Shanahan, 2005; Valentino, Hutchings, & Williams, 2004)

Presidential behavior (Bucy & Newhagen, 1999)

Foreign countries (Perry, 1990)

Government (Becker & Whitney, 1980)

- Acquiring criteria for judgments about
  – Current events (Iyengar & Kinder, 1987)
  – Expectations for marriage (Segrin & Nabi, 2002) and romantic partners (Eggermont, 2004)
  – Satisfaction with one's own body (Harrison & Fredrickson, 2003)

Triggering

- Making judgments about
  – The media in general (Gunther & Christen, 2002; Gunther & Schmitt, 2004)
  – Media credibility (Flanagin & Metzger, 2000; Johnson & Kaye, 1998; S. T. Kim, Weaver, & Willnat, 2000), news stories (Grabe, Zhou, Lang, & Bolls, 2000; Sundar & Nass, 2001), and advertising (Groenendyk & Valentino, 2002)
  – Reality of stories on television (Dorr, 1980), about media texts (A. Hall, 2003) and about public service announcements (Andsager, Austin, & Pinkleton, 2001)
  – Characters in media stories (Kirsh & Olczak, 2000)
  – Moral issues, such as the degree of punishment of violent actions (Krcmar & Cooke, 2001)

Altering

- Altering attitudes (Goffman, 1974, 1979; Kisielius & Sternthal, 1984; T. Newcomb, 1953; Solomon, 1989)
  – Cognitive consistency (Festinger, 1957)
  – Elaboration likelihood (Petty & Cacioppo, 1981)
  – Information integration (Fishbein & Ajzen, 1975)
- Media enjoyment as an attitude (Nabi & Krcmar, 2004)

Conditioning

- Reinforcement of existing attitudes (Klapper, 1960)
  – Cognitive consistency (Festinger, 1957)
  – Elaboration likelihood (Petty & Cacioppo, 1981)
  – Information integration (Fishbein & Ajzen, 1975)
- Media enjoyment as an attitude (Nabi & Krcmar, 2004)

Table 17.4   Affect Effects

Acquiring

- Learning appropriate emotional responses (Goleman, 1995)

Triggering

- Triggering certain emotional reactions, such as
  - Fear (C. R. Berger, 2000; J. Bryant, Carveth, & Brown, 1981; J. Cantor, 2002; J. Cantor & Hoffner, 1990; J. Cantor & Sparks, 1984; J. Cantor & Wilson, 1988; M. G. Cantor, 1994; Comisky & Bryant, 1982; N. D. Feshbach & Roe, 1968; Geen & Rokosky, 1973; Groebel & Krebs, 1983; Gunter & Furnham, 1984; Hare & Blevings, 1975; Himmelweit, Oppenheim, & Vince, 1958; Ogles & Hoffner, 1987; Sapolsky & Zillmann, 1978; S. L. Smith & Wilson, 2002; Tannenbaum & Gaer, 1965; von Feilitzen, 1975; Zillmann, 1991a, 1991b; Zillmann & Cantor, 1977)
  - Empathy (Zillmann, 1991a, 1991b, 1996)
  - Humor (C. M. King, 2000)

Altering

- Managing affect
  - Moods (M. H. Davis & Kraus, 1989; Mares & Cantor, 1992; Zillmann, 1988)
  - Increasing enjoyment of media experience (Csikszentmihalyi, 1988; Denham, 2004; Green & Brock, 2000; Knobloch, Patzig, Mende, & Hastall, 2004; Oliver, Weaver, & Sargent, 2000; Raney, 2002, 2004; Raney & Bryant, 2002; Sherry, 2004; Vorderer, Klimmt, & Ritterfeld, 2004; Vorderer, Knobloch, & Schramm, 2001; Zillmann & Cantor, 1972; Zillmann, Taylor, & Lewis, 1998)
  - Lessening emotional reactions (Cline, Croft, & Courrier, 1973; Gunter, 1985; Lazarus, Speisman, Mordkoff, & Davison, 1962; Mullin & Linz, 1995; Sander, 1995; Speisman, Lazarus, Mordkoff, & Davison, 1964; Thomas, 1982; Thomas, Horton, Lippincott, & Drabman, 1977; Van der Voort, 1986)

Conditioning

- Conditioning of emotional reactions (Zajonc, 1980)

Table 17.5   Physiological Effects

Triggering

- Triggering arousal, such as
  - Increasing heart rate and blood pressure (Detenber, Simons, & Bennett, 1998; Detenber, Simons, & Reiss, 2000; A. Lang, Schwartz, Chung, & Lee, 2004; A. Lang, Zhou, Schwartz, Bolls, & Potter, 2000; R. F. Potter, 2000; E. F. Schneider, Lang, Shin, & Bradley, 2004; Suckfill, 2000)
  - Skin conductance (Detenber et al., 2000; Sundar & Wagner, 2002)
  - Sexual arousal (Harris & Scott, 2002)

Conditioning

- Deadening arousal through habituation and narcoticization
- Transferring physiological arousal to other areas (Zillmann, 1983)

Table 17.6   Behavioral Effects

Acquiring

- Learning behavioral sequences through observation

Triggering

- Triggering behaviors, such as

   – Harmful behaviors

      Eating disorders (Bissell & Zhou, 2004; Botta, 1999; Harrison, 2000; Harrison & Cantor, 1997)

      Imitation of aggression (N. E. Miller & Dollard, 1941)

      Risk-taking behaviors, such as problem drinking and driving, delinquency (vandalizing, trespassing, truancy), reckless driving, and drug use are related to exposure to violent television in the form of violent drama, realistic crime shows, and contact sports among adolescents (Krcmar & Greene, 2000)

   – Prosocial behaviors

      Calls to an AIDS hotline increased dramatically the hour after a soap opera subplot delivered HIV prevention messages (Kennedy, O'Leary, Beck, Pollard, & Simpson, 2004)

      Pro-environmental behavior (Holbert, Kwak, & Shah, 2003)

      Political participation and civic engagement (De Vreese & Semetko, 2002; Hardy & Scheufele, 2005; Mastin, 2000; Newhagen, 1994; Scheufele, 2002; Scheufele, Shanahan, & Kim, 2002; Wilkins, 2000)

Altering

- Reducing inhibitions to behave aggressively (Andison, 1977; Baker & Ball, 1969; Bandura, 1994; Carlson, Marcus-Newhall, & Miller, 1990; Chaffee, 1972; Comstock, Chaffee, Katzman, McCombs, & Roberts, 1978; Grimes, Bergen, Nicholes, Vernberg, & Fonagy, 2004; Hearold, 1986; Liebert, 1972; Liebert & Baron, 1972, 1973; Liebert & Poulos, 1975; Liebert & Schwartzberg, 1977; Lovaas, 1961; Maccoby, 1964; Paik & Comstock, 1994; Scharrer, 2001; Sherry, 2001; Shirley, 1973; Slater, 2003; Stein & Friedrich, 1975; Tannenbaum & Zillmann, 1975; Wood, Wong, & Chachere, 1991)

Conditioning

- Using the media habitually (Freedman & Sears, 1966; Himmelweit, Swift, & Jaeger, 1980; LaRose & Eastin, 2002; McIntosh, Schwegler, & Terry-Murray, 2000; Shah, McLeod, & Yoon, 2001; Sherry, 2001; Slater, 2003)
- Dependency theory—people will become more dependent on media that meet more of their needs (Ball-Rokeach & DeFleur, 1976)
- Conditioning media addiction (Himmelweit, Oppenheim, & Vince, 1958; Jhally, 1987; Kaplan, 1972; LaRose, Lin, & Eastin, 2003; Maccoby, 1954; Mander, 1978; J. M. McLeod, Ward, & Tancill, 1965; Winn, 1977)

cognitive is a term that has been applied to simple information acquisition as well as to the construction of knowledge in a person's mind through the application of inference and generalization. And perhaps the most contested category of all is that of attitudes; an attitude could be an opinion, a belief, a value, a perception, a feeling about something, and perhaps several other things. The inconsistency and fuzziness in definitions of effects are a large part of the motivation to create a template. To make a template useful, we must have clear, consistent definitions.

Macro-Level Template

Up to this point, this chapter has focused on mass media effects on individuals. This is because the literature on how the mass media have influenced individuals is much larger and much more visible than the literature on larger aggregates. Some scholars have criticized this lack of attention to more macro-level effects. For example, Shoemaker and Reese (1996) pointed out that the dominance of psychological studies and the paucity of sociological studies bias the accumulation of findings about the mass media. Also, Mills (1959) argued that we cannot understand larger social structures simply by adding up data about individuals. We need to examine the nature of media influence on more macro-level units.

The different types of effects and the functions were developed with examples of research on individuals, so the MET appears to be a categorization scheme for research only on individuals. However, I believe it also has value as an organization scheme for larger aggregates.

I will make a distinction among three types of macro-level units: the public, institutions, and society. It appears that among these three macro units, mass media influence has been examined more with the public than with the other two. Also, with the public, it is possible to use type of effect as an organizing dimension (see Table 17.7). The literature examining how the mass media influence the public can be grouped by cognitions, beliefs, attitudes, emotions, and behaviors. While there is no macro analogy with physiology, the other five types of individual-level effects match up with the macro unit of the public. With institutions, the organizational dimension would seem to be the institution itself. And with society, there are few studies, making an organizational scheme less needed (see Table 17.8).

One important characteristic that the individual-level effects and the macro-level effects share is their patterning over time. Regardless of the level of effect, it is useful to think in terms of baselines and fluctuations. The only difference is the unit that is being influenced by the mass media. With macro-level effects, the unit is an aggregate or a nonhuman entity.

Using the Media Effects Template

Given the structure of the template, we can look for patterns to learn more about the nature of media-influenced effects on individuals. In the following sections, I will discuss two patterns. First, I will make a distinction between cell and compound effects. Second, I will argue that some of these effects are fundamental, and others are derived from the fundamental effects.

Table 17.7 Variety of Media Effects on Macro Units

Effects on Public Knowledge

- Speed of information flow (DeFleur & Larsen, 1958)
- Diffusion of information in the culture (Rogers, 1962)
  - Fertility (Hornik & McAnany, 2001)
  - Drunk driving (Yanovitzky, 2002)
- Knowledge gap (Tichenor, Donohue, & Olien, 1970; Rucinski, 2004)
- Reduction in shared cultural knowledge (Tewksbury, 2003)

Effects on Public Attitudes

- Propaganda theory (Lasswell, 1927)
- Public opinion formation (Lippmann, 1922)
- Two-step flow (E. Katz & Lazarsfeld, 1955)
- Political action groups influence media workers who create messages that affect the public at large (Andsager, 2000)
  - Race relations (Domke, 2000)
  - National Organization for Women (Barker-Plummer, 2002)
- Hierarchy of persuasive effects (Rice & Atkin, 1989)
- Audience-centered marketing theory (Dervin, 1989)

Effects on Public Beliefs

- Heightened fear of crime and being victimized (Gerbner, Gross, Morgan, & Signorielli, 1980)
- Public perceptions about institutions (Fan, Wyatt, & Keltner, 2001)
- Manufacturing consent (Herman & Chomsky, 1988)
- Promote a consensus through indexing the news (W. L. Bennett, 1990)
- Erosion of social trust (Cappella, 2002; Putnam, 2000)

Effects on Public Emotions

- Moral panic (Chiricos, 1996; S. Cohen, 1972)

Effects on Public Behavior

- Social movements:
  - Student protests against the Vietnam War were influenced by the media coverage of it (Gitlin, 1980)
  - Feminist movement (Lind & Salo, 2002)
- Effects on civil disorder (B. D. Singer, 1970; Spilerman, 1976)
- Adoption of innovations (Rogers & Shoemaker, 1971)
- Reduction in civic engagement and social capital (Putnam, 2000)
- Spiral of silence (Moy, Domke, & Stamm, 2001; Scheufele, Shanahan, & Lee, 2001)

Cell Effects and Compound Effects

If we look at the effects in the MET cell by cell, we can see that many effects are neatly classified within one cell. Let's refer to these as cell effects because their experience by individuals is contained within a particular cell. An example of a cell

Table 17.8   Variety of Media Effects on Institutions and Society

Effects on Society

- Functional theory (Merton, 1949; C. R. Wright, 1949)
- Entertainment theory (Mendelsohn, 1966)
- Ritual theory (Carey, 1975a, b)
- Mass media create a public forum where ideas are negotiated (S. Hall, 1982)
- Media exert a hegemonic influence on society (Adorno & Horkheimer, 1972)
- Media change social structures (Innis, 1950, 1951)
- Form of a medium changes experience with society (McLuhan, 1964)
- Information society (Mattelart, 2003)

Effects on Economic System

- Affluent society (Galbraith, 1976)
- Culture of narcissism (Lasch, 1978)
- One-dimensional man (Marcuse, 1964)
- Consumer culture theory (Ewen, 1976)
- Globalization (Schiller, 1969)

Effects on Political System

- e-democracy (Chadwick, 2006)
- The press effect (Jamieson & Waldman, 2003)

Effects on Government Policy and Actions

- Media shape behaviors of political candidates (G. E. Lang & Lang, 1983)
- CNN effect (P. Robinson, 2001)
- Foreign aid (Van Belle, 2003)
- Political scandals (J. Thompson, 2000; Tumber & Waisbord, 2004)
- Regulation (or nonregulation) of media content such as violence (C. A. Cooper, 1996; W. J. Potter, 2003)

Effect on Mass Media

- Media logic (Altheide & Snow, 1979)
- Media as culture industries (Hay, 1989; Jhally, 1987)

effect is the acquisition of a fact as a result of a media exposure. Another example is the triggering of a particular behavior as a result of a media exposure.

There are also other effects that cannot be cleanly classified within one cell. Let's refer to these as compound effects because their experience by individuals is spread out over more than one cell. An example of a compound effect is the cultivation effect, which has been conceptualized as a belief about the real world (e.g., the world is mean and violent), a behavioral pattern (e.g., not walking alone in one's neighborhood at night), and a faulty estimate of risk (e.g., overestimating the percentage of crimes that are violent).

There are several ways these cells can be configured for compound effects: vertical integration, horizontal integration, and conglomeration. Vertical integration refers to an effect that involves two or more cells in the same column of the MET. An example of this would be the cultivation effect. This effect assumes people have real-world information, attitudes, and beliefs on a topic—let's say the criminal justice system. From exposure to media messages, those information structures, attitudes, and beliefs are altered. Thus, this affect is predominantly one where the media alter existing things in the person, and those "things" are from different cells in the same column. Furthermore, it is assumed that information, attitudes, and beliefs are all related to one another on a given topic, such that when one is altering, the others are altered; thus, these three actions across these three cells are integrated, and hence this is an example of vertical integration. Notice how this analysis of cultivation highlights the consideration of assumptions in cultivation research that multiple types of effects are integrated with one another.

Horizontal integration refers to an effect that involves two or more cells on the same line in the MET. Conglomeration refers to an effect that involves two or more cells that are not all on the same line or in the same column.

This language and the MET could be useful in model building. For example, a scholar could examine findings on a body of attitudinal effects (all one row in the MET) and look for connections across acquiring, triggering, altering, and conditioning (the columns). By making those connections, the scholar is constructing a horizontal explanation. Such an explanation could be a more general theory of media influence on all functions of attitudes. Or a media scholar might be interested in constructing a more general theory of media conditioning, so this scholar would work down the conditioning column and make connections about how the media condition cognitions, which in turn influence attitudes and beliefs, which in turn influence behaviors over time.

Primary and Derived Effects

In this section, I will present an argument that the cognitive and physiological effects are more primary and that the other three types of effects are essentially derived from the primary effects. Thus, I argue that attitudinal, affective, and behavioral effects will not occur unless there is first some cognitive or physiological process.

I have two reasons to support this argument. First, the six types of effects differ in the sense of how dependent they are on one another. To illustrate, some types of effects are strongly influenced and even dependent on another type. Cognitions influence belief formation (Tversky & Kahneman, 1973; Wyer & Albarracin, 2005), affect (Isen, 2000), and attitude formation and change (Chaiken, Liberman, & Eagly, 1989; Petty & Cacioppo, 1986; Wegener & Carlston, 2005). Beliefs influence attitudes (Fishbein & Ajzen, 1975; Kruglanski & Stroebe, 2005), and attitudes influence beliefs (Marsh & Wallace, 2005; McGuire, 1990). Behaviors influence attitudes (Festinger, 1957; J. M. Olson & Stone, 2005), and attitudes influence behavior (Ajzen & Fishbein, 1977, 2005), both consciously (Allport, 1935; Dulany, 1968) and unconsciously (Bargh, 1997). Affect influences attitudes (Clore & Schnall, 2005; Zajonc, 1968) as well as behaviors (Johnson-Laird & Oatley, 2000).

In the set of six types of media effects, cognitive and physiological effects are relatively independent from the others in the sense that they can occur with no antecedent from the other four, but the other four are dependent on an antecedent from cognitive effects or physiology or both. For example, a person can be exposed to a media message and learn a fact. That is a purely cognitive effect. The person can then do something with that fact and derive another type of effect. Media-influenced attitudes begin with the media providing information to a person in the form of an attitude, which then either (a) is retained by the person (much like the retention of factual information) as his or her own attitude or (b) triggers a thought process of evaluation. Likewise, media-influenced beliefs begin with the media providing information to a person in the form of a belief, which then either (a) is retained by the person (much like the retention of factual information) as his or her own belief or (b) triggers a thought process of pattern construction and generalization from the pattern elements to the world. In their chapter titled "Cognitive Processes in Attitude Formation and Change" in the *Handbook of Attitudes,* Wegener and Carlston (2005) argued that the "cognitive process has been at the heart of research on attitudes virtually since that research began" (p. 493). And more generally, they said, "If the human brain is involved, a process is cognitive, and because the human brain is almost always involved, few human activities fall outside the cognitive umbrella" (p. 494).

Media-influenced affective effects begin with the media stimulating a physiological reaction, which is then labeled in a cognitive process, either consciously or unconsciously. Media-influenced behavioral effects begin with an idea planted in a person's mind about a behavioral element or a behavioral sequence and a physiological reaction that is needed to energize the action. Some of the behavioral effects are automatic, that is, requiring only the energy to enact (e.g., imitation) and circumvent the thinking processes. Other behavioral effects require a significant degree of cognition as people think about how to behave, construct a sequence of novel acts, and rehearse the sequence before actually performing it. The manifestation consists of behaviors, but to understand the manifestation, we need to understand the process leading up to it.

My second reason to support this distinction between primary and derived types is that derived effects are typically more complex than primary effects in that they require more drive energy to undertake and complete successfully. Furthermore, the derived effects get their drive energy from the primary effects. For example, behaving aggressively requires more energy than imagining one's self behaving aggressively. Crossing the line between thinking about something and doing something requires arousal, and that is a physiological effect. Another example is changing one's attitude about something. This requires more energy to reevaluate and rethink than to keep the same attitude. It requires drive energy to do the reevaluation and rethinking. The cognitive state of dissonance has been found to create such drive energy. Humans experience a drive for consistency and will be motivated to expend the energy needed to achieve this goal of consistency.

In essence, what I am arguing is that future research and conceptualizing will likely have their greatest impact if scholars work most in the areas of the primary effects because then their work will radiate out to the derived effects. Also, scholars who develop models of compound effects need to build their explanations from the primary effects; if they focus only on derived effects, those explanations will be less compelling.

Conclusion

This chapter attempts to organize the large literature of media effects. The chapter begins with conceptualizations of media effect and media influence, and then it builds to an MET that is a matrix that can provide addresses for the different effects. One dimension of the matrix is composed of the six types of media effects: cognitions, beliefs, attitudes, affects, physiology, and behaviors. The second dimension of the matrix is composed of the four media-influenced functions of acquiring, triggering, altering, and conditioning. This template is altered to organize more macro-level effects on the public and institutions.

Table 17.9   Assumptions Underlying the Mass Media Effects Line of Thinking

Assumption 1: Media effects can be either categorical or continuous.

1.1:   A few effects are truly categorical. This means that a person experiences an effect or does not; either there is clear evidence that an effect has occurred or there is not.

1.2:   Almost all media-influenced effects vary by degree on a continuum. This means that people experience varying levels of the effect and that there are degrees of strength in evidence of these effects.

Assumption 2: We will never be able to determine a nonarbitrary threshold along any continuum of levels of a particular effect. Therefore, the experience of an effect or evidence of an effect cannot be defined in terms of crossing a threshold.

Assumption 3: Media effects are best studied when the individual is both the unit of measurement and the unit of analysis. This puts the focus on change (or nonchange) within the individual rather than averages across groups of individuals.

Assumption 4: People are constantly being exposed to mass media messages either directly or indirectly. Therefore, the influence of the mass media is constant and ongoing.

Assumption 5: Mass media influence occurs as a manifested or process effect. Manifested effects spontaneously occur and can be observed relatively easily. Process effects are latent patterns that build up over time. They are not easy to observe.

Assumption 6: There are four patterns of mass media influence:

6.1:   Long-term alterations to a baseline (upward sloping or downward sloping)

6.2:   Long-term reinforcing of a baseline's position

6.3:   Immediate shift of the baseline to a new level that is sustained

6.4:   Fluctuations off a person's baseline during a media exposure with a return to the baseline

Assumption 7: The wide variety of effects documented in the mass media literature can be usefully organized into a Media Effects Template (MET), which has two dimensions of effect type (cognition, attitude, affect, physiology, and behavior) and media influence function (acquiring, triggering, altering, and conditioning). The MET can be used with a variety of targets, including individuals, institutions, and society.

Table 17.10   Media Effects Propositions

Effect 1: An individual's baseline is established and maintained by the influences of three sets of factors: media exposure habits, characteristics about the person, and characteristics of the environment.

Effect 2: Fluctuations from the effect baseline are influenced by three sets of factors: particular media exposures, characteristics about the person (especially states), and characteristics of the particular environment.

Effect 3: Exposure states are associated with the degree of media power in influencing an effect. The media exert their greatest power when audiences experience the messages in the automatic and transported states. In contrast, the media power is lower in the attentional and self-reflexive states, where audience members more consciously make decisions and thereby exert more power in filtering and constructing meaning.

Table 17.11   Structured Glossary of Terms About Mass Media Effects on Individuals

Micro effect—effect on an individual person.

Macro effect—effect on an aggregate of people, culture, or an institution.

Baseline pattern effect—is the best estimate of a person's degree of effect at any given time. It is formed over the long term by the constant interaction of three types of factors: psychological traits of the person, sociological experiences of the person, and media exposure patterns.

Fluctuation pattern effect—is observed in research studies when there is a change between a person's preexposure and postexposure effect level score. The larger the difference, the larger the influence of the media exposure on the effect level. Fluctuation changes can be in the direction to increase the level of an effect or to decrease the level. In either case, fluctuation changes are usually temporary. They are typically traceable to particular interpretations that the person made about the message.

Reinforcement pattern effect—through repeated exposures of the same type of messages, a person's baseline position is made more weighty; that is, it becomes much more resistant to change over time, and it loses its elasticity, thus rendering fluctuations more minor and more rare.

Type of effect—refers to six categories of effects: cognitive, attitudinal, belief, affective, physiological, and behavioral.

- Cognitive effect—media exposure exercising an influence on an individual's mental processes or the product of those mental processes; typically involves the acquisition, processing, and storage of information.
- Attitudinal effect—media exposure exercising an influence on an individual's evaluative judgments; typically involves providing people with elements to evaluate or shaping standards of evaluation.
- Belief effect—media exposure exercising an influence on an individual's judgments about the probability of existence or occurrence of things.
- Affective effect—media exposure exercising an influence on an individual's feelings; typically involves providing people with messages that trigger and shape feelings.

- Physiological effect—media exposure exercising an influence on an individual's automatic bodily responses to stimuli; typically involves triggering immediate reactions and shaping those reactions over time.
- Behavioral effect—media exposure exercising an influence on an individual doing something; typically involves attracting people to media messages and conditioning habits.

Media-influenced functions—generic ways the mass media can influence individuals. There are four in this conceptualization: acquiring, triggering, altering, and conditioning.

Media Effects Template (MET)—a two-dimensional scheme that crosses the six types of effects with the four media-influenced functions.

CHAPTER 18

Designing Media Effects Studies

This chapter further elaborates the lineation general perspective line of thinking about mass media effects by focusing on operational issues that become important when moving from conceptual concerns into the design of research studies. To this end, I present a generic five-step model for designing Target-Degree strategy studies. This design model is a hybrid because it attempts to take the strongest elements from a variety of traditional methods of experiment and survey as well as qualitative approaches to research. Specifically, I incorporate the idea of differential treatments from experimental design, multiple measures from survey design, and a phenomenological approach from qualitative methods.

Focus on One Effect

This design model begins with a clear focus on the effect that is being studied in this particular research design. Thus, the use of the Target-Degree strategy for designing research studies requires the identification of a conceptual definition and conceptual positioning.

The conceptual definition is an extremely important starting place. It clarifies the focal idea of the research, and this clarity then positions the planned study strongly into the existing literature. When there is no careful articulation of the conceptual definition in studies, those studies can only be grouped loosely by topic area, like effects of violent messages or effects of political ads. When positioning is done by message, there is a low level of clarity, and this makes synthesis across findings much more difficult. This is because a message type could be associated with a variety of effects. For example, violent messages have been associated with a learning effect, a disinhibition effect, a fear effect, a cultivation effect, and a desensitization effect. Thus, position by message does little to reduce ambiguity as to effect.

The conceptual definition needs to highlight one effect and explicate what that one effect is. In this explication, the researchers need to articulate clearly what they believe the role of media is in the process of influence that brings about evidence of this effect. The Media Effects Template (MET; see Table 17.1) can help in this task by providing fundamental addresses for effects. The MET can also be used as context to compare and contrast effects; this comparing and contrasting of contiguous effects helps position the focal effect of a particular study. Study designers need to access relevant empirical literatures to consider as many measures and procedures as possible to determine which are the best and which to avoid. The challenge of accessing a complete set of studies on a particular effect is enhanced when those studies are organized by MET addresses. Also, in situations when there is no published literature on a particular effect, study designers can read across rows and down columns to identify the most relevant contiguous literatures.

Select a Media Factor of Influence

When designing media effects studies, it is essential to identify some factor of the media that will be tested for its influence. This factor then becomes the focal media factor in the study. If the study is to be an experiment, then this factor is what is varied to create differential treatments. If the study is a survey, this factor becomes the central message element in a cluster of other message elements.

Because many media factors appear in the effects literature, the challenge lies not in identifying an interesting message factor to test. For example, researchers have

Table 18.1   Explaining Acquisition of Facts Effect

Baseline Factors

Message Factors

- People can learn better when presented with concrete examples rather than abstract principles (Zillmann, 1999).
- The media present messages by diverting people's attention away from the abstract principles with the emphasis on the concrete visualizations of particulars (Corner, 1999).

Audience Factors

- Increased when people already have a good deal of information on the topic (Huang, 2000; Valentino, Hutchings, & Williams, 2004)
- Cognitive styles (particularly those high on verbalizing) (Mendelson & Thorson, 2004)
- Capacity to process messages; related to skills and developmental level (Fisch, 2000)
- Long-term attentional patterns (S.-H. Kim, Scheufele, & Shanahan, 2005)

Fluctuation Factors

Message Factors

- Amount of information
  - Redundant information (Fox, 2004; van der Molen & Klijn, 2004; van der Molen & van der Voort, 2000)
  - Too many elements confuse people and reduce acquisition (Gibbons, Vogl, & Grimes, 2003).
  - Too many simultaneous sources of messages split attention and learning decreases (Armstrong, 2002).
  - There are limits to how much information an individual can process at a single time (A. Lang, 2000).
- Type of information
  - Atypical information elements (Shapiro & Fox, 2002)
  - Visual intensity of information (Bolls & Lang, 2003)
  - Layout of information (Eveland, Cortese, Park, & Dunwoody, 2004; Grabe, Zhou, Lang, & Bolls, 2000)
  - Arousing elements (Bolls, Lang, & Potter, 2001)
- Structure of information
  - Information gaps in structure create drive for continuity and closure (Levin & Simons, 2000; Metzger, 2000).
- Framing of the information (Shah, Kwak, Schmierbach, & Zubric, 2004; Shen, 2004; Valentino, Buhr, & Beckmann, 2001)

The Medium

- Memory for ad is related to the medium in which it is viewed.
  - Sundar, Narayan, Obregon, and Uppal (1999) ran an experiment and found that people remember ads more in newspapers than online.

- Increases in learning are related to the way people interact with computers in social situations (Bracken & Lombard, 2004).

Audience Factors

- Reasons for message exposures (Eveland, 2001, 2002)
- High motivation for retaining information (Huang, 2000)
- High interest in a topic (Graber, 1988)
- Higher attention to messages
  - This leads to more cognitive elaboration of messages (Eveland, 2001; Eveland & Dunwoody, 2000).
  - Attention is increased when perceived message sensation value is high (Morgan, 2003).
- Emotional state (Newhagen, 1998)
- Activation of associative networks in memory (Shrum, 2002)
- People use mental shortcuts when processing information (Tversky & Kahneman, 1973).

found many factors influencing the acquisitions facts from the media (see Table 18.1) and there are long lists of influential factors found for many other media effects. Instead, the challenge lies in selecting the factor that is likely to exert the strongest influence on a particular effect. Thus, we need to consider calibration of influence. Because our research field has limited resources, we need to select variables that matter most and leave more trivial predictors in the background. Of course, we can never know for sure which variables are more important and which are more trivial until we conduct the empirical tests. However, my argument is that we have produced a literature large enough to make fairly good decisions about calibration.

In making our selections of media influence factors, we also need to think of patterns of influence and how this message variable will fit into that pattern. Specifically, we need to consider that some of these message factors should be related to fluctuations (the immediate media message, exposure as well as other states in the individual, and the exposure situation) and others to baseline (long-term conditioning, habits of media exposure, traits, and information-processing skill levels). This raises the issues of level and timing.

Level

The level of the media factor ranges from a medium itself at the most general end of the continuum, through a meta-genre of content (such as all news, entertainment, or ads), through genres (such as action-adventure or romance), through a narrative (one story in its entirety), down to a particular message characteristic (such as humor or one character). For example, it might be the medium itself that exerts an influence (Centerwall, 1989; McLuhan, 1964; Meyrowitz, 1985), certain characteristics of a medium (McClure & Patterson, 1974; Munsterberg, 1916), or particular content that dominates a medium (Gerbner & Gross, 1976). Most of the thinking and research is that there are particular characteristics about genres, messages, and message elements that exert an influence.

I am not arguing at this time that the factors from one level are more powerful or more interesting than the factors of other levels. Instead, I am arguing for conscious selection and clear positioning. This means that we must recognize that as we select a content element to study, that selected element is being abstracted from a content array of more macro and more micro elements that are all linked to the focal selection, so we should not ignore the array.

Timing

Study designers need to consider whether they want to present one treatment or multiple treatments over time. A one-treatment design is the easiest but also the least useful for illuminating the nature of media influence on effects. The one-treatment design has utility only for testing a fluctuation effect. Designs gain strength to the extent that they increase treatments over time along with measurements over time, so it is possible to plot the *pattern* of influence with multiple exposures.

Measurement

Some effects offer an obvious manifestation, such as aggressive behavior or learning of a fact. However, most effects will require the study designer to develop measures to elicit evidence—that is, the evidence will not spontaneously and naturally exhibit itself; it must be elicited. In designing those measures, researchers should be guided by seven recommendations: focus on what participants know, consider targets' meanings, conduct more naturalistic observation, consider exposure states, take targets' history relevant to the particular effect, use active over attribute variables, and try to generate continuous distributions on as many variables as possible.

Focus on What Targets Know

This guideline is the most primary one, such that if researchers fail to follow this, none of the other guidelines will matter. This primary guideline is as follows: Ask participants questions about only those things they are able to answer. Specifically, this means that researchers should have a defensible expectation that their study participants have a trace memory and that they are able to access that memory during the data gathering.

What makes this recommendation so important is that mass media effects researchers frequently ask their study participants about mundane behaviors for which they have no trace memory or adequate heuristics for constructing anything near an accurate answer. These are behaviors that are performed so automatically that they require almost no mental effort, so people do not pay much, if any, attention to the details of the experience while it is happening. As a result, there is little, if any, recollection that can be accessed. When researchers then ask participants to recall the experience, participants have nothing to recall and must instead use heuristics to construct their responses. Researchers then are not measuring recall but instead are measuring the use of a variety of cognitive heuristics. For example, Ferguson (1992) conducted a study where he had people sit in a room and watch TV with a remote control device (RCD) in their hand while they purportedly waited to be called to begin a research study in another room. He recorded how often the participants changed channels. Then later, after the "other" study was completed, he asked participants how many times they changed channels during the previous TV viewing session. He found a zero correlation; that is, everyone was making wild guesses, and participants were as likely to underestimate their channel changes as they were to overestimate them. Therefore, it is foolhardy to expect people to report accurately their mundane behaviors performed in everyday rituals.

It is also unlikely that people who watch a TV show will have an accurate recollection of the occurrence of elements. To illustrate this point, I conducted an experiment with some colleagues (W. J. Potter, Pashupati, Pekurny, Hoffman, & Davis, 2002) where we were looking at differences in how people interpret violence in television programs. We showed our participants one of three versions of the same television show edited to vary the number of violent acts. One treatment had 63 acts of violence, a second treatment had 43 acts, and a third show had 13 acts. After the viewing, we asked our participants to write down how many acts of violence they had just witnessed in the show. None of the participants could recall more than about a dozen acts, and the distribution of estimates in all three groups overlapped considerably, leading us to conclude that participants do not keep a running tabulation of acts that occur in the shows they watch. Therefore, it would seem useless to ask participants about particular elements they encountered in media messages unless those particular elements were not only highly salient but also rare.

It is also suspect to ask participants to express how much attention they pay to media messages. Yet, the mass media effects literature contains many examples of highly suspect measures. One example of this is a measure of attention to TV, such as Rouner's (1984) Attention Scale that uses a 5-point Likert-type scale ranging from (1) *no attention at all* to (5) *very close attention.* It asks questions about how much attention is paid to the story line, the characters' appearance, the personal qualities of the characters, and the values and morals displayed by the characters. How can respondents go about making such judgments? What context do they use for comparison? This measure is highly suspect, but despite its questionable nature, this scale has been used by other researchers (J. Kim & Rubin, 1997).

Another example of highly suspect self-measures is in the area of emotional reactions. Of course, it is likely that people can recall instances of extremely strong emotional reactions to certain media content, such as strong fear reactions (see J. Cantor, 2002), but it is not likely that people can accurately report on more mundane emotional reactions. Sparks, Pellechia, and Irvine (1999) criticized 15 years of mass media studies of viewers' emotional reactions to frightening messages that are based on the assumption that self-reports of negative emotions are accurate. They conducted a study and found that certain viewers report low levels of negative affect in response to frightening films but exhibit significantly higher physiological arousal. These are people who repress their feelings; researchers cannot trust self-report emotional data from them.

At best, these faulty measures generate responses on elements that did not exist before the participant read the researcher's question and felt the demand to answer. Some participants' attitudes about X and beliefs about Y might not have existed until they were asked to express an attitude or a belief and did so. What respondents put on the questionnaire may be accurate reflections about their new attitudes and beliefs, but should these newly generated attitudes and beliefs be averaged together with the long-held attitudes and beliefs of other participants who were able to achieve accurate recollections?

Another problem is that participants might not have a trace memory of something, so they provide a wild guess. Such wild guesses usually create random distributions that are then found to have no predictive power; in this case, their faultiness is rendered moot. But the worst-case situation may be when a person is asked about X and Y for which there is no memory. The person uses a heuristic to come up with a "quick and dirty" estimate for X and then uses the same heuristic to estimate Y. When researchers correlate the X responses with the Y responses, they find a fairly strong correlation. But this finding is likely to be spurious; that is, the correlation coefficient is not an accurate reflection of the degree to which X and Y are related conceptually. Instead, the correlation coefficient is an indication of the degree to which participants used the same heuristic to make a wild guess about both X and Y.

Because much of media exposure and the experiences surrounding it are so habitual and mundane, people are not likely to have an accurate idea for many of the things we typically measure. The trap is that because participants have so much experience with something, they think they can provide accurate answers. But it is the high degree of contact with something that leads people to lose their perspective on it and have faulty impressions. So we as researchers need to think carefully about the quality of data that participants can provide.

We need to get past our reliance on self-report measures. Oftentimes, there are stronger measures that we can access if we take some time to think creatively and do a bit more work. One example is with the belief effect that the media have made us materialistic. We could ask people to rate themselves on a scale of 1 to 10 to indicate how materialistic they are and then use the average as a general measure of materialism. But it would be far more accurate to look at aggregate economic data of consumer expenditures over time. We could look at consumption patterns and map them onto increases in media power and messages as well as onto gross national product for consumer goods (instead of public goods). We can then look at increases in what we throw away (nonrecyclables, which indicate that which is no longer useful to us or anyone). Also, the rise in psychotherapy and depression medication indicates that something is wrong—that is, we just cannot meet the expectations we have for ourselves. The constant flow of mass media messages urging consumption and continually portraying high affluence makes many of us feel that there is more to life than we are able to attain.

Consider Targets' Meaning

The Groups-Effect strategy places people in treatment groups where differences across the group means (reflecting the meaning in the media treatment message) are the focus of the explanation and the individual interpretations are either ignored as error variation or not measured at all. In contrast, the Target-Degree strategy places the locus of meaning with the person instead of with the message. People are asked for their interpretations of meaning, and those distributions of interpretation variables become an important set of factors to test.

Thus, with the Target-Degree strategy, we need to recognize that the rationality we use as scholars to construct studies and explain phenomena is often not the same rationality that people use in their everyday lives to make mundane decisions. That is, what appears to be rational to us as scholars is not rational to people making decisions in their everyday lives, where they must be governed by a different set of goals and values. Once we understand those different goals and ways of thinking, we may come to understand that there is a different logic operating in the nonacademic real world.

I am using the term *nonrational* in two senses. One sense of the term is nonintellectual, as in the dichotomy of rational-emotional. People often make decisions guided by their feeling processes over their thinking processes. A second sense of the term is nonlogical. People often make decisions that do not follow any logical reasoning. Some decisions are based on little or no evidence; those decisions are made in an intuitive leap. Often, these nonrational decisions are not in the person's best interest—that is, they are stupid or wrong or self-destructive. Still, decisions are made in nonrational ways.

We as rational researchers putting together our logical, formal designs for research studies need to acknowledge that people are not always like that in their everyday lives. On many topics, people feel it is not worth the mental effort to gather more evidence and engage in logical, ordered reasoning. Some people do not have the mental skills to undertake much mental reasoning without feeling overwhelmed or frustrated.

Human thinking is complex and not always rational, especially in situations when people feel overwhelmed with information and need to achieve efficiency over accuracy, when people do not feel much involvement in the information-processing task, and when people are in a state of automaticity. These conditions are not rare. To the contrary, with people's exposures to media messages every day, these conditions are likely to be very prevalent. Therefore, ignoring nonrational models of information processing seriously limits our ability to understand how people filter, construct meaning making, and are influenced by media exposures.

Rational models emphasize structure, direction, and a progression. Nonrational models are more open to multiple paths, some of which are recursive and some of which skip steps. Thus, nonrational models are more complex in their need to incorporate idiosyncrasies. I recommend backing off from structured models and instead focus on calibrating the relative influence of various factors and sets of factors on levels of effects. If a scholar truly believes in a rational model, then he or she must test for structure, and the degree of influence of a factor is likely to change depending on where it is tested in the model. In fact, the nature of testing structured models is to play around with the positioning of factors to find where their influence is strongest and place the factor at that location. However, when we do not have a presumption of structure, then we can still ask the following question: In a situation where lots of factors are present, which are the most influential ones?

Instead of using this type of model to structure an explanation of media effects, I draw more from the perspective of Kurt Lewin, who took a broad view on explaining human experience. He used the idea of life-space to refer to a person's total psychological environment. This includes a person's "needs, goals, unconscious influences, memories, beliefs, events of a political, economic, and social nature, and anything else that might have a direct effect on behavior" (Marrow, 1969, p. 35). All of these factors within a person's life-space constitute a system of interrelationships. The situation is organic and evolving where all factors with influence are in constant interaction with one another. The focus is shifted to looking at what factors are the most salient within a cycle of influence over repeated exposures of immersion in a media-saturated environment.

Conduct More Naturalistic Observations

We need to shift studies more into a naturalistic realm. This is more than simply moving studies out of the laboratory and into a person's familiar settings. It also requires more sensitivity to the degree of awareness audience members have in their everyday exposure situations and how much of that awareness can be captured in measurement instruments. Thus, achieving a highly naturalistic research design requires shifting from paper-and-pencil self-reports to more insightful observation by trained scholars.

Consider Exposure States

In documenting these exposures, we must take into account exposure states. Because the experience of any given media message is different for individuals across exposure states, it is highly likely that the effects will also be different across exposure states. For example, the acquisition of an information effect can take place in all four exposure states. In the attentional state, the information in the message is attended to consciously but may or may not be cataloged into long-term memory. In the self-reflexive state of exposure, the audience member is very active in pursuing a goal for a particular kind of information, so he or she is likely to be more active in filtering and evaluating the information, then carefully cataloging what is deemed the most useful information found, and quickly purging the rest. In the transported state, a person is likely to catalog information with emotional tags rather than informational ones. And in the automatic state, the person's algorithm makes cataloging decisions outside of the person's consciousness. Readers may disagree with the particular predictions I have made in this example; however, my point is that it is likely that there are differences, although making predictions about what those differences are at this time is highly speculative. For this reason, we need to factor exposure states into our research designs.

Models that do not take into consideration multiple exposure states are limited. For example, McQuail (2005) presented a model of media effects that has what he calls "filter conditions" that can prevent attention. He said that "attention is important because without it there can be no effect" (p. 475). This linear, logical model is a popular type of model. It makes logical sense, but it is limited in its ability to explain a full range of media effects. A great deal of media influence takes place in nonattentional states.

Not only do we as researchers need to examine the influence that different exposure states have on effects; we also need to be careful that we achieve correspondence on this feature between how we conceptualize media exposure and how we operationalize it in a research study. To illustrate this point, consider the following example. Let's say researchers design an experiment to test the acquisition of an information effect. They show their participants some documentaries and then administer a test afterward. In this case, it is likely that the participants were in an attentional state during the exposure to the documentaries as well as during the testing period—likely, but not certain. To be certain, we need to measure to find out which exposure state they were in during the exposure and then post hoc put them in groups and compare means on the posttest across groups. There is likely to be a range of performance scores on the posttest, and perhaps the variable of exposure state can help explain some of that variance.

Developing good measures of exposure states is a challenging task. We cannot simply ask someone to circle his or her state from a list of these four technical terms. We need to develop such a scale to measure exposure states, even though this is a most challenging task. Until we develop such a scale, we need to at least avoid the more serious problems of validity that would occur with obvious shifts in attentional states. These shifts occur frequently in survey work. For example, we frequently ask people to recall how much TV they watch. Most of respondents' TV exposure is likely to be in the automatic state (where the TV is on in the background while they do other things in the foreground) or in the transported state (while they watch their favorite shows). However, the survey experience puts respondents in the attention or even in the self-reflexive state.

Take Each Target's History

A key characteristic in the Target-Degree strategy is to contextualize any media exposure treatment in the target's history. People are not blank slates when they start their participation in research studies. Instead, people differ fundamentally in terms of their history of exposure to the mass media, how they have filtered those experiences, what they have retained, how that retained information is organized, and their skills of using that retained information in cognitive processing. Thus, they have clusters of beliefs, attitudes, and moods that are likely to affect strongly their experience of any treatment material in an experiment. Also, by the time people have reached college (the source of many of the experimental participants in mass media published research), they have been subjected to almost two decades of constant conditioning by the media, family, and other institutions. People are continually exposed to a stream or flow of messages, and any one message does not stand alone but must be interpreted in the context of this flow. Raymond Williams (1974) was among the first to argue that individual television programs do not exist as discrete entities in the minds of viewers. Rather, a kind of flow across texts is the central experience of the medium (p. 95)—a fact that accounts for much of television's critical significance. This flow occurs both in a day's viewing and across the episodes of a series. H. Newcomb and Hirsch (1984) picked up on this idea and called for the analysis of viewing strips or flow texts rather than analyzing an individual program. Producers are trying to create in each individual audience member what R. Williams (1990) called flow. This is when the audience member continues an exposure while having one message replace another and where a message is interrupted by other messages. Williams was concerned with the negative impact flow has on meaning construction by audiences who are exposed to an endless random juxtaposition of different texts. Thus, people at different points in a flow will not all "see" the same thing in a given media message.

The Target-Degree strategy research tries to tap into the history of the individual and where he or she is in the flow of media exposure as a way of assessing where each individual is at the beginning of an experiment. This information thus forms the context from which we can explain what happens (or does not happen) to the research participant during the media exposure. This includes history with media exposures, traits, lifestyles, and states. There are always a large number of variables that can be considered in this category; researchers cannot measure all of these, so designers must make selections. These selections should be guided by an awareness of which of these factors has been found in past research studies to have the strongest predictive values of this particular media effect.

Perhaps the most important explanatory factor of influence is mass media exposure. It can be both a baseline and a fluctuation factor. When it is a fluctuation factor, it can simply be measured by the typical questions used, such as, How much time did you spend watching TV yesterday? But when it is a baseline factor, there needs to be more attention to long-term patterns. If Harry and Cindy both viewed 3 hours of TV a day last week, this does not mean that both have the same long-term exposure to TV: What if Harry were 13 and Cindy were 70 years old? Also, there needs to be more concern over the type of content. The meaning lies in the way stories are told. Frequency of exposure to a story tells us about the degree of reinforcement of the meaning, not the meaning itself. Finally, there needs to be more attention paid to the exposure amounts in context. For example, if a person has viewed 100 hours of violent movies, it makes a difference if the overall movie attendance were 110 hours or 2,000 hours. For more on this point, see W. J. Potter and Chang (1990).

Active Over Attribute Variables

Attribute variables are useful in the early formative stages of a research field, but one of the things that allows a field to evolve beyond exploration is the identification of active influences that are cleaner predictors conceptually and usually stronger predictors empirically. The shift of attention from attribute to active variables is a sign of increasing precision.

Two variables—gender and age—are frequently used in mass media effects research and have provided some value in the past, but it is time to get beyond simple grouping by gender and age. It is time to think more about what we are assuming these variables indicate and shift away from these attributes to look for more active factors. For example, sex is a very easy attribute variable to measure and use. If a researcher is willing to assume uniformity within a sex value (i.e., all females are exactly the same), then it makes sense to stay with the attribute-type variable. But typically sex is used to represent some pattern of socialization, that is, an active influence on a person's belief system. Testing sex as a predictor variable has some value in the exploratory phase of research because it is better to test its effect than to ignore it. But the active element in the sex variable is usually something like gender role socialization, and this is what should be measured. Using biological sex as a surrogate for gender role socialization guarantees that the prediction will be fuzzy at best because not all people of the same biological sex have the same degree or type of gender role socialization.

A child's age has been used as a grouping variable indicating the child's developmental maturity. We need to focus more on a person's abilities than on a person's presumed developmental maturity. A person's level of developmental maturity is a useful measure of potential. While all people at the same development level may have the same potential, not everyone has acted on that potential; there is a range of ability. When designing research studies, it seems much more useful to include factors that measure a person's information-processing abilities than his or her potentials.

There is evidence that certain people are cognitively developed to a level to achieve certain things but that they do not exercise their abilities to achieve that potential. For example, Piaget's theory says that children are fully developed cognitively and therefore are capable of adult thinking (formal operations) at age 13. However, P. M. King (1986) conducted a review of the published literature that tested the formal reasoning abilities of adults and concluded that "a rather large proportion of adults do not evidence formal thinking, even among those who have been enrolled in college" (p. 6). This conclusion holds up over the 25 studies she analyzed, including a variety of tests of formal reasoning ability and a variety of samples of adults 18 to 79 years old. In one third of the samples, less than 30% of the respondents exhibited reasoning at the fully formal level, and in almost all samples, no more than 70% of the adults were found to be fully functioning at the formal level.

Ability to reason morally is not always shown to be more advanced with age. For example, Van der Voort (1986) found no evidence that children judge violent behavior more critically in a moral sense as they age. He found no reduction in the approval of the good guys' behavior. And as children aged, they were even more likely to approve of the violent actions of the bad guys. So while children acquire additional cognitive abilities with age, they do not necessarily acquire additional moral insights. There is a range of moral development among people of any given age.

Continuous Distributions Over Categories

To use the power of quantitative analyses, one should use continuous distributions rather than categorical distinctions. Also, because many of our variables are continuous to begin with, it makes little sense to subdivide them into categories, especially when such divisions are made with arbitrary cut points.

Working with continuous distributions, of course, presents its own set of challenges. For example, we need to test them for normalcy. Also, when we try to correlate across distributions, we need to test for nonlinear relationships as well as symmetry.

Analyses

As for the analysis stage, the Target-Degree strategy is delineated most clearly from the Groups-Differences strategy in terms of the focus on the target rather than the group in the analysis. This leads to considerations of distributions of change, determination of media influence on that change, participant-determined contingent analyses, and the use of many variables in those analyses.

Focus on the Target as Unit

With the Target-Degree strategy, the unit of analysis is the target or, better yet, the target's change score on an effect measure. That is, for each target, there should be a change score computed that indicates any change from before to after exposure to a particular media factor of influence. This will result in a distribution of change scores. The focus of the analyses then is explaining the variance in that distribution of change scores in a multivariate manner.

The media do exert influence on groups of people and macro structures in society. That is an important area of study. But so is the examination of media influence on individuals. However, when the focus is the individual, it would seem wise to keep the focus on the individual as much as possible in the analysis. One way to get better at this is to break with the practice of moving quickly to aggregate analyses, which is required by experiments and analysis of variance (ANOVA). The simplest way to do this is to compute change scores (level of an effect before and then after a media exposure). The change score reflects the degree of fluctuation of the individual. Thus, the person is compared at two points in time rather than aggregated in a group where the focus shifts to comparing group means across groups. Related to this recommendation is the suggestion that it is better to treat continuous distributions in the analyses as distributions and not to arbitrarily divide them into categories.

Distribution of Change

Researchers need to consider the pattern of the effect, that is, the baseline position at a given time, baseline changes over time, fluctuations during media exposures, or a loss of elasticity to fluctuations over time. Some researchers may be more concerned with the baseline and pose questions such as the following: What is the level of the baseline on a particular effect? What are the factors of influence that explain that baseline level? and How stable is that level—that is, does it change over time or does it get more fixed over time? Other researchers will be more concerned with the fluctuations and pose questions such as the following: Do fluctuations occur off the baseline for a particular effect? If there are fluctuations, what are the factors of influence that are most associated with those fluctuations? Notice that the baseline is foundational to all these questions.

Determine Influence of Media Factors on Change/Nonchange

The analysis's focus on prediction should be less on predicting differences in group means and more on predicting the change (or nonchange) across the distribution of effects change scores. This is the focus of the analysis in the Target-Degree strategy, which makes it a much better strategy for answering questions such as the following: Which participants exhibited the most change on effects? What factors of influence are most responsible for those changes in effects scores?

Participant-Determined Contingent Analyses

The standard practice in Groups-Effect studies is for researchers to select a characteristic or two about the participants (usually a demographic such as gender or age) and build it in as an independent variable. This in essence sets up a contingent test, that is, a test to see if the effect is contingent on the participant's demographic. Testing for such contingencies is a strength of the Groups-Effect strategy. Contingent tests are essentially tests of how general the influence is on the particular effect.

Researchers using the Target-Degree strategy can also plan to test contingencies a priori in designing their studies. In addition, I recommend that researchers construct contingent groups to test a posteriori. One way of doing this is to look at the distribution of change scores and divide participants into perhaps three groups of no change, low change, and high change, and then look for patterns of predictors in each of the three groups. If the same pattern holds for all three groups, then the set of predictors is general to all levels of the effect. But more likely, there may be a set of predictors that is most influential in holding people to no change, another set that is responsible for little change, and yet a third set of predictors that explains a high level of change.

Another way to construct groups is by interpretation patterns—that is, participants who exhibit an X pattern of interpretation are likely to exhibit a different level of effect than participants who exhibit non-X patterns of interpretations. These are only two examples of how contingent analyses can be constructed after the data are gathered and patterns are spotted. These types of contingent analyses are likely to generate a good deal of insight. Of course, the construction of contingent groups in an a posteriori manner is usually just as arbitrary (unless the distribution is multimodal) as in an a priori manner. However, the results of a contingent analysis can indicate the degree to which an influence is linear; this finding will help in the design of a more powerful test using the full distribution.

Multivariate Analyses

The processes of effects from exposure to media violence are complex. For us to have a good chance of increasing our understanding of that complexity, we must take a truly multivariate approach. Multivariate analyses have several important advantages. First, they allow us to deal with many variables at the same time, thus giving us a better chance of explaining the complexity of media influence. Second, multivariate relationships are more stable than are estimates of univariate values across samples (Basil, Brown, & Bocarnea, 2002). A useful guide to this task is the work of Malamuth and his colleagues (Malamuth, Linz, Heavey, Barnes, & Acker, 1995; Malamuth, Sockloskie, Koss, & Tanaka, 1991), who have been developing a confluence model of sexual aggression. This model illustrates how researchers can theorize and then test how different variables work together in a complex interlocking process of influence.

How do we ensure that we have identified the large set of factors of influence potentially relevant to a particular effect—let's call it effect X? The natural starting place is to conduct a review of the literature on effect X. A review of the literature on a particular effect will uncover those factors that have been tested and found to have an influence on that effect—this is one of the most useful products of Groups-Differences strategy research. However, there may be additional untested factors that do not show up in the literature search on that particular effect. To help uncover these additional possible factors, the MET (see Table 17.1) can be a useful tool. In using this template, we begin by locating the X effect and then consider contiguous effects by column and row. These contiguous effects are likely to have large literatures that identify their own factors of influence. Furthermore, it is likely that the most contiguous effects will have lists of factors of influence with a significant degree of overlap with the literature on the X effect. To illustrate, let's say we are interested in running a study to test the effect of factual acquisition. We review the literature on factual acquisition and come up with a list like that displayed in Table 18.1. Because factual acquisition is a cognitive effect, we could check out other cognitive effects, such as inferring patterns (see Table 18.2). Also, factual information is an acquiring effect, and we might want to check out contiguous acquiring effects, such as the acquiring of attitudes (see Table 18.3) across the row to consider similar effects that might also share similar factors of influence. By following this procedure, we can systematically expand our list of probable factors of influence and thus make our tests much more powerful with the inclusion of many more factors. When researchers are able to approach a full set of possibilities for factors of influence, their tests will be more complete, and the results of their analyses will be more explanatory.

After we have identified a large set of possible factors of influence for a particular effect, we need to organize the factors into sets—one set for explanators of baseline and another to explain the fluctuations. Because the baseline is foundational to the Target-Degree strategy, researchers will need to devise some measures of the baseline regardless of the type of effect they plan to study. Even studies that will focus on fluctuation effects will need baseline measures to use as context to plot the fluctuations.

Some factors of influence operate primarily on forming and shaping the baseline. Over the long term, there is the constant interaction of factors of influence—psychological traits of the person, sociological experiences of the person, and media exposure patterns—that account for the level of the baseline. This is why it is so important to take a person's history. Without an understanding of a person's baseline, there is little context to understand any temporary fluctuation effect. A fluctuation change cannot

Table 18.2   Explaining Inferring Patterns Effect

Baseline Factors

Message Factors

- Degree to which messages are consistent across media and over time (Gerbner, Gross, Signorielli, Morgan, & Jackson-Beeck, 1979; Hawkins & Pingree, 1981; Liebert, Neale, & Davidson, 1973; Nisbet et al., 2002; Tan, 1981)

- Type of portrayals; people who expose themselves to one type of portrayal more than others will be influenced more by that type of information in constructing patterns (Fan, Wyatt, & Keltner, 2001; Segrin & Nabi, 2002; Sotirovic, 2001a, 2001b).

Audience Factors

- Existing schema (W. J. Potter, Pashupati, Pekurny, Hoffman, & Davis, 2002; W. J. Potter & Tomasello, 2003)

- Existing beliefs (Scott, 2003)

- Personality characteristics
   - Level of intelligence (Perloff, 2002)
   - Self-perceptions of knowledge (Salwen & Dupagne, 2001)
   - Trait hostility (Kirsh & Olczak, 2000)
   - Degree of societal awareness (Valentino, Hutchings, & Williams, 2004)

- Typical exposure patterns (Chory-Assad & Tamborini, 2003; S. Davis & Mares, 1998; Ex, Janssens, & Korzilius, 2002; Romer, Jamieson, & Aday, 2003)

- Demographics
   - Gender (Kwak, Zinkhan, & Dominick, 2002)
   - Age and developmental level
   - Race and culture (Appiah, 2002; Oliver, 1999; Oliver & Fonash, 2002; Oliver, Jackson, Moses, & Dangerfield, 2004)
   - Level of education (Peiser & Peter, 2000, 2001; Scharrer, 2002)

Fluctuation Factors

Message Factors

- Exposure to particular content (Kirsh & Olczak, 2000; Rossler & Brosius, 2001)
- Exemplars in messages (Busselle, 2001; Zillmann, 2002)

Audience Factors

- Processing strategy (K. Greene, Krcmar, Rubin, Walters, & Hale, 2002; Shrum, 2001)
- Ego involvement with an issue (Perloff, 2002)

Table 18.3   Explaining Attitude Acquisition Effect

Baseline Factors

Message Factors

- Frequency of exposure to a particular attitude (Naples, 1981; Sutherland & Galloway, 1981)

Audience Factors

- Age: Ads have stronger effect on younger children (Buijzen & Valkenburg, 2000).
- Sensation seeking (M. T. Stephenson, 2003)
- Gender role socialization (Andsager, Austin, & Pinkleton, 2002)
- Degree of societal awareness (Valentino, Hutchings, & Williams, 2004)

Fluctuation Factors

Message Factors

- Degree of involvement of message (Nabi & Hendriks, 2003)
- Product spokesperson (Mehta & Davis, 1990; Berscheid & Walster, 1974; Whipple & Courtney, 1980; Wilcox, Murphy, & Sheldon, 1985)
- Credibility of source of message (Groenendyk & Valentino, 2002)
- Perceived realism (Andsager, Austin, & Pinkleton, 2001)
- Humor (Duncan & Nelson, 1985; Wu, Crocker, & Rogers, 1989)
- Visuals (Edell, 1988; S. Lee & Barnes, 1990)
- Nonverbal elements (Hallahan, 1994)
- Music (Gorn, 1982; Park & Young, 1986)
- Techniques of persuasiveness (Nabi, 2003; Pfau, Holbert, Zubric, Pasha, & Lin, 2000; Pfau et al., 2001; Pfau et al., 2004; Sopory & Dillard, 2002; Sotirovic, 2001a, 2001b; Tal-Or, Boninger, Poran, & Gleicher, 2004)

Audience Factors

- Positive affective reactions to ad and product (Burke & Edell, 1989; Holbrook & Westwood, 1989; Stout & Leckenby, 1986)
- Prior attitudes (Dolich, 1969)
- Prior knowledge (Sujan, 1985)
- Experience with product (Kolter, 1988; C. J. Thompson, Locander, & Pollio, 1989)
- Involvement with purchase decision (Park & Young, 1986)
- Mood (M. P. Gardner & Hill, 1988)
- Processing strategy—people automatically process messages, and messages enter a person's mind through the peripheral route (elaboration likelihood model) and thus are not subject to counterarguing (Chang, 2002; Slater & Rouner, 2002).

Environmental Factors

- Degree of clutter (Keller, 1991; Kent & Machleit, 1992)
- Influence from program in which TV ad appeared (Goldberg & Gorn, 1987; Hsia, 1977)

be attributed only to the immediate exposure. For example, a person who is 20 years old and exhibits an X effect during exposure to a particular media message is influenced not only by that particular exposure but also by almost 20 years of media exposures. Therefore, the way to understand the influence of the particular exposure is to look at it in the context of a long-term pattern of media exposures. In short, a person's level at the top of a spike on a fluctuation effect is explained by the combination of the baseline position plus the power of the media message to create the fluctuation.

Individual interpretations of a media message are important. These individual interpretations are a good explanation for fluctuation effects. But we also need to explain the individual interpretations themselves—that is, why do different people construct different meanings for the same media message? To explain the reasons for the individual interpretations, we need to consider baseline factors, such as previous experience and knowledge of the type of message, and degree of information-processing skills, especially analysis, evaluation, grouping, induction, deduction, and synthesis.

The dynamic and organic nature of the situation, however, does not mean that it is without form or structure. It does have a structure, but it is a different structure than that presented in linear models. Also, it does not mean that the situation is so fluid that it is not amenable to research designs that can generate interesting and predictive findings. What it *does* mean is that we need to conceptualize the phenomenon in a different way and design research studies in a different way. The same research tools that have been used in the past are still useful in testing media effects under lineation theory. The tools and the building materials are the same; it is the architecture that is different.

Reporting Findings

As a research field matures, it needs to move beyond description and into explanation. The descriptive stage is an essential first step and cannot be skipped. The product of the descriptive-type research—what are the media effects and which factors are associated with which effects—provides the required building blocks of explanations, but of course, they are not explanations themselves.

To move this research beyond description and into explanation, the reporting of findings needs to be more than the listing of levels, fluctuation sizes, and factors associated with those levels and sizes. The challenge of explanation is to convey a calibration of the power of the set of factors of influence on individuals and to show how those factors work together to account for changes (or nonchanges).

Explanation itself is not categorical but can be thought of as having three stages—what I will call calibration, interactions, and structures—each building on the previous one. The first step on this path to explanation is calibration; that is, researchers need to move beyond whether a factor appeared to have an influence on an effect process. Instead, we also need to gauge the relative degree of influence in the context of other factors.

It is no longer sufficient merely to report that a variable showed an influence on the dependent measure; we need to see a rank ordering of the individual influences of each of the independent variables as well as the interactions among them. The rank orderings would provide valuable information to guide the weighting of factors in scales of risk. The resulting scale scores then would give us a better sense of the probability of the effect occurring. For example, Sopory and Dillard (2002) conducted a meta-analysis of the literature testing the persuasive impact of metaphors. They found that the overall effect of the metaphor-literal comparison for attitude change was $r = .07$, which they concluded supports the claim that metaphors are more persuasive in general than literal claims. Under optimal conditions, the relationship is much stronger ($r = .42$); optimal conditions include the use of a single metaphor that is novel, had a familiar target, and was used early in a message. This is an example of measuring the strength of a factor; notice that the range of strength shows the importance of looking at a factor in the context of other factors.

To complete this step well, we do not need to have a precise rank ordering of many different factors. That would be too much to ask for, especially at this later exploratory stage of our research field. Instead, it is more reasonable to arrive at an assessment of what factors are worthwhile. While calibration of factors of influence can be regarded as a form of explanation over description, there are more steps along this explanatory path.

A second step to a higher degree of explanation is to examine interactions among factors of influence. Sometimes the interactions can make a factor rank very high in a rank ordering of influences when, in fact, the particular factor is an intersection for other influences. For example, X factor may be highly related to an effect level, but when we recompute that relationship while partialling out the influence of factor Y, the initial relationship might be reduced and even disappear. In this example, the relationship between factor X and the effect was *spuriously* high; once we partialled out the interactive influence of Y on the relationship, we found that the actual relationship between X by itself and the effect was negligible. Another reason to test for interactions is to identify factors that seem to be weak by themselves but gain power when paired with another variable. To illustrate, let's say factors A and B each are related weakly to an effect. But if we test the combination of A and B together on the effect, we find a strong relationship; what we have found is that when either A or B occurs by itself, the level of the effect is not likely to change, but when you put both A and B into the situation, the likelihood of an effect-level change is much greater.

Rarely does a factor exert an influence on an effect without interacting with other factors (for some examples, see Table 18.4). Bandura (2002) is one theoretician who acknowledged that many factors (such as the reality of the portrayals and whether the models are rewarded) are simultaneously interacting in this complex process of influence. He speculated that "reciprocality does not mean that the different sources of influences are of equal strength. Some may be stronger than others" (p. 61), but he did not elaborate on this point by specifying what those might be.

Thus, it is important to design effects experiments with more attention to interactions. Understandably, experiments limit their examination to a small set of key variables. The isolation of a key factor while controlling the influence of others is an important strength of the experimental methodology. This strength is what is

Table 18.4   Examples of Interactions in Media Violence Research

Message-Viewer Interactions

Gender: There is an interaction between gender and the influence of reality programming, presentational style, and humor.

- Hapkiewicz and Stone (1974) ran an experiment on 180 elementary school children and found no significant differences on film (real-life aggression, aggressive cartoon, or nonaggressive film) but did find an interaction with sex. Boys who viewed the realistic aggressive film were significantly more aggressive in play than boys who viewed other films.
- Alvarez, Huston, Wright, and Kerkman (1988) found that children (ages 5 to 11) exhibited sex differences in their attention to violence. Boys' visual attention was generally higher. Girls preferred programs with low action, not high action.
- As for humor, Mueller and Donnerstein (1977) found that males were not affected by listening to a humorous audiotape, but females reduced their level of arousal after listening to the low-arousing tape.

Age: There is an interaction between age and perceptions of reality. J. C. Wright, Huston, Reitz, and Piemyat (1994) found that by age 5, children can distinguish between factuality of programming—that is, tell the difference between fictional programs and news or documentary—and that they get better at this with age. The learning comes not in believing TV is fiction; 5-year-olds know this. The learning comes in figuring out what is nonfiction.

Race: Baron (1979) found that pain cues from a same-race victim had a stronger effect on participants' subsequent aggressive behavior. For example, with White participants, pain cues were less effective in inhibiting subsequent aggression from nonangry Whites and less facilitating of aggression from angry Whites.

Culture: There appear to be cultural differences in an interaction with heroes and seriousness. Gunter (1985) found that American viewers rated violence by villains as more serious, while in contrast, British viewers rated violence by heroes as more serious.

Locus of control: Prerost (1987) ran an experiment on 144 female undergraduates in a 2 × 2 × 3 design of locus of control (internal and external), arousal of anger (arousal, nonarousal), and jokes (neutral humor, aggressive humor, and nonhumorous jokes). Locus of control was significant, with internals using humor to reduce anger. Internals who were angered enjoyed the aggressive humor most.

Intoxication: Schmutte and Taylor (1980) found that high-pain feedback only reduced the aggression of nonintoxicated participants, while highly intoxicated participants still behaved aggressively.

Message Elements Interaction

Punishment-justification: Bryant, Carveth, and Brown (1981) ran an experiment with two treatment groups. One group was exposed to programs offering a clear triumph of justice—the transgressive acts were punished by personal vengeance, or retribution was provided by an affiliated agent or through legal restitution. The

(Continued)

Table 18.4 (Continued)

other group saw an equal number of violent acts where there was a preponderance of injustice—the majority of transgressive acts went unpunished. The viewers in the unpunished condition developed significantly increased levels of anxiety. So it appears there is an interaction between justification and punishment.

Strategy-success: Lando and Donnerstein (1978) found an interaction between problem-solving strategy of a filmed model and success/failure of the strategy. Neither characteristic was significant by itself. Those participants who saw a successful aggressive model *and* those who saw an unsuccessful nonaggressive model both showed the most aggressiveness subsequent to the viewing.

Pain-humor: Deckers and Carr (1986) found ratings of pain to be related to the degree of funniness of newspaper cartoons. Pain ratings were superior to aggression ratings in predicting cartoon funniness.

Realism-consequences: Gunter (1985) found that when consequences of the violence are shown, viewers think it is much more serious. However, this finding only holds with relatively realistic content and not fantasy.

Motive-role: A viewer's interpretation of motive is shaped by the role of a character, and this relates to judgments of violence.

- Lincoln and Levinger (1972) showed their experimental respondents a picture of a White police officer grabbing an African American man by the shirt. When subjects were told that the action took place at a peace rally, the action was rated as violent, but when respondents were told nothing, they assumed that the police officer was subduing a criminal, and the action was not rated as violent.

Fantasy-humor: Sprafkin, Gadow, and Grayson (1988) ran an experiment on 26 emotionally disturbed children (6 to 9 years old) where they were exposed to either six aggressive cartoons or six control cartoons. The control cartoons resulted in more nonphysical aggression from participants. The aggressive cartoons showed fantasy characters in repeated humorous acts of aggression. The nonaggressive cartoons featured a realistic animated drama that was suspenseful throughout a narrative adventure. Therefore, the "control" materials were likely to be perceived as more realistic and arousing.

responsible for our high degree of confidence that certain individual variables influence particular effects, for example, disinhibition. However, when violence appears on the television screen, many contextual factors appear simultaneously, and all are available to influence viewers' interpretations of the meaning of the message. Therefore, we need to focus more attention on interactions. We need to know which factors interact, if the presence of some amplifies the effect of particular others, or if the influence of some cancels out the influence of others.

Until we have more guidance from the results of multivariate experiments that focus on interactions, we are left with arbitrarily constructing scales of risk. Gerbner and his colleagues were forced to do this several decades ago when they first developed a violence index, which contains three elements: "the percent of programs with any violence at all, the frequency and rate of violent episodes, and the number of roles calling for characterizations as violents, victims, or both" (e.g., see Gerbner & Gross, 1976, p. 185). To compute their index, they took the rate figure, doubled it, and then added it to the prevalence percentage and the number of roles involved in violence. They said that the "index itself is not a statistical finding but serves as a convenient illustrator of trends and facilitates gross comparisons" (p. 185). While the elements that are used to construct the scale are relevant indicators of the number of violent portrayals on television, the problem is that there is no discernible logic guiding the way that these measures with different metrics are assembled into a single scale that would reflect how the relative degree of risk for negative effects would change when content patterns change. Therefore, it is very difficult to understand what the resulting score from such an index means.

The problem Gerbner and his colleagues had three decades ago is still with us today. Although the experimental literature has elaborated the list of contextual variables that viewers use to interpret the meaning of violence, we still do not have a sense of the relative importance of these factors in contributing to risk. In sum, the theories and the experimental research have been very useful in identifying contextual characteristics that lead to risks, but they are weak in modeling processes of influence to explain how those risk factors work together.

A third step in this explanatory path—beyond calibration and interactions—is structure. The strength of a factor and its behavior in interactions are often influenced by its position in a process. This is why structural equations are so useful in explaining phenomena; that is, they consider the relative strengths of factors alone as well as in interactions, and they consider the predictive power of each variable in particular locations in the process of influence.

When these tasks are accomplished using the language of baselines, fluctuations, and addresses in the MET, the findings can be made more accessible to scholars, students, and the general public. Scholars will be in a better position to identify relevant literatures, select the most useful operationalizations, and position their findings at the appropriate place in the emerging synthesis across studies. Students will better focus on the big picture of mass media effects literature and be able to contextualize particular findings in a much more parsimonious manner. Finally, the general public will have findings crafted and presented in a way that will provide clearer answers to the form of their questions about mass media influence.

Conclusion

This chapter provides a perspective on how to shift from a Groups-Differences to a Target-Degree strategy when designing media effects studies. It presents a five-step set of guidelines that call for focusing on one effect, selecting a particular media factor of influence, avoiding measurement traps, focusing the analysis, and reporting results in a way that makes them more useful for scholars, students, and the general public.

Table 18.5   Media Effects Propositions

Effect 1: An individual's baseline is established and maintained by the influences of three sets of factors: media exposure habits, characteristics about the person, and characteristics of the environment.

   1.1: The influence of media in the establishment of effect baselines is greater when

- Messages are consistent.
- Exposure is greater, that is, there is exposure to a higher number of messages.
- Exposure is in the automatic state.

   1.2: The influence of a person's characteristics in the establishment of effect baselines is greater when

- Individuals are at middle levels of certain key personality traits, such as tolerance for uncertainty.
- Individuals are at low levels of certain key personality traits, such as locus of control, field independence, and extroversion.
- Individuals have low levels of meaning construction skills.
- Individuals have weak knowledge structures.

   1.3: The influence of the environment in the establishment of effect baselines is greater when

- The individual has fewer options to media exposure.
- Media messages resonate with real-life experiences.

Effect 2: Fluctuations from the effect baseline are influenced by three sets of factors: particular media exposures, characteristics about the person (especially states), and characteristics of the particular environment.

   2.1: The influence of media in these fluctuations is greater when the messages violate expectations or break with the formula.

   2.2: The influence of a person's characteristics in bringing about fluctuations is greater when the individual has less experience with that type of message or medium.

   2.3: The influence of the environment in bringing about fluctuations is greater when

- Factors in the environment support change.
- Sanctions for change are small or nonexistent.

Effect 3: Exposure states are associated with the degree of media power in influencing an effect.

   3.1: The media exert their greatest power of conditioning audience members when they are in the automatic and transported exposure states. The media exercise this power gradually over the long term in the way they establish effect baselines.

   3.2: Audience members have the greatest control over the process of influence when they are in the self-reflexive exposure state.

Effect 4: Audience members who have a well-developed understanding of a narrative line will be better able to pick up on the story line at any given point, follow the action, and have more accurate expectations for what will happen.

- As for efficiency, people with a greater understanding of the narrative line will be required to expend less mental effort in following the new message compared with people with less of an understanding of the narrative line. Thus, habitual users of this message will find it easy to continue in their habitual use.
- As for effectiveness, people with a greater understanding of the narrative line will have more competency at matching meaning and will therefore be better able to follow the meaning constructed by producers.

PART VI

Conclusion

CHAPTER 19

Integration of Explanations

Now that all the ideas in the lineation general framework have been laid out in detail in the previous 18 chapters, I will leave you with the big picture. It is my hope that this big-picture perspective will provide you with a clear understanding of what ideas need to be the focus of our thinking and research if we are to evolve from a Generating-Findings to a Mapping-Phenomenon perspective for our scholarly field. In this chapter, I will focus your attention on the two sets of ideas from which all other ideas stem. The first set includes five ideas that are unique to this framework. The second set includes three ideas that can integrate thinking across all four facets of the mass media phenomenon and thus begin the formation of the rim (recall the bicycle wheel metaphor) of the scholarly field. A more delineated rim will help provide direction for each spoke of research. Also, a more delineated rim is essential for providing scholars with the context needed to integrate the many diverse findings that are currently scattered throughout our various literatures.

Unique Ideas

In this section, I focus attention on five ideas I regard as unique to this general framework. By *unique,* I do not mean that these ideas originated with me or that they appear only in this general framework. Instead, I mean that these ideas are given a degree of salience in this general framework that they have not had in the literature to this point. Also, these ideas are defined and organized in a different way than they have been thus far in the literature.

The most fundamental of these five ideas lies in the way I have defined our phenomenon of interest. The other four ideas each address the nature of one of the four facets of the phenomenon—organizations, audiences, content, and effects.

Mass Media

The mass media are organizations that distribute messages with the purpose of creating and maintaining audiences. They use technologically driven channels to make their messages available and attractive to prescribed niche audiences with known needs. The key elements in this definition were chosen to clarify the central essence of the mass media in a way to explain their values and practices in a message-saturated culture.

What makes this definition different from many other definitions in the literature is that the mass media are not defined in terms of audience size or type. Also, the definition does not key on the type of channel. Instead, the definition is keyed to *how the channel is used.* The focus is on the sender. To be a mass medium, the sender's primary intention must be to condition audiences into a habitual exposure pattern; that is, the mass media are much less interested in attracting people for one exposure than they are in trying to get people into a position where they will be exposed regularly to their messages. Thus, the *mass* media want to preserve their audiences so they can maintain their revenue streams and amortize their initially high costs of attracting the audience in our message-saturated culture.

The mass media organizations use technologically driven channels, but that definitional element is secondary to their motives and practices. The technology of the channels is such that it is used to replicate their messages and make them available to all members of their targeted audiences simultaneously and repeatedly. However, technology by itself is not a critical element in the definition because the technology can be used in non-mass-like ways, such as videotaping a family member's birthday party, using computer software to self-publish one's book of poetry, or recording one's original song and sending it to one's three closest friends.

Economic Foundation

Mass media organizations are regarded as being fundamentally concerned with economic matters. By *economic,* I do not mean that the pursuit is only financial rewards; instead, I mean economic in the broad sense—that is, the concern is with acquiring, manipulating, and exchanging resources. The mass media, of course, can be examined from many different perspectives—historical, political, anthropological, sociological, educational, legal, and critical, to name a few of the most popular. All of these perspectives produce valuable insights into the nature of the mass media. However, I argue that it is from the economic perspective that we achieve the most fundamental understanding of the mass media—an understanding that helps us view the media from all the other possible perspectives.

By an economic perspective, I am not conceptualizing media organizations in a narrow way of aggressively competing for money in a capitalistic system. Money is important, but it is only one resource among many. Other resources include talent, ideas, production materials, channel space, prestige, influence, and the like. Mass media organizations are constantly negotiating for all of these every day in different markets. The way these negotiations and exchanges take place lies at the heart of the mass media. Examining these exchanges and practices reveals their motives and values.

Most of the mass media organizations are commercial businesses, and as such, the drive for maximizing the utilization of resources is paramount. This drive permeates all decisions. Of course, these organizations have interests in achieving other goals, such as educating the public and creating artistic expression. But these other goals are not ends; instead, the achieving of these other goals is important only insofar as they can serve as tools to achieve the more fundamental economic goal. For example, a commercial book publisher will want its books to achieve artistic recognition through awards such as the National Book Award and Pulitzer Prizes. However, the awards are not the ends but instead the means to acquire the resources of respect in the book publishing industry, attractiveness to high-talent writers, and attractiveness to the readers and the book-buying public. That is, awards put the mass media organizations in a stronger negotiating position for resources in several different markets.

Many mass media organizations are *not* commercial enterprises; these are created and run by cultural, educational, political, and religious institutions that are motivated primarily to achieve goals that are not economic. However, these institutions are still faced with getting over the initial economic hurdle before they can begin achieving their other goals. If these noncommercial mass media organizations cannot attract and maintain particular kinds of audiences in an economically viable way, they have no chance of achieving their educational, political, religious, or cultural goals.

The economic perspective is also foundational to understanding audiences. Every day, people make thousands of filtering decisions about media messages, most of which are decisions to filter out messages. This filtering is governed by an algorithm that is keyed to an economic consideration, that is, a comparison of costs to benefits. There are times when people are inaccurate in their quick, intuitive assessments of costs and benefits, so they make faulty judgments. However, the essence of the judgment process is primarily economic.

Audience Exposure States

Potential audience members live in a message-saturated culture where they must avoid paying attention to more than a very small percentage of the messages in their everyday environments. Thus, their minds stay on a kind of automatic pilot most of the time, and in this exposure state, they are governed by algorithms that have been programmed substantially by the mass media through a long history of exposures.

This does not mean that there are not times when audience members are in an attentional state, where they consciously decide to expose themselves to a particular message and pay attention to that message during the exposure. Also, there are times when people are swept away by messages or when they are very analytical and examine messages in a self-reflexive state. The point is that there are several exposure states (automatic, attentional, transported, and self-reflexive), and people have a qualitatively different experience in each of those states. The research and thinking to date have largely ignored the differences across states. Typically, researchers assume that their respondents experience the media in an attentional state, where respondents are consciously aware of their motives and able to self-report their experiences and effects accurately. Of course, there are likely times when this assumption is a valid one; however, it is not likely that this assumption holds very often.

Narrative Line

For most media researchers, scholarship on media content is limited to the messages themselves. Researchers using the quantitative methodology of content analysis have a micro focus as they count the occurrence of certain elements, such as demographic characteristics of people in the stories or the number of times a violent act is presented. This research is valuable for documenting the prevalence of certain characteristics in media messages. But the meaning of the messages resides more in the story formulas, especially in the arc of the story. Qualitative scholars do a better job of assessing meaning by linking messages to genres, cultures, or types of audiences. In this lineation general framework, I have argued for a deeper analysis where scholars use message elements to infer how producers navigated their way through the maze of options when designing their messages. The producer's path through the maze of options is the narrative line.

By studying media content through narrative line analyses, we can focus attention more on the decisions, formulas, and conventions used by producers; this, in turn, reveals those producers' values. We can build greater understanding about how producers attract audiences, hold their attention, and reinforce their exposure experiences. Also, we can build greater understanding about the way algorithms guide audience members through not just the filtering process but also the processes of meaning matching and meaning construction. These are the concerns that make the content facet of the mass media phenomenon so fascinating.

Continuous Effects

Media influence is constant and pervasive on each individual as well as on larger structures such as institutions, the public, and culture. This constant media influence on individuals is not limited to sudden, observable changes in behaviors, attitudes, emotions, physiology, or cognitions; those are manifest effects. There are also process effects that continually shape a person's baseline. There are three fundamental patterns of mass media–influenced effects: temporary fluctuations, baseline alterations, and baseline reinforcement. The easiest to spot are the temporary fluctuation effects, which are the abrupt changes that are short-lived. This is what our research to date has had as its focus. A second type of effect is the alteration to a person's baseline, which is a gradual change over a long period of time and therefore much more difficult to measure. Baselines are shaped by long-term media exposures as well as enduring characteristics about the person (traits, lifestyles, skills, etc.) and his or her environment. The third type of effect is the reinforcement of a person's baseline. Exposure to media messages and real-world influences conditions people into habits that become harder and harder to change as time passes. Ways of thinking become more fixed and harder to change. Behavioral patterns become stronger and stronger habits. This conditioning makes the baseline appear unchanged because the effects level remains the same, but there is change just the same—that is, the baseline is reinforced, making it less elastic for fluctuation effects and less likely to have its level altered over time. This third pattern of effect, which is likely to be the most difficult to measure by using current research methods, is also likely to be the most prevalent and most profound.

Rim Ideas

This section focuses attention on the rim, that is, the flow of ideas across the spokes from the different quadrants. The rim illustrates how the major ideas connect to one another and form themes. In this section, I will focus on three themes: audience attraction/conditioning, meaning, and dynamic manifestations of effects.

Audience Attraction/Conditioning

The idea of audience attraction/conditioning originates in the media organization's facet and moves through the other three facets, tying explanations in those other three facets to the organization's central goal and strategies of attracting an audience and conditioning that audience for habitual, repeat exposures. To achieve this audience attraction and eventual conditioning, producers use story formulas. The purpose of story formulas is to provide rules for attracting audiences and holding their attention. Producers know what these story formulas are. Media workers' talents are in direct proportion to their ability to use the formulas to attract and hold audiences. The holding of attention is achieved when the messages give the audience members a perception of high value, which means high payoff at a relatively low cost to them. Audience members weigh what they pay (in terms of money, time, and mental energy) against what they receive in return (in terms of satisfying their existing needs for information and emotional experiences). The greater the perceived benefits from the exposure in comparison to perceived costs, the stronger the conditioned drive to seek additional exposures of this message type. Therefore, producers must use the story formulas well continually to meet and exceed audience expectations.

Media effects are contingent on attraction. With nonexposure, there can be no effect of media influence. Effects require exposure, but several qualitatively different exposure states alter the experience of an effect. Most of the time, people experience media messages in a state of automaticity, where they are guided by automatic algorithms. These are typically programmed by the mass media through repeated exposures over the long term. In contrast, audience members who are not highly conditioned are likely to make filtering and meaning construction decisions in the attentional or self-reflexive state and therefore keep more control over the process of influence by exerting a greater degree of influence on programming their algorithms. People who are less conditioned by the media are more likely to experience media effects much more in line with their own goals, especially when their personal goals diverge from the mass media's goals.

If we look at the attraction/conditioning idea only within the effects facet, we would likely ask the following question: Why would the audience members agree to the constant and aggressive conditioning? This would appear as a negative effect that audience members would want to avoid because it takes the power away from them to make exposure decisions and turns over the power to the mass media. Furthermore, the conditioning is likely to come with a lot of negative by-products, such as loss of resources (time displacement) and socialization of unhealthy beliefs. But if we look at this from within the audience facet, we see that audiences find this conditioning very beneficial. The conditioning leads to efficient filtering decisions. Media habits help provide structure to a life. Media conditioning reinforces an efficient set of everyday routines where people feel they are in the capable hands of experts who will tell them the news that is important, introduce them to products that will help solve their problems, and provide them with entertainment that will help make their lives happier and more interesting. Also, the conditioning reinforces a small set of story formulas, thus making them more highly accessible and simpler to understand over time. This lowers psychic costs, which in turn raises the value of the exposures for audience members.

Meaning

By using story formulas, producers try to make the surface meaning of messages as transparent as possible. This means they make the messages appear very simple to match meaning. When audience members see this type of simple message, they feel that they can automatically access an algorithm with almost no psychic effort, thus keeping their exposure costs low. For example, when people read a newspaper, their attention is drawn more quickly to a small colorful graphic than to a long story of words, believing the graphic (pie chart, histogram, etc.) will deliver as much information as the story while requiring much less effort from them to process.

Producers know that by following standard story formulas, they can present an easy-to-access meaning, which will keep information-processing costs down and thus attract larger audiences. Also, when producers lower the costs to audiences for processing messages, audience members experience an increase in the perception of value. And producers know that when meaning is continually matched (rather than constructed), people are more likely to enter and stay in an automatic state of exposure. Producers want to avoid requiring audience members to construct meaning, not because producers are necessarily megalomaniacs who want to define the world for everyone. Instead, producers want to make the processing of the messages as simple as possible to achieve maximum perceptions of value from the maximum number of potential audience members.

Audience members "read" the messages through the formulas quickly and intuitively. Most of this reading is done in a state of automaticity or transportation where people match meaning, that is, read surface symbols in media messages and match them automatically to meanings stored in simple associative networks (SANs). In the attentional state, the reading requires more effort because there is more attention paid to recognizing symbols and trying to assess their meaning. In the self-reflexive state, a good deal of psychic energy is required to encounter the message much more analytically, and the reading of symbols takes place in much more depth. The meanings are not just matched; they are also constructed.

When people are initially exposed to a message, they make a quick evaluation of the potential value of that message. For messages that are encountered in the state of automaticity, either the message triggers a person's attention or it does not. The few messages that do trigger a person's attention are then attended to initially for purposes of evaluation. In this quick evaluation, the person assesses two qualities of the messages (benefits to the person and costs to the person) and compares those qualities. If the comparison is favorable (costs are outweighed by benefits), then the person continues the exposure but stays in the evaluative state. The exposure continues as the filtering algorithm automatically runs, thus making a continual series of value comparisons that are experienced emotionally. As long as the emotions are positive, the exposure flow continues.

During the exposure to the unfolding story line, there are many opportunities for the audience to terminate the exposure. This is especially the case with television, where the stories are continually interrupted with breaks for commercials; however, this also applies to messages that do not have such breaks. When the flow of the message is continuous, audience members continually monitor the value either consciously or unconsciously. People do conscious monitoring when they are in the message-seeking mode—that is, they have a motive for searching, and they are governed by that motive. Thus, they keep asking themselves if they are getting what they are seeking. But evaluation of messages also continually takes place in the unconscious mode, such as when the exposure takes place in the state of automaticity. Here there is an intuitive feeling about value that is unsystematically derived. It is more of a feeling than a cognitive evaluation.

Evaluating a satisfying resolution to a story also can be done consciously or unconsciously. The resolution of a seeking behavior is success; that is, the person gets what he or she has been seeking, usually information. But when a person is flowing along in the state of automaticity, there is an intuitive expectation for how the story should be resolved. When the expectation seems met, the person is satisfied with the resolution. But when the resolution does not meet the audience's expectation, the audience is frustrated or disappointed.

The better that audience members understand a formula, the more efficiently they will be able to expose themselves to the message and the more effectively they will be able to understand the story. For this reason, producers who stick closest to the formula in designing their messages will provide audiences with the lowest costing experiences. However, this lack of creativity in the design of messages is likely to reduce the payoff to the audience, who will find the story predictable, thus offering nothing new and only a minimal emotional kick. Thus, there is usually a trade-off. However, skilled producers know how to work off the formula and thereby give audiences something new while asking their audience members to expend only minimal additional resources. Even if a producer is very skilled, the decision about the value of the message rests with the audience members' perceptions, more so than with the producer's skill.

Dynamic Manifestations of Media Effects

Mass media researchers have focused most of their attention on effects. In fact, E. Katz and Lazarsfeld (1955) argued that the study of media effects, broadly defined, was the "over-riding interest of mass media research" (pp. 18–19), and since then, other respected scholars have credited this type of research as the reason why communications exists as an academic discipline (Chaffee & Rogers, 1997; Jensen & Rosengren, 1990; Rogers, 1994; Schramm, 1997). Effects are important, but to understand effects well, we first need to understand the content that stimulates those effects and the audience members who exhibit those effects. Also, because effects change audience members over time, those members end up looking for different content or looking for different things in the same content, so the content changes, which leads to changes in effects over time. It is all linked together.

The more that producers and programmers can increase audience members' risk of an attraction effect, the lower is their own economic risk. This does not necessarily mean that there is a trade-off between the interests of the organization and the interests of the audience. To the extent that the audience members want particular exposures, the attraction effect is positive—that is, it successfully shows those audience members where the desired message is.

This is usually a win-win situation. That is, audience members get their needs met by exciting, low-cost messages, and producers build audiences. However, this is not always a win-win situation. There are times when audiences are conditioned by producers to do things counter to their best interests, that is, to automatically and habitually expose themselves to a series of mass media messages when they would be better spending their resources elsewhere. Also, the attraction to media messages has by-products that the mass media did not intend but that nevertheless result in negative effects on audience members. For example, mass media organizations know there is a market for violence in films, television series, novels, and lyrics in music. Many media organizations produce this type of message to satisfy the market and increase their revenue. Also, particular mass media organizations argue that they are motivated to entertain people, and this is what people want for entertainment. Because certain audiences are continually attracted to violence, those audience members feel they are having their entertainment desires satisfied. However, these audience members are also susceptible to many other effects as by-products of their violent message exposure. That is, the risk of fear and desensitization effects is increased. In this situation, it is a win for the mass media organization but a loss for many audience members who continually expose themselves to these messages.

The risk of negative effects is not attributable solely to media message factors. Many of the influences on a person's baseline are traits of the individual. Also, a person's baseline is influenced by socialization patterns from parents, siblings, friends, and the institutions of education, religion, and the criminal justice system. Of course, many of these seemingly "non" media factors are themselves influenced by media practices and messages. Thus, the phenomenon of media effects is a complex system of interacting influences constantly in play. This is why it is important for media researchers to assess risk with process effects in addition to manifestation effects.

Mass media organizations are businesses with the goal of maximizing value for their owners. Their business strategy is designed to help them make economic exchanges where they are net winners (getting more in return for the resources they give up) in the building and maintaining of audiences. To build their audiences, the media businesses need content to attract and hold people. They construct messages by using their tried-and-tested formulas that provide a favorable economic exchange for audience members—that is, providing a high payoff for the investment of minimal resources.

Programmers are constantly assessing risk. To them, risk is the probability of a media message not attracting and holding an audience and thereby generating enough income resources to warrant the expenditure of resources required to produce and market the messages. This is a very different conception of risk compared with the risk assessment by audience members. To the extent that the gap between risk for audience members and risk for media businesses is reduced, the system works better.

It is the responsibility of researchers to reduce this gap by generating evidence that clearly shows where audience members are most susceptible to effects that will harm them significantly. Until researchers can convincingly demonstrate the degree to which certain media messages increase this risk to individuals, there is no chance that media business managers will be motivated to respond to criticism about harmful content, even if they want to behave responsibly. Media programmers need to be shown convincing evidence of harm to audience members *and* that there are options for change that are in their best interests, that is, alternatives that will serve to reduce their own risk of financial harm. Until we as researchers can make our case convincingly, media programmers will continue to treat these audience risks as unimportant by-products that are external to their decisions (for decision-making externalities, see Hamilton, 1998).

Ultimately, it comes down to a question of who controls the attraction/conditioning, meaning, and risk dynamics. As of now, control is primarily in the hands of the people in the media industries. M. G. Cantor (1994) reminds us that while ultimate control over what is available rests with those who own or manage the means of distribution, "only those who are able to reach profitable markets are successful in the struggle to get their message on the air and in print" (p. 168).

If power is defined by the control of resources, then the greatest *potential* power rests with the audience with all its time, money, and psychic energy. The industries have the power to market messages and thereby dominate channels of information, but the audience has the power to withhold their resources from the media organizations. However, this audience power is widely dispersed, so while the audience accounts for the largest pool of resources in the aggregate, the audience is not organized as an aggregate to exercise central control in the exchange of those resources. In contrast, mass media organizations are much more organized and single-minded than are audiences, so they are able to *exercise* a greater degree of control in the economic exchanges of resources. If audiences were organized to that degree, they would clearly exert far more power than the organization. The difference comes in at the individual level, where people have control over the use of their resources but often do not exercise this power; instead, they allow media conditioning to create algorithms that they follow without thinking. We could debate the degree to which this is bad or good from a normative point of view. Those debates are beyond the scope of this book. What I argue here is that we need to understand better the elements in the economic exchanges, especially the information-processing demands of the audiences, the algorithms that guide that processing, and the configurations of authors of the codes in those algorithms. This knowledge will then lead to a better informed debate.

Finally, scholars have the ability to exercise a great deal of power by influencing the way people look at things. In this case, mass media scholars can influence audience members to examine more carefully their practices and assumptions. To do this, scholars need to give audiences fresh perspectives on the phenomenon and a richer language to use in talking about all the fascinating elements in the phenomenon. And media scholars have to do more than tell people what exposures to avoid; scholars need to show people how to use the media as tools to achieve their own goals.

Individuals can change their attitudes and behaviors and thereby make their lives better. The more people who do this, the more markets will change. When markets change, industries will respond with different messages to meet the newer configuration of needs. But the only way scholars can get the process moving more strongly in this direction is to get beyond categorical thinking that oversimplifies the phenomenon, get beyond debates that generate more heat than light, follow the phenomenon wherever it takes us, and break with our past conditioning as researchers to embrace the risk of constructing new meanings that better capture the fascinating complexity of the mass media.

References

Abelman, R., & Atkin, D. (2000). What children watch when they watch TV: Putting theory into practice. *Journal of Broadcasting & Electronic Media, 44,* 143–154.

Abelson, R. P. (1981). Psychological status of the script concept. *American Psychologist, 36,* 715–729.

Abercrombie, N. (1996). *Television and society.* Cambridge, UK: Polity.

Abrahamson, D. (1998). The visible hand: Money, markets, and media evolution. *Journalism & Mass Communication Quarterly, 75,* 14–18.

Adams, E. E., & Baldasty, G. J. (2001). Syndicated service dependence and a lack of commitment to localism: Scripps newspapers and market subordination. *Journalism & Mass Communication Quarterly, 78,* 519–532.

Adorno, T., & Horkheimer, M. (1972). *Dialectic of enlightenment.* New York: Herder & Herder.

Ajzen, I., & Fishbein, M. (1977). Attitude-behavior relations: A theoretical analysis and review of empirical research. *Psychological Bulletin, 84,* 888–918.

Ajzen, I., & Fishbein, M. (2005). The influence of attitudes on behavior. In D. Albarracin, B. T. Johnson, & M. P. Zanna (Eds.), *The handbook of attitudes* (pp. 173–221). Mahwah, NJ: Lawrence Erlbaum.

Albarracin, D., Johnson, B. T., & Zanna, M. P. (Eds.). (2005). *The handbook of attitudes.* Mahwah, NJ: Lawrence Erlbaum.

Albarracin, D., Zanna, M. P., Johnson, B. T., & Kumkale, G. T. (2005). Attitudes: Introduction and scope. In D. Albarracin, B. T. Johnson, & M. P. Zanna (Eds.), *The handbook of attitudes* (pp. 3–19). Mahwah, NJ: Lawrence Erlbaum.

Albarran, A. B., & Dimmick, J. (1996). Concentration and economies of multiformity in the communication industries. *Journal of Media Economics, 9*(4), 41–50.

Allen, R. C. (1987). *Channels of discourse.* London: Allen & Unwin.

Allport, G. W. (1935). Attitudes. In C. Murchison (Ed.), *Handbook of social psychology* (pp. 798–884). Worcester, MA: Clark University Press.

Althaus, S. L., & Tewksbury, D. (2002). Agenda setting and the "new" news: Patterns of issue importance among readers of the paper and online versions of the *New York Times. Communication Research, 29,* 180–207.

Altheide, D. L. (1976). *Creating reality: How TV news distorts events.* Beverly Hills, CA: Sage.

Altheide, D. L. (1985). *Media power.* Beverly Hills, CA: Sage.

Altheide, D. L., & Snow, R. P. (1979). *Media logic.* Beverly Hills, CA: Sage.

Altheide, D. L., & Snow, R. P. (1991). *Media worlds in the postjournalism era.* New York: Aldine/de Gruyter.

Althusser, L. (1970). *For Marx* (B. Brewster, Trans.). New York: Vintage.

Alvarez, M. M., Huston, A. C., Wright, J. C., & Kerkman, D. D. (1988). Gender differences in visual attention to television form and content. *Journal of Applied Developmental Psychology, 9,* 459–475.

Anderson, A. A., Deuser, W. E., & DeNeve, K. M. (1995). Hot temperatures, hostile affect, hostile cognition, and arousal: Tests of a general model of affective aggression. *Personality and Social Psychology Bulletin, 21,* 434–448.

Anderson, D. R., Lorch, E. P., Field, D. E., Collins, P. A., & Nathan, J. G. (1986). Television viewing at home: Age trends in visual attention and time with TV. *Child Development, 57,* 1024–1033.

Anderson, J. R. (1976). *Language, memory, and thought.* Hillsdale, NJ: Lawrence Erlbaum.

Anderson, J. R. (1983). *The architecture of cognition.* Cambridge, MA: Harvard University Press.

Anderson, J. R. (1992). Automaticity and the ACT* theory. *American Journal of Psychology, 105,* 165–180.

Andison, F. S. (1977). TV violence and viewer aggression: A cumulation of study results. *Public Opinion Quarterly, 41,* 314–331.

Andsager, J. L. (2000). How interest groups attempt to shape public opinion with competing news frames. *Journalism & Mass Communication Quarterly, 77,* 577–592.

Andsager, J. L., Austin, E. W., & Pinkleton, B. E. (2001). Questioning the value of realism: Young adults' processing of messages in alcohol-related public service announcements and advertising. *Journal of Communication, 51,* 121–142.

Andsager, J. L., Austin, E. W., & Pinkleton, B. E. (2002). Gender as a variable in interpretation of alcohol-related messages. *Communication Research, 29,* 246–269.

Ang, I. (1985). *Watching* Dallas: *Soap operas and the melodramatic imagination.* New York: Methuen.

Appiah, O. (2002). Black and White viewers' perception and recall of occupational characters on television. *Journal of Communication, 52,* 776–793.

Armstrong, G. B. (2002). Experimental studies of the cognitive effects of the use of television as background to intellectual activities. In A. V. Stavros (Ed.), *Advances in communications and media research* (Vol. 1, pp. 21–56). New York: Nova Science Publishers.

Bae, H.-S. (2000). Product differentiation in national TV newscasts: A comparison of the cable all-news networks and the broadcast networks. *Journal of Broadcasting & Electronic Media, 44,* 62–77.

Bagdikian, B. H. (1983). *The media monopoly.* Boston: Beacon.

Bagdikian, B. H. (1992). *The media monopoly* (4th ed.). Boston: Beacon.

Bagdikian, B. H. (2000). *The media monopoly* (6th ed.). Boston: Beacon.

Baker, R. K., & Ball, S. J. (1969). *Violence and the media.* Washington, DC: Government Printing Office.

Ball-Rokeach, S. J., & DeFleur, M. (1976). A dependency model of mass-media effects. *Communication Research, 3,* 3–21.

Banaji, M. R., Blair, I. V., & Glaser, J. (1997). Environments and unconscious processes. In R. S. Wyer (Ed.), *Advances in social cognition* (pp. 63–74). Mahwah, NJ: Lawrence Erlbaum.

Bandura, A. (1973). *Aggression: A social learning analysis.* Upper Saddle River, NJ: Prentice Hall.

Bandura, A. (1994). Social cognitive theory of mass communication. In J. Bryant & D. Zillmann (Eds.), *Media effects* (pp. 61–90). Hillsdale, NJ: Lawrence Erlbaum.

Bandura, A. (2001). Social cognitive theory of mass communication. *Media Psychology, 3,* 265–299.

Bandura, A. (2002). Social cognitive theory of mass communication. In J. Bryant & D. Zillmann (Eds.), *Media effects: Advances in theory and research* (2nd ed.). Mahwah, NJ: Lawrence Erlbaum.

Bantz, C. R., McCorkle, S., & Baade, R. C. (1980). The news factory. *Communication Research, 7,* 45–68.

Baran, S. J., & Davis, D. K. (2000). *Mass communication theory: Foundations, ferment, and future* (2nd ed.). Belmont, CA: Wadsworth.

Bargh, J. A. (1984). Automatic and conscious processing of social information. In R. S. Wyer & T. K. Srull (Eds.), *Handbook of social cognition* (Vol. 3, pp. 1–43). Hillsdale, NJ: Lawrence Erlbaum.

Bargh, J. A. (1994). The four horsemen of automaticity: Awareness, intention, efficiency, and control in social cognition. In R. S. Wyer & T. K. Srull (Eds.), *Handbook of social cognition* (2nd ed., pp. 1–40). Hillsdale, NJ: Lawrence Erlbaum.

Bargh, J. A. (1997). The automaticity of everyday life. In R. S. Wyer (Ed.), *Advances in social cognition* (pp. 1–61). Mahwah, NJ: Lawrence Erlbaum.

Bargh, J. A., Chaiken, S., Raymond, P., & Hymes, C. (1996). The automatic evaluation effect: Unconditional automatic attitude activation with a pronunciation task. *Journal of Experimental Social Psychology, 32,* 185–210.

Barker-Plummer, B. (2002). Producing public voice: Resource mobilization and media access in the National Organization for Women. *Journalism & Mass Communication Quarterly, 79,* 188–205.

Barnes, B. E., & Thomson, L. M. (1994). Power to the people(meter): Audience measurement technology and media specialization. In J. S. Ettema & D. C. Whitney (Eds.), *Audiencemaking: How the media create the audience* (pp. 75–94). Thousand Oaks, CA: Sage.

Barnhurst, K. G., & Mutz, D. (1997). American journalism and the decline in event-centered reporting. *Journal of Communication, 47*(4), 27–53.

Baron, R. A. (1979). Effects of victim's pain cues, victim's race, and level of prior instigation upon physical aggression. *Journal of Applied Social Psychology, 9*(2), 103–114.

Barsalou, L. W. (1992). *Cognitive psychology: An overview for cognitive scientists.* Hillsdale, NJ: Lawrence Erlbaum.

Barthes, R. (1968). *Elements of semiology.* New York: Hill & Wang.

Barthes, R. (1975). *The pleasure of the text* (R. Miller, Trans.). New York: Hill & Wang.

Barthes, R. (1977). *Image-music-text* (S. Heath, Trans.). London: Fontana.

Bartlett, F. A. (1932). *A study in experimental and social psychology.* New York: Cambridge University Press.

Barwise, T. P., Ehrenberg, A. S. C., & Goodhardt, G. J. (1982). Glued to the box? Patterns of TV repeat-viewing. *Journal of Communication, 32*(4), 22–29.

Basil, M. D. (1992, May). *A "new world" of media effects.* Paper presented to the mass communication division at the annual conference of the International Communication Association, Miami, FL.

Basil, M. D., Brown, W. J., & Bocarnea, M. C. (2002). Differences in univariate values versus multivariate relationships: Findings from a study of Diana, Princess of Wales. *Human Communication Research, 28,* 501–514.

Bass, A. Z. (1969). Refining the gatekeeper concept. *Journalism Quarterly, 46,* 69–71.

Bassili, J. N., & Brown, R. D. (2005). Implicit and explicit attitudes: Research, challenges, and theory. In D. Albarracin, B. T. Johnson, & M. P. Zanna (Eds.). *The handbook of attitudes* (pp. 543–574). Mahwah, NJ: Lawrence Erlbaum.

Bates, B. J. (1998). Valuation of media properties. In A. Alexander, J. Owers, & R. Carveth (Eds.), *Media economics: Theory and practice* (2nd ed., pp. 73–94). Mahwah, NJ: Lawrence Erlbaum.

Battles, K., & Hilton-Morrow, W. (2002). Gay characters in conventional spaces: *Will and Grace* and the situation comedy genre. *Critical Studies in Media Communication, 19,* 87–105.

Baudrillard, J. (1983). *In the shadow of the silent majorities.* New York: Semiotexte.

Baumeister, R. F., & Sommer, K. L. (1997). Consciousness, free choice, and automaticity. In R. S. Wyer (Ed.), *Advances in social cognition* (pp. 75–81). Mahwah, NJ: Lawrence Erlbaum.

Beaudoin, C. E., & Thorson, E. (2004). Testing the cognitive mediation model: The roles of news reliance and three gratifications sought. *Communication Research, 31,* 446–471.

Becker, L. B., & Whitney, D. C. (1980). Effects of media dependencies: Audience assessments of government. *Communication Research, 7,* 95–120.

Bennett, S. E. (1989). Trends in Americans' political information, 1967–1987. *American Politics Quarterly, 17,* 422–435.

Bennett, W. L. (1990). Toward a theory of press-state relationship in the United States. *Journal of Communication, 40*(2), 103–125.

Berelson, B., Lazarsfeld, P. F., & McPhee, W. N. (1954). *Voting: A study of opinion formation in a presidential campaign.* Chicago: University of Chicago Press.

Berger, C. R. (1991). Communication theories and other curios. *Communication Monographs, 58,* 101–113.

Berger, C. R. (2000). Quantitative depictions of threatening phenomena in news reports: The scary world of frequency data. *Human Communication Research, 26,* 27–52.

Berger, P. L., & Luckmann, T. (1966). *The social construction of reality.* Garden City, NY: Anchor.

Berkowitz, D., & Limor, Y. (2003). Professional confidence and situational ethics: Assessing the social-professional dialectic in journalistic ethics decisions. *Journalism & Mass Communication Quarterly, 80,* 783–801.

Berkowitz, D., & TerKeurst, J. V. (1999). Community as interpretive community: Rethinking the journalist-source relationship. *Journal of Communication, 49,* 125–136.

Berkowitz, L. (1965). Some aspects of observed aggression. *Journal of Personality and Social Psychology, 2,* 259–269.

Berkowitz, L. (1984). Some effects of thoughts on anti- and prosocial influences of media events: A cognitive-neoassociationistic analysis. *Psychological Bulletin, 95,* 410–427.

Berkowitz, L. (1997). Some thoughts extending Bargh's argument. In R. S. Wyer (Ed.), *Advances in social cognition* (pp. 83–94). Mahwah, NJ: Lawrence Erlbaum.

Berkowitz, L. (2000). *Causes and consequences of feelings.* New York: Cambridge University Press.

Berman, R. (1981). *Advertising and social change.* Beverly Hills, CA: Sage.

Berscheid, E., & Walster, E. (1974). Physical attractiveness. In L. Berkowitz (Ed.), *Advances in experimental social psychology* (pp. 157–215). New York: Academic Press.

Bettelheim, B. (1975). *The uses of enchantment: The meaning and importance of fairy tales.* New York: Knopf.

Bettig, R. V., & Hall, J. L. (2003). *Big media, big money: Cultural texts and political economics.* New York: Rowman & Littlefield.

Bickham, D. S., Vandewater, E. A., Huston, A. C., Lee, J. H., Caplovitz, A. G., & Wright, J. C. (2003). Predictors of children's electronic media use: An examination of three ethnic groups. *Media Psychology, 5,* 107–137.

Bickham, D. S., Wright, J. C., & Huston, A. C. (2001). Attention, comprehension, and the educational influences of television. In D. G. Singer & J. L. Singer (Eds.), *Handbook of children and the media* (pp. 101–119). Thousand Oaks, CA: Sage.

Bilandzic, H., & Buselle, R. (2006, June). *Experiential engagement in filmic narratives and enjoyment: The role of transportation, identification, and perceived realism.* Paper presented at the annual conference of the International Communication Association, Dresden, Germany.

Biocca, F. A. (1988). Opposing conceptions of the audience. In J. A. Anderson (Ed.), *Communication yearbook* (Vol. 11, pp. 51–80). Newbury Park, CA: Sage.

Bissell, K. L., & Zhou, P. (2004). Must-see TV or ESPN: Entertainment and sports media exposure and body-image distortion in college women. *Journal of Communication, 54*, 5–21.

Blumer, H. (1946). The field of collective behavior. In A. M. Lee (Ed.), *New outline of the principles of sociology* (pp. 167–222). New York: Barnes & Noble.

Blumler, J. G., & McQuail, D. (1968). *Television in politics: Its uses and influence.* London: Faber.

Bochner, A. P. (1985). Perspectives on inquiry: Representation, conversation, and reflection. In M. L. Knapp & G. R Miller (Eds.), *Handbook of interpersonal communication* (pp. 27–58). Newbury Park, CA: Sage.

Bolls, P. D., & Lang, A. (2003). I saw it on the radio: The allocation of attention to high-imagery radio advertisements. *Media Psychology, 5*, 33–55.

Bolls, P. D., Lang, A., & Potter, R. F. (2001). The effects of message valence and listener arousal on attention, memory, and facial muscular responses to radio advertisements. *Communication Research, 28*, 627–651.

Boorstin, D. (1961). *The image.* New York: Atheneum.

Borardus, E. S. (1931). *Fundamentals of social psychology.* New York: Century Press.

Botta, R. A. (1999). Television images and adolescent girls' body image disturbance. *Journal of Communication, 49*, 22–41.

Botta, R. A. (2000). The mirror of television: A comparison of black and white adolescents' body image. *Journal of Communication, 50*, 144–159.

Bower, R. T. (1985). *The changing television audience in America.* New York: Columbia University Press.

Boyd-Barrett, O. (1977). Media imperialism: Towards an international framework for the analysis of media systems. In J. Curren, M. Gurevitch, & J. Woollacott (Eds.), *Mass communication and society* (pp. 116–135). Beverly Hills, CA: Sage.

Bracken, C. D., & Lombard, M. (2004). Social presence and children: Praise, intrinsic motivation, and learning with computers. *Journal of Communication, 54*, 22–37.

Brewer, W. H., & Lichtenstein, E. H. (1981). Event schemas, story schemas, and story grammars. In J. Long & A. Baddeley (Eds.), *Attention and performance, IX* (pp. 363–379). Hillsdale, NJ: Lawrence Erlbaum.

Brewer, W. H., & Nakamura, G. V. (1984). The nature and functions of schemas. In R. S. Wyer & T. K. Srull (Eds.), *Handbook of social cognition* (Vol. 1, pp. 119–160). Hillsdale, NJ: Lawrence Erlbaum.

Broadbent, D. E. (1958). *Perception and communication.* Oxford, UK: Pergamon.

Brooks, P. (1995). *The melodramatic imagination: Balzac, Henry James, melodrama, and the mode of excess.* New Haven, CT: Yale University Press.

Bryant, J., Carveth, R. A., & Brown, D. (1981). Television viewing and anxiety: An experimental examination. *Journal of Communication, 31*(1), 106–119.

Bryant, J., & Zillmann, D. (Eds.). (2002). *Media effects: Advances in theory and research* (2nd ed.). Mahwah, NJ: Lawrence Erlbaum.

Bryant, P. E., & Kopytynska, H. (1976). Spontaneous measurement by young children. *Nature, 260*, 773–774.

Bucy, E. P., & Newhagen, J. E. (1999). The emotional appropriateness heuristic: Processing televised presidential reactions to the news. *Journal of Communication, 49*, 59–79.

Budd, M., Craig, S., & Steinman, C. (1999). *Consuming environments: Television and commercial culture.* New Brunswick, NJ: Rutgers University Press.

Buijzen, M., & Valkenburg, P. M. (2000). The impact of television advertising on children's Christmas wishes. *Journal of Broadcasting & Electronic Media, 44,* 456–470.

Bundesen, C., & Habekost, T. (2005). Attention. In K. Lamberts & R. L. Goldstone (Eds.), *Handbook of cognition* (pp. 105–129). Thousand Oaks, CA: Sage.

Burke, M. C., & Edell, J. A. (1989). The impact of feelings on ad-based affect and cognition. *Journal of Marketing Research, 26*(1), 69–83.

Busselle, R. W. (2001). Television exposure, perceived realism, and exemplar accessibility in the social judgment process. *Media Psychology, 3,* 43–67.

Butler, J. G. (2002). *Television: Critical methods and applications* (2nd ed.). Mahwah, NJ: Lawrence Erlbaum.

Cantor, J. (2002). Fright reactions to mass media. In J. Bryant & D. Zillmann (Eds.), *Media effects: Advances in theory and research* (2nd ed., pp. 287–306). Mahwah, NJ: Lawrence Erlbaum.

Cantor, J., & Hoffner, C. (1990). Children's fear reactions to a televised film as a function of perceived immediacy of depicted threat. *Journal of Broadcasting & Electronic Media, 34,* 421–442.

Cantor, J., & Sparks, G. C. (1984). Children's fear responses to mass media: Testing some Piagetian predictions. *Journal of Communication, 34*(2), 90–103.

Cantor, J., & Wilson, B. J. (1988). Helping children cope with frightening media presentations. *Current Psychology: Research & Reviews, 7,* 58–75.

Cantor, M. G. (1994). The role of the audience in the production of culture: A personal research perspective. In J. S. Ettema & D. C. Whitney (Eds.), *Audiencemaking: How the media create the audience* (pp. 159–170). Thousand Oaks, CA: Sage.

Cantril, H. (1940). *The invasion from Mars: A study of the psychology of panic.* Princeton, NJ: Princeton University Press.

Cappella, J. N. (2002). Cynicism and social trust in the new media environment. *Journal of Communication, 52,* 229–241.

Cappella, J. N., & Jamieson, K. H. (1997). *The spiral of cynicism: The press and the public good.* New York: Oxford University Press.

Carey, J. (1975a). A cultural approach to communications. *Communications, 2,* 1–22.

Carey, J. (1975b). Culture and communications. *Communication Research, 2,* 173–191.

Carlson, M., Marcus-Newhall, A., & Miller, N. (1990). Effects of situational aggression cues: A quantitative review. *Journal of Personality and Social Psychology, 58,* 622–633.

Carragee, K. M. (1990). Interpretive media study and interpretive social science. *Critical Studies in Mass Communication, 7,* 81–96.

Cartwright, D. (1949). Some principles of mass persuasion. *Human Relations, 2,* 253–267.

Cassata, M., Skill, T., & Boadu, S. (1979). In sickness and in health. *Journal of Communication, 24*(2), 73–80.

Castells, M. (1996). *The rise of the network society.* Oxford, UK: Blackwell.

Centerwall, B. S. (1989). Exposure to television as a cause for violence. In G. Comstock (Ed.), *Public communication and behavior* (Vol. 2, pp. 1–58). San Diego: Academic Press.

Chadwick, A. (2006). *Internet politics: States, citizens, and new communication technologies.* New York: Oxford University Press.

Chaffee, S. (1972). The interpersonal context of mass communication. In F. G. Kline & P. J. Tichenor (Eds.), *Current perspectives in mass communication research* (pp. 95–120). Beverly Hills, CA: Sage.

Chaffee, S. (1977). Mass media effects: New research perspectives. In D. Lerner & L. M. Nelson (Eds.), *Communication research: A half-century appraisal* (pp. 210–241). Honolulu: University Press of Hawaii.

Chaffee, S. (1991). *Communication concepts 1: Explication.* Newbury Park, CA: Sage.

Chaffee, S., & Rogers, E. M. (Eds.). (1997). *The beginnings of communication study in America: A personal memoir.* Thousand Oaks, CA: Sage.

Chaiken, S., Liberman, A., & Eagly, A. H. (1989). Heuristic and systematic processing within and beyond the persuasion context. In J. S. Uleman & J. A. Bargh (Eds.), *Unintended thought* (pp. 212–252). New York: Guilford.

Chaiken, S., Wood, W., & Eagly, A. H. (1996). Principles of persuasion. In E. T. Higgins & A. W. Kruglanski (Eds.), *Social psychology: Handbook of basic principles* (pp. 702–742). New York: Guilford.

Chang, C. (2002). Self-congruency as a cue in different advertising-processing contexts. *Communication Research, 29,* 503–536.

Chan-Olmsted, S. M., & Albarran, A. B. (1998). A framework for the study of global media exomics. In A. B. Albarran & Chan-Olmsted (Eds.), *Global media economics: Commercialization, concentration and integration of world media markets* (pp. 3–16). Ames: Iowa State University Press.

Chan-Olmsted, S. M., & Ha, L. S. (2003). Internet business models for broadcasters: How television stations perceive and integrate the Internet. *Journal of Broadcasting & Electronic Media, 47,* 597–617.

Chan-Olmsted, S. M., & Kim, Y. (2001). Perceptions of branding among television station managers: An exploratory analysis. *Journal of Broadcasting & Electronic Media, 45,* 75–91.

Chan-Olmsted, S. M., & Park, J. S. (2000). From on-air to online world: Examining the content and structures of broadcast TV stations' Web sites. *Journalism & Mass Communication Quarterly, 77,* 321–339.

Chater, N., Heit, E., & Oaksford, M. (2005). Reasoning. In K. Lamberts & R. L. Goldstone (Eds.), *Handbook of cognition* (pp. 297–320). Thousand Oaks, CA: Sage.

Chiricos, T. (1996). *Justice with prejudice: Race and criminal justice in America.* New York: Harrow & Heston.

Chory-Assad, R. M., & Tamborini, R. (2003). Television exposure and the public's perceptions of physicians. *Journal of Broadcasting & Electronic Media, 47,* 197–215.

Christ, W. G., & Potter, W. J. (1998). Media literacy, media education, and the academy. *Journal of Communication, 48*(1), 5–15.

Clark, H. H., & Marshall, C. R. (1981). Definite reference and mutual knowledge. In A. K. Joshi, B. Webber, & I. Sag (Eds.), *Elements of discourse understanding* (pp. 10–63). Cambridge, UK: Cambridge University Press.

Cline, V. B., Croft, R. G., & Courrier, S. (1973). Desensitization of children to television violence. *Journal of Personality and Social Psychology, 27*(3), 260–265.

Clore, G. L., & Schnall, S. (2005). The influence of affect on attitudes. In D. Albarracin, B. T. Johnson, & M. P. Zanna (Eds.), *The handbook of attitudes* (pp. 437–489). Mahwah, NJ: Lawrence Erlbaum.

Cohen, E. L. (2002). Online journalism as market-driven journalism. *Journal of Broadcasting & Electronic Media, 46,* 532–548.

Cohen, S. (1972). *Folk devils and moral panics.* London: McGibbon & Kee.

Coleridge, S. T. (1847). *Biographia literaria* (Vol. 2). London: William Pickering.

Collins, A. M., & Loftus, E. F. (1975). A spreading-activation theory of semantic processing. *Psychological Review, 82,* 407–428.

Collins, A. M., & Quillian, M. R. (1969). Retrieval time from semantic memory. *Journal of Verbal Learning and Verbal Memory, 8,* 240–247.

Combs, B., & Slovic, P. (1979). Newspaper coverage of causes of death. *Journalism Quarterly, 56,* 837–843.

Comisky, P., & Bryant, J. (1982). Factors involved in generating suspense. *Human Communication Research, 9,* 49–58.

Comrie, M. (1999). Television news and broadcasting deregulation in New Zealand. *Journal of Communication, 49*(2), 42–54.

Comstock, G., Chaffee, S., Katzman, N., McCombs, M., & Roberts, D. (1978). *Television and human behavior.* New York: Columbia University Press.

Comstock, G., & Scharrer, E. (1999). *Television: What's on, who's watching, and what it means.* New York: Academic Press.

Cooper, B. (2002). *Boys Don't Cry* and female masculinity: Reclaiming a life & dismantling the politics of normative heterosexuality. *Critical Studies in Media Communication, 19,* 44–63.

Cooper, C. A. (1996). *Violence on television: Congressional inquiry, public criticism and industry response.* New York: University Press of America.

Corner, J. (1999). *Critical ideas in television studies.* Oxford, UK: Clarendon.

Coser, L. A. (1956). *The functions of social conflict.* New York: Free Press.

Coser, L. A., Kadushin, C., & Powell, W. W. (1982). *Books: The culture and commerce of publishing.* New York: Basic Books.

Coulson, D. C., Riffe, D., Lacy, S., & St. Cyr, C. R. (2001). Media and public affairs: Erosion of television coverage of city hall? Perceptions of TV reporters on the beat. *Journalism & Mass Communication Quarterly, 78,* 81–92.

Craig, D. A. (2003). The promise and peril of anecdotes in news coverage: An ethical analysis. *Journalism & Mass Communication Quarterly, 80,* 802–817.

Craik, F. I. M., & Lockhart, R. S. (1972). Levels of processing: A framework for memory research. *Journal of Verbal Learning and Verbal Behavior, 11,* 671–684.

Croteau, D., & Hoynes, W. (2000). *Media society: Industries, images, and audiences* (2nd ed.). Boston: Pine Forge Press.

Croteau, D., & Hoynes, W. (2001). *The business of media: Corporate media and the public interest.* Boston: Pine Forge Press.

Csikszentmihalyi, M. (1988). The flow experience and its significance for human psychology. In M. Csikszentmihalyi & I. S. Csikszentmihalyi (Eds.), *Optimal experience: Psychological studies of flow in consciousness* (pp. 15–35). New York: Cambridge University Press.

Cwalina, W., Falkowski, A., & Kaid, L. L. (2000). Role of advertising in forming the image of politicians: Comparative analysis of Poland, France, and Germany. *Media Psychology, 2,* 119–146.

D'Alessio, D., & Allen, M. (2000). Media bias in presidential elections: A meta-analysis. *Journal of Communication, 50,* 133–156.

David, P., Morrison, G., Johnson, M. A., & Ross, F. (2002). Body image, race, and fashion models: Social distance and social identification in third-person effects. *Communication Research, 29,* 270–294.

Davis, D. K. (1990). News and politics. In D. L. Swanson & D. Nimmo (Eds.), *New directions in political communication* (pp. 181–208). Newbury Park, CA: Sage.

Davis, M. H., & Kraus, L. A. (1989). Social contact, loneliness and mass media use: A test of two hypotheses. *Journal of Applied Social Psychology, 19,* 1100–1124.

Davis, S., & Mares, M.-L. (1998). Effects of talk show viewing on adolescents. *Journal of Communication, 48*(2), 69–86.

Davison, W. P. (1983). The third person effect in communication. *Public Opinion Quarterly, 47,* 1–15.

Deckers, L., & Carr, D. E. (1986). Cartoons varying in low-level pain ratings, not aggression ratings, correlate positively with funniness ratings. *Motivation and Emotion, 10,* 207–216.

Deetz, S. (1973). Words without things: Toward a social phenomenology of language. *Quarterly Journal of Speech, 59,* 40–51.

DeFleur, M. (1970). *Theories of mass communication.* New York: David McKay.

DeFleur, M. L., & Ball-Rokeach, S. (1975). *Theories of mass communication* (3rd ed.). New York: David McKay.

DeFleur, M. L., & Larsen, O. N. (1958). *The flow of information.* New York: Harper & Brothers.

Denham, B. E. (2004). Toward an explication of media enjoyment: The synergy of social norms, viewing situations, and program content. *Communication Theory, 14,* 370–387.

Dervin, B. (1989). Changing conceptions of the audience. In R. E. Rice & C. Atkin (Eds.), *Public communication campaigns* (2nd ed.). Beverly Hills, CA: Sage.

Dervin, B., Grossberg, L., O'Keefe, B. J., & Wartella, E. (Eds.). (1989). *Rethinking communication.* Newbury Park, CA: Sage.

de Saussure, F. (1966). *Course in general linguistics.* New York: McGraw-Hill.

de Saussure, F. (1983). *Course in general linguistics.* London: Duckworth.

Detenber, B. H., Simons, R. F., & Bennett, G. G., Jr. (1998). Roll 'em! The effects of picture motion on emotional responses. *Journal of Broadcasting & Electronic Media, 42,* 113–127.

Detenber, B. H., Simons, R. F., & Reiss, J. E. (2000). The emotional significance of color in television presentations. *Media Psychology, 2,* 331–355.

De Vreese, C. H., & Semetko, H. A. (2002). Cynical and engaged: Strategic campaign coverage, public opinion, and mobilization in a referendum. *Communication Research, 29,* 615–641.

Dobos, J., & Dimmick, J. (1988). Factor analysis and gratification constructs. *Journal of Broadcasting & Electronic Media, 32,* 335–350.

Dolich, I. J. (1969). Congruence relationships between self images and product brands. *Journal of Marketing Research, 6,* 80–83.

Dominick, J. R., Sherman, B. L., & Messere, F. (2000). *Broadcasting, cable, the Internet, and beyond.* Boston: McGraw-Hill.

Domke, D. (2000). Strategic elites, the press, and race relations. *Journal of Communication, 50,* 115–140.

Donaldson, M. (1978). *Children's minds.* Glasgow, UK: Fontana/Collins.

Donohew, L., & Tipton, L. (1973). A conceptual model of information seeking, avoiding, and processing. In P. Clark (Ed.), *New models for mass communication research* (pp. 243–268). Beverly Hills, CA: Sage.

Dorr, A. (1980). When I was a child I thought as a child. In S. B. Withey & R. P. Abeles (Eds.), *Television and social behavior: Beyond violence and children* (pp. 191–230). Hillsdale, NJ: Lawrence Erlbaum.

Douglas, S. (1987). *Inventing American broadcasting, 1899–1922.* Baltimore: Johns Hopkins University Press.

Doyle, G. (2002). *Understanding media economics.* London: Sage.

D'Souza, D. (1991). *Illiberal education: The politics of race and sex on campus.* New York: Free Press.

Dulany, D. E. (1968). Awareness, rules, and propositional control: A confrontation with S-R behavior theory. In T. Dixon & D. Horton (Eds.), *Verbal behavior and behavior theory* (pp. 340–387). New York: Prentice Hall.

Duncan, C. P., & Nelson, J. E. (1985). Effects of humor in a radio advertising experiment. *Journal of Advertising, 14,* 33–40.

Dyer, R. (1998). *Stars.* London: British Film Institute.

Eagly, A. H., & Chaiken, S. (1993). Attitude structure and function. In D. Gilbert, S. T. Fiske, & G. Lindsey (Eds.), *Handbook of social psychology* (Vol. 2, pp. 269–322). Boston: McGraw-Hill.

Eagly, A. H., & Chaiken, S. (1998). Attitude structure and function. In D. T. Gilbert, S. T. Fiske, & G. Lindsey (Eds.), *Handbook of social psychology* (4th ed., Vol. 1, pp. 269–322). Boston: McGraw-Hill.

Eastman, S. T. (1993). *Broadcast/cable programming: Strategies and practices* (4th ed.). Belmont, CA: Wadsworth.

Eastman, S. T. (1998). Programming theory under strain: The active industry and the active audience. In M. E. Roloff & G. D. Paulson (Eds.), *Communication yearbook* (Vol. 11, pp. 323–377). Thousand Oaks, CA: Sage.

Eco, U. (1966). Narrative structure in Fleming. In E. del Buono & U. Eco (Eds.), *The Bond affair.* London: MacDonald.

Edell, J. A. (1988). Effects in advertisements: A review and synthesis. In S. Hecker & D. W. Stewart (Eds.), *Nonverbal communication in advertising* (pp. 11–28). Lexington, MA: D. C. Heath.

Edman, I. (1939). *Arts and the man.* New York: Norton.

Eggermont, S. (2004). Television viewing, perceived similarity and adolescents' expectations of a romantic partner. *Journal of Broadcasting & Electronic Media, 48,* 244–265.

Ehrenberg, A. S. C., Goodhardt, G. J., & Barwise, T. P. (1990). Double jeopardy revisited. *Journal of Marketing, 54,* 82–91.

Ehrenberg, A. S. C., & Wakshlag, J. (1987). Repeat viewing with people-meters. *Journal of Advertising Research, 27,* 9–13.

Ellis, D. G. (1995). Fixing communicative meaning: A coherentist theory. *Communication Research, 22,* 515–544.

Ellis, J. (1992). *Visible fictions: Cinema, television, video.* Boston: Routlege.

Erdelyi, M. H., & Zizak, D. M. (2004). Beyond gizmo subliminality. In L. J. Schrum (Ed.), *The psychology of entertainment media: Blurring the lines between entertainment and persuasion* (pp. 13–43). Mahwah, NJ: Lawrence Erlbaum.

Ettema, J. S. (1982). The organizational context of creativity: A case study from public television. In J. S. Ettema & D. C. Whitney (Eds.), *Individuals in mass media organizations: Creativity and constraint* (pp. 91–106). Beverly Hills, CA: Sage.

Ettema, J. S., & Whitney, D. C. (Eds.). (1994). *Audiencemaking: How the media create the audience.* Thousand Oaks, CA: Sage.

Evans, J. St B. T. (1998). Matching bias in conditional reasoning: Do we understand it after 25 years? *Thinking and Reasoning, 4,* 45–82.

Evans, J. St B. T., Legrenzi, P., & Firotto, V. (1999). The influence of linguistic form on reasoning: The case of matching bias. *Quarterly Journal of Experimental Psychology, 52A,* 185–216.

Eveland, W. P., Jr. (2001). The cognitive mediation model of learning from the news: Evidence from nonelection, off-year election, and presidential election contexts. *Communication Research, 28,* 571–601.

Eveland, W. P., Jr. (2002). News information processing as mediator of the relationship between motivations and political knowledge. *Journalism & Mass Communication Quarterly, 79,* 26–40.

Eveland, W. P., Jr., Cortese, J., Park, H., & Dunwoody, S. (2004). How Web site organization influences free recall, factual knowledge, and knowledge structure density. *Human Communication Research, 30,* 208–233.

Eveland, W. P., Jr., & Dunwoody, S. (2000). Examining information processing on the World Wide Web using think aloud protocols. *Media Psychology, 2,* 219–244.

Ewen, S. (1976). *Captains of consciousness.* New York: McGraw-Hill.

Ex, C. T. G. M., Janssens, J. M. A. M., & Korzilius, H. P. L. M. (2002). Young females' images of motherhood in relation to television viewing. *Journal of Communication, 52,* 955–971.

Fan, D. P., Wyatt, R. O., & Keltner, K. (2001). The suicidal messenger: How press reporting affects public confidence in the press, the military, and organized religion. *Communication Research, 28,* 826–852.

Fazio, R. (1990). Multiple processes by which attitudes guide behavior: The MODE model as an integrative framework. In M. Zanna (Ed.), *Advances in experimental social psychology* (Vol. 23, pp. 75–109). New York: Academic Press.

Fazio, R., Sanbonmatsu, D. M., Powell, M. C., & Kardes, F. R. (1986). On the automatic activation of attitudes. *Journal of Personality and Social Psychology, 50,* 229–238.

Ferguson, D. A. (1992). Channel repertoire in the presence of remote control devices, VCRs, and cable television. *Journal of Broadcasting & Electronic Media, 36,* 83–91.

Ferguson, D. A., & Perse, E. M. (1993). Media and audience influences on channel repertoire. *Journal of Broadcasting & Electronic Media, 37,* 31–47.

Ferguson, D. A., & Perse, E. M. (2000). The World Wide Web as a functional alternative to television. *Journal of Broadcasting & Electronic Media, 44,* 155–174.

Feshbach, N. D., & Roe, K. (1968). Empathy in six- and seven-year-olds. *Child Development, 39,* 133–145.

Feshbach, S. (1961). The stimulating versus cathartic effects of a vicarious aggressive activity. *Journal of Abnormal and Social Psychology, 63,* 381–385.

Festinger, L. (1957). *A theory of cognitive dissonance.* Evanston, IL: Row, Peterson.

Fisch, S. M. (2000). A capacity model of children's comprehension of educational content on television. *Media Psychology, 2,* 63–91.

Fischer, C. (1992). *America's calling.* Berkeley: University of California Press.

Fishbein, M., & Ajzen, I. (1975). *Belief, attitude, intention, and behavior: An introduction to theory and research.* Reading, MA: Addison-Wesley.

Fishman, M. (1980). *Manufacturing the news.* Austin: University of Texas Press.

Fiske, J. (1986). Television: Polysemy and popularity. *Critical Studies in Mass Communication, 3,* 391–408.

Fiske, J. (1989). *Television culture.* New York: Routledge.

Fiske, S. T., & Taylor, S. E. (1991). *Social cognition* (2nd ed.). New York: McGraw-Hill.

Flanagin, A. J., & Metzger, M. J. (2000). Perceptions of Internet credibility. *Journalism & Mass Communication Quarterly, 77,* 515–540.

Flanagin, A. J., & Metzger, M. J. (2001). Internet use in the contemporary media environment. *Human Communication Research, 27,* 153–181.

Fortunato, J. A. (2005). *Making media content: The influence of constituency groups on mass media.* Mahwah, NJ: Lawrence Erlbaum.

Foster, J. K., & Jelicic, M. (Eds.). (1999). *Memory: Systems, process, or function?* New York: Oxford University Press.

Foucault, M. (1984). *The Foucault reader* (P. Rabinow, Ed.). New York: Pantheon.

Fox, J. R. (2004). A signal detection analysis of audio/video redundancy effects in television news video. *Communication Research, 31,* 524–536.

Fredin, E. S., & David, P. (1998). Browsing and the hypermedia interaction cycle: A model of self-efficacy and goal dynamics. *Journalism & Mass Communication Quarterly, 75,* 35–54.

Freedman, J. L., & Sears, D. (1966). Selective exposure. In L. Berkowitz (Ed.), *Advances in experimental social psychology.* New York: Academic Press.

Freud, S. (1922). *Beyond the pleasure principle.* London: Hogarth.

Friedman, T. L. (2007). *The world is flat: A brief history of the twenty-first century, Release 3.0.* New York: Farrar, Straus and Giroux.

Frijda, N. H., & Zeelenberg, M. (2001). Appraisal: What is the dependent? In K. R. Scherer & A. Schorr (Eds.), *Appraisal processes in emotion: Theory, methods, research* (pp. 141–155). Oxford, UK: Oxford University Press.

Fulk, J., & DeSanctis, G. (1999). Articulation of communication technology and organizational form. In G. DeSanctis & J. Fulk (Eds.), *Shaping organizational form: Communication, connection, and community* (pp. 5–32). Thousand Oaks, CA: Sage.

Fursich, E. (2002). Nation, capitalism, myth: Covering news of economic globalization. *Journalism & Mass Communication Quarterly, 79,* 353–373.

Galbraith, J. K. (1976). *The affluent society.* New York: New American Library.

Gans, H. J. (1979). *Deciding what's news.* New York: Vintage.

Gant, C., & Dimmick, J. (2000). Making local news: A holistic analysis of sources, selection criteria, and topics. *Journalism & Mass Communication Quarterly, 77,* 628–638.

Gardner, H. (1983). *Frames of mind: The theory of multiple intelligences.* New York: Basic Books.

Gardner, M. P., & Hill, R. P. (1988). Consumers' mood states: Antecedents and consequences of experimental versus informational strategies for brand choice. *Psychology and Marketing, 5*(2), 169–182.

Gardner, W. L., & Cacioppo, J. T. (1997). Automaticity and social behavior: A model, a marriage, and a merger. In R. S. Wyer (Ed.), *Advances in social cognition* (pp. 133–141). Mahwah, NJ: Lawrence Erlbaum.

Garner, A., Sterk, H. M., & Adams, S. (1998). Narrative analysis of sexual etiquette in teenage magazines. *Journal of Communication, 48*(4), 59–78.

Garramone, G. M., & Atkin, C. K. (1986). Mass communication and political socialization: Specifying the effects. *Public Opinion Quarterly, 50*(1), 76–86.

Garrison, B. (2000). Journalists' perceptions of online information-gathering problems. *Journalism & Mass Communication Quarterly, 77,* 500–514.

Geen, R. G., & Rokosky, J. J. (1973). Interpretations of observed aggression and their effect on GSR. *Journal of Experimental Research in Personality, 6,* 289–292.

Geiger, S., & Newhagen, J. (1993). Revealing the black box: Information processing and media effects. *Journal of Communication, 43*(4), 42–50.

Gerbner, G. (1969). Towards "Cultural Indicators": The analysis of mass mediated message systems. *AV Communication, 27*(2), 171–180.

Gerbner, G. (1983). The importance of being critical—in one's own fashion. *Journal of Communication, 33*(3), 355–362.

Gerbner, G., & Gross, L. (1976). Living with television: The violence profile. *Journal of Communication, 26*(2), 173–199.

Gerbner, G., Gross, L., Morgan, M., & Signorielli, N. (1980). The "mainstreaming" of America: Violence profile No. 11. *Journal of Communication, 30*(3), 10–29.

Gerbner, G., Gross, L., Signorielli, N., Morgan, M., & Jackson-Beeck, M. (1979). The demonstration of power: Violence profile No. 10. *Journal of Communication, 29*(3), 177–196.

Gibbons, J. A., Vogl, R. J., & Grimes, T. (2003). Memory misattributions for characters in a television news story. *Journal of Broadcasting & Electronic Media, 47,* 99–112.

Gibson, R., & Zillmann, D. (2000). Reading between the photographs: The influence of incidental pictorial information on issue perception. *Journalism & Mass Communication Quarterly, 77,* 355–366.

Giddens, A. (1981). *A contemporary critique of historical materialism: Vol. 1. Power, property and the state.* Basingstoke, UK: Macmillan.

Gigerenzer, G., & Murray, D. J. (1987). *Cognition as intuitive statistics.* Hillsdale, NJ: Lawrence Erlbaum.

Gitlin, T. (1980). *The whole world is watching: The role of the news media in the making and unmaking of the new left.* Berkeley: University of California Press.

Gladwell, M. (2005). *Blink: The power of thinking without thinking.* New York: Little, Brown.

Goffman, E. (1974). *Frame analysis: An essay on the organization of experience.* New York: Harper & Row.

Goffman, E. (1979). *Gender advertisements.* New York: Harper Colophon Books.

Golan, G., & Wanta, W. (2001). Second-level agenda setting in the New Hampshire primary: A comparison of coverage in three newspapers and public perceptions of candidates. *Journalism & Mass Communication Quarterly, 78,* 247–259.

Goldberg, M. E., & Gorn, G. J. (1987). Happy and sad TV programs: How they affect reactions to commercials. *Journal of Consumer Research, 14,* 387–403.

Goldman, W. (1983). *Adventures in the screen trade: A personal view of Hollywood and screenwriting.* New York: Warner.

Goleman, D. (1995). *Emotional intelligence.* New York: Bantam.

Gomery, D. (1998). Media ownership: Concepts and principles. In A. Alexander, J. Owers, & R. Carveth (Eds.), *Media economics: Theory and practice* (2nd ed., pp. 45–52). Mahwah, NJ: Lawrence Erlbaum.

Goodhardt, G. J., Ehrenberg, A. S. C., & Collins, M. A. (1975). *The television audience: Patterns of viewing.* Westmead, UK: Saxon House.

Gorn, G. J. (1982). The effects of music in advertising on choice behavior: A classical conditioning approach. *Journal of Marketing, 46*(1), 94–101.

Grabe, M. E. (2002). Maintaining the moral order: A functional analysis of "The Jerry Springer Show." *Critical Studies in Media Communication, 19,* 311–328.

Grabe, M. E., Zhou, S., Lang, A., & Bolls, P. D. (2000). Packing television news: The effects of tabloids on information processing and evaluative responses. *Journal of Broadcasting & Electronic Media, 44,* 581–598.

Graber, D. A. (1988). *Processing the news: How people tame the information tide* (2nd ed.). New York: Longman.

Graesser, A. C., & Nakamura, G. V. (1982). The impact of a schema on comprehension and memory. In G. H. Bower (Ed.), *The psychology of learning and motivation* (Vol. 16, pp. 60–109). New York: Academic Press.

Gramsci, A. (1971). *Selections from the prison notebooks.* New York: International Publishers.

Granovetter, M. (1985). Economic action and social structure: The problem of embeddedness. *American Journal of Sociology, 91*(3), 481–510.

Granovetter, M. (1992). Problems of explanation in economic sociology. In N. Nohria & R. G. Eccles (Eds.), *Networks and organizations: Structure, form, and action* (pp. 25–56). Boston: Harvard Business School Press.

Green, M. C., & Brock, T. C. (2000). The role of transportation in the persuasiveness of public narratives. *Journal of Personality and Social Psychology, 79,* 701–721.

Green, M. C., Garst, J., & Brock, T. C. (2004). The power of fiction: Determinants and boundaries. In L. J. Shrum (Ed.), *The psychology of entertainment media: Blurring the lines between entertainment and persuasion* (pp. 161–176). Mahwah, NJ: Lawrence Erlbaum.

Greenberg, B. S. (1964). Person-to-person communication in the diffusion of a news event. *Journalism Quarterly, 41,* 489–494.

Greenberg, B. S. (1988). Some uncommon television images and the drench hypothesis. In S. Oskamp (Ed.), *Television as a social issue* (pp. 88–102). Newbury Park, CA: Sage.

Greenberg, B. S., & Brand, J. E. (1993). Cultural diversity on Saturday morning television. In G. Berry & J. K. Asamen (Eds.), *Children and television in a changing socio-cultural world* (pp. 132–142). Newbury Park, CA: Sage.

Greenberg, B. S., Mastro, D., & Brand, J. E. (2002). Minorities and the mass media: Television into the 21st century. In J. Bryant & D. Zillmann (Eds.), *Media effects: Advances in theory and research* (2nd ed., pp. 333–352). Mahwah, NJ: Lawrence Erlbaum.

Greenberg, B. S., & Parker, E. (Eds.). (1965). *The Kennedy assassination and the American public.* Stanford, CA: Stanford University Press.

Greene, J. O. (1989). Action assembly theory: Metatheoretical commitments, theoretical propositions, and empirical applications. In B. Dervin, L. Grossberg, B. J. O'Keefe, & E. Wartella (Eds.), *Rethinking communication* (Vol. 2, pp. 117–128). Newbury Park, CA: Sage.

Greene, K., Krcmar, M., Rubin, D. L., Walters, L. H., & Hale, J. L. (2002). Elaboration in processing adolescent health messages: The impact of egocentrism and sensation seeking on message processing. *Journal of Communication, 52,* 812–831.

Greenwald, A. G. (1968). Cognitive learning, cognitive response to persuasion, and attitude change. In A. Greenwald, T. Brock, & T. Ostrom (Eds.), *Psychological foundations of attitudes* (pp. 147–170). New York: Academic Press.

Griffin, R. J., Neuwirth, K., Dunwoody, S., & Giese, J. (2004). Information sufficiency and risk communication. *Media Psychology, 6,* 23–61.

Grimes, T., Bergen, L., Nicholes, K., Vernberg, E., & Fonagy, P. (2004). Is psychopathology the key to understanding why some children become aggressive when they are exposed to violent television programming? *Human Communication Research, 30,* 153–181.

Groebel, J., & Krebs, D. (1983). A study of the effects of television on anxiety. In C. D. Spielberger & R. Diaz-Guerrero (Eds.), *Cross-cultural anxiety* (Vol. 2, pp. 89–98). New York: Hemisphere.

Groenendyk, E. W., & Valentino, N. A. (2002). Of dark clouds and silver linings: Effects of exposure to issue versus candidate advertising on persuasion, information retention, and issue salience. *Communication Research, 29,* 295–319.

Gross, K., & Aday, S. (2003). The scary world in your living room and neighborhood: Using local broadcast news, neighborhood crime rates, and personal experience to test agenda setting and cultivation. *Journal of Communication, 53,* 411–426.

Grossberg, L. (1993). Can cultural studies find true happiness in communication? *Journal of Communication, 43,* 89–97.

Grossberg, L., Wartella, E., & Whitney, D. C. (1998). *Mediamaking: Mass media in a popular culture.* Thousand Oaks, CA: Sage.

Gunter, B. (1985). *Dimensions of television violence.* Aldershot, England: Gower Publishing.

Gunter, B., & Furnham, A. (1984). Perceptions of television violence: Effects of programme genre and type of violence on viewers' judgements of violent portrayals. *British Journal of Social Psychology, 23,* 155–164.

Gunther, A. C., & Chia, S. C.-Y. (2001). Predicting pluralistic ignorance: The hostile media perception and its consequences. *Journalism & Mass Communication Quarterly, 78,* 688–701.

Gunther, A. C., & Christen, C. T. (2002). Projection of persuasive press? Contrary effects of personal opinion and perceived news coverage on estimates of public opinion. *Journal of Communication, 52,* 177–195.

Gunther, A. C., & Schmitt, K. (2004). Mapping boundaries of the hostile media effect. *Journal of Communication, 54,* 55–70.

Gunther, A. C., & Storey, J. D. (2003). The influence of presumed influence. *Journal of Communication, 53,* 199–215.

Hall, A. (2003). Reading realism: Audiences' evaluations of the reality of media texts. *Journal of Communication, 53,* 624–641.

Hall, S. (1980). Encoding and decoding in the television discourse. In S. Hall, D. Hobson, A. Lowe, & P. Willis (Eds.), *Culture, media, language* (pp. 128–138). London: Hutchinson.

Hall, S. (1982). The rediscovery of "ideology": Return of the repressed in media studies. In M. Gurevitch, T. Bennett, J. Curran, & J. Woollacott (Eds.), *Culture, society, and the media.* London: Routledge.

Hallahan, K. (1994, August). *Product news versus advertising: An exploration within a student population.* Paper presented at the annual conference of the Association for Education in Journalism and Mass Communication, Atlanta, GA.

Hamilton, J. T. (1998). *Channeling violence: The economic market for violent television programming.* Princeton, NJ: Princeton University Press.

Hammond, K. R. (1996). *Human judgment and social policy: Irreducible uncertainty, inevitable error, unavoidable justice.* New York: Oxford University Press.

Hampton, J. A. (1982). A demonstration of intransitivity in natural concepts. *Cognition, 12,* 151–164.

Hapkiewicz, W. G., & Stone, R. D. (1974). The effect of realistic versus imaginary aggressive models on children's interpersonal play. *Child Study Journal, 4*(2), 47–58.

Hardt, H. (1992). *Critical communication studies: Communication, history and theory in America.* New York: Routledge.

Hardy, B. W., & Scheufele, D. A. (2005). Examining differential gains from Internet use: Comparing the moderating role of talk and online interactions. *Journal of Communication, 55,* 71–84.

Hare, R. D., & Blevings, G. (1975). Defense responses to phobic stimuli. *Biological Psychology, 3,* 1–13.

Haridakis, P. M. (2002). Viewer characteristics, exposure to television violence, and aggression. *Media Psychology, 4,* 323–352.

Harris, R. J. (2004). *A cognitive psychology of mass communication* (4th ed.). Mahwah, NJ: Lawrence Erlbaum.

Harris, R. J., & Scott, C. L. (2002). Effects of sex in the media. In J. Bryant & D. Zillmann (Eds.), *Media effects: Advances in theory and research* (2nd ed., pp. 307–331). Mahwah, NJ: Lawrence Erlbaum.

Harrison, K. (2000). The body electric: Thin-ideal media and eating disorders in adolescents. *Journal of Communication, 50,* 119–143.

Harrison, K., & Cantor, J. (1997). The relationship between media consumption and eating disorders. *Journal of Communication, 47*(1), 40–67.

Harrison, K., & Fredrickson, B. L. (2003). Women's sports media, self-objectification, and mental health in Black and White adolescent females. *Journal of Communication, 53,* 216–232.

Hashway, R. M., & Duke, L. I. (1992). *Cognitive styles: A primer to the literature.* Lewiston, NY: Edwin Mellen Press.

Hawkins, R. P., & Pingree, S. (1981). Uniform messages and habitual viewing: Unnecessary assumptions in social realty effects. *Human Communication Research, 7,* 291–301.

Hawkins, R. P., Pingree, S., Bruce, L., & Tapper, J. (1997). Strategy and style in attention to television. *Journal of Broadcasting & Electronic Media, 41,* 245–264.

Hawkins, R. P., Pingree, S., Hitchon, J. B., Gilligan, E., Kahlor, L., Gorham, B. W., et al. (2002). What holds attention to television? Strategic inertia of looks at content boundaries. *Communication Research, 29,* 3–30.

Hay, J. (1989). Advertising as a cultural text: Rethinking message analysis in a recombinant culture. In B. Dervin, L. Grossberg, B. J. O'Keefe, & E. Wartella (Eds.), *Rethinking Communication* (Vol. 2, pp. 129–152). Newbury Park, CA: Sage.

Healy, J. M. (1999). *Endangered minds: Why children don't think and what we can do about it.* New York: Simon & Schuster.

Hearold, S. (1986). A synthesis of 1043 effects of television on social behavior. In G. Comstock (Ed.), *Public communication and behavior* (Vol. 1, pp. 65–133). Orlando, FL: Academic Press.

Heeter, C. (1988). The choice process model. In C. Heeter & B. Greenberg (Eds.), *Cable-viewing* (pp. 11–32). Norwood, NJ: Ablex.

Heeter, C., & Greenberg, B. (1985). Cable program choice. In D. Zillmann & J. Bryant (Eds.), *Selective exposure to communication* (pp. 203–224). Hillsdale, NJ: Lawrence Erlbaum.

Henning, B., & Vorderer, P. (2001). Psychological escapism: Predicting the amount of television viewing by need for cognition. *Journal of Communication, 51,* 100–120.

Herald, D. T. (2006). *Genreflecting: A guide to popular reading interests* (6th ed.). Westport, CT: Libraries Unlimited.

Herman, E., & Chomsky, N. (1988). *Manufacturing consent: The political economy of mass media.* New York: Pantheon.

Hiebert, R. E., & Gibbons, S. J. (2000). *Exploring mass media for a changing world.* Mahwah, NJ: Lawrence Erlbaum.

Himmelweit, H. T., Oppenheim, A. N., & Vince, P. (1958). *Television and the child.* Oxford, UK: Oxford University Press.

Himmelweit, H. T., Swift, B., & Jaeger, M. E. (1980). The audience as critic: A conceptual analysis of television entertainment. In P. H. Tannenbaum (Ed.), *The entertainment functions of television* (pp. 67–106). Hillsdale, NJ: Lawrence Erlbaum.

Hirsch, E. D., Jr. (1987). *Cultural literacy: What every American needs to know.* Boston: Houghton Mifflin.

Hirsch, P. M., & Thompson, T. A. (1994). The stock market as audience: The impact of public ownership on newspapers. In J. S. Ettema & C. C. Whitney (Eds.), *Audiencemaking: How the media create the audience* (pp. 142–158). Thousand Oaks, CA: Sage.

Hoffner, C., & Buchanan, M. (2002). Parents' responses to television violence: The third-person perception, parental mediation, and support for censorship. *Media Psychology, 4,* 231–252.

Hoffner, C., Plotkin, R. S., Buchanan, M., Anderson, J. D., Kamigaki, S. K., Hubbs, L. A., et al. (2001). The third-person effect in perceptions of the influence of television violence. *Journal of Communication, 51,* 283–299.

Holbert, R. L., Kwak, N., & Shah, D. V. (2003). Environmental concern, patterns of television viewing, and pro-environmental behaviors: Integrating models of media consumption and effects. *Journal of Broadcasting & Electronic Media, 47,* 177–196.

Holbert, R. L., Shah, D. V., & Kwak, N. (2003). Political implications of prime-time drama and sitcom use: Genres of representation and opinions concerning women's rights. *Journal of Communication, 53,* 45–60.

Holbrook, M. B., & Westwood, R. A. (1989). The role of emotion in advertising revisited: Testing a typology of emotional responses. In P. Cafferata & A. M. Tybout (Eds.), *Cognitive and affective responses to advertising* (pp. 353–371). Lexington, MA: D. C. Heath.

Hollenbeck, A., & Slaby, R. (1979). Infant visual and vocal responses to television. *Child Development, 50,* 41–45.

Hollifield, C. A., Kosicki, G. M., & Becker, L. B. (2001). Organizational vs. professional culture in the newsroom: Television news directors' and newspaper editors' hiring decisions. *Journal of Broadcasting & Electronic Media, 45,* 92–117.

Hollis, M., & Nell, E. D. (1975). *Rational economic man.* New York: Cambridge University Press.

Holmstrom, A. J. (2004). The effects of the media on body image: A meta-analysis. *Journal of Broadcasting & Electronic Media, 48,* 196–217.

Holsti, O. R. (1969). *Content analysis for the social sciences and humanities.* Reading, MA: Addison-Wesley.

Hornik, R., & McAnany, E. (2001). Theories and evidence: Mass media effects and fertility change. *Communication Theory, 11,* 454–471.

Horton, D., & Wohl, R. R. (1956). Mass communication and para-social interaction. *Psychiatry, 19,* 215–229.

Hoskins, C., McFadyen, S., & Finn, A. (2004). *Media economics: Applying economics to new and traditional media.* Thousand Oaks, CA: Sage.

Hovland, C. I. (1954). Effects of the mass media of communication. In G. Lindzey (Ed.), *Handbook of social psychology* (pp. 1062–1103). Reading, MA: Addison-Wesley.

Hovland, C. I., Janis, I. L., & Kelley, H. H. (1953). *Communication and persuasion: Psychological studies of opinion change.* New Haven, CT: Yale University Press.

Hsia, H. J. (1977). Redundancy: Is it the lost key to better communication? *AV Communication Review, 25*(1), 63–85.

Huang, L.-N. (2000). Examining candidate information search processes: The impact of processing goals and sophistication. *Journal of Communication, 50,* 93–114.

Huh, J., Delorme, D. E., & Reid, L. N. (2004). The third-person effect and its influence on behavioral outcomes in a product advertising context: The case of direct-to-consumer prescription drug advertising. *Communication Research, 31,* 568–599.

Hume, D. (1969). *A treatise of human nature.* New York: Penguin. (Original work published 1739)

Hyman, H. (1955). *Survey design and analysis: Principles, cases and procedures.* Glencoe, IL: Free Press.

Hyman, H., & Sheatsley, P. (1947). Some reasons why information campaigns fail. *Public Opinion Quarterly, 11,* 412–423.

Innis, H. A. (1950). *Empire and communications.* Oxford, UK: Oxford University Press.

Innis, H. A. (1951). *The bias of communication.* Toronto: University of Toronto Press.

Isen, A. M. (2000). Positive affect and decision making. In M. Lewis & J. M. Haviland-Jones (Eds.), *Handbook of emotions* (2nd ed., pp. 417–435). New York: Guilford.

Iyengar, S. (1991). *Is anyone responsible? How television frames political issues.* Chicago: University of Chicago Press.

Iyengar, S. (1997). Overview: The effects of news on the audience. In S. Iyengar & B. Reeves (Eds.), *Do the media govern?* (pp. 211–216). Thousand Oaks, CA: Sage.

Iyengar, S., & Kinder, D. R. (1987). *News that matters: Television and American opinion.* Chicago: University of Chicago Press.

James, W. (1890). *Association* (Vol. 1). New York: Holt.

James, W. (1894). The physical basis of emotion. *Psychological Review, 1,* 516–529.

Jamieson, K. H., & Waldman, P. (2003). *The press effect: Politicians, journalists, and the stories that shape the political world.* New York: Oxford University Press.

Janowitz, M. (1968). The study of mass communication. In D. L. Sills (Ed.), *International encyclopedia of the social sciences* (Vol. 3, pp. 41–53). New York: Macmillan.

Jeffres, L. W. (1997). *Mass media effects* (2nd ed.). Prospect Heights, IL: Waveland.

Jensen, K. B., & Rosengren, K. E. (1990). Five traditions in search of the audience. *European Journal of Communication, 5,* 207–238.

Jhally, S. (Ed.). (1987). *The codes of advertising: Fetishism and the political economy of meaning in the consumer society.* New York: St. Martin's.

Jhally, S., & Livant, B. (1986). Watching as working: The valorization of audience consciousness. *Journal of Communication, 36*(3), 124–143.

Jo, E., & Berkowitz, L. (1994). A priming effect analysis of media influences: An update. In J. Bryant & D. Zillmann (Eds.), *Media effects: Advances in theory and research* (pp. 43–60). Hillsdale, NJ: Lawrence Erlbaum.

Johnson, T. J., & Kaye, B. K. (1998). Cruising is believing? Comparing Internet and traditional sources on media credibility measures. *Journalism & Mass Communication Quarterly, 75,* 325–340.

Johnson-Laird, P. N. (1983). *Mental models: Towards a cognitive science of language, inference, and consciousness.* Cambridge, UK: Cambridge University Press.

Johnson-Laird, P. N., & Oatley, K. (2000). Cognitive and social construction of emotions. In M. Lewis & J. M. Haviland-Jones (Eds.), *Handbook of emotions* (2nd ed., pp. 458–475). New York: Guilford.

Juanillo, N. K., Jr., & Scherer, C. W. (1991, May). *Patterns of family communication and health lifestyle.* Paper presented at the annual conference of the International Communication Association, Chicago.

Kahneman, D. (1973). *Attention and effort.* Englewood Cliffs, NJ: Prentice Hall.

Kahneman, D., & Tversky, A. (1973). On the psychology of prediction. *Psychological Review, 80,* 237–251.

Kamhawi, R., & Weaver, D. (2003). Mass communication research trends from 1980 to 1999. *Journalism & Mass Communication Quarterly, 80,* 7–27.

Kaminsky, S. M. (1974). *American film genres.* Dayton, OH: Pflaum.

Kaminsky, S. M., & Mahan, J. H. (1985). *American television genres.* Chicago: Nelson-Hall.

Kaplan, D. (1972, July/August). The psychopathology of TV watching. *Performance.*

Karlin, S. (1991, October 14). The new producers. *Mediaweek,* p. 18.

Katz, D. (1960). The functional approach to the study of attitudes. *Public Opinion Quarterly, 24,* 163–204.

Katz, E. (1987). Communication research since Lazarsfeld. *Public Opinion Quarterly, 51*(Suppl.), S25–S45.

Katz, E., Blumler, J. G., & Gurevitch, M. (1974). Utilization of mass communication by the individual. In J. G. Blumler & E. Katz (Eds.), *The uses of mass communication* (pp. 19–32). Beverly Hills, CA: Sage.

Katz, E., Gurevitch, M., & Haas, H. (1973). On the use of the mass media for important things. *American Sociological Review, 38,* 164–181.

Katz, E., & Lazarsfeld, P. F. (1955). *Personal influence: The part played by people in the flow of mass communications.* Glencoe, IL: Free Press.

Katzman, N. (1972). Television soap operas: What's been going on anyway? *Public Opinion Quarterly, 26*(2), 130–137.

Kaye, B. K., & Johnson, T. J. (2002). Online and in the know: Uses and gratifications of the Web for political information. *Journal of Broadcasting & Electronic Media, 46,* 54–71.

Keller, K. L. (1991). Memory and evaluation effects in competitive advertising environments. *Journal of Consumer Research, 17,* 463–476.

Kellerman, K., & Lim, T.-S. (1989). Conversational acquaintance: The flexibility of routinized behaviors. In B. Dervin, L. Grossberg, B. J. O'Keefe, & E. Wartella (Eds.), *Rethinking communication* (Vol. 2, pp. 172–187). Newbury Park, CA: Sage.

Kennedy, M. G., O'Leary, A., Beck, V., Pollard, K., & Simpson, P. (2004). Increases in calls to the CDC National STD and AIDS hotline following AIDS-related episodes in a soap opera. *Journal of Communication, 54,* 287–301.

Kent, R. J., & Machleit, K. A. (1992). The effects of postexposure test expectation in advertising experiments utilizing recall and recognition measures. *Marketing Letters, 3*(1), 17–26.

Key, V. O. (1961). *Public opinion and American democracy.* New York: Knopf.

Kilmer, P. D. (2001). "Madstones," clever toads, and killer tarantulas: Fairy-tale briefs in wild west newspapers. *Journalism & Mass Communication Quarterly, 78,* 799–835.

Kim, H. S. (2002). Gatekeeping international news: An attitudinal profile of U. S. television journalists. *Journal of Broadcasting & Electronic Media, 46,* 431–452.

Kim, J., & Rubin, A. M. (1997). The variable influence of audience activity on media effects. *Communication Research, 24,* 107–135.

Kim, S.-H., Scheufele, D. A., & Shanahan, J. (2002). Think about it this way: Attribute agenda-setting function of the press and the public's evaluation of a local issue. *Journalism & Mass Communication Quarterly, 79*, 7–25.

Kim, S.-H., Scheufele, D. A., & Shanahan, J. (2005). Who cares about the issues? Issue voting and the role of news media during the 2000 U.S. presidential election. *Journal of Communication, 55*, 103–121.

Kim, S. T., Weaver, D., & Willnat, L. (2000). Media reporting and perceived credibility of online polls. *Journalism & Mass Communication Quarterly, 77*, 846–864.

Kimchi, R. (1992). Primacy of wholistic processing and global/local paradigm: A critical review. *Psychological Bulletin, 112*, 24–38.

King, C. M. (2000). Effects of humorous heroes and villains in violent action films. *Journal of Communication, 50*, 5–24.

King, P. M. (1986). Formal reasoning in adults: A review and critique. In R. A. Mines & K. S. Kitchenor (Eds.), *Adult cognitive development: Methods and models* (pp. 1–21). New York: Praeger.

Kirsh, S. J., & Olczak, P. V. (2000). Violent comic books and perceptions of ambiguous provocation situations. *Media Psychology, 2*, 47–62.

Kisielius, J., & Sternthal, B. (1984). Detecting and explaining vividness effects in attitudinal judgments. *Journal of Marketing Research, 21*, 54–64.

Klapper, J. T. (1960). *The effects of mass communication.* Glencoe, IL: Free Press.

Klayman, J., & Brown, K. (1993). Debias the environment instead of the judge: An alternative approach to reducing error in diagnostic (and other) judgment. *Cognition, 49*, 97–122.

Klein, P. (1971, January). The men who run TV aren't stupid . . . *New York*, 20–29.

Klein, P. (1975). The television audience and mediocrity. In A. Wells (Ed.), *Mass media and society* (pp. 74–77). Palo Alto, CA: Mayfield.

Knobloch, S. (2003). Mood adjustment via mass communication. *Journal of Communication, 53*, 233–250.

Knobloch, S., Patzig, G., Mende, A.-M., & Hastall, M. (2004). Affective news: Effects of discourse structure in narratives of suspense, curiosity, and enjoyment while reading news and novels. *Communication Research, 31*, 259–287.

Knobloch, S., & Zillmann, D. (2002). Mood management via the digital jukebox. *Journal of Communication, 52*, 351–366.

Kolter, P. (1988). *Marketing management* (6th ed.). Englewood Cliffs, NJ: Prentice Hall.

Krcmar, M., & Cooke, M. C. (2001). Children's moral reasoning and their perceptions of television violence. *Journal of Communication, 51*, 300–316.

Krcmar, M., & Greene, K. (2000). Connections between violent television exposure and adolescent risk taking. *Media Psychology, 2*, 195–217.

Krosnick, J. A., Judd, C. M., & Wittenbrink, B. (2005). The measurement of attitudes. In D. Albarracin, B. T. Johnson, & M. P. Zanna (Eds.), *The handbook of attitudes* (pp. 21–76). Mahwah, NJ: Lawrence Erlbaum.

Kruglanski, A. W., & Stroebe, W. (2005). The influence of beliefs and goals on attitudes: Issues of structure, function, and dynamics. In D. Albarracin, B. T. Johnson, & M. P. Zanna (Eds.), *The handbook of attitudes* (pp. 323–368). Mahwah, NJ: Lawrence Erlbaum.

Kruschke, J. K. (2005). Category learning. In K. Lamberts & R. L. Goldstone (Eds.), *Handbook of cognition* (pp. 183–201). Thousand Oaks, CA: Sage.

Ku, G., Kaid, L. L., & Pfau, M. (2003). The impact of Web site campaigning on traditional news media and public information processing. *Journalism & Mass Communication Quarterly, 80*, 528–547.

Kuhn, T. (1970a). *The essential tension: Selected studies in scientific tradition and change.* Chicago: University of Chicago Press.

Kuhn, T. (1970b). *The structure of scientific revolutions* (2nd ed.). Chicago: University of Chicago Press.

Kwak, H., Zinkhan, G. M., & Dominick, J. R. (2002). The moderating role of gender and compulsive buying tendencies in the cultivation effects of TV shows and TV advertising: A cross cultural study between the United States and South Korea. *Media Psychology, 4,* 77–111.

Lampinen, J. M., Neuschatz, J. S., & Payne, D. G. (1998). Memory illusions and consciousness: Examining the phenomonology of true and false memories. *Current Psychology, 16,* 118–124.

Lando, H. A., & Donnerstein, E. I. (1978). The effects of a model's success or failure on subsequent aggressive behavior. *Journal of Research in Personality, 12,* 225–234.

Lang, A. (2000). The limited capacity model of mediated message processing. *Journal of Communication, 50,* 46–70.

Lang, A., Borse, J., Wise, K., & David, P. (2002). Captured by the World Wide Web: Orienting to structural and content features of computer-presented information. *Communication Research, 29,* 215–245.

Lang, A., Potter, R. F., & Bolls, P. D. (1999). Something for nothing: Is visual encoding automatic? *Media Psychology, 1,* 145–163.

Lang, A., Schwartz, N., Chung, Y., & Lee, S. (2004). Processing substance abuse messages: Production pacing, arousing content, and age. *Journal of Broadcasting & Electronic Media, 48,* 61–88.

Lang, A., Zhou, S., Schwartz, N., Bolls, P. D., & Potter, R. F. (2000). The effects of edits on arousal, attention and memory for television messages: When an edit is an edit can an edit be too much? *Journal of Broadcasting & Electronic Media, 44,* 94–109.

Lang, G. E., & Lang, K. (1983). *The battle for public opinion.* New York: Columbia University Press.

Lang, G. E., & Lang, K. (1991). Watergate: An exploration of the agenda setting process. In D. L. Protess & M. McCombs (Eds.), *Agenda setting: Readings on media, public opinion, and policymaking* (pp. 277–289). Hillsdale, NJ: Lawrence Erlbaum. (Original work published 1981)

LaRose, R., & Eastin, M. S. (2002). Is online buying out of control? Electronic commerce and consumer self-regulation. *Journal of Broadcasting & Electronic Media, 46,* 249–264.

LaRose, R., & Eastin, M. S. (2004). A social cognitive theory of Internet uses and gratifications: Toward a new model of media attendance. *Journal of Broadcasting & Electronic Media, 48,* 358–377.

LaRose, R., Lin, C. A., & Eastin, M. S. (2003). Unregulated Internet usage: Addiction, habit, or deficient self-regulation? *Media Psychology, 5,* 225–253.

Larson, S. G., & Bailey, M. (1998). ABC's "Person of the Week": American values in television news. *Journalism & Mass Communication Quarterly, 75,* 487–499.

Lasch, C. (1978). *The culture of narcissism.* New York: Norton.

Lasswell, H. D. (1927). *Propaganda techniques in the World War.* New York: Peter Smith.

Lasswell, H. D. (1948). The structure and function of communication in society. In L. Bryson (Ed.), *The communication of ideas* (pp. 37–51). New York: Harper.

Laurel, B. (1993). *Computers as theatre.* Reading, MA: Addison-Wesley.

Lazarsfeld, P. F. (1948). Communication research and the social psychologist. In W. Dennis (Ed.), *Current trends in social psychology* (pp. 218–273). Pittsburgh: University of Pittsburgh Press.

Lazarsfeld, P. F., Berelson, B., & Gaudet, H. (1944). *The people's choice.* New York: Columbia University Press.

Lazarus, R. S., Speisman, J. C., Mordkoff, A. M., & Davison, L. A. (1962). A laboratory study of psychological stress produced by a motion picture film. *Psychological Monographs: General and Applied, 76*(34), Whole No. 553.

Lee, K. M. (2004). Presence, explicated. *Communication Theory, 14,* 27–50.

Lee, S., & Barnes, J. H., Jr. (1990). Using color preferences in magazine advertising. *Journal of Advertising Research, 29*(6), 25–30.

Leiss, W., Kline, S., & Jhally, S. (1988). *Social communication in advertising: Persons, products, & images of well-being.* Scarborough, Ontario: Nelson Canada.

Levin, D. T., & Simons, D. J. (2000). Perceiving stability in a changing world: Combining shots and integrating views in motion pictures and the real world. *Media Psychology, 2,* 357–380.

Levi-Strauss, C. (1955). Structural study of myth. *Journal of American Folklore, 68,* 428–443.

Levi-Strauss, C. (1968). *Structural anthropology.* Harmondsworth, UK: Penguin.

Levy, M. R. (1977). Experiencing television news. *Journal of Communication, 27,* 112–177.

Lewin, K. (1935). *A dynamic theory of personality.* New York: McGraw-Hill.

Liebert, R. M. (1972). Television and social learning: Some relationships between viewing violence and behaving aggressively (overview). In J. P. Murray, E. A. Rubinstein, & G. A. Comstock (Eds.), *Television and social behavior: Television and social learning* (Vol. 2, pp. 1–42). Washington, DC: Government Printing Office.

Liebert, R. M., & Baron, R. A. (1972). Short-term effects of television aggression on children's aggressive behavior. In J. P. Murray, E. A. Rubinstein, & G. A. Comstock (Eds.), *Television and social behavior: Reports and papers: Vol. 2. Television and social learning.* Washington, DC: Government Printing Office.

Liebert, R. M., & Baron, R. A. (1973). Some immediate effects of televised violence on children's behavior. *Developmental Psychology, 6,* 469–475.

Liebert, R. M., Neale, J. M., & Davidson, E. S. (1973). *The early window: Effects of television on children and youth.* New York: Pergamon.

Liebert, R. M., & Poulos, R. W. (1975). Television and personality development: The socializing effects of an entertainment medium. In A. Davids (Ed.), *Child personality and psychopathology: Current topics* (Vol. 2, pp. 61–97). New York: John Wiley.

Liebert, R. M., & Schwartzberg, N. S. (1977). Effects of mass media. *Annual Review of Psychology, 28,* 141–173.

Lin, C. A., & Jeffres, L. W. (2001). Comparing distinctions and similarities across websites of newspapers, radio stations, and television stations. *Journalism & Mass Communication Quarterly, 78,* 555–573.

Lincoln, A., & Levinger, G. (1972). Observers' evaluations of the victim and the attacker in an aggressive incident. *Journal of Personality and Social Psychology, 22,* 202–210.

Lind, R. A., & Rockler, N. (2001). Competing ethos: Reliance on profit versus social responsibility by laypeople planning a television newscast. *Journal of Broadcasting & Electronic Media, 45,* 118–134.

Lind, R. A., & Salo, C. (2002). The framing of feminists and feminism in news and public affairs programs in US electronic media. *Journal of Communication, 52,* 211–228.

Lipari, L. (1999). Polling as ritual. *Journal of Communication, 49,* 83–102.

Lippmann, W. (1922). *Public opinion.* New York: Macmillan.

Lipschultz, J. H., & Hilt, M. L. (2002). *Crime and local television news: Dramatic, breaking, and live from the scene.* Mahwah, NJ: Lawrence Erlbaum.

Litman, B. R. (1998). The economics of television networks: New dimensions and new alliances. In A. Alexander, J. Owers, & R. Carveth (Eds.), *Media economics: Theory and practice* (2nd ed., pp. 131–149). Mahwah, NJ: Lawrence Erlbaum.

Littlejohn, S. W. (1999). *Theories of human communication* (6th ed.). Belmont, CA: Wadsworth.

Livingstone, S. M. (1993). The rise and fall of audience research: An old story with a new ending. *Journal of Communication, 43,* 5–12.

Lo, V.-H., & Wei, R. (2002). Third-person effect, gender, and pornography on the Internet. *Journal of Broadcasting & Electronic Media, 46,* 13–33.

Lombard, M., & Ditton, R. (1997). At the heart of it all: The concept of presence. *Journal of Computer Mediated Communication, 3*(2). Retrieved March 23, 2007, from http://jcmc.indiana.edu/v013/issue2/lombard.html

Lombard, M., Reich, R. D., Grabe, M. E., Bracken, C. C., & Ditton, T. B. (2000). Presence and television: The role of screen size. *Human Communication Research, 26,* 75–98.

Lovaas, O. I. (1961). Effect of exposure to symbolic aggression on aggressive behavior. *Child Development, 32,* 37–44.

Lowery, S. A., & DeFleur, M. L. (1988). *Milestones in mass communication research* (2nd ed.). White Plains, NY: Longman.

Lucas, C. J., & Schmitz, C. D. (1988). Communication media and current events knowledge among college students. *Higher Education Amsterdam, 17*(2), 139–149.

Lucas, K., & Sherry, J. L. (2004). Sex differences in video game play: A communication-based explanation. *Communication Research, 31,* 499–523.

Maccoby, E. E. (1954). Why do children watch TV? *Public Opinion Quarterly, 18,* 239–244.

Maccoby, E. E. (1964). Effects of the mass media. In M. L. Hoffman & L. W. Hoffman (Eds.), *Review of child development research* (pp. 323–348). New York: Russell Sage Foundation.

Maier, S. R. (2003). Numeracy in the newsroom: A case study of mathematical competence and confidence. *Journalism & Mass Communication Quarterly, 80,* 921–936.

Malamuth, N. M., Linz, D., Heavey, C. L., Barnes, G., & Acker, M. (1995). Using the confluence model of sexual aggression to predict men's conflict with women: A 10-year follow-up study. *Journal of Personality and Social Psychology, 69,* 353–369.

Malamuth, N. M., Sockloskie, R. J., Koss, M. P., & Tanaka, J. S. (1991). Characteristics of aggressors against women: Testing a model using a national sample of college students. *Journal of Consulting and Clinical Psychology, 59,* 670–681.

Mander, J. (1978). *Four arguments for the elimination of television.* New York: Morrow.

Mansfield, E. (1970). *Microeconomics: Theory and applications* (2nd ed.). New York: Norton.

Marcuse, H. (1964). *One-dimensional man.* Boston: Beacon.

Mares, M.-L., & Cantor, J. (1992). Elderly viewers' responses to televised portrayals of old age: Empathy and mood management versus social comparison. *Communication Research, 19,* 459–478.

Marrow, A. J. (1969). *The practical theorist: The life and work of Kurt Lewin.* New York: Basic Books.

Marsh, K. L., & Wallace, H. M. (2005). The influence of attitudes on beliefs: Formation and change. In D. Albarracin, B. T. Johnson, & M. P. Zanna (Eds.), *The handbook of attitudes* (pp. 369–395). Mahwah, NJ: Lawrence Erlbaum.

Mason, A., & Meyers, M. (2001). Living with Martha Stewart media: Chosen domesticity in the experience of fans. *Journal of Communication, 51,* 801–823.

Mastin, T. (2000). Media use and civic participation in the African-American population: Exploring participation among professionals and nonprofessionals. *Journalism & Mass Communication Quarterly, 77,* 115–127.

Mattelart, A. (2003). *The information society: An introduction* (S. G. Taponier & J. A. Cohen, Trans.). Thousand Oaks, CA: Sage.

McAllister, M. P. (2002). Television news plugola and the last episode of *Seinfeld. Journal of Communication, 52,* 383–401.

McClure, R. D., & Patterson, T. E. (1974). Television news and political advertising: The impact of exposure on voter beliefs. *Communication Research, 1,* 3–31.

McCombs, M. E., & Shaw, D. L. (1972). The agenda setting function of the press. *Public Opinion Quarterly, 36,* 176–187.

McCombs, M. E., & Shaw, D. L. (1993). The evolution of agenda setting theory: 25 years in the marketplace of ideas. *Journal of Communication, 43*(2), 58–66.

McDevitt, M. (2003). In defense of autonomy: A critique of the public journalism critique. *Journal of Communication, 53,* 155–164.

McDonald, D. G. (2004). Twentieth century media effect research. In J. D. H. Downing, D. McQuail, P. Schlesinger, & E. Wartella (Eds.), *The Sage handbook of media studies* (pp. 183–200). Thousand Oaks, CA: Sage.

McGarrigle, J., & Donaldson, M. (1975). Conservation accidents. *Cognition, 3,* 341–350.

McGuire, W. J. (1986). The myth of massive media impact: Savaging and salvagings. In G. Comstock (Ed.), *Public communication and behavior* (Vol. 1, pp. 173–257). Orlando, FL: Academic Press.

McGuire, W. J. (1990). Dynamic operations of thought systems. *American Psychologist, 45,* 504–512.

McIntosh, W. D., Schwegler, A. F., & Terry-Murray, R. M. (2000). Threat and television viewing in the United States, 1960–1990. *Media Psychology, 2,* 35–46.

McKenzie, C. R. M. (2005). Judgment and decision making. In K. Lamberts & R. L. Goldstone (Eds.), *Handbook of cognition* (pp. 321–338). Thousand Oaks, CA: Sage.

McKenzie, C. R. M., & Mikkelsen, L. A. (2000). The psychological side of Hempel's paradox of confirmation. *Psychonomic Bulletin and Review, 7,* 360–366.

McLeod, D. M., Detenber, B. H., & Eveland, W. P., Jr. (2001). Behind the third-person effect: Differentiating perceptual processes for self and others. *Journal of Communication, 51,* 678–695.

McLeod, J. M., & Becker, L. B. (1974). Testing the validity of gratification measures through political effects analysis. In J. G. Blumler & E. Katz (Eds.), *The uses of mass communications: Current perspectives on gratifications research* (pp. 137–164). Beverly Hills, CA: Sage.

McLeod, J. M., & Becker, L. B. (1981). The uses and gratifications approach. In D. D. Nimmo & K. R. Sanders (Eds.), *Handbook of political communication* (pp. 67–99). Beverly Hills, CA: Sage.

McLeod, J. M., & Reeves, B. (1980). On the nature of media effects. In S. B. Withey & R. P. Abeles (Eds.), *Television and social behavior: Beyond violence and children* (pp. 17–54). Hillsdale, NJ: Lawrence Erlbaum.

McLeod, J. M., Sotirovic, M., Voakes, P. S., Guo, Z., & Huang, K. Y. (1998). A model of public support for First Amendment rights. *Communication Law and Policy, 3,* 479–514.

McLeod, J. M., Ward, L. S., & Tancill, K. (1965). Alienation and uses of mass media. *Public Opinion Quarterly, 29,* 583–594.

McLuhan, M. (1962). *The Gutenberg galaxy: The making of typographic man.* Toronto: University of Toronto Press.

McLuhan, M. (1964). *Understanding media: The extensions of man.* New York: New American Library.

McManus, J. H. (1994). *Market-driven journalism: Let the citizen beware?* Thousand Oaks, CA: Sage.

McPhee, W. N. (1963). *Formal theories of mass behavior.* New York: Free Press.

McQuail, D. (1987). *Mass communication theory: An introduction.* London: Sage.

McQuail, D. (1989). Communication research: Past, present and future. In M. Ferguson (Ed.), *Public communication: The new imperatives* (pp. 135–151). London: Sage.

McQuail, D. (2000). *McQuail's mass communication theory* (4th ed.). London: Sage.

McQuail, D. (2005). *McQuail's mass communication theory* (5th ed.). London: Sage.

McQuail, D., Blumler, J. D., & Brown, J. R. (1972). The television audience: A revised perspective. In D. McQuail (Ed.), *Sociology of mass communications* (pp. 135–165). Harmondsworth, UK: Penguin.

McQuail, D., & Windahl, S. (1981). *Communication models for the study of mass communications.* London: Longman.

McQuail, D., & Windahl, S. (1993). *Communication models* (2nd ed.). London: Longman.

Mead, G. H. (1934). *Mind, self and society.* Chicago: University of Chicago Press.

Mehta, A., & Davis, C. M. (1990, August). *Celebrity advertising: Perception, persuasion and processing.* Paper presented to the Association for Education in Journalism and Mass Communication, Minneapolis, MN.

Meirick, P. C. (2004). Topic-relevant reference groups and dimension of distance: Political advertising and first- and third-person effects. *Communication Research, 31,* 234–255.

Meltzoff, A. N. (1988). Imitation of televised models by infants. *Child Development, 59,* 1221–1229.

Mendelsohn, H. (1966). *Mass entertainment.* New Haven, CT: College & University Press.

Mendelson, A. L., & Thorson, E. (2004). How verbalizers process the newspaper environment. *Journal of Communication, 54,* 474–491.

Merton, R. K. (1949). *Social theory and social structure.* Glencoe, IL: Free Press.

Merton, R. K. (1967). *On theoretical sociology.* New York: Free Press.

Metallinos, N. (1996). *Television aesthetics: Perceptual, cognitive, and compositional bases.* Mahwah, NJ: Lawrence Erlbaum.

Metzger, M. J. (2000). When no news is good news: Inferring closure for news issues. *Journalism & Mass Communication Quarterly, 77,* 760–787.

Meyrowitz, J. (1985). *No sense of place: The impact of electronic media on social behavior.* New York: Oxford University Press.

Meyrowitz, J. (1994). Medium theory. In D. Crowley & D. Mitchell (Eds.), *Communication theory today* (pp. 50–77). Stanford, CA: Stanford University Press.

Mill, J. S. (1843). *A system of logic, ratiocinative and inductive.* London: J. W. Parker.

Miller, G. A., Galanter, E., & Pribram, K. H. (1960). *Plans and the structure of behavior.* New York: Holt, Rinehart & Winston.

Miller, N. E., & Dollard, J. (1941). *Social learning and imitation.* New Haven, CT: Yale University Press.

Mills, C. W. (1957). *The power elite.* New York: Oxford University Press.

Mills, C. W. (1959). *The sociological imagination.* New York: Oxford University Press.

Minsky, M. A. (1975). Framework for representing knowledge. In P. H. Winston (Ed.), *The psychology of computer vision.* New York: McGraw-Hill.

Moore, C., & Fry, D. (1986). The effect of the experimenter's intention on the child's understanding of conservation. *Cognition, 22,* 283–298.

Morgan, S. E. (2003). Associations between message features and subjective evaluations of the sensation value of antidrug public service announcements. *Journal of Communication, 53,* 512–526.

Morley, D. (1980). *The nationwide audience.* London: British Film Institute.

Morley, D. (1992). *Television, audiences and cultural studies.* London: Routledge.

Motion Picture Association of America. (n.d.). *Anti-piracy.* Retrieved June 15, 2005, from http://www.mpaa.org/anti%2Dpiracy/

Moy, P., Domke, D., & Stamm, K. (2001). The spiral of silence and public opinion on affirmative action. *Journalism & Mass Communication Quarterly, 78,* 7–25.

Moy, P., & Scheufele, D. A. (2000). Media effects on political and social trust. *Journalism & Mass Communication Quarterly, 77,* 744–759.

Mueller, C., & Donnerstein, E. (1977). The effects of humor-induced arousal upon aggressive behavior. *Journal of Research in Personality, 11,* 73–82.

Mullin, C. R., & Linz, D. (1995). Desensitization and resensitization to violence against women: Effects of exposure to sexually violent films on judgments of domestic violence victims. *Journal of Personality and Social Psychology, 69,* 449–459.

Munsterberg, H. (1916). *The photoplay: A psychological study.* New York: Appleton & Company.

Murphy, S. T., & Zajonc, R. B. (1993). Affect, cognition, and awareness: Affective priming with optimal and suboptimal stimulus exposures. *Journal of Personality and Social Psychology, 64,* 723–739.

Nabi, R. (1999). A cognitive-functional model for the effects of discrete negative emotions on information processing, attitude change, and recall. *Communication Theory, 9,* 292–320.

Nabi, R. (2003). "Feeling" resistance: Exploring the role of emotionally evocative visuals in inducing inoculation. *Media Psychology, 5,* 199–223.

Nabi, R., Biely, E. N., Morgan, S. J., & Stitt, C. R. (2003). Reality-based television programming and the psychology of its appeal. *Media Psychology, 5,* 303–330.

Nabi, R., & Hendriks, A. (2003). The persuasive effect of host and audience reaction shots in television talk shows. *Journal of Communication, 53,* 527–543.

Nabi, R., & Krcmar, M. (2004). Conceptualizing media enjoyment as attitude: Implications for mass media effects research. *Communication Theory, 14,* 288–310.

Nabi, R., & Sullivan, J. L. (2001). Does television viewing relate to engagement in protective action against crime? A cultivation analysis from a theory of reasoned action perspective. *Communication Research, 28,* 802–825.

Naples, M. J. (1981). *Effective frequency: The relationship between frequency and advertising effectiveness.* New York: Association of National Advertisers.

Napoli, P. M. (2003). *Audience economics: Media institutions and the audience marketplace.* New York: Columbia University Press.

Natarajan, K., & Hao, X. (2003). An Asian voice? A comparative study of Channel News Asia and CNN. *Journal of Communication, 53,* 300–314.

National Television Violence Study (Vol. 1). (1997). Thousand Oaks, CA: Sage.

Neath, I., & Surprenant, A. M. (2005). Mechanisms of memory. In K. Lamberts & R. L. Goldstone (Eds.), *Handbook of cognition* (pp. 221–238). London: Sage.

Negroponte, N. (1995). *Being digital.* New York: Knopf.

Neuendorf, K. A. (2001). *Content analysis guidebook.* Thousand Oaks, CA: Sage.

Neuman, W. R. (1991). *The future of the mass audience.* New York: Cambridge University Press.

Newcomb, H. (1984). On the dialogic aspects of mass communication. *Critical Studies in Mass Communication, 1,* 34–50.

Newcomb, H., & Alley, R. S. (1982). The producer as artist: Commercial television. In J. S. Ettema & D. Charles Whitney (Eds.), *Individuals in mass media organizations: Creativity and constraint* (pp. 69–89). Beverly Hills, CA: Sage.

Newcomb, H., & Hirsch, P. M. (1984). *Television as a cultural forum: Implications for research.* In W. Rowland & B. Watkins (Eds.), *Interpreting television* (pp. 58–73). Beverly Hills, CA: Sage.

Newcomb, T. (1953). An approach to the study of communicative acts. *Psychological Review, 60,* 393–404.

Newhagen, J. E. (1994). Self efficacy and call-in political television show use. *Communication Research, 21,* 366–379.

Newhagen, J. E. (1998). TV news images that induce anger, fear, and disgust: Effects on approach-avoidance and memory. *Journal of Broadcasting & Electronic Media, 42,* 265–276.

Newstead, S. E., & Evans, J. St B. T. (1993). Mental models as an explanation of belief bias effects in syllogistic reasoning. *Cognition, 46,* 93–97.

Niedenthal, P. M. (1990). Implicit perception of affective information. *Journal of Experimental Social Psychology, 26,* 505–527.

Nisbet, M. C., Scheufele, D. A., Shanahan, J., Moy, P., Brossard, D., & Lewenstein, B. V. (2002). Knowledge, reservations, or promise? A media effects model for public perceptions of science and technology. *Communication Research, 29,* 584–608.

Noelle-Neumann, E. (1974). The spiral of silence: A theory of public opinion. *Journal of Communication, 24,* 24–51.

Noelle-Neumann, E. (1984). *The spiral of silence: Public opinion—our social skin.* Chicago: University of Chicago Press.

Noelle-Neumann, E. (1991). The theory of public opinion: The concept of spiral of silence. In J. Anderson (Ed.), *Communication yearbook* (Vol. 14, pp. 256–287). Newbury Park, CA: Sage.

Nohria, N. (1992). Is a network perspective a useful way of studying organizations? In N. Nohria & R. G. Eccles (Eds.), *Networks and organizations: Structure, form, and action* (pp. 1–22). Boston: Harvard Business School Press.

Norman, D. A. (1976). *Memory and attention: An introduction to human information processing.* New York: John Wiley.

Oaksford, M., & Chater, N. (1991). Against logicist cognitive science. *Mind and Language, 6,* 1–38.

Oaksford, M., & Chater, N. (1998). *Rationality in an uncertain world.* Hove, UK: Psychology Press.

Ogles, R. M., & Hoffner, C. (1987). Film violence and perceptions of crime: The cultivation effect. In M. L. McLaughlin (Ed.), *Communication yearbook* (Vol. 10, pp. 384–394). Thousand Oaks, CA: Sage.

Oliver, M. B. (1999). Caucasian viewers' memory of Black and White criminal suspects in the news. *Journal of Communication, 49,* 46–60.

Oliver, M. B., & Fonash, D. (2002). Race and crime in the news: Whites' identification and misidentification of violent and nonviolent criminal suspects. *Media Psychology, 4,* 137–156.

Oliver, M. B., Jackson, R. L., II, Moses, N. N., & Dangerfield, C. L. (2004). The face of crime: Viewers' memory of race-related facial features of individuals pictured in the news. *Journal of Communication, 54,* 88–104.

Oliver, M. B., & Kalyanaraman, S. (2002). Appropriate for all viewing audiences? An examination of violent and sexual portrayals in movie previews featured on video rentals. *Journal of Broadcasting & Electronic Media, 46,* 283–299.

Oliver, M. B., Weaver, J. B., III, & Sargent, S. L. (2000). An examination of factors related to sex differences in enjoyment of sad films. *Journal of Broadcasting & Electronic Media, 44,* 282–300.

Olson, J. M., & Stone, J. (2005). The influence of behavior on attitudes. In D. Albarracin, B. T. Johnson, & M. P. Zanna (Eds.), *The handbook of attitudes* (pp. 223–271). Mahwah, NJ: Lawrence Erlbaum.

Olson, S. R. (1999). *Hollywood planet: Global media and the competitive advantage of narrative transparency.* Mahwah, NJ: Lawrence Erlbaum.

Osgood, C. E., Suci, G. J., & Tannenbaum, P. H. (1957). *The measurement of meaning.* Urbana: University of Illinois Press.

Owen, B. M., & Wildman, S. W. (1992). *Video economics.* Cambridge, MA: Harvard University Press.

Owers, J., Carveth, R., & Alexander, A. (1998). An introduction to media economics theory and practice. In A. Alexander, J. Owers, & R. Carveth (Eds.), *Media economics: Theory and practice* (2nd ed., pp. 1–43). Mahwah, NJ: Lawrence Erlbaum.

Ozanich, G. W., & Writh, M. O. (1998). Mergers and acquisitions: A communications industry overview. In A. Alexander, J. Owers, & R. Carveth (Eds.), *Media economics: Theory and practice* (2nd ed., pp. 95–107). Mahwah, NJ: Lawrence Erlbaum.

Packard, V. (1957). *The hidden persuaders.* Philadelphia: David McKay Company.

Padioleau, J. (1985). *Le Monde et le Washington Post.* Paris: PUF.

Paik, H., & Comstock, G. (1994). The effects of television violence on antisocial behavior: A meta-analysis. *Communication Research, 21,* 516–546.

Paivio, A. (1986). *Mental representations: A dual-coding approach.* New York: Oxford University Press.

Palmgreen, P., & Rayburn, J. D. (1985). An expectancy-value approach to media gratifications. In K. E. Rosengren (Ed.), *Media gratification research* (pp. 61–72). Beverly Hills, CA: Sage.

Papacharissi, Z., & Rubin, A. M. (2000). Predictors of Internet use. *Journal of Broadcasting & Electronic Media, 44,* 175–196.

Parameswaran, R. (2002). Reading fictions of romance: Gender, sexuality, and nationalism in postcolonial India. *Journal of Communication, 52,* 832–851.

Parenti, M. (1986). *Inventing reality: The politics of the mass media.* New York: St. Martin's.

Park, C. W., & Young, S. M. (1986). Consumer response to television commercials: The impact of involvement and background music on brand attitude formation. *Journal of Marketing Research, 23,* 11–24.

Parkin, F. (1972). *Class, inequality and political order.* London: Paladin.

Pashler, H. (1998). *The psychology of attention.* Cambridge: MIT Press.

Pauly, J. J., & Eckert, M. (2002). The myth of "the local" in American journalism. *Journalism & Mass Communication Quarterly, 79,* 310–326.

Payne, D. G., Klin, C. M., Lampinen, J. M., Neuschatz, J. S., & Lindsay, D. S. (1999). Memory applied. In F. T. Durso, R. S. Nickerson, R. W. Schvaneveldt, S. T. Dumais, D. S. Lindsay, & M. T. H. Chi (Eds.), *Handbook of applied cognition* (pp. 83–113). New York: John Wiley.

Peiser, W., & Peter, J. (2000). Third-person perception of television-viewing behavior. *Journal of Communication, 50,* 25–45.

Peiser, W., & Peter, J. (2001). Explaining individual differences in third-person perception: A limits/possibilities perspective. *Communication Research, 28,* 156–180.

Pekurny, R. (1982). Coping with television production. In J. S. Ettema & D. C. Whitney (Eds.), *Individuals in mass media organizations: Creativity and constraint* (pp. 131–143). Beverly Hills, CA: Sage.

Perloff, R. M. (2002). The third-person effect. In J. Bryant & D. Zillmann (Eds.), *Media effects: Advances in theory and research* (2nd ed., pp. 489–506). Mahwah, NJ: Lawrence Erlbaum.

Perry, D. K. (1990). News reading, knowledge about, and attitudes toward foreign countries. *Journalism Quarterly, 67,* 353–358.

Perse, E. M. (1994). Uses of erotica. *Communication Research, 20,* 488–515.

Perse, E. M. (2001). *Media effects and society.* Mahwah, NJ: Lawrence Erlbaum.

Peters, A. K., & Cantor, M. G. (1982). Screen acting as work. In J. S. Ettema & D. C. Whitney (Eds.), *Individuals in mass media organizations: Creativity and constraint* (pp. 53–68). Beverly Hills, CA: Sage.

Peterson, C. R., & Beach, L. R. (1967). Man as an intuitive statistician. *Psychological Bulletin, 68,* 29–46.

Petty, R. E., & Cacioppo, J. T. (1981). *Attitudes and persuasion: Classic and contemporary approaches.* Dubuque, IA: W. C. Brown.

Petty, R. E., & Cacioppo, J. T. (1986). *Communication and persuasion: Central and peripheral routes to attitude change.* New York: Springer-Verlag.

Petty, R. E., & Wegener, D. T. (1998). Attitude change: Multiple roles for persuasion variables. In D. Gilbert, S. Fiske, & G. Lindzey (Eds.), *Handbook of social psychology* (pp. 323–390). New York: McGraw-Hill.

Pfau, M., Compton, J., Parker, K. A., Wittenberg, E. M., An, C., Ferguson, M., et al. (2004). The traditional explanation for resistance versus attitude accessibility: Do they trigger distinct or overlapping processes of resistance? *Human Communication Research, 30,* 329–360.

Pfau, M., Holbert, R. L., Zubric, S. J., Pasha, N. H., & Lin, W.-K. (2000). Role and influence of communication modality in the process of resistance to persuasion. *Media Psychology, 2,* 1–33.

Pfau, M., Szabo, A., Anderson, J., Morrill, J., Zubric, J., & Wan, H.-H. (2001). The role and impact of affect in the process of resistance to persuasion. *Human Communication Research, 27,* 216–252.

Phillips, L. D. (1983). A theoretical perspective on heuristics and biases in probabilistic thinking. In P. C. Humphreys, O. Svenson, & A. Vari (Eds.), *Analyzing and aiding decision processes* (pp. 525–543). Amsterdam: North Holland.

Piaget, J., & Inhelder, B. (1969). *The psychology of the child.* New York: Basic Books.

Picard, R. G. (1989). *Media economics: Concepts and issues.* Newbury Park, CA: Sage.

Picard, R. G. (1998). The economics of the daily newspaper industry. In A. Alexander, J. Owers, & R. Carveth (Eds.), *Media economics: Theory and practice* (2nd ed., pp. 111–129). Mahwah, NJ: Lawrence Erlbaum.

Picard, R., & Brody, J. H. (2000). The structure of the newspaper industry. In A. N. Greco (Ed.), *The media and entertainment industries: Readings in mass communications* (pp. 46–75). Boston: Allyn & Bacon.

Pietila, V. (1994). Perspectives on our past: Charting the histories of mass communication studies. *Critical Studies in Mass Communication, 11,* 346–361.

Pifer, L. K. (1991, November). *Scientific literacy and political participation.* Paper presented at the annual conference of the Midwest Association of Public Opinion Research, Chicago.

Plack, C. J. (2005). Auditory perception. In K. Lamberts & R. L. Goldstone (Eds.), *Handbook of cognition* (pp. 71–104). London: Sage.

Plaisance, P. L., & Skewes, E. A. (2003). Personal and professional dimensions of news work: Exploring the link between journalists' values and roles. *Journalism & Mass Communication Quarterly, 80,* 833–848.

Poindexter, P. M., & McCombs, M. E. (2001). Revisiting the civic duty to keep informed in the new media environment. *Journalism & Mass Communication Quarterly, 78,* 113–126.

Poindexter, P. M., Smith, L., & Heider, D. (2003). Race and ethnicity in local television news: Framing, story assignments, and source selections. *Journal of Broadcasting & Electronic Media, 47,* 524–536.

Pomerantz, J. R., & Lockhead, G. R. (1991). Perception of structure: An overview. In G. R. Lockhead & J. R. Pomerantz (Eds.), *The perception of structure* (pp. 1–20). Washington, DC: American Psychological Association.

Pool, M. M., Koolstra, C. M., & van der Voort, T. H. A. (2003). The impact of background radio and television on high school students' homework performance. *Journal of Communication, 53,* 74–87.

Porter, M. M. (1980). *Competitive strategy: Techniques for analyzing industries and competitors.* New York: Free Press.

Porter, M. M. (1985). *Competitive advantage.* New York: Free Press.

Posner, M. I. (1982). Cumulative development of attentional theory. *American Psychologist, 37,* 168–179.

Postman, N. (1985). *Amusing ourselves to death.* New York: Penguin.

Potter, R. F. (2000). The effects of voice changes on orienting and immediate cognitive overload in radio listeners. *Media Psychology, 2,* 147–177.

Potter, W. J. (1991). Examining cultivation from a psychological perspective: Component subprocesses. *Communication Research, 18,* 77–102.

Potter, W. J. (1996). *An analysis of thinking and research about qualitative methods.* Mahwah, NJ: Lawrence Erlbaum.

Potter, W. J. (1997). The problem of indexing risk of viewing television aggression. *Critical Studies in Mass Communication, 14,* 228–248.

Potter, W. J. (1999). *On media violence.* Thousand Oaks, CA: Sage.

Potter, W. J. (2003). *The 11 myths of media violence.* Thousand Oaks, CA: Sage.

Potter, W. J. (2004). *Theory of media literacy: A cognitive approach.* Thousand Oaks, CA: Sage.

Potter, W. J. (2005). *Media literacy* (3rd ed.). Thousand Oaks, CA: Sage.

Potter, W. J., & Chang, I. K. (1990). Television exposure measures and the cultivation hypothesis. *Journal of Broadcasting & Electronic Media, 34,* 313–333.

Potter, W. J., Cooper, R., & Dupagne, M. (1993). The three paradigms of mass media research in mainstream journals. *Communication Theory, 3,* 317–335.

Potter, W. J., Cooper, R., & Dupagne, M. (1995). Is media research prescientific? Reply to Sparks's critique. *Communication Theory, 5,* 280–286.

Potter, W. J., Pashupati, K., Pekurny, R. B., Hoffman, E., & Davis, K. (2002). Perceptions of television: A schema explanation. *Media Psychology, 4,* 27–50.

Potter, W. J., & Riddle, K. (2006, November). *A content analysis of the mass media effects literature.* Paper presented at the annual convention of the National Communication Association, San Antonio.

Potter, W. J., & Riddle, K. (2007). Profile of mass media effects research in scholarly journals. *Journalism & Mass of Communication Quarterly, 84,* 90–104.

Potter, W. J., & Smith, S. (2000). The context of graphic portrayals of television violence. *Journal of Broadcasting & Electronic Media, 44,* 301–323.

Potter, W. J., & Tomasello, T. K. (2003). Building upon the experimental design in media violence research: The importance of including receiver interpretations. *Journal of Communication, 53,* 315–329.

Potter, W. J., & Ware, W. (1987). An analysis of the contexts of antisocial acts on prime-time television. *Communication Research, 14,* 664–686.

Potter, W. J., & Ware, W. (1989). The frequency and context of prosocial acts on primetime television. *Journalism Quarterly, 66,* 359–366, 529.

Powdermaker, H. (1950). *Hollywood the dream factory.* Boston: Little, Brown.

Powell, W. W. (1982). From craft to corporation: The impact of outside ownership on book publishing. In J. S. Ettema & D. C. Whitney (Eds.), *Individuals in mass media organizations: Creativity and constraint* (pp. 33–52). Beverly Hills, CA: Sage.

Powell, W. W. (1990). Neither market nor hierarchy: Network forms of organization. *Research in Organizational Behavior, 12,* 295–336.

Power, P., Kubey, R., & Kiousis, S. (2002). Audience activity and passivity. In W. B. Gudykunst (Ed.), *Communication yearbook* (Vol. 26, pp. 116–159). Mahwah, NJ: Lawrence Erlbaum.

Prerost, G. J. (1987). Health locus of control, humor, and reduction in aggression. *Psychological Reports, 61,* 887–896.

Price, V., & Tewksbury, D. (1997). New values and public opinion: A theoretical account of media priming and framing. In G. A. Barnett & F. J. Boster (Eds.), *Progress in communication sciences: Advances in persuasion* (Vol. 13, pp. 173–212). Greenwich, CT: Ablex.

Propp, V. (1968). *Morphology of the folk tale* (2nd ed.). Austin, TX: University of Texas Press.

Protess, D. L., Cook, F. L., Doppelt, J. C., Errema, J. S., Gordon, M. T., Leff, D. R., et al. (1991). *The journalism of outrage: Investigating reporting and agenda building in America.* New York: Guilford.

Putnam, R. D. (2000). *Bowling alone: The collapse and revival of American community.* New York: Simon & Schuster.

Radway, J. (1984). *Reading the romance.* Chapel Hill: University of North Carolina Press.

Radway, J. (1987). *Reading the romance: Women, patriarchy and popular literature.* London: Verso.

Raney, A. A. (2002). Moral judgment as a predictor of enjoyment of crime drama. *Media Psychology, 4,* 305–322.

Raney, A. A. (2004). Expanding disposition theory: Reconsidering character liking, moral evaluations, and enjoyment. *Communication Theory, 14,* 348–369.

Raney, A. A., & Bryant, J. (2002). Moral judgment and crime drama: An integrated theory of enjoyment. *Journal of Communication, 52,* 402–415.

Reeves, B., & Borgman, C. L. (1983). A bibliometric evaluation of core journals in communication research. *Human Communication Research, 10,* 119–136.

Reeves, B., & Nass, C. (1996). *The media equation: How people treat computers, television, and new media like real people and places.* New York: Cambridge University Press.

Reisenzein, R. (2001). Appraisal processes conceptualized from a schema-theoretic perspective: Contributions to a process analysis of emotions. In K. R. Scherer & A. Schorr (Eds.), *Appraisal processes in emotion: Theory, methods, research* (pp. 187–201). Oxford, UK: Oxford University Press.

Ressmeyer, T. J., & Wallen, D. J. (1991, November). *Where do people go to learn about science? Informal science education in Europe and the United States.* Paper presented at the annual conference of the Midwest Association for Public Opinion Research, Chicago.

Rheingold, H. (1991). *Virtual reality.* New York: Summit.

Rice, R. E., & Atkin, C. (1989). *Public communication campaigns* (2nd ed.). Beverly Hills, CA: Sage.

Rice, R. E., Borgman, C. L., & Reeves, B. (1988). Citation networks of communication journals, 1977–1985: Cliques and positions, citations made and citations received. *Human Communication Research, 15,* 256–283.

Riffe, D., & Freitag, A. (1997). A content analysis of content analyses: Twenty-five years of *Journalism Quarterly. Journalism & Mass Communication Quarterly, 74,* 873–882.

Riffe, D., Lacy, S., & Fico, F. G. (1998). *Analyzing media messages: Using quantitative content analysis in research.* Mahwah, NJ: Lawrence Erlbaum.

Riley, J. W., & Riley, M. W. (1959). Mass communication and the social system. In R. K. Merton (Ed.), *Sociology today.* New York: Basic Books.

Rimal, R. N. (2001). Perceived risk and self-efficacy as motivators: Understanding individuals' long-term use of health information. *Journal of Communication, 51,* 633.

Rimal, R. N., & Real, K. (2003). Perceived risk and efficacy beliefs as motivators of change: Use of the risk perception attitude (RPA) framework to understand health behaviors. *Human Communication Research, 29,* 370–399.

Rios, D. I., & Gaines, S. O., Jr. (1998). Latino use for cultural maintenance. *Journalism & Mass Communication Quarterly, 75,* 746–761.

Rips, L. J., Shoben, E. J., & Smith, E. E. (1973). Semantic distance and the verification of semantic relations. *Journal of Verbal Learning and Verbal Behavior, 12,* 1–20.

Roberts, D. F., & Maccoby, N. (1985). Effects of mass communication. In G. Lindzey & E. Aronson (Eds.), *Handbook of social psychology* (Vol. 2, 3rd ed., pp. 539–599). New York: Random House.

Roberts, M., Wanta, W., & Dzwo, T.-H. (2002). Agenda setting and issue salience online. *Communication Research, 29,* 452–465.

Robinson, M. J. (1976). Public affairs television and the growth of political malaise: The case of "The selling of the Pentagon." *American Political Science Review, 70,* 409–432.

Robinson, P. (2001). Theorizing the influence of media on world politics. *European Journal of Communication, 16*(4), 523–544.

Rodgers, S., & Thorson, E. (2003). A socialization perspective on male and female reporting. *Journal of Communication, 53,* 658–675.

Rogers, E. M. (1962). *Diffusion of innovations.* New York: Free Press.

Rogers, E. M. (1986). *Communication technology.* New York: Free Press.

Rogers, E. M. (1994). *A history of communication study: A biographical approach.* New York: Free Press.

Rogers, E. M., & Shoemaker, F. (1971). *Communication of innovations: A cross-cultural approach.* New York: Free Press.

Romer, D., Jamieson, K. H., & Aday, S. (2003). Television news and the cultivation of fear of crime. *Journal of Communication, 53,* 88–104.

Rosch, E. H., & Lloyd, B. L. (1978). *Cognition and categorization.* Hillsdale, NJ: Lawrence Erlbaum.

Rosenberg, B., & Herald, D. T. (1991). *Genreflecting: A guide to reading interests in genre fiction* (3rd ed.). Englewood, CO: Libraries Unlimited.

Rosenberg, M. (1968). *The logic of survey analysis.* New York: Basic Books.

Rosenberg, M. J., & Hovland, C. I. (1960). Cognitive, affective, and behavioral components of attitudes. In M. J. Rosenberg, C. I. Hovland, W. J. McGuire, R. P. Abelson, & J. W. Brehm (Eds.), *Attitude organization and change: An analysis of consistency among attitude components* (pp. 1–16). New Haven, CT: Yale University Press.

Rosengren, K. E. (1974). Uses and gratifications: A paradigm outlined. In J. G. Blumler & E. Katz (Eds.), *The uses of mass communications: Current perspectives of gratifications research* (pp. 269–286). Beverly Hills, CA: Sage.

Rosengren, K. E., Wenner, L. A., & Palmgreen, P. (Eds.). (1985). *Media gratifications research: Current perspectives.* Beverly Hills, CA: Sage.

Rosengren, K. E., & Windahl, S. (1989). *Media matter.* Norwood, NJ: Ablex.

Roskos-Ewoldsen, D. R., Roskos-Ewoldsen, B., & Carpentier, F. R. D. (2002). Media priming: A synthesis. In J. Bryant & D. Zillmann (Eds.), *Media effects: Advances in theory and research* (2nd ed., pp. 97–120). Mahwah, NJ: Lawrence Erlbaum.

Rossler, P., & Brosius, H.-B. (2001). Do talk shows cultivate adolescents' views of the world? A prolonged-exposure experiment. *Journal of Communication, 51,* 143–163.

Rothenbuhler, E. W., & Streck, J. M. (1998). The economics of the music industry. In A. Alexander, J. Owers, & R. Carveth (Eds.), *Media economics: Theory and practice* (2nd ed., pp. 199–221). Mahwah, NJ: Lawrence Erlbaum.

Rouner, D. (1984). Active television viewing and the cultivation hypothesis. *Journalism Quarterly, 61,* 168–174.

Rubin, A. M. (1984). Ritualized and instrumental television viewing. *Journal of Communication, 34,* 67–77.

Rubin, A. M., Haridakis, P. M., & Eyal, K. (2003). Viewer aggression and attraction to television talk shows. *Media Psychology, 5,* 331–362.

Rubin, A. M., & Perse, E. M. (1987). Audience activity and television news gratifications. *Communication Research, 14,* 58–84.

Rubin, A. M., Perse, E. M., & Powell, E. (1990). Loneliness, parasocial interaction and local TV news viewing. *Communication Research, 14,* 246–268.

Rubin, A. M., & Step, M. M. (2000). Impact of motivation, attraction, and parasocial interaction on talk radio listening. *Journal of Broadcasting & Electronic Media, 44,* 635–654.

Rubin, A. M., & Windahl, S. (1986). The uses and dependency model of mass communication. *Critical Studies in Mass Communication, 3,* 184–199.

Rucinski, D. (2004). Community boundedness, personal relevance, and the knowledge gap. *Communication Research, 31,* 472–495.

Rumelhart, D. E. (1984). Schemata and the cognitive system. In R. S. Wyer & T. K. Srull (Eds.), *Handbook of social cognition* (Vol. 1, pp. 161–188). Hillsdale, NJ: Lawrence Erlbaum.

Ryan, J., & Peterson, R. A. (1982). The product image: The fate of creativity in country music songwriting. In J. S. Ettema & D. C. Whitney (Eds.), *Individuals in mass media organizations: Creativity and constraint* (pp. 11–32). Beverly Hills, CA: Sage.

Ryan, M., & Tankard, J. W., Jr. (1977). *Basic news reporting.* Palo Alto, CA: Mayfield.

Sallot, L. M. (2002). What the public thinks about public relations: An impression management experiment. *Journalism & Mass Communication Quarterly, 79,* 150–171.

Sallot, L. M., Steinfatt, T. M., & Salwen, M. B. (1998). Journalists' and public relations practitioners' news values: Perceptions and cross-perceptions. *Journalism & Mass Communication Quarterly, 75,* 366–377.

Salwen, M. B., & Dupagne, M. (2001). Third-person perception of television violence: The role of self-perceived knowledge. *Media Psychology, 3,* 211–230.

Salwen, M. B., & Dupagne, M. (2003). News of Y2K and experiencing Y2K: Exploring the relationship between the third-person effect and optimistic bias. *Media Psychology, 5,* 23–48.

Sampedro, V. (1998). Grounding the displaced: Local media reception in a transnational context. *Journal of Communication, 48*(2), 125–143.

Sander, I. (1995, May). *How violent is TV-violence? An empirical investigation of factors influencing viewers' perceptions of TV-violence.* Paper presented at the annual conference of the International Communication Association, Albuquerque, NM.

Sapolsky, B. S., & Zillmann, D. (1978). Experience and empathy: Affective reactions to witnessing childbirth. *Journal of Social Psychology, 105,* 131–144.

Scannell, P. (1996). *Radio, television and modern life.* Oxford, UK: Blackwell.

Schachter, S., & Singer, J. (1962). Cognitive, social, and physiological determinants of emotional state. *Psychological Review, 69,* 379–399.

Schacter, D. L., & Tulving, E. (1994). What are the memory systems of 1994? In D. L. Schacter & E. Tulving (Eds.), *Memory systems 1994* (pp. 1–38). Cambridge: MIT Press.

Schank, R. C., & Abelson, R. P. (1977). *Scripts, plans, goals and understanding.* Hillsdale, NJ: Lawrence Erlbaum.

Schank, R. C., & Abelson, R. P. (1995). Knowledge and memory: The real story. In R. S. Wyer Jr. (Ed.), *Advances in social cognition* (Vol. 8, pp. 1–85). Hillsdale, NJ: Lawrence Erlbaum.

Scharrer, E. (2001). Tough guys: The portrayal of hypermasculinity and aggression in television police dramas. *Journal of Broadcasting & Electronic Media, 45,* 615–634.

Scharrer, E. (2002). Third-person perception and television violence: The role of out-group stereotyping in perceptions of susceptibility to effects. *Communication Research, 29,* 681–704.

Scheufele, D. A. (1999). Framing as a theory of media effects. *Journal of Communication, 49,* 103–122.

Scheufele, D. A. (2002). Examining differential gains from mass media and their implications for participatory behavior. *Communication Research, 29,* 46–65.

Scheufele, D. A., Shanahan, J., & Kim, S.-H. (2002). Who cares about local politics? Media influences on local political involvement, issue awareness, and attitude strength. *Journalism & Mass Communication Quarterly, 79,* 427–444.

Scheufele, D. A., Shanahan, J., & Lee, E. (2001). Real talk: Manipulating the dependent variable in spiral of silence research. *Communication Research, 28,* 304–324.

Schiller, H. I. (1969). *Mass communication and American empire.* New York: Kelley.

Schimmack, U., & Crites, S. L., Jr. (2005). The structure of affect. In D. Albarracin, B. T. Johnson, & M. P. Zanna (Eds.), *The handbook of attitudes* (pp. 397–435). Mahwah, NJ: Lawrence Erlbaum.

Schmutte, G. T., & Taylor, S. P. (1980). Physical aggression as a function of alcohol and pain feedback. *Journal of Social Psychology, 110,* 235–244.

Schneider, E. F., Lang, A., Shin, M., & Bradley, S. D. (2004). Death with a story: How story impacts emotional, motivational, and physiological responses to first-person shooter video games. *Human Communication Research, 30,* 361–375.

Schneider, W., & Shiffrin, R. M. (1977). Controlled and automatic human information processing: I. Detection, research and attention. *Psychological Review, 84,* 1–66.

Schramm, W. (1954). *The processes and effects of mass communication.* Urbana: University of Illinois Press.

Schramm, W. (1973). Channels and audiences. In I. De Sola Pool, F. W. Frey, W. Schramm, N. Maccoby, & E. B. Parker (Eds.), *Handbook of communication* (pp. 116–140). Chicago: Rand McNally.

Schramm, W. (1997). The forefathers of communication study in America. In S. H. Chaffee & E. M. Rogers (Eds.), *The beginnings of communication study in America: A personal memoir* (pp. 3–121). Thousand Oaks, CA: Sage.

Schramm, W., Lyle, J., & Parker, E. B. (Eds.). (1961). *Television in the lives of our children.* Stanford, CA: Stanford University Press.

Schudson, M. (2003). *The sociology of news.* New York: Norton.

Schwartz, T. (1974). *The responsive cord.* New York: Anchor.

Scott, D. W. (2003). Mormon "family values" versus television: An analysis of the discourse of Mormon couples regarding television and popular media culture. *Critical Studies in Media Communication, 20,* 317–333.

Segrin, C., & Nabi, R. L. (2002). Does television viewing cultivate unrealistic expectations about marriage? *Journal of Communication, 52,* 247–263.

Semetko, H. A., & Valkenburg, P. M. (2000). Framing European politics: A content analysis of press and television news. *Journal of Communication, 50,* 93–109.

Severin, W. J., & Tankard, J. W., Jr. (2001). *Communication theories: Origins, methods, and uses in the mass media* (5th ed.). New York: Longman.

Shah, D. V., Kwak, N., Schmierbach, M., & Zubric, J. (2004). The interplay of news frames on cognitive complexity. *Human Communication Research, 30,* 102–120.

Shah, D. V., McLeod, J. M., & Yoon, S.-H. (2001). Communication, context, and community: An exploration of print, broadcast, and Internet influences. *Communication Research, 28,* 464–506.

Shank, R. C. (1982). *Dynamic memory: A theory of reminding and learning in computers and people.* Cambridge, UK: Cambridge University Press.

Shanks, D. R. (2005). Implicit learning. In K. Lamberts & R. L. Goldstone (Eds.), *Handbook of cognition* (pp. 202–220). London: Sage.

Shannon, C., & Weaver, W. (1949). *The mathematical theory of communication.* Urbana: University of Illinois Press.

Shapiro, M. A., & Fox, J. R. (2002). The role of typical and atypical events in story memory. *Human Communication Research, 28,* 109–135.

Shen, F. (2004). Chronic accessibility and individual cognitions: Examining the effects of message frames in political advertisements. *Journal of Communication, 54,* 123–137.

Shepard, R. N. (1987). Toward a universal law of generalization for psychological science. *Science, 237,* 1317–1323.

Sherif, M., & Hovland, C. I. (1961). *Social judgment: Assimilation and contrast effects in communication and attitude change.* New Haven, CT: Yale University Press.

Sherry, J. L. (2001). The effects of violent video games on aggression: A meta-analysis. *Human Communication Research, 27,* 409–431.

Sherry, J. L. (2004). Flow and media enjoyment. *Communication Theory, 14,* 328–347.

Shiffrin, R. M. (1988). Attention. In R. A. Atkinson, R. J. Hernstein, G. Lindzey, & R. D. Luce (Eds.), *Stevens' handbook of experimental psychology: Vol. 2. Learning and cognition* (pp. 739–811). New York: John Wiley.

Shiffrin, R. M., & Dumais, S. T. (1981). The development of automatism. In J. R. Anderson (Ed.), *Cognitive skills and their acquisition* (pp. 111–140). Hillsdale, NJ: Lawrence Erlbaum.

Shirley, K. W. (1973). *Television and children: A modeling analysis review essay.* Unpublished doctoral dissertation, University of Kansas.

Shoemaker, P. J., Eichholz, M., Kim, E., & Wrigley, B. (2001). Individual and routine forces in gatekeeping. *Journalism & Mass Communication Quarterly, 78,* 233–246.

Shoemaker, P. J., & Reese, S. D. (1990). Exposure to what? Integrating media content and effects studies. *Journalism Quarterly, 67,* 649–652.

Shoemaker, P. J., & Reese, S. D. (1996). *Mediating the message: Theories of influences on mass media content* (2nd ed.). White Plains, NY: Longman.

Shoemaker, P. J., Tankard, J. W., Jr., & Lasorsa, D. L. (2004). *How to build social science theories.* Thousand Oaks, CA: Sage.

Shotter, J., & Gergen, K. J. (1994). Social construction: Knowledge, self, others, and continuing the conversation. In S. Deetz (Ed.), *Communication yearbook* (Vol. 17, pp. 3–33). Thousand Oaks, CA: Sage.

Shrum, L. J. (2001). Processing strategy moderates the cultivation effect. *Human Communication Research, 27,* 94–120.

Shrum, L. J. (2002). Media consumption and perceptions of social reality: Effects and underlying processes. In J. Bryant & D. Zillmann (Eds.), *Media effects: Advances in theory and research* (2nd ed., pp. 69–95). Mahwah, NJ: Lawrence Erlbaum.

Shugart, H. A. (2003). Reinventing privilege: The new (gay) man in contemporary popular media. *Critical Studies in Media Communication, 20,* 67–91.

Shum, M. S., & Ripps, L. J. (1999). The respondent's confession: Autobiographical memory in the context of surveys. In M. G. Sirken, D. J. Herrmann, S. Schechter, N. Schwarz, J. M. Tanur, & R. Rourangeau (Eds.), *Cognition and survey research* (pp. 95–109). New York: John Wiley.

Sigal, L. V. (1973). *Reporters and officials: The organization and politics of newsmaking.* Lexington, MA: D. C. Heath.

Simon, H. A. (1957). *Administrative behavior* (2nd ed.). Totowa, NJ: Littlefield, Adams.

Simons, R. F., Detenber, B. H., Cuthbert, B. N., Schwartz, D. D., & Reiss, J. E. (2003). Attention to television: Alpha power and its relationship to image motion and emotional content. *Media Psychology, 5,* 283–301.

Singer, B. D. (1970). Mass media and communications processes in the Detroit riots of 1967. *Public Opinion Quarterly, 34,* 236–245.

Singer, E., & Endreny, P. (1987). Reporting hazards: The benefits and costs. *Journal of Communication, 37*(3), 10–26.

Skinner, B. F. (1953). *Science and human behavior.* New York: Free Press.

Skinner, B. F. (1974). *About behaviorism.* New York: Knopf.

Slater, M. (2003). Alienation, aggression, and sensation seeking as predictors of adolescent use of violent film, computer, and Website content. *Journal of Communication, 53,* 105–121.

Slater, M., & Rouner, D. (2002). Entertainment-education and elaboration likelihood: Understanding the processing of narrative persuasion. *Communication Theory, 12,* 173–191.

Slattery, K., Doremus, M., & Marcus, L. (2001). Shifts in public affairs reporting on the network evening news: A move toward the sensational. *Journal of Broadcasting & Electronic Media, 45,* 290–302.

Smiley, J. (2005). *Thirteen ways of looking at the novel.* New York: Knopf.

Smith, E. R. (1994). Procedural knowledge and processing strategies in social cognition. In R. S. Wyer & T. K. Srull (Eds.), *Handbook of social cognition* (2nd ed., Vol. 1, pp. 99–152). Hillsdale, NJ: Lawrence Erlbaum.

Smith, E. R. (1999). New connectionist models of mental representation: Implications for survey research. In M. G. Sirken, D. J. Herrmann, S. Schechter, N. Schwarz, J. M. Tanur, & R. Rourangeau (Eds.), *Cognition and survey research* (pp. 251–264). New York: John Wiley.

Smith, M. E., & Gevins, A. (2004). Attention and brain activity while watching television: Components of viewer engagement. *Media Psychology, 6,* 285–305.

Smith, R. E., & Swinyard, W. R. (1982). Information response models: An integrated approach. *Journal of Marketing, 46,* 81–93.

Smith, R. E., & Swinyard, W. R. (1988). Cognitive response to advertising and trial: Belief strength, belief confidence and product curiosity. *Journal of Advertising, 17*(3), 3–14.

Smith, S. L., & Wilson, B. J. (2002). Children's comprehension of and fear reactions to television news. *Media Psychology, 4,* 1–26.

Smythe, D. W. (1954). Reality as presented by television. *Public Opinion Quarterly, 18*(2), 143–156.

So, C., & Chan, J. (1991, August). *Evaluating and conceptualizing the field of mass communication: A survey of the core scholars.* Paper presented at the annual meeting of the AEJMC, Boston.

Soderlund, G. (2002). Covering urban vice: The *New York Times,* "White slavery," and the construction of journalistic knowledge. *Critical Studies in Media Communication, 19,* 438–460.

Solomon, D. S. (1989). A social marketing perspective on communication campaigns. In R. E. Rice & C. K. Atkin (Eds.), *Public communication campaigns* (2nd ed., pp. 87–104). Newbury Park, CA: Sage.

Soong, R. (1988). The statistical reliability of people meter ratings. *Journal of Advertising Research, 28,* 50–56.

Sopory, P., & Dillard, J. P. (2002). The persuasive effects of metaphor: A meta-analysis. *Human Communication Research, 28,* 382–419.

Sotirovic, M. (2001a). Effects of media use on complexity and extremity of attitudes toward the death penalty and prisoners' rehabilitation. *Media Psychology, 3,* 1–24.

Sotirovic, M. (2001b). Media use and perceptions of welfare. *Journal of Communication, 51,* 750–774.

Soukup, E. (2006, May 22). Trailers: Seen any good books lately? *Newsweek,* p. 9.

Sparks, G. G. (1995a). Is media research prescientific? Comments concerning the claim that mass media research is "prescientific": A response to Potter, Cooper, and Dupagne. *Communication Theory, 5,* 273–280.

Sparks, G. G. (1995b). Is media research prescientific? A final reply to Potter, Cooper, and Dupagne. *Communication Theory, 5,* 286–289.

Sparks, G. G. (2006). *Media effects research: A basic overview* (2nd ed.). Belmont, CA: Thomson Wadsworth.

Sparks, G. G., Pellechia, M., & Irvine, C. (1999). The repressive coping style and fright reactions to mass media. *Communication Research, 26,* 176–192.

Speisman, J. C., Lazarus, R. S., Mordkoff, A., & Davison, L. (1964). Experimental reduction of stress based on ego-defense theory. *Journal of Abnormal and Social Psychology, 68,* 367–380.

Spilerman, S. (1976). Structural characteristics and severity of racial disorders. *American Sociological Review, 41,* 771–792.

Sprafkin, J., Gadow, K. D., & Grayson, P. (1988). Effects of cartoons on emotionally disturbed children's social behavior in school settings. *Journal of Psychological Psychiatry, 29,* 91–99.

Srull, T. K., & Wyer, R. S., Jr. (1979). The role of category accessibility in the interpretation of information about persons: Some determinants and implications. *Journal of Personality and Social Psychology, 37,* 1660–1672.

Staller, K. M. (2003). Constructing the runaway youth problem: Boy adventures to girl prostitutes, 1960–1978. *Journal of Communication, 53,* 330–346.

Stein, A. H., & Friedrich, L. K. (1975). Television content and young children's behavior. In J. P. Murray, E. A. Rubinstein, & G. A. Comstock (Eds.), *Television and social behavior: Vol. 2. Television and social learning.* Washington, DC: Government Printing Office.

Steiner, P. O. (1952). Program patterns and preferences, and the workability of competition in radio broadcasting. *Quarterly Journal of Economics, 66,* 194–223.

Stempel, G. H., III. (1981). Content analysis. In G. H. Stempel III & B. H. Westley (Eds.), *Research methods in mass communication* (pp. 119–131). Englewood Cliffs, NJ: Prentice Hall.

Stephenson, M. T. (2003). Examining adolescents' responses to antimarijuana PSAs. *Human Communication Research, 29,* 343–369.

Stephenson, W. (1967). *Play theory of mass communication.* Chicago: University of Chicago Press.

Stevenson, R. L. (1992). Defining international communication as a field. *Journalism Quarterly, 69,* 543–553.

Stout, P. A., & Leckenby, J. D. (1986). Measuring emotional response to advertising. *Journal of Advertising, 15*(4), 35–42.

Suckfill, M. (2000). Film analysis and psychophysiology: Effects of moments of impact and protagonists. *Media Psychology, 2,* 269–301.

Sujan, M. (1985). Consumer knowledge: Effects on evaluation strategies mediating consumer judgments. *Journal of Consumer Research, 12*(1), 31–46.

Sundar, S. S., Narayan, S., Obregon, R., & Uppal, C. (1999). Does Web advertising work? Memory for print vs. online media. *Journalism & Mass Communication Quarterly, 75,* 822–835.

Sundar, S. S., & Nass, C. (2001). Conceptualizing sources in online news. *Journal of Communication, 51,* 52–72.

Sundar, S. S., & Wagner, C. B. (2002). The World Wide Wait: Exploring physiological and behavioral effects of download speed. *Media Psychology, 4,* 173–206.

Sutherland, M., & Galloway, J. (1981). Role of advertising: Persuasion or agenda setting? *Journal of Advertising Research, 21*(5), 215–229.

Tal-Or, N., Boninger, D. S., Poran, A., & Gleicher, F. (2004). Counterfactual thinking as a mechanism in narrative persuasion. *Human Communication Research, 30,* 301–328.

Tan, A. S. (1981). *Mass communication theories and research.* Columbus, OH: Grid Publishing.

Tannenbaum, P., & Gaer, E. P. (1965). Mood changes as a function of stress of protagonist and degree of identification in film-viewing situations. *Journal of Personality and Social Psychology, 2,* 612–616.

Tannenbaum, P., & Zillmann, D. (1975). Emotional arousal in the facilitation of aggression through communication. In L. Berkowitz (Ed.), *Advances in experimental social psychology* (Vol. 8, pp. 149–192). New York: Academic Press.

Taylor, S. E., & Crocker, J. (1981). Schematic bases of social information processing. In E. T. Higgins, C. P. Herman, & M. P. Zanna (Eds.), *Social cognition: The Ontario Symposium* (Vol. 1, pp. 89–134). Hillsdale, NJ: Lawrence Erlbaum.

Tewksbury, D. (2003). What do Americans really want to know? Tracking the behavior of news readers on the Internet. *Journal of Communication, 53,* 694–710.

Tewksbury, D., Jones, J., Peske, M. W., Raymond, A., & Vig, W. (2000). The interaction of news and advocacy frames: Manipulating audience perceptions of a local public policy issue. *Journalism & Mass Communication Quarterly, 77,* 804–829.

Tewksbury, D., Moy, P., & Weis, D. S. (2004). Preparations for Y2K: Revisiting the behavioral components of the third-person effect. *Journal of Communication, 54,* 138–155.

Thomas, M. H. (1982). Physiological arousal, exposure to a relatively lengthy aggressive film, and aggressive behavior. *Journal of Research in Personality, 16,* 72–81.

Thomas, M. H., Horton, R. W., Lippincott, E. C., & Drabman, R. S. (1977). Desensitization to portrayals of real-life aggression as a function of exposure to television violence. *Journal of Personality and Social Psychology, 35,* 450–458.

Thompson, C. J., Locander, W. B., & Pollio, H. R. (1989). Putting consumer experience back into consumer research: The philosophy and method of existential-phenomenology. *Journal of Consumer Research, 16*(2), 133–146.

Thompson, J. (1995). *The media and modernity: A social theory of the media.* Stanford, CA: Stanford University Press.

Thompson, J. (2000). *Political scandals.* Cambridge, UK: Polity.

Thomsen, S. R., McCoy, J. K., Gustafson, R. L., & Williams, M. (2002). Motivations for reading beauty and fashion magazines and anorexic risk in college-age women. *Media Psychology, 4,* 113–135.

Thurstone, L. L. (1928). Attitudes can be measured. *American Journal of Sociology, 33,* 529–544.

Tichenor, P., Donohue, G. A., & Olien, C. N. (1970). Mass media flow and differential growth of knowledge. *Public Opinion Quarterly, 34,* 159–170.

Todorov, T. (1975). *The fantastic: A structural approach to a literary genre* (R. Howard, Trans.). Ithaca, NY: Cornell University Press.

Todorov, T. (1977). *The poetics of prose.* Oxford, UK: Blackwell.

Traudt, P. J. (2005). *Media, audiences, effects.* Boston: Pearson.

Treisman, A. M. (1964). The effect of irrelevant material on the efficiency of selective listening. *American Journal of Psychology, 77,* 533–546.

Tsfati, Y. (2003). Does audience skepticism of the media mater in agenda setting? *Journal of Broadcasting & Electronic Media, 47,* 157–176.

Tuchman, G. (1978). *Making news: A study in the construction of reality.* New York: Free Press.

Tuggle, C. A., & Huffman, S. (2001). Live reporting in television news: Breaking news or black holes? *Journal of Broadcasting & Electronic Media, 45,* 335–344.

Tulving, E., & Pearlstone, Z. (1966). Availability versus accessibility of information in memory for words. *Journal of Verbal Learning and Verbal Behavior, 5,* 381–391.

Tumber, H., & Waisbord, S. (2004). Political scandals and media across democracies. *American Behavioral Scientist, 47,* 1031–1039.

Tunstall, J. (1977). *The media are American: Anglo-American media in the world.* New York: Columbia University Press.

Turner, V. (1977, Summer). Process, system, and symbol: A new anthropological synthesis. *Daedalus,* pp. 61–80.

Turow, J. (1982). Unconventional programs on commercial television: An organizational perspective. In J. S. Ettema & D. C. Whitney (Eds.), *Individuals in mass media organizations: Creativity and constraint* (pp. 107–129). Beverly Hills, CA: Sage.

Turow, J. (1984). *Media industries: The production of news and entertainment.* New York: Longman.

Turow, J. (1989). Television and institutional power: The case of medicine. In B. Dervin, L. Grossberg, B. J. O'Keefe, & E. Wartella (Eds.), *Rethinking communication* (Vol. 2, pp. 454–473). Newbury Park, CA: Sage.

Tversky, A. (1972). Elimination by aspects: A theory of choice. *Psychological Review, 79,* 281–299.

Tversky, A., & Kahneman, D. (1973). Availability: A heuristic for judging frequency and probability. *Cognitive Psychology, 4,* 207–232.

Tversky, A., & Kahneman, D. (1974). Judgment under uncertainty: Heuristics and biases. *Science, 185,* 1124–1131.

Uleman, J. S., Newman, L. S., & Moskowitz, G. B. (1996). People as spontaneous interpreters: Evidence and issues from spontaneous trait inference. In M. P. Zanna (Ed.), *Advances in experimental social psychology* (Vol. 28, pp. 211–279). San Diego: Academic Press.

Underwood, D., & Stamm, K. (2001). Are journalists really irreligious? A multidimensional analysis. *Journalism & Mass Communication Quarterly, 78,* 771–786.

Valentino, N. A., Buhr, T. A., & Beckmann, M. N. (2001). When the frame is the game: Revisiting the impact of "strategic" campaign coverage on citizens' information retention. *Journalism & Mass Communication Quarterly, 78,* 93–112.

Valentino, N. A., Hutchings, V. L., & Williams, D. (2004). The impact of political advertising on knowledge, Internet information seeking, and candidate preference. *Journal of Communication, 54,* 337–354.

Valkenburg, P. M., & Janssen, S. C. (1999). What do children value in entertainment programs? A cross-cultural investigation. *Journal of Communication, 49,* 3–21.

Valkenburg, P. M., & Soeters, K. E. (2001). Children's positive and negative experiences with the Internet: An exploratory survey. *Communication Research, 28,* 652–675.

Valkenburg, P. M., & Vroone, M. (2004). Developmental changes in infants' and toddlers' attention to television entertainment. *Communication Research, 31,* 288–311.

Van Belle, D. A. (2003). Bureaucratic responsiveness to news media: Comparing the influence of the NYT and network TV news coverage on US foreign and civil allocations. *Political Communication, 20*(3), 263–285.

van der Molen, J. H. W., & Klijn, M. E. (2004). Recall of television versus print news: Retesting the semantic overlap hypothesis. *Journal of Broadcasting & Electronic Media, 48,* 89–107.

van der Molen, J. H. W., & van der Voort, T. H. A. (2000). The impact of television, print, and audio on children's recall of the news: A study of three alternative explanations for the dual-coding hypothesis. *Human Communication Research, 26,* 3–26.

Van der Voort, T. H. A. (1986). *Television violence: A child's-eye view.* Amsterdam: North-Holland.

Vavrus, M. D. (2002). Domesticating patriarchy: Hegemonic masculinity and television's "Mr. Mom." *Critical Studies in Media Communication, 19,* 352–375.

Volosinov, V. (1986). *Marxism and the philosophy of language.* Cambridge, MA: Harvard University Press.

von Feilitzen, C. (1975). Findings of Scandinavian research on child and television in the process of socialization. *Fernsehen und Bildung, 9,* 54–84.

Vorderer, P., Klimmt, C., & Ritterfeld, U. (2004). Enjoyment: At the heart of media entertainment. *Communication Theory, 14,* 388–408.

Vorderer, P., & Knobloch, S. (2000). Conflict and suspense in drama. In D. Zillmann & P. Vorderer (Eds.), *Media entertainment: The psychology of its appeal* (pp. 59–72). Mahwah, NJ: Lawrence Erlbaum.

Vorderer, P., Knobloch, S., & Schramm, H. (2001). Does entertainment suffer from interactivity? The impact of watching an interactive TV movie on viewers' experience of entertainment. *Media Psychology, 3,* 343–363.

Wahl-Jorgensen, K. (2002). The normative-economic justification for public discourse: Letters to the editor as a "wide open" forum. *Journalism & Mass Communication Quarterly, 79,* 121–133.

Walker, J. R., & Eastman, S. T. (2003). On-air promotion effectiveness for programs of different genres, familiarity, and audience demographics. *Journal of Broadcasting & Electronic Media, 47,* 618–637.

Wasko, J. (2003). *How Hollywood works.* Thousand Oaks, CA: Sage.

Waterman, D. (1992). "Narrowcasting" and "broadcasting" on nonbroadcast media: A program choice model. *Communication Research, 19,* 3–28.

Waters, K. (2001). Vibrant, but invisible: A study of contemporary religious periodicals. *Journalism & Mass Communication Quarterly, 78,* 307–320.

Weaver, D., & Wilhoit, C. G. (1996). *The American journalist in the 1990s: US news people at the end of an era.* Mahwah, NJ: Lawrence Erlbaum.

Weaver, D. H. (1998). *The global journalist.* Creskill, NJ: Hampton Press.

Webster, J. G. (2005). Beneath the veneer of fragmentation: Television audience polarization in a multichannel world. *Journal of Communication, 55,* 366–382.

Webster, J. G., & Lin, S.-F. (2002). The Internet audience: Web use as mass behavior. *Journal of Broadcasting & Electronic Media, 46,* 1–12.

Webster, J. G., & Phalen, P. F. (1994). Victim, consumer, or commodity? Audience models in communication policy. In J. Ettema & D. C. Whitney (Eds.), *Audiencemaking: How media create the audience* (pp. 19–37). Thousand Oaks, CA: Sage.

Webster, J. G., & Phalen, P. F. (1997). *The mass audience: Rediscovering the dominant model.* Mahwah, NJ: Lawrence Erlbaum.

Webster, J. G., & Wakshlag, J. (1985). Measuring exposure to television. In D. Zillmann & J. Bryant (Eds.), *Selective exposure to communication* (pp. 35–62). Hillsdale, NJ: Lawrence Erlbaum.

Wegener, D. T., & Carlston, D. E. (2005). Cognitive processes in attitude formation and change. In D. Albarracin, B. T. Johnson, & M. P. Zanna (Eds.), *The handbook of attitudes* (pp. 493–542). Mahwah, NJ: Lawrence Erlbaum.

Weiss, W. (1969). Effects of the mass media of communication. In G. Lindzey & E. Aronson (Eds.), *Handbook of social psychology* (Vol. 2, 2nd ed., pp. 77–195). Reading, MA: Addison-Wesley.

Westley, B. H., & MacLean, M. (1957). A conceptual model for mass communication research. *Journalism Quarterly, 34,* 31–38.

Which actress made a movie that grossed over $200 million? (2007, July 9). *Newsweek,* pp. 72–73.

Whipple, T. W., & Courtney, A. E. (1980). How to portray women in TV commercials. *Journal of Advertising Research, 20*(2), 53–59.

White, D. M. (1950). The gatekeepers: A case study in the selection of news. *Journalism Quarterly, 27,* 383–390.

Whitehead, A. N. (1911). *An introduction to mathematics.* New York: Holt.

Whitney, D. C. (1982). Mass communicator studies: Similarity, difference, and level of analysis. In J. S. Ettema & D. C. Whitney (Eds.), *Individuals in mass media organizations: Creativity and constraint* (pp. 241–254). Beverly Hills, CA: Sage.

Wilcox, G. B., Murphy, J. H., & Sheldon, P. S. (1985). Effects of attractiveness of the endorser on the performance of testimonial ads. *Journalism Quarterly, 62,* 515–532.

Wildman, S. S. (2006). Paradigms and analytical frameworks in modern economics and media economics. In A. B. Albarran & S. M. Chan-Olmsted (Eds.), *Handbook of media management and economics* (pp. 67–90). Mahwah, NJ: Lawrence Erlbaum.

Wiley, N. (2000). Movies and the mind: A pragmatist approach. *Interdisciplinary Journal for Germanic Linguistics and Semiotic Analysis, 5,* 93–126.

Wilkins, K. G. (2000). The role of media in public disengagement from political life. *Journal of Broadcasting & Electronic Media, 44,* 569–580.

Williams, D. (2002). Synergy bias: Conglomerates and promotion in news. *Journal of Broadcasting & Electronic Media, 46,* 453–472.

Williams, R. (1974). *Television: Technology and cultural form.* New York: Schocken.

Williams, R. (1977). A lecture on realism. *Screen, 18*(1), 61–74.

Williams, R. (1990). *Technology and cultural form.* London: Routledge.

Winn, M. (1977). *The plug-in drug.* New York: Viking.

Wood, W., Wong, F. Y., & Chachere, J. G. (1991). Effects of media violence on viewers' aggression in unconstrained social interaction. *Psychological Bulletin, 109,* 371–383.

Woods, D. D., & Cook, R. I. (1999). Perspectives on human error: Hindsight biases and local rationality. In F. T. Durso, R. S. Nickerson, R. W. Schvaneveldt, S. T. Dumais, D. S. Lindsay, & M. T. H. Chi (Eds.), *Handbook of applied cognition* (pp. 141–171). New York: John Wiley.

Wright, C. R. (1949). *Mass communication: A sociological perspective.* New York: Random House.

Wright, C. R. (1960). Functional analysis and mass communication. *Public Opinion Quarterly, 24,* 605–620.

Wright, J. C., Huston, A. C., Reitz, A. L., & Piemyat, S. (1994). Young children's perceptions of television reality: Determinants and developmental differences. *Developmental Psychology, 30,* 229–239.

Wright, K. (2000). Computer-mediated social support, older adults, and coping. *Journal of Communication, 50,* 100–118.

Wu, B. T. W., Crocker, K. E., & Rogers, M. (1989). Humor and comparatives in ads for high- and low-involvement products. *Journalism Quarterly, 66,* 653–661.

Wyatt, J. (1994). *High concept: Movies and marketing in Hollywood.* Austin, TX: University of Texas Press.

Wyer, R. S., Jr. (2004). *Social comprehension and judgment: The role of situation models, narratives, and implicit theories.* Mahwah, NJ: Lawrence Erlbaum.

Wyer, R. S., Jr., & Albarracin, D. (2005). Belief formation, organization, and change: Cognitive and motivational influences. In D. Albarracin, B. T. Johnson, & M. P. Zanna (Eds.), *The handbook of attitudes* (pp. 273–322). Mahwah, NJ: Lawrence Erlbaum.

Wyer, R. S., Jr., & Srull, T. K. (1989). *Memory and cognition in its social context.* Hillsdale, NJ: Lawrence Erlbaum.

Yanovitzky, I. (2002). Effects of news coverage on policy attention and actions: A closer look into the media-policy connection. *Communication Research, 29,* 422–451.

Young, M. E., & Wasserman, E. A. (2005). Theories of learning. In K. Lamberts & R. L. Goldstone (Eds.), *Handbook of cognition* (pp. 161–182). Thousand Oaks, CA: Sage.

Young, S. D. (2000). Movies as equipment for living: A developmental analysis of the importance of film in everyday life. *Critical Studies in Media Communication, 17,* 447–468.

Zajonc, R. (1968). Attitudinal effects of mere exposure. *Journal of Personality and Social Psychology Monographs, 9*(2, Pt. 2), 1–27.

Zajonc, R. (1980). Feeling and thinking: Preferences need no inferences. *American Psychologist, 35,* 151–175.

Zillmann, D. (1983). Transfer of excitation in emotional behavior. In J. T. Cacioppo & R. E. Petty (Eds.), *Social psychophysiology: A sourcebook* (pp. 215–242). New York: Guilford.

Zillmann, D. (1988). Mood management through communication choices. *American Behavioral Scientist, 31,* 327–340.

Zillmann, D. (1991a). Empathy: Affect from bearing witness to the emotions of others. In J. Bryant & D. Zillmann (Eds.), *Responding to the screen* (pp. 135–167). Hillsdale, NJ: Lawrence Erlbaum.

Zillmann, D. (1991b). Television viewing physiological arousal. In J. Bryant & D. Zillmann (Eds.), *Responding to the screen* (pp. 103–133). Hillsdale, NJ: Lawrence Erlbaum.

Zillmann, D. (1996). The psychology of suspense in dramatic exposition. In P. Vorderer, H. J. Wulff, & M. Friedrichsen (Eds.), *Suspense: Conceptualizations, theoretical analyses, and empirical explorations* (pp. 199–232). Mahwah, NJ: Lawrence Erlbaum.

Zillmann, D. (1999). Exemplification theory: Judging the whole by some of its parts. *Media Psychology, 1,* 69–94.

Zillmann, D. (2002). Exemplification theory of media influence. In J. Bryant & D. Zillmann (Eds.), *Media effects: Advances in theory and research* (2nd ed., pp. 19–41). Mahwah, NJ: Lawrence Erlbaum.

Zillmann, D., & Brosius, H.-B. (2000). *Exemplification in communication: The influence of case reports on the perception of issues.* Mahwah, NJ: Lawrence Erlbaum.

Zillmann, D., & Bryant, J. (1985). Affect, mood and emotion as determinants of selective exposure. In D. Zillmann & J. Bryant (Eds.), *Selective exposure to communication* (pp. 157–190). Hillsdale, NJ: Lawrence Erlbaum.

Zillmann, D., & Cantor, J. R. (1972). Directionality of transitory dominance as a communication variable affecting humor appreciation. *Journal of Personality and Social Psychology, 24,* 191–198.

Zillmann, D., & Cantor, J. R. (1976). A disposition theory of humour and mirth. In A. J. Chapman & H. C. Foot (Eds.), *Humour and laughter: Theory, research and applications* (pp. 93–115). London: John Wiley.

Zillmann, D., & Cantor, J. R. (1977). Affective responses to the emotions of a protagonist. *Journal of Experimental Social Psychology, 13,* 155–165.

Zillmann, D., Taylor, K., & Lewis, K. (1998). News as nonfiction theater: How dispositions toward the public cast of characters affect reactions. *Journal of Broadcasting & Electronic Media, 42,* 153–169.

Zillmann, D., & Weaver, J. B. (1997). Psychoticism in the effect of prolonged exposure to gratuitous media violence on the acceptance of violence as a preferred means of conflict resolution. *Personality and Individual Differences, 22,* 613–627.

Zipf, G. K. (1949). *Human behaviour and the principle of least effort: An introduction to human ecology.* Cambridge, MA: Addison-Wesley.

Author Index

Subject Index

About the Author

W. James Potter is a professor in the Department of Communication at the University of California at Santa Barbara, where he teaches courses in media literacy, media content, and media effects. A holder of a Ph.D. in Communication and another in Instructional Systems, he has also taught at Western Michigan University, Florida State University, Indiana University, UCLA, and Stanford University. He is a former editor of the *Journal of Broadcasting & Electronic Media*. He is the author of numerous scholarly articles, book chapters, and a dozen books, including the following titles: *Media Literacy* (4th ed.), *On Media Violence, Theory of Media Literacy: A Cognitive Approach, How to Publish Your Communication Research* (edited with Alison Alexander), and *The 11 Myths of Media Violence.*